Regenerating London

London's regeneration is closely linked to debates about globalisation, sustainability, urban renaissance, community and social inclusion. *Regenerating London* explores in a scholarly but accessible text the different ways in which these key ideas are shaping the metropolis's urban fabric and future. It also considers how urban policy practices are helping to influence the broader conceptual debates about urban change and regeneration in London.

The use of select case material in the book helps to highlight the paradoxes and contradictions in urban policy ideas and practices in London, and enables detailed evaluation of the limits and potential of contemporary forms of sustainable urban regeneration.

Rob Imrie, Loretta Lees and Mike Raco are members of the Cities Group in the Department of Geography, King's College London.

Regenerating London

Governance, sustainability and community in a global city

Edited by
Rob Imrie, Loretta Lees and Mike Raco

Routledge
Taylor & Francis Group

LONDON AND NEW YORK

First published 2009 by Routledge
2 Park Square, Milton Park, Abingdon, Oxon OX14 4RN

Simultaneously published in the USA and Canada
by Routledge
270 Madison Avenue, New York, NY 10016, USA

Routledge is an imprint of the Taylor & Francis Group, an informa business

Typeset in Univers by Saxon Graphics Ltd, Derby
Printed and bound in Great Britain by
TJ International Ltd, Padstow, Cornwall

British Library Cataloguing in Publication Data
A catalogue record for this book is available from the British Library

Library of Congress Cataloging-in-Publication Data
Regenerating London : governance, sustainability and community in a global
city / edited by Rob Imrie, Loretta Lees and Mike Raco.
    p.cm.
  Includes bibliographical references and index.
  1. Urban renewal—England—London. 2. City planning—England—London. 3.
Community development—England—London. 4. London (England)—Social
conditions. 5. London (England)—Economic conditions. I. Imrie, Robert, 1958–
II. Lees, Loretta. III. Raco, Mike.
  HT178.G72.R44 2008
  307.3'41609421—dc22   2008023486

ISBN13: 978-0-415-43366-2 Hardback
ISBN13: 978-0-415-43367-9 Paperback
ISBN13: 978-0-203-88671-7 eBook

ISBN10: 0-415-43366-5 Hardback
ISBN10: 0-415-43367-3 Paperback
ISBN10: 0-203-88671-2 eBook

Contents

Preface   vii

Notes on the editors   ix

Notes on the contributors   x

Part I: The dimensions of urban change in London

1   London's regeneration   3
ROB IMRIE, LORETTA LEES AND MIKE RACO

2   Planning London: a conversation with Peter Hall   24

3   Regenerating a global city   40
TIM BUTLER AND CHRIS HAMNETT

4   Governing London: the evolving institutional and planning landscape   58
MARK TEWDWR-JONES

Part II: Prestige projects and the sustainable city

5   Figuring city change: understanding urban regeneration and Britain's Thames Gateway   75
MICHAEL KEITH

6   'An exemplar for a sustainable world city': progressive urban change and the redevelopment of King's Cross   93
ROB IMRIE

7   Local government and the politics of flagship regeneration in London: the development of Paddington   112
MIKE RACO AND STEVEN HENDERSON

8   The 2012 Olympic Games and the reshaping of East London   132
GAVIN POYNTER

Part III: Sustainability, inclusion and social mixing

9   The rebirth of high-rise living in London: towards a sustainable, inclusive, and liveable urban form   151
RICHARD BAXTER AND LORETTA LEES

Contents

10 London's Blue Ribbon Network: riverside renaissance along
the Thames   173
MARK DAVIDSON

11 The promotion of London as a 'walkable city' and
overlapping walks of life   192
JENNIE MIDDLETON

12 Social housing and regeneration in London   212
PAUL WATT

Part IV: Community governance and urban change

13 Regenerating the South Bank: reworking community and
the emergence of post-political regeneration   237
GUY BAETEN

14 The disputed place of ethnic diversity: an ethnography of
the redevelopment of a street market in East London   254
NICK DINES

15 From a 'society of fear' to a 'society of respect': the
transformation of Hackney's Holly Street Estate   273
TONY MANZI AND KEITH JACOBS

16 Young people and the regeneration of the King's Cross
Ten Estates   289
NINA BROWN AND LORETTA LEES

Part V: Conclusions

17 London: regeneration or rebirth?   313
ALLAN COCHRANE

Bibliography   323
Index   343

Preface

The objective of this book is to provide a scholarly yet accessible text about contemporary urban regeneration in London. London, as the dominant metropolitan centre, not just in the UK but also, arguably, worldwide, is a place where the diverse dimensions and complexities of contemporary urban processes and change are evident. The sheer size of London, its entanglement in global relations and processes, and the diverse range of its socio-political and cosmopolitan structures provide an important context through which to explore the different ways in which the urban fabric of the metropolis is shaped by urban regeneration and its programmes, policies and outcomes. Such a book is timely because the changing social, economic and political structures of cities are a major concern to the UK government, in a context whereby urban areas are the focus of much debate about urban renaissance, sustainable development, community-led regeneration and socially inclusive neighbourhoods.

London's regeneration is closely linked to concepts of, and debates about, globalisation, sustainability, governance and community, and the book explores, through case examples, the different ways in which these terms are entwined with regeneration politics, policy and practice. The terms 'globalisation' and 'sustainability' are especially evident in urban policy documents and practices, and they provide the over-arching frames of reference that are guiding urban development and regeneration in London and elsewhere. Seeking to enhance London's global city status, and achieve a sustainable urban environment, is, however, dependent, so some argue, on new ways of developing and delivering urban regeneration, and a main focus of the book will be to describe the changing structures of urban governance in London, and to evaluate the different ways in which these are influencing policy innovation and change.

Much policy innovation is related to a sustainable urban renaissance premised on socially inclusive places and neighbourhoods, in which social interaction and mixing ought to be, so some argue, created through purposive policy and practice. Thus, a focus of the book is discussion of the shaping of urban regeneration agendas in London around concepts of social inclusion that have, as a remit, the creation of safe and secure places, the diminution of social polarisation and the physical development of spaces that respond to the diverse needs of London's changing demographic and cosmopolitan social structures. The use of select case material enables discussion to highlight paradoxes and contradictions in urban policy ideas and practices in London, and to describe and evaluate the limits and potential of contemporary forms of urban regeneration in the city.

In bringing the book to publication, we are indebted to a number of people. Foremost, we would like to thank the contributors to the book for their willingness to be involved, and their responsiveness to the various deadlines that we set. We are particularly grateful to a team of referees that looked at each of the chapters, and who provided useful comments and observations. We would also like to thank reviewers of the original book proposal for constructive comments, and to the editorial team at Routledge for their patience with us in the editing of the book. Our thanks also to Peter Howard for providing some excellent photographs, and to Rob Hydon for facilitating the production of some of the book's maps. Finally, we would like to acknowledge the intellectual support and guidance provided by the members of the Cities Group in the Department of Geography at King's College London.

At the time of writing and completing this book Ken Livingstone was still Mayor of London. On the date we submitted the book to the publishers, Boris Johnson had just been voted in as the new mayor, and at a time in which he has still to put into place regeneration policies and programmes for London. We await his policies related to all that is discussed in this book.

Rob Imrie, Loretta Lees and Mike Raco, May 2008

Notes on the editors

Rob Imrie is Professor of Geography at King's College London. He is co-author of *Inclusive Design* (Spon Press, London, 2001), author of *Disability and the City* (Sage, Oxon, 1996), *Accessible Housing: Disability, Design and Quality* (Routledge, London, 2006) and co-editor of *British Urban Policy* (1993, Paul Chapman Publishing, London; 1999; second edition, Sage, London) and *Urban Renaissance* (2003, Policy Press, Bristol). He was previously professor of Geography at Royal Holloway University of London.

Loretta Lees is Professor of Geography at King's College London. She is co-author of *Gentrification* (Routledge, New York, 2008), editor of *The Emancipatory City? Paradoxes and Possibilities* (Sage, London, 2004) and co-author of *Researching Human Geography* (Arnold, London, 2002). She is also editor of the urban geography section of the *International Encyclopedia of Human Geography* (Elsevier, forthcoming). She has published on gentrification, urban public space, architecture and urban renaissance/regeneration issues more generally.

Mike Raco is Reader in Human Geography at King's College London. He has published widely on the topics of urban and regional governance and regeneration. He is author of *Building Sustainable Communities* (Policy Press, Bristol, 2007) and co-editor of *Urban Renaissance* (Policy Press, Bristol, 2003). His background is in geography, planning and urban studies, and he previously lectured at the universities of Reading and Glasgow.

Notes on the contributors

Guy Baeten is Reader in Geography at the Department of Social and Economic Geography, University of Lund, Sweden. He has previously been affiliated with the University of Strathclyde, Glasgow, the University of Oxford and the University of Leuven, Belgium. He specialises in European urban geography and has published articles in leading journals on urban issues in the UK, Belgium and Sweden.

Richard Baxter was an ESRC-ODPM graduate student in Geography at King's College London. His PhD was titled 'High-rise living in London: towards an urban renaissance?' He is the author of 'The residential high-rise in London: towards an urban renaissance' (ESRC/ODPM Postgraduate Research Programme, Working Paper 18, 2005).

Nina Brown was an ESRC-CASE graduate student in Geography at King's College London. Her PhD was titled 'Young people, place and urban regeneration: the case of the King's Cross Ten Estates'. Her research interests are in urban education, urban regeneration and the geography of young people.

Tim Butler is Professor of Geography at King's College London. He is the co-author of *Understanding Inequality* (Sage, London, 2007), co-editor of *Multicultures and Cities* (Museum Tusculanum Press, Copenhagen, 2005), co-author of *London Calling: The Middle Classes and the Remaking of Inner London* (Berg, Oxford, 2003), editor of *Eastern Promise: Education and Social Renewal in London's Docklands* (Lawrence and Wishart, London, 2000) and author of *Gentrification and the Middle Classes* (Ashgate, Aldershot, 1997). He has worked on the gentrification of London and on the regeneration of East London for a number of years. He is also interested in the role of education markets in class formation and urban regeneration. Before coming to King's College London he was Professor of Urban Sociology at the University of East London.

Allan Cochrane is Professor of Urban Studies at the Open University. His recent published work includes *Understanding Urban Policy* (Blackwell, Oxford, 2007), and over the past couple of years he has been trying to make sense of the changing nature of urban and regional governance, with a particular interest in the south-east of England, building on the co-authored book *Rethinking the Region* (Routledge, London, 1998). He is also co-editor of *Comparing Welfare States* (Sage, London, 2001), and *Security: Welfare, Crime and Society* (Open University Press, Maidenhead, forthcoming).

Mark Davidson is a Research Fellow at the Urban Research Centre, University of Western Sydney. His research interests include gentrification, housing inequalities, urban development and planning practice, urban politics and sustainability. His contribution to this book was written whilst a postdoctoral fellow at Dartmouth College, USA. He completed his PhD at King's College London. He has previously published on new-build gentrification and the role of capital within this process. He is currently researching the implementation of social sustainability objectives in urban policy in Vancouver and Sydney, and place-making practices in Sydney Olympic Park.

Nick Dines was until recently a Research Associate in the Geography Department at King's College London where he conducted research on housing aspirations among ethnic minorities in east London. Prior to this post he was research fellow in the Institute of Community Health Studies, Queen Mary University of London. He is the co-author of *Public Spaces, Social Relations and Well-being in East London* (Policy Press, Bristol, 2006). He currently lives in Rome, Italy, where he is completing a monograph on urban renewal and spatial conflict in the historic centre of Naples during the 1990s.

Peter Hall is Professor of Planning and Regeneration at the Bartlett School of Architecture and Planning, University College London. From 1991 to 1994 he was Special Adviser on Strategic Planning to the Secretary of State for the Environment, with special reference to London and South-East regional planning, including Thames Gateway and the Channel Tunnel Rail Link. In 1998–9 he was a member of the Deputy Prime Minister's Urban Task Force. In 2004 he was appointed Chair of ReBlackpool, the Blackpool Urban Regeneration Company. He is author, co-author or editor of over thirty-five books on urban and regional planning and related topics – most recently, *London Voices London Lives* (Policy Press, Bristol, 2007). He received the Gold Medal of the Royal Town Planning Institute in 2003 and the Balzan International Prize in 2005.

Chris Hamnett is Professor of Geography at King's College London. He is the author of *Unequal City: London in the Global Arena* (Routledge, London, 2003), author of *Winners and Losers: Home Ownership in Modern Britain* (UCL Press, London, 1999), co-author of *Shrinking the State: The Political Underpinnings of Privatisation* (Cambridge University Press, Cambridge, 1998) and co-author of *Cities, Housing and Profits* (Hutchinson, London, 1992). He has worked on housing, gentrification and social polarisation for many years, especially in London. Before moving to King's College London he worked at the Open University.

Steven Henderson is a lecturer in Urban Regeneration and Planning at the University of Wolverhampton. He has written articles on peri-urban expansion, sustainable brownfield development and area-based regeneration. His background is in geography and planning.

Keith Jacobs is a senior lecturer in Sociology at the University of Tasmania. He has published widely on housing and urban policy issues and is the author of *The Dynamics of Local Housing Policy: A Study of Council Housing Renewal in the London Borough of Hackney* (Ashgate, Aldershot, 1999) and co-editor of *Social Constructionism in Housing Research* (Ashgate, Aldershot, 2004). His research interests include migration, housing policy, urban sociology and discourse-based research methodologies. He is currently writing a book on the subjective experiences of migrants who have settled in Australia.

Michael Keith is Director of the Centre for Urban and Community Research and Professor of Sociology at Goldsmiths College, University of London. His work focuses on issues of multiculture, city transformation and contemporary urbanism and he is the author, most recently, of *After the Cosmopolitan: Multicultural Cities and the Future of Racism* (Routledge, Oxon, 2005). He was formerly also a politician in east London and served as leader of the council in a London borough, for six years as the chair of Thames Gateway London Partnership, and as a member of the government's Commission for Integration and Cohesion, which reported in 2007.

Tony Manzi is Principal Lecturer in Housing at the University of Westminster, London. He is co-author of *Creating and Sustaining Mixed Income Communities: A Good Practice Guide* (Joseph Rowntree Foundation, York, 2006 and 2007), co-editor of *Social Constructionism in Housing Research* (Ashgate, London, 2004) and co-author of *Temporary Housing: A Good Practice Guide* (Chartered Institute of Housing, Coventry, 1998). His current research interests are in housing and neighbourhood governance, social theory and the management of change.

Jennie Middleton is a Research Associate in the ERSC Centre for Business Relationships, Accountability, Sustainability and Society (BRASS) at Cardiff University where she is conducting research on sustainable communities, lifestyles and consumption. Prior to this post she was an ESRC Postdoctoral Fellow in the Department of Geography, Royal Holloway University of London. She completed her PhD in the Geography Department at King's College London. Her doctoral research examined everyday urban walking in London.

Gavin Poynter is Professor of Social Sciences in the School of Social Sciences, Media and Cultural Studies at the University of East London and he is chair of London East Research Institute (LERI). He has authored *Restructuring in the Service Industries* (Routledge, London, 2000) and written widely on urban regeneration and social and economic change. With colleagues in LERI, he is currently engaged in several research projects related to 'London 2012'.

Mark Tewdwr-Jones is Professor of Spatial Planning and Governance and Director of Research at University College London's Bartlett School. His background is in urban planning, politics and film, and his research interests comprise spatial development, politics and place identity. He has published more than ten books, including *The European Dimension of British Planning* (Spon Press, London, 2001), *The Planning Polity* (Routledge, London, 2002), *Planning Futures* (Routledge, London, 2002), *Territory, Identity and Spatial Planning* (Routledge, Oxon, 2006) and *Decent Homes for All* (Routledge, Oxon, 2007). He is currently pursuing research on post-war urban development and filmic representation, and spatial planning.

Paul Watt is a lecturer in Sociology at Birkbeck, University of London. He has researched and published on urban social inequality and exclusion, housing, employment, neighbourhoods and community, plus more recently on citizenship education. He is co-author of *Understanding Social Inequality* (Sage, London, 2007). His background is in sociology and urban studies.

Part I

The dimensions of urban change in London

Chapter 1

London's regeneration

Rob Imrie, Loretta Lees and Mike Raco

Introduction

> Here is a city of diversity. The contrasts which can be found are more
> extreme than those of most other cities, for overlaid on locally inspired
> social and geographical differentiations that are intrinsic to all cities are
> the intensifying and complicating forces of the capital's national and
> international roles.
>
> (Hoggart, 1991: 5)

Nearly twenty years ago now, colleagues of ours in Geography at King's College
London published an edited volume titled *London: A New Metropolitan Geography*
(Hoggart and Green, 1991). In that book, they argued that London was being
'renewed' at a rapid pace. In this book, we show that the pace has stepped up
significantly and in qualitatively different ways. Hoggart and Green (1991) suggested
that inner London was not being 'Americanised', or becoming a polarised or working-
class city. They argued instead that the real risk was of inner London becoming
gentrified and almost exclusively reserved for middle to upper income and/or class
strata. In this book, which is focused specifically on regeneration in London, we
explore the growing tensions between a globally focused growth agenda and the
broader pressures associated with the city's social reproduction, such as housing
affordability, sustainability and the provision of public services.

The rationale for the book is to advance understanding of London through
the context of urban regeneration, a topic that has barely been a subject matter or
topic of concern. Thus, there is a plethora of books about social and economic
changes in London, and much exploration of urban and regional planning policies
and programmes, but little within this genre that focuses on the specificities of
urban regeneration (see, for example, Buck *et al.*, 2002; Hall, 1989; Thornley, 1992).
Likewise, much has been written about the social histories of London, and there
are numerous literary accounts of the life and times of London's population (Ackroyd,
2000; Hall, 2007; Picard, 1997; Porter, 1989; Rasmussen, 1960). This book seeks to
build on these contributions by developing the argument that the making of

London's geographies has always been related closely to interventions in, and actions upon, physical spaces in the capital and, as such, much more focus on the topic is warranted.

In this book we use the term 'urban regeneration' as a normative concept that is rooted in British urban policy. It refers to those policies and strategies that have been designed to deal with urban decline, decay and social and economic transformation in London. Urban regeneration implies an integrated perspective on the problems and potentials of cities. Roberts (2000: 17) defines it as a 'comprehensive and integrated vision and action which leads to the resolution of urban problems and which seeks to bring about a lasting improvement in the economic, physical, social and environmental condition of an area that has been subject to change'. Couch *et al.* (2003: 2) state that urban regeneration is 'concerned with the re-growth of economic activity where it has been lost; the restoration of social function where there has been dysfunction, or social inclusion where there has been exclusion; and the restoration of environmental quality or ecological balance where it has been lost'.

The chapters in the book seek to develop, in a variety of ways, at least three interrelated understandings of urban regeneration in London. First, policy approaches to London's regeneration have to be understood as part of the capital's interplay with broader, national state policy programmes and forms of restructuring of welfare provision. In Cochrane's (2007) terms, urban, spatial, policies and programmes are closely entwined with (national) social policy measures and interventions. Second, the regeneration of London has also to be set, and understood, within the broadcloth of international relations and transnational processes relating to the capital's position as a global city and as a pre-eminent player in the global economy. Third, while in aggregate terms urban regeneration in London seems to be successful in facilitating economic and cultural regeneration, it is faring much less well in terms of social inclusion and social sustainability, and may well be implicated in contributing to the widening of social and economic inequalities.

As such, much of the rhetoric, and some of the substance, of urban regeneration in London is connected to attaining sustainability as the basis to solving economic, social and environmental problems. This commitment is influenced by the complexity, even the uniqueness, of London's social and economic contexts, and by a politics of urban change that, in Dikeç's (2007) terms, requires an analysis of regeneration as part of a political project of active state and corporate interventions in social and welfare spending programmes. Such interventions, while influenced by the specific geographies of London, do not preclude possibilities of policy learning and we hope that by outlining and discussing a number of urban regeneration programmes in London (some of which have been completed, some of which are still underway, some that are large scale and some small scale) the book will inform ideas about, and practices of, regeneration elsewhere.

This introductory chapter sets the context for the volume by outlining the key dimensions of London's regeneration, and discussing the ways in which they are entwined with, and influenced by, what we argue are the core concerns of contemporary urban regeneration policies: sustainability, community and the governance of policy delivery. We divide the chapter into five further parts. First, we outline the main dimensions of urban regeneration in London, and highlight some of the key continuities and changes in the city's development politics and strategies, and the role of regeneration projects in reflecting and reproducing London's socio-economic geographies. This is followed by three sections that consider, respectively, the ways in which London's regeneration is influenced by issues of sustainability, community and governance. We conclude by outlining the structure and content of the book's chapters.

The dimensions of regeneration in London

The making of London's socio-cultural and political geographies has always been related closely to interventions in, and actions upon, its physical spaces. London changed out of all recognition during the eighteenth and nineteenth centuries as a result of major building and infrastructure projects. Developments, such as the construction of the railways, contributed to the displacement of tens of thousands of people and heralded the opening up of new working-class neighbourhoods or 'railway suburbs', such as East Ham and Walthamstow. London was also a focal point for mega projects, and during this period, major public places, streets and buildings were constructed, including Regent Street, the Crystal Palace, the National Gallery and the British Museum. Such was the ferment and pace of change that contemporary observers lamented that the city's character was being lost as 'there is always building and rebuilding' (Ackroyd, 2000: 522; see also Hunt, 2004).

This observation has parallels with more recent, post-1945 phases of building and urban regeneration, in which a host of design, development and construction processes have been at the heart of the capital's changing social and economic geographies. Patrick Abercrombie's plan for London, published in 1944, set a context for population dispersal and the building of major inner city housing estates. Later, in the 1950s, prestige projects dotted the London landscape, with major new buildings, such as the Royal Festival Hall, defining the city's character. By the mid 1960s, London's global dominance was increasingly manifest in the construction of new property, a trend that intensified in the 1980s. Today, London's landscape is peppered with major regeneration sites and schemes, and the propagation of a range of infrastructure and renewal projects, such as Cross Rail, the Olympic Games, Paddington Basin and King's Cross. These are, arguably, as ambitious, if not more so, than some of the predecessors of earlier periods.

These ambitions are part of a broader socio-political process in London that places urban regeneration at the fulcrum of the capital's economic competitiveness. Like cities elsewhere, regeneration is being 'put to work' by politicians as part of a strategy to remove obstacles to economic growth and to create the social and physical infrastructure required to compete for inward investment.

There is nothing new about this. It is part of a continuing emphasis in London's recent regeneration history, or what Cochrane (2007) describes as a 'growth first' logic. The attainment of such status is being driven by major property-led regeneration, characterised by the provision of urban infrastructure, such as roads, office parks, retail centres, new dwellings and telecommunications. These interventions, so the regeneration logic goes, will enable London to engage in place marketing, diversify local labour and housing markets, and capture flows of global investment.

Such sentiments are part of policy approaches that conceive of regeneration as closely entwined with globalisation and London's global city status. Mayor Johnson (and Mayor Livingstone before him) and the coterie of politicians and policy officials in the Department of Communities and Local Government (DCLG), Greater London Authority (GLA) and the London Development Agency (LDA) subscribe to a particular narrative about London's global development. Beck (1996: 17) refers to this narrative as 'globalism', that is, an ideology based on 'the naive idea that the world market is the patent medicine for all of society's ills'. On the front page of the LDA's (2008a) website it is suggested that 'it's our job to ensure that London remains a global success story'. For the LDA, it is clear that London is 'a global city both in a world-class league but also increasingly in a league of its own. It is faced with the challenges and opportunities that are presented by being in that class' (LDA, 2008b).

The global city emphasis here extends to urban policy and the role of regeneration projects as catalysts for the city's growth. Growth is conceived of as part of interlocking spatial scales, in which a cascade or trickle-down of economic benefits will follow from the inflow of investment. In the GLA's (2004a: 3) terms, 'The Mayor, London Development Agency and Transport for London will . . . ensure that the development of London as a global business centre supports the spatial and economic development of Europe and the UK and that London's growth supports the future growth of the core cities.' This growth logic is aligned to specific spatial plans and strategies that have identified twenty-eight 'opportunity areas' as sites where growth is to be concentrated and special efforts made to spread the benefits of development to (deprived) local communities. The sites include King's Cross, Shoreditch, Elephant and Castle, Wembley, Paddington and the Isle of Dogs.

These pronouncements suggest that the globalism agenda is part of a development politics in London based on 'picking winners' and investments in selective, strategic infrastructure projects. As Brenner (2004) notes, states and development agencies are increasingly focusing on new rounds of spatial selectivity in which those areas and sectors that are seen to be successful are being supported through new rounds of state spending and macroeconomic support. The sentiments expressed by the GLA are a manifestation of this development politics. It presents a case for further state investment in the capital to off-set a number of 'costs' associated with its recent expansion and development, and to provide some 'distributional justice' in terms of national government spending patterns and priorities. The argument is that London's future development and sustainability should be a national priority if the UK's wider economic competitiveness is to be maintained. In short, spatial policy's role is not to redistribute resources across the space economy but to select and support places that are 'global winners' (see also Jones, 1997).

This approach to regeneration is not without contradictions, not least in relation to the sustainability of the manufacturing base of the capital. The spatial development plan for London notes that 'in the highly competitive London land market, manufacturing, wholesale distribution and a number of other industrial activities rely on the planning system to sustain adequate development capacity to meet their strategic needs'. However, as later chapters show, there are tensions between the global development imaginations being put forward and the need to create alternative spaces for different types of industries and activities. The role of manufacturing and 'bad neighbour' firms, for instance, is understated in, and even written out of, the globalism discourse. They have been airbrushed out of policy imaginations and frameworks to the extent that predictions of their demise become self-fulfilling prophecies (see Berry *et al.*, 1968; Imrie *et al.*, 1995).

At the same time, there is a growing recognition, at least in policy discourses, that regeneration is not reducible solely to a physical product or process. Organisations like the World Bank (2002) suggest that the facilitation of city competitiveness requires the regeneration of dated social and political organisations, and a policy emphasis on developing the skills and competencies of urban populations by recourse to social capital building programmes. In this context, the understanding of what regeneration is, or ought to be, is interlinked to education and labour market programmes, and other supply-side policies that provide a basis for urban competitiveness. The LDA (2006: 6) is in the vanguard of this process, and has recently restated the case: 'It is broadly recognised that for London to be a sustainable world-class city, it must ensure that all of its residents have the opportunity to make a positive contribution to London's economic performance and success.'

This observation is part of a political and policy context that conceives of regeneration as propagating the socially inclusive city, in which people will be provided with the resources to help them to gain access to the opportunities provided by the capital's economic growth. This formulation is interesting for the way that it places an onus on individuals to acquire competencies and skills that, in turn, will permit them, so it is alleged, to share in the fruits of economic growth. Regeneration, in this formula, eschews a re-distributive (economic) model for one that revolves around individuals' adaptability to the market opportunities that the 'growth first' logic is generating for London. This chimes with New Labour's broader exhortations for citizens to become 'active' in regeneration, in which communities 'must be fully engaged in the process from the start and . . . everyone must be included' (DETR, 2000a: 4; see also section 4 below).

Regeneration, through capacity building of this type, represents an active process of making people and making places, and much of this in London is occurring through specific institutional, political and legal processes, usually inter-ventions in spatial development by powerful state and corporate organisations and networks. These can be thought of, in part, as 'practices of articulation', in which, as Dikeç (2007: 9) suggests, particular spaces, and particular people within those spaces, become 'constituted as objects of urban policy intervention'. The spaces of regeneration in London are constituted in a variety of ways, including what Dean (2007) characterises as the exercise of authoritarian liberalism, in which the propa-gation of models of social pathology, and punishment of deviant groups and indi-viduals, are to the fore. Thus, neighbourhood renewal programmes include 'punitive sovereignty' and 'target hardening' programmes that seek to clear the streets of particular groups, while securing them for conspicuous consumption.

The emphasis on social control within London's regeneration politics is, we would argue, particularly salient in a context where juxtaposed inequalities and processes of social polarisation are greater than in any comparable city in Europe (see Hamnett, 2003; May *et al.*, 2007). As Power and Houghton (2007:114) argue 'London is by far the most complex, most diverse and most socially mixed city in Britain – a jigsaw of such vast scale and minuscule pieces that no one quite grasps its totality'. This complexity and diversity is growing with the dramatic turnaround in London's population. From its peak of 8.6 million in 1939 the city consistently lost population in the post-war period, in large part because of active central government decentralisation programmes (for example the Abercrombie Plan). By 1983 it stood at just 6.8 million and only in 1989 did the population start to grow again. However, by 2006 London's population was estimated to be 7.57 million and the projections are that by 2026 it could reach 8.7 million. London's diversity is one of its greatest historical and contemporary strengths. Today it is one of the world's most multi-racial cities with 25 per cent of its population foreign born and over 300 languages spoken by London's schoolchildren (GLA, 2004a).

The city's growing material divisions match this breadth of social diver-sity. Despite the strength of London's financial services and claims that 'London is by far the wealthiest area of the European Union' (Government Office for London, 2008: 1), large parts of the city have yet to recover from the de-industrialisation of the 1970s and 1980s in which approximately 500,000 jobs disappeared (Turok and Edge, 1998). The GLA's survey of inequalities across the city in 2002 painted a bleak picture (GLA, 2002a). Despite ten years of sustained economic growth, over a third of children (36 per cent) and 30 per cent of working adults in inner London were living in poverty. Black and minority ethnic (BME) communities have suffered dispro-portionately from marginalisation, with 73 per cent of Pakistani and Bangladeshi children, for example, growing up in poor households, and employment rates amongst all BME communities averaging only 59 per cent. The contrasts in official unemployment figures for London also make powerful reading, with a rate of only 5.1 per cent for 'white' Londoners, as compared to 24.1 per cent for Bangladeshis and 18.9 per cent for Black Africans.

At the same time as inner London contains the highest concentrations of professional and highly paid employment positions in the country, overall unemployment rates are 9.5 per cent, the highest of any sub-region of England and in 2007 four inner London boroughs were listed amongst the top ten most deprived local authority areas in England (see figure 1.1). Whilst much of the attention has been on these spatial and ethnic divisions, it should be noted that material inequalities are manifest in other ways. The gender pay gap in London, for example, is greater than in Great Britain as a whole, with the full-time average pay of female workers being only 77 per cent that of males. The quality and provision of education varies enormously with only 41 per cent of children in the inner London borough of Greenwich achieving five or more A–C Grades at GCSE level as compared to the English average of 57 per cent and that of outer London boroughs, such as Redbridge, where the figure is 71.7 per cent (Mayor of London, 2007).

It is important to recognise that since the early 1980s regeneration policy has not only failed to address such inequalities but has also played a significant role in creating and reproducing them. In some ways there have been real and tangible successes. New development landscapes have emerged in London, often on de-industrialised sites, and the long-term population decline of the city has been reversed. However, the extent to which this has improved the quality of life for the majority of the city's residents is highly questionable. Perhaps the best example of regeneration policy's failures can be found in Tower Hamlets where inequalities have mushroomed despite public and private sector investment of over £10 billion in the Canary Wharf development and the in-migration or creation of over 80,000 jobs. A report in 2005, for example, found that 'the average pay of a male worker in the parliamentary constituency that includes London's Canary Wharf financial district rose 22 per cent to more than £101,000' (Thornton, 2005: 1).

In contrast, two-thirds of Tower Hamlet's children are growing up in households officially defined as 'poor' and economic inactivity rates are as high

Rank	Local authority
1	Liverpool
2	Hackney (London)
3	Tower Hamlets (London)
4	Manchester
5	Knowsley
6	Newham (London)
7	Easington
8	Islington (London)
9	Middlesbrough
10	Birmingham

1.1
**The top ten most
deprived places in
England, 2007**

Source: DCLG, 2007a

as 46 per cent (Borough of Tower Hamlets, 2008). The borough still ranks as the third poorest local authority area in England even though it lies at the centre of Europe's most ambitious, spectacular and long-running regeneration project. It is in this context of policy failure that debates have increasingly focused on issues of sustainability and sustainable community building and it is to these new agendas that the chapter now turns.

Sustaining success: planning for a sustainable London

During the 2000s, the discourse of sustainability has come to dominate development agendas in London and beyond. A key focus for such debates has been the spatial development plan for London, known as *The London Plan* (see chapter 4 for a wider discussion of the Plan and where it fits into broader development frameworks for the city). It claims to establish new development priorities for London that are 'set within an overarching policy of sustainable development' (Mayor of London, 2006a: xxi). Sustainability here is principally elided with new forms of *balanced* development that can 'rebalance the distribution of economic benefits . . . direct[ing] growth to where it is most needed, providing more affordable housing . . . and promoting equal access to all London's opportunities' (Mayor of London, 2006a: 9). The process of re-balancing does not, therefore, involve an active redistribution of resources from London's wealthier residents, but the opening up of new 'opportunities' to the city's poorest. At certain moments, balance is discussed in terms of the ways in which planning policy can support economic development. At other times, the emphasis is on social balance and community mixing as the basis for what is termed sustainable community building, whereas in other contexts balance is used to legitimate the construction of exclusive and expensive urban spaces in order to encourage the in-migration of a creative, entrepreneurial and relatively mobile class of workers into deprived neighbourhoods.

The extent to which these objectives are mutually supportive, or run counter to each other, is not directly discussed. The desirability of growth per se, or its impacts on London's populations, is not questioned or challenged. Instead, 'sustainability-oriented' planning strategies 'predict and provide' for the inevitability of future expansion and celebrate it as an essential ingredient in the city's attempts to sustain and enhance its global city status. Thus, the aim of policy is 'to accommodate the expected growth of the city in a sustainable way, within London's boundaries and without encroaching on London's own precious green spaces' (Mayor of London, 2006a: 8). This is to be achieved through the construction of 'a more compact city [that] will enable the more effective use of scarce resources, including land, energy, transport infrastructure, water and construction materials' (Mayor of London, 2006a: xxi).

These understandings of sustainability reflect broader changes in spatial policy discourses in the UK and beyond, in which there is growing recognition that economic growth is as dependent upon the availability of high quality 'social' infrastructure, such as housing and high quality public services, as it is on the presence or absence of entrepreneurs and businesses (see Jonas and Ward, 2007; Krueger and Savage, 2007). It is this recognition of the importance of state spending and welfare policy interventions that has generated a specific 'politics of sustainability' in London. Public and private sector elites have sought to build a political consensus that calls for London's sustainable development to be treated as a national priority. The LDA (2006), for example, now sees its strategic role as one of 'sustaining success' and advocates major state-funded investment in infrastructure as a way of ensuring that the longer term economic development of the city and its wider 'contribution' to the UK economy can be sustained in the longer term (see Raco, 2007a).

In this context, the discourse of sustainability is primarily being used as a discursive vehicle in and through which alliances and city-wide agendas are being forged in order to open up 'the possibility of finding new ways of mobilising resources though the new machineries of governance' (Allen and Cochrane, 2007: 9). Business groups, such as London First, have enthusiastically adopted the sustainability label in order to challenge and contest the agendas of national government. They claim, for example, that London represents a special case as it contributes 18.3 per cent of the UK's GDP, despite having 12.4 per cent of the population. They also note that London has been responsible for nearly 40 per cent of the growth in the UK's exports from 2000 to 2004, and contributes over £80 billion to the UK Treasury whilst receiving lower public spending per head when compared to other parts of the UK, although these figures are highly contested.[1] Such arguments may take on a new salience in the context of the global credit crunch and economic slowdown that is now taking place that could have a major impact on the very sectors that have underpinned economic growth in the 1990s and 2000s. Over the coming decade the politics of 'sustaining success' may become an increasingly important objective for policy-makers and other elite groups across London.

At the same time, despite the promotion of globalisation discourses, the city's development politics has ironically become increasingly insular, with less of a focus on its responsibilities to places beyond its boundaries (see Massey, 2004, 2007). There is little recognition, for example, of the city's impacts on the regional geographies of the UK and the longer-term sustainability of regional economies. London sucks in skilled workers and investment from across the spatial economy and possesses the greatest concentrations of wealth and economic activity in the country. It also attracts skilled workers from around the world, often from countries that can ill-afford to lose them. Approximately 30 per cent of jobs in London are now filled by workers born outside of the UK, something that is having a significant effect on donor countries (see LSE, 2007; Raco, 2007b). As a global centre of international finance, City of London firms also invest in a range of international projects, many of which are fuelling economic growth and resource exploitation across the globe. A broader conceptualisation of sustainability would, at least, acknowledge the socio-economic and environmental consequences of London's development.

Sustainable urban regeneration in the London context has, therefore, come to mean a variety of things. As later chapters will demonstrate, the outcome in practical terms is a potpourri of policy measures, targets, programmes and projects that revolve around the increasingly used but nebulous notion of 'sustainable community-building'. The emphasis is partly focused on the ways in which the physical environment can become a development asset that can be used to attract rather than repel mobile global investment. However, there is a growing concern with principles drawn from new urbanism, such as high density living, urban villages, walkable places and mixed-tenure housing (LDA, 2006). Likewise, themes about liveable places, averting threats of terrorism and related issues of security and safety have become paramount in London's regeneration proposals and projects. Bluefield waterfront areas and post-industrial brownfield sites represent particularly important opportunity spaces and, as later chapters will show, new developments are springing up on such sites across the city (see GLA, 2004a; Pinch and Munt, 2002). As the next section demonstrates, this emphasis on the creation of 'sustainable communities' represents the latest in a long line of 'community-oriented' initiatives in the city and the changing policies of central government.

London's regeneration and the 'turn to community'

Ideas about 'community' have long been associated with urban regeneration initiatives in London. In 1945, the London County Council Town Planning Committee endorsed Abercrombie's Greater London Plan and announced seven tasks in reconstruction, one of which was the creation of balanced communities in London, each comprising of several neighbourhood units. But in recent years the notion of community has become a much more central focus. Under a Labour government there has been both a 'turn to community' as the preferred mode of governance in urban regeneration and a focus on building inclusive or mixed communities at the neighbourhood level. These moves are both related but also different. They are related in that they are both focused on mediating the perceived erosion of 'community', that is social interaction and civic engagement, and stimulating social inclusion. This is underlain by a communitarian discourse that aims to rebind individuals with their broader society, to kick-start moral responsibility, cooperation, consensus and mutual trust (see Putnam, 2000). They are different in that the turn to community is about including community in decision-making, which is public participation in local planning and urban regeneration initiatives, whereas creating sustainable (mixed) communities is about social engineering at the neighbourhood level.

Central government's broader commitment to partnership has been complemented by a 'turn to community' in urban regeneration policy. As Imrie and Raco (2003: 6-7) argue, this turn is related to New Labour's rejection of universal, expensive and bureaucratic forms of governance that stifle devolved management and individual choice (see Deakin, 2001) and their belief that social and economic inequality can only be solved by partnerships between government and civil society. Government has advocated that local communities should play a larger role in urban regeneration partnerships (e.g. DETR, 2000a), the rationales being fourfold:

1   They have a better idea of their own localized problems and solutions to them.
2   Participation empowers them against social exclusion.
3   Their local knowledge is a valuable resource to enhance the expertise of urban regeneration partnerships.
4   This serves democratic and accountability ends (Maginn, 2004: 5).

However, as Paddison (2001: 202) has argued, bringing the community into the practice of urban regeneration, particularly in a major city such as London, is a 'demonstrably more fraught exercise than governments have assumed it to be'. A number of the chapters in this book discuss community participation with respect to a wide variety of regeneration programmes across inner London. Each of these examples has their own governance structure, constructions of community and achievements and/or failures. There are lessons here to be learned. First, all communities are characterised by boundaries of inclusion and exclusion, sometimes conflicted, sometimes not. Second, the consistent factor in the success of community participation is not only the energy and commitment of the local community but also the way that local authorities, developers, housing associations and other organisations enact participation. Third, London has a rich history of political action from which communities can see how best to develop effective strategies for their participation.

Key policy concerns with respect to community are over how the overwhelming tensions within London's global city growth can be managed in such a way that the social polarisation and inequity that has deepened over the past thirty years can be managed (see Buck *et al.*, 2002; Hamnett 2003). Many of the policies directed at London aim to build upon its diversity, paying special attention to inclusion of all constituent groups. As the London Plan states:

> Urban renaissance is about making the city a place where people want to live, rather than a place from which they want to escape. A successful and sustainable city needs to be both beautiful and environmentally responsible, both compact and polycentric, with distinctive communities and neighbourhoods. But above all, it must be a fair city, respecting and celebrating the diversity of its people.
>
> (GLA, 2002b: ix).

Mixed communities policy (see ODPM, 2006b) is underlain by the notion that diversity and mixing are seen to be sources of economic renewal and cultural vitality, for when people mix and mingle, sharing and combining ideas from different vantage points, they innovate and generate progress (see Florida 2005) and they learn from each other producing a 'creative trickle down' (see Peck, 2005: 766).

Here 'community' is an object of policy, a thing to be worked on, but also a thing to be created, an end in itself (Imrie and Raco, 2003: 6). As Uitermark (2003: 531) argues:

> It is frequently suggested by planners and politicians alike, that a policy that promotes 'social mixing' could strengthen the social tissue of a disadvantaged neighbourhood, thus saving its inhabitants from living in an environment that allegedly inhibits social and economic integration.

But as Holcomb and Beauregard (1981: 3) noted some time ago now 'although it is often assumed that the benefits of revitalisation will "trickle down" to the lower and working classes in a manner similar to that hypothesized for the housing market . . . in fact they are almost completely captured by the middle and upper classes'. Nevertheless as Rose (2004: 281) says:

> [s]ince the image of the 'liveable city' has become a key aspect of a city's ability to compete in a globalized, knowledge-based economy, post-industrial cities have a growing interest in marketing themselves as being built on a foundation of 'inclusive' neighbourhoods capable of harmoniously supporting a blend of incomes, cultures, age groups and lifestyles.

The current wave of 'mixed communities' policy-led regeneration in London is a result of serious concern over the increasing gap between rich and poor that has widened more quickly in London than in the rest of Britain (see Green, 1994; Edwards and Flatley, 1996) and in that other global city – New York (Fainstein, Gordon and Harloe, 1992: ch 5; see also above). The result could be 'a city of dystopia where inequality, crime, violence, fear and social control are locked in a vicious circle, with the urban riot and "white flight" as its climax' (Hebbert, 1998: 163). The theme of social breakdown that was a subtext throughout the debate over the abolition of the Greater London Council (GLC) was reborn when the GLA was elected. It drew on national government concerns about growing social exclusion and social breakdown in the UK as a whole (e.g. SEU, 1998). It also drew on the lessons learned from the free market disregard for social policy and social issues in the regeneration of London's Docklands (Brownill, 1990) and the weak trickle down effects of Docklands' regeneration to the adjacent parts of the East End (Ambrose, 1994). As the GLA (2002a: ix) stated:

> London is the most dynamic, cosmopolitan and diverse of our major cities, and one of a handful of truly 'world cities' . . . However London's formidable wealth-generating capacity coexists with truly staggering levels of economic disadvantage.

The building of mixed communities in London, especially in those comprehensive regeneration programmes that seek to redevelop large-scale social housing as mixed-income communities, is liable to undo the relatively large safety net of social housing in the capital that Buck *et al.* (2002) argue mitigates against the growth of the truly excluded in London and that Massey (2007) argues is a unique articulation in the global city of London – market capitalism embedded in the remains of a social democratic settlement (see also DeFillipis and North, 2004). The different chapters in this book that focus on mixed communities and social mixing in London assert two things, first, that the policy discourse on mixed communities/social mixing is being used as a form of state-led 'positive' gentrification (see Lees *et al.*, 2008), and second, many of the claims made about social mixing and mixed communities are not supported by any significant evidence. However, the emphasis on community represents only one part of a wider set of shifts in the governance of regeneration in London and it is these broader processes that the next section addresses.

Institutional assemblages and the governance of urban regeneration

London is a prime location for flagship, high-profile regeneration projects that reflect its symbolic and political pre-eminence and its buoyant market conditions (see Gyford, 1999). In recent years, as noted above, this has found expression in the vision of London as a 'global city' and broader debates over the types of urban spaces and environments that the city requires in order to sustain and enhance this role. This broader focus, however, generates tensions within London over the extent to which the governance of regeneration should primarily be a bottom-up process, delivered and funded by the city's elected local authorities or a city-wide, strategically focused process that works on London as a unified space of action. As later chapters will show, these tensions are reflected in, and reproduced by, a series of institutional divisions and political arguments over the appropriate form and character of development in the city and this section will explore some of these key relationships and dynamics.

One of the most significant factors shaping governance in London relates to what Allen and Cochrane (2007) define as its 'institutional assemblages' or the collection of formal and informal organisations that govern and manage the city. London has complex governance assemblages, including development agencies, metropolitan and borough-wide elected institutions, national organisations, the media, elite public and private sector groups, and a vibrant civil society. This complexity is such that, for some commentators, London is an 'ungovernable city', too large and diverse to manage and shape in a coherent and strategic fashion (see Travers, 2004). An extraordinarily complex range of elected and non-elected agencies exist alongside the thirty-two London boroughs (and the Corporation of London). London also possesses the headquarters of one-third of the Fortune 500 top global companies in the world, as well as national quango agencies and the executive departments of national government (London First, 2007).

It is not only the presence of such institutions that makes governance relationships in the city complex, but also the diverse and fragmented agendas and modes of accountability that governance organisations possess. In many ways, London is an archetype of the wider shift from local government to local governance. This has implications for urban regeneration policy for, as later chapters show, major projects require the support and involvement not only of the LDA and other development agencies, but also landowners, investors, conservationists, environmental consultants, transport bodies, engineers and local communities. While this is similar for urban policy-making in other cities, in London the relations between such agencies are made much more complex by the fragmented development politics in the city, and the scale of the physical problems that need to be addressed. Gordon and Buck (2004) suggest that this fragmentation is compounded by the city's history of weak institutional coordination and the incongruence between its institutional boundaries and its wider 'functional' urban region. Despite the presence of so many institutions, so they suggest, London suffers from a governance deficit in terms of its organisational and institutional capacities to deliver urban regeneration.

In addition, London's governance has always had a complex relationship with national government. On the one hand there is little doubt that what happens in London has a significant impact on development politics and practices elsewhere in the UK. The introduction of the Labour government's *Planning Bill* in 2008, for example, and its proposals for the introduction of a new, powerful development quango named the Infrastructure Planning Commission, has emerged in large part because of the perception that strategically important development projects in London have been thwarted by local community-based opposition and an overly bureaucratic, old-fashioned and slow planning system (see London First, 2007; DCLG, 2008a). This London-focused politics has also had a major impact on the governance of other policy fields such as education reforms and macroeconomic policy (see Massey, 2007).

On the other hand, the status of London as a capital city has significant implications for the autonomy of its agencies, particularly in relation to urban regeneration. Regeneration programmes such as the London Docklands, or the 2012 Olympics, have primarily been designed to act as flagship exemplars of broader development ideologies and national state projects. As London's global status, economy and population have expanded in the 1990s and 2000s, so regeneration projects are increasingly promoted in terms of their strategic national importance in supporting the UK's global economic competitiveness. Their impacts on the quality of life and opportunities of communities within London have often been seen as less of a priority. Indeed, London has become so commonly associated with images of growth and prosperity that it can be easy to overlook the level of deprivation that exists in some of its most deprived neighbourhoods.

There have also been ongoing political disputes within London about the appropriate powers and objectives of different tiers of government. Traditionally, London has been represented as a polycentric city, made up of diverse 'interconnected villages' (see Gyford, 1999; Hall, 1974). However, since 1889 it has also possessed metropolitan authorities, including the London County Council (1889–1965), the Greater London Council (1965–1986) and, since 2000, the Mayor and the Greater London Authority (see chapter 3). These bodies have consistently sought to legitimate themselves by adopting 'strategic' development agendas and establishing London-wide development priorities. At the same time the sub-metropolitan boroughs, which act as local planning authorities, also have a duty to prioritise the development needs of *their own* constituents.

These tensions are compounded by the tendency of national governments to create centrally funded quangos to oversee regeneration projects in the capital. In delivering the Olympics, for example, it was decided that a new organisation, the Olympic Delivery Authority, was required, as existing agencies were seen to lack the capacities to ensure that the development would be delivered on time (see chapter 8 in this volume). Similarly, in east London, a London Thames Gateway Urban Development Corporation has been set up with the aim of bringing 'single-minded' development to the East End (see Raco, 2005). The irony is that every time a 'strategic' quango agency is established, London's institutional assemblages become even more complex and disjointed. The modern history of governance in London has been forged in and through these institutional tensions and complexities.

These complexities reflect and reproduce competing *governmentalities* in the city over what London means as a place and a space of intervention. The mayor (Ken Livingstone at the time of writing), the Labour government and private sector elites have been pushing for a more 'structurally coherent' (*cf.* Harvey, 1989) set of arrangements in which the governance of London becomes more cohesive and development planning focused on the delivery of large-scale, global projects and investments. However, the boroughs and local communities in London retain a significant influence over development planning (see, for example, chapter 7, in this volume). The attempt to establish a dominant global city imagination has encouraged some London boroughs to create new working relationships and partnerships, such as Barnet's *Successful City Suburbs* campaign or the recently formed, cross-borough *South London Partnership*. Such bodies seek to highlight and promote alternative, suburban-focused governmentalities of the city in direct response to what has been seen as an inner London dominated set of political discourses.

Coordinating the development politics of London in this context is a difficult and challenging process. Since 2000, debates over the efficacy and justice of flagship development plans, such as the London Olympics and Crossrail, have surfaced in some parts of the city in relation to who should cover their significant long-term costs. Outer London boroughs, in particular, are suggesting that support for such projects mean that their needs and priorities are being sidelined to promote London's global centre (see Young, 2006). These political divisions across the city were reflected by the outcome of the May 2008 mayoral elections. The support base of the winning Conservative candidate, Boris Johnson, was overwhelmingly concentrated in the suburban London boroughs (in Bromley and Bexley, for example, he gained 60.80 per cent of the vote). Mayor Living-stone's vote was much higher in the more deprived inner London boroughs and in many ways the election results can be seen as a reflection of the complex, contested and multiple governmentalities that shape the politics of regeneration and development in the city. Such contestations are likely to become greater if, as current trends predict, inequalities grow and polarisation expands.

Overview of the book

The book is divided into five parts and comprises sixteen further chapters. The rest of Part I provides an overview of social, economic and governance changes in London and their interrelationships with urban change and regeneration. Chapter 2 sets the scene for the book by outlining the viewpoints of one of the most prolific commentators about urban change in London. The editors of the book interviewed Peter Hall in mid 2007, and chapter 2 provides a flavour of what he feels are the main issues and challenges relating to London's regeneration. As Hall suggests, the problem of, and for, London is to regenerate against a back-ground of booming growth, which, as he argues, makes the place 'absolutely special'. Hall highlights the growing income inequalities in London, what he refers to as the emergence of 'a super-class, a hyper-class, and maybe a hyper hyper-class of extraordinarily rich people', in contrast to those 'working for a minimum wage, sometimes less, and living in extraordinarily poor conditions, almost undocumented'.

In chapter 3, Tim Butler and Chris Hamnett identify the main physical, social and cultural transformations that have occurred in London post 1945, and assess to what extent these have contributed to London's resurgence as a major global centre. They consider the ways in which London's traditional and predomi-nantly upmarket urban centres have been remodelled to adapt to the new circum-stances, as well as how old industrial areas or buildings have been transformed to meet the perceived requirements of a post-industrial economy. Part of the chapter's focus is housing inequality in which the authors note that unless it is addressed, then, for many Londoners, urban regeneration will be experienced not so much as gentrification but urban degeneration as they pay more of their salaries for less accommodation in a situation where people live in private squalor surrounded by public affluence.

Mark Tewdwr-Jones, in chapter 4, outlines the history of post-war governance changes in London. He considers the problems with governing a large city that has global city status, and examines the attempt to manage growth and change within and across the London city region area. The chapter provides an evaluation of the concept of vision and strategy making through new spatial strategies in London. A focus is the discussion of developments in the governance of London related to the office of the Mayor of London, and the strange anomaly where the office-holder may possess some of the powers necessary to set a clear vision for the city but, as a result of the fragmentation of power between central and local interests, often lacks many of the implementation roles that are necessary to turn spatial visions into practical realities.

Part II focuses on the interrelationships between policy debates about sustainability and prestige property development and large-scale or mega projects in London. Here, the book explores the different ways in which prestige regeneration projects are being shaped by, and are shaping, issues relating to sustainable urbanism and community activation and participation. In chapter 5, Michael Keith focuses on one of the most significant regeneration projects for years, the redevelopment of the Thames Gateway. He notes that its future is related to a paradox between long-term public interests and short-term rational outcomes. The latter relates to the supply of infrastructure to ensure the deliveries of a viable sustainable community, the former to fiscal spending and Treasury austerity. For Keith, the latter is unlikely to meet the expectations of the former. He suggests that one ought to open up thinking about fiscal risk related to experiments with infrastructure investment that, as he says, 'recognises the potential for innovation in instruments of regeneration that can accommodate the paradox of the Thames Gateway rather than guarantee its failure'.

In chapter 6, Rob Imrie investigates how far property developers are responding to the government's exhortations, first outlined in the Urban White Paper (DETR, 2000a), to incorporate community values and viewpoints into the development process. Referring to the redevelopment of King's Cross, the data suggest less a new context of progressive consultative and participative processes, and much more the propagation of a rhetoric about the sensitivity of the development process to the viewpoints and wishes of (some) place-based groups. Community engagement in King's Cross is akin to what Amin (2005: 614) refers to as 'a conformist civic particularism'. Despite the language of participation, expressed by the developer and other actors, the organisation of the project's key components, including the developer's approach to community engagement, has not challenged power inequalities or the hierarchical social relations of the development process. In this respect, community engagement in King's Cross falls short of the inclusive policy agenda that the Urban White Paper originally outlined as integral to urban regeneration.

Mike Raco and Steven Henderson, in chapter 7, explore the delivery and governance of one of London's most significant flagship projects, the regeneration of Paddington. The authors suggest that the project is being influenced, primarily, by the politics and contexts of the Borough of Westminster City; that it is the actions of the local authority, first and foremost, that are shaping and structuring the development processes and priorities. The chapter demonstrates that no understanding of the development would be complete without an examination of its emergence in and through the local, sub-metropolitan politics of development in Westminster and it calls for a broader conceptualisation of the governance of urban regeneration in the capital. Their data suggest that site-specific knowledge is critical to the effective planning of flagship development projects and that local authorities are well placed to carry out the key role of facilitating development and defining the contours of political engagement and debate.

In chapter 8, Gavin Poynter's discussion of the 2012 Olympics shows how a sporting mega-event has become closely associated with achieving a range of non-sports related legacies – cultural, social, economic and environmental. He argues that this prestige project has contributed to the creation of a new form of state intervention and city governance, representing a significant break from the neo-liberal model that was dominant in the late twentieth century. One of his core arguments is that the complex, hierarchical governance structures for 2012 reflects the adaptive capacities of the state in contemporary capitalism; rather than weakening its influence it has strengthened its capacity to define and determine the social, economic and cultural agenda of the 2012 legacy. The chapter relates such observations to the complex patterns of community engagement associated with the 2012 event, and critically evaluates the potential for achieving a positive or sustainable Olympic legacy for east London.

Part III evaluates the translation of sustainability into policies and programmes of social inclusion and social mixing. It also offers some suggestions about future sustainable forms of urban living in London, for example, in chapter 9, Richard Baxter and Loretta Lees consider the significance of a new genre of sustainable residential high-rises that are beginning to emerge in London. Drawing on a survey of, and interviews with, high-rise residents in inner London, the chapter outlines the factors influencing residents' perceptions of the liveability and sustainability of London's high-rises. As the authors note, such knowledge is key to regenerating existing high-rise social housing, and ensuring that the new generation of high-rises are liveable, sustainable, socially inclusive and successful components in the regeneration of their local areas. Their data suggest that if well designed and managed, the residential high-rise can make an important contribution to developing sustainable urban environments. The chapter also provides evidence that public sector high-rises can be as successful as those that are privately owned, but that certain elements have to be in place for this to occur.

Mark Davidson, in chapter 10, examines how the GLA's vision of transforming London's derelict and abandoned riverside spaces into a desirable Blue Ribbon Network has been implemented, and with what effects. Mayor Ken Livingstone, and his urban affairs advisor Richard Rogers, wanted the Blue Ribbon Network to become a space of social mixing, a place where London's diverse communities could harmoniously live and mix together. This vision meshed neatly with New Labour's urban renaissance programme, for the goals of attractive urban spaces, social mixing and cohesive communities were shared by both national and metropolitan governments. However, Davidson's research, conducted in three Thames-side neighbourhoods, shows that the inclusive spaces and society envisaged in the Blue Ribbon Network policy are not being realised. As he suggests, if the Blue Ribbon Network is to become a space which unites London's communities, plays a part in addressing the city's social inequities, and develops into an attractive public space, then a significantly greater commitment to dealing with the causes of social exclusion has to be made.

In chapter 11, Jennie Middleton looks at London's policies for walking, as part of a sustainability strategy to promote social interaction. Drawing upon research findings on the walking experiences of residents in the inner London boroughs of Islington and Hackney, she argues that the relationship between walking and social interaction is oversimplified in London's policy for walking. The complexities in the social dimensions of pedestrian movement reveal how walking does not facilitate social exchange and mixing in a straightforward way. For example engaging with debates that assert that there is an over-privileging of face-to-face interaction in constructions of 'community' (Young, 1990; Larsen *et al.* 2006), the chapter illustrates the significance of walking in maintaining existing social relations as opposed to creating new ones. The implications of these findings are discussed in relation to the promotion of walking for engendering social mixing in London.

Paul Watt, in chapter 12, evaluates London's pronounced and persistent housing problem despite its twenty-first-century global city status. He does so by outlining aspects of urban policy under New Labour in relation to social housing and social exclusion, and by discussing the main dimensions of change within social housing in London. He provides an account of how social housing in London is distinctive relative to the rest of England, and examines how area-based initiatives have tried to address the needs of tenants in council-built housing estates in London with particular reference to New Labour's flagship programme, the New Deal for Communities. As Paul Watt shows, social housing is unlikely to be produced at the levels to meet the needs of the many thousands of ill-housed ordinary Londoners. He concludes that if this remains the case, then any area-based initiatives that attempt to foster 'sustainable communities' in council-built estates will face an uphill struggle.

Part IV outlines and evaluates the interrelationships between regeneration schemes and local communities, by focusing on the dynamics of sub-national and community governance, and the different ways in which they influence, and are influenced by, the shaping of regeneration programmes and outcomes. In chapter 13, Guy Baeten focuses on a key site in London, the South Bank, to observe and analyse the emergence of what he refers to as 'post-political urban regeneration'. He argues that political debates and programmes, as part of urban renewal efforts, appear to be disappearing into a plethora of scientific and technical discourses, and that regeneration policies are being depoliticised through a range of 'post political regeneration tactics'. He develops this observation by discussing the politics of redevelopment in one part of the South Bank, Coin Street, and a place that initially resisted property-led regeneration, but now seems to be embracing it. In Baeten's words, the South Bank has come full circle:

what was impossible in a time of politics – the development of a business and leisure district – will be realised in post-political times.

Nick Dines, in chapter 14, discusses some of the key struggles over the meaning and shape of public space in contemporary London, with a focus on the proposed redevelopment of Queens Market in the London borough of Newham. The chapter explores local people's discussions of the current market and how a perceived threat to its existence enhanced reflections about the market as a public space, and led to organised opposition to the scheme to redevelop it. The chapter analyses the different public representations of the market among promoters and opponents of redevelopment, and how these are cut across by particular understandings of diversity. In doing so, the chapter attempts to unpack the contested significance of ethnic diversity in the context of urban regeneration, from the everyday experience of interaction and a resource that is mobilised by campaigners, to the gentrifying trajectory that is inherent in the redevelopment scheme.

In chapter 15, Tony Manzi and Keith Jacobs evaluate the Comprehensive Estates Initiative (CEI), a housing renewal policy adopted by the London Borough of Hackney in the 1990s. They focus on one estate, Holly Street, and consider its legacies and suggest that it is an example of how the local state has engaged with territorialising components of neo-liberal policy making. The authors note Holly Street is illustrative of how regeneration policy has since developed in London and beyond. It was characterised by collective goals, such as community empowerment, but was also dependent on individualistic mechanisms, such as private finance and voluntary sector involvement, and, as the authors argue, this created tensions. For Manzi and Jacobs, the legacy of Holly Street, and the CEI more generally, is one whereby community involvement strategies, active resident participation, institutional partnerships and attempts to engender wider socio-economic regeneration are only meaningful if they are underpinned by substantial financial investment and by an enduring institutional momentum.

Nina Brown and Loretta Lees, in chapter 16, focus on the complexity of regenerating communal spaces on the Ten Estates, King's Cross, and the social-spatial exclusion of young people in and around the area. The chapter has two main concerns that frame the study. The first is the marginalisation, if not outright exclusion, of young people from the decision-making about the urban regeneration of their estates. The second is the way that a design-led regeneration has further excluded young people from the public spaces around their homes. The authors outline the failures, missed opportunities and successes, which relate to young people's interrelationships with urban regeneration decision-making processes. The chapter suggests that while young people are central to the visions of urban renaissance, as key users of public space, they are awkwardly balanced between, on the one hand, policies to provide amenity and public space provision and, on the other hand, programmes related to youth protection and regulation.

Part V of the book is an overarching, concluding piece by Allan Cochrane. He reflects on the previous chapters and speculates about London's urban future, discussing themes related to changing property markets, the politics of regeneration, security and the city, new social divisions and new patterns of governance and policy development and delivery. Cochrane develops the point that London's regeneration is neither singular nor reducible to a particular type or approach. In some contexts, regeneration is 're-growth', opening up new investment opportunities for developers, even if it also requires some engagement with local interests. In other contexts, regeneration implies an active process of state-led renewal. In some cases, however, this may have similar results and a similar focus to 're-growth' as stress is placed on ways of remaking places in ways that help generate opportunity for profitable redevelopment. For Cochrane, however, the main challenge for London's regeneration is to take on a different set of meanings, as an active programme of social renewal that, as he suggests, ought to draw in people and places that might otherwise be actively disadvantaged or sidelined by the political and policy processes of urban change.

Note

1 UK Treasury figures for 2006/2007 show that spending per head in London (at £8,404) was greater than the English average (£7,121) and higher than that spent in any other English region.

Chapter 2

Planning London: a conversation with Peter Hall

Editors: What makes regeneration in London 'unique' or different to other places, different cities?

Peter Hall: If you take a spectrum, with London at one end and places at the other end that are old one-industry mill towns, then what characterises London and makes it absolutely unique is its own extraordinary economic success: you are regenerating against the background of colossal pressures of population increase, economic growth, severe housing shortages, problems with transport infrastructure and also very much increasing income inequality, due to the rises in very high incomes, which make London different from anywhere else. Core cities, like Birmingham, Manchester, Leeds, and Newcastle, have some of these characteristics mixed up with some of the characteristics of the one-industry towns. But in London the problem is to regenerate against this background of booming growth, which makes it absolutely special.

Editors: What are the continuities and contrasts in the regeneration agendas of today and those of earlier periods, such as the 1960s and 1970s?

Peter Hall: There are changes in degree rather than kind. In the early 1960s London was booming and many of the problems we identify now – population growth, economic growth, strains on the transport system – were evident then and hitting the headlines as they are now. The Victoria Line on the London Underground system was an example of a piece of infrastructure that was put in because of a perceived desperate need at that very point. But the difference now is globalisation and all that happened as a result of the deregulation of the City of London in 1986, the so-called 'big bang'. This should not be exaggerated because London was always a global financial centre. What really did make a difference was that the Thatcher government deliberately destroyed the cosy, 'Old Boy' quality of that City of London world. And that did something very extraordinary, because it lifted London as an economic centre, almost away from the rest of the UK and maybe away from the rest of the planet. It wasn't just financial services. In other sectors such as architecture and the media, London now competes with a small number of other cities, such as New York and Los Angeles. These characteristics of the London economy have become much more evident, even exaggerated, in the last twenty years.

Editors: Are there similarities in the problems faced by regeneration agencies and policy-makers in London and other major international centres, such as New York and Tokyo?

Peter Hall: There are some shared approaches, resulting from shared problems, in any city that is sharing these characteristics of growth against the background of the global economy, and New York and Los Angeles would certainly be the most obvious comparisons I can think of. Among these are the problems of accommodating growth, including the fact that some of the growth inevitably will be diverted into a much wider 'mega-city region'. One can very clearly see that in the New York region as well as in southern California, just as you can in south-east England. Also the problems of increasing income inequality, arising in part from immigration from all over the world of low-skilled people, or sometimes high skilled-people working in low-skilled jobs. What it does mean is that you have at one extreme whatever you want to call it, a super-class, a hyper-class, and maybe a hyper hyper-class of extraordinarily rich people whose lifestyles are the talk of the media. On the other hand you have a kind of underclass of people, who are very obscure and difficult to research, working for a minimum wage, sometimes perhaps even below it, and living in extraordinarily poor conditions, almost undocumented. These features are very much shared with those other so-called global cities, and they distinguish London and those other cities from cities in their own countries. You do not find that to the same degree at all in Manchester or in Leeds, for instance, or in successful American cities like Boston.

Editors: Given these changing circumstances what should the policy responses be?

Peter Hall: Well, the first thing I think I would tend to go at – but it's something that's beaten every single politician, every single policy analyst – is to try and get at the heart of the problem of why we have huge amounts of immigration side by side with very high rates of localised unemployment in London. Now we've all gone round in circles on this, and certainly we went round in circles on the *Working Capital* team, but I'm not sure that we're any closer on this one. It is just as if parts of the labour force have simply contracted out of the labour market, and it may well be that they have done so, while the people who are coming in are doing very many different jobs, some of them very much below their capacities. This is a perversion of the theory of comparative advantage, as by doing jobs below their capacities these immigrant workers are actually doing the jobs much better than the competition might.

Editors: Isn't one logical policy response to the problems of rapid growth to reduce growth? Shouldn't jobs in London be decentralised as part of a stronger spatial or regional policy agenda?

Peter Hall: The objectives of policy should be two-pronged. First of all I do think that we can make south-east England much more of a multi-centred region than it is even now. And we can extend that phenomenon progressively outwards through the government's Sustainable Communities strategy that already reaches out as far as Corby, which is eighty-two miles from London. If it can get eighty-two miles there's probably no reason why it shouldn't get a hundred miles to Leicester or Birmingham, and begin to regenerate Midland cities, not all of which are doing at all badly anyway. So that's one approach to this, to increase the poly-centricity of the Greater South East – or, rather, the Greater South, because you could also go down west, towards Bristol and even perhaps South Wales.

The second is, undoubtedly, to try in every way you can through public policy, to enhance the role of the provincial core cities, and again this is fairly conventional wisdom. There are things you can do here, like moving part of the BBC to Manchester, like biasing research funding to the universities away from London, Oxford and Cambridge, towards the big northern civic universities, building up strong research centres: a thoroughly good principle, because you've got public levers that you can pull there. If strong research centres are established in Manchester or Newcastle then the smart people will go if they are offered the salaries. And there are other areas of public policy that you can develop in that way.

Editors: Would you describe that as a spatial policy?

Peter Hall: It is a spatial policy. But I am pessimistic, because London is unique. Places like Manchester and Leeds are not doing the same job and probably will not do so. The kinds of very special financial services that London and New York specialise in are just not replicated easily elsewhere. So there is a limit to what these other cities can do. They can do useful other functions, they can grow these functions, but they'll never do these special global functions. So trying to work out what they can do and pump those jobs out is, I think, a second priority. The third priority, which is most difficult of all for the north, is the city region approach: spreading development out from the cores of the cities into their surrounding regions. Certainly the first two elements of this strategy, the spreading of the south-east and developing the core cities to their maximum potential, have got to be part of a regional strategy.

Editors: Would it require a different sort of national politics for this vision to take shape?

Peter Hall: It would have been very desirable if John Prescott's dream had come true and we now had elected regional assemblies. I think that was probably a great political catastrophe, not much noticed by the Blair government because at the time that government was suffering bigger catastrophes than that. But it was certainly a great turning point when that north-east ballot rejected a strong regional assembly, because you don't have the same political power from largely non-elected and very obscure authorities. Although the RDAs are more noticeable, say in the north-west of England than they are in the south, no one can claim that they are a centre for debate in every pub in the north-west of England, nor is the Regional Assembly, which is barely visible.[1] And compared with the German or Spanish positions with their programmes of progressive decentralisation to the regions, we've failed, despite the best of good intentions on the part of the Blair government.

Editors: Can we talk about metropolitan regional governance in London?

Peter Hall: I have contradictory feelings about this. Although I am critical of a lot of what Ken Livingstone [the Mayor of London at the time of this interview] has done, on the whole I support his general aim of seeing himself as a kind of champion of London and of its continuing economic growth, because if you haven't got a strong, prosperous city you've failed as a mayor or any kind of politician. And he certainly hasn't failed that way. I think he is failing to deal fully with some of the consequences. I think he is also right in deliberately trying to continue the policy of diverting growth to the east side of London, because that is where both the potential and the need is. He took over the policy and he is trying hard to make it work, although there are lots of questions about how effective the policy is. For me, the great failure is that the administrative structure is so complex and so, in a way, self-contradictory, that it's holding the job up or at least it's not helping it. There are just too many cooks stirring the broth and tripping over each other, to a ludicrous degree.

I think that Labour governments can be so careful about democracy that they actually end up with paralysis. I've always felt that you actually need someone to do things down there in the Gateway now. Some things are getting done, but it's taken an unbelievably long time when you consider how old this initiative is: Michael Heseltine started it in March 1991, and it's now sixteen years on with far too little to show for it, and what little we can see is not actually in Thames Gateway, it's the completion of the much older Docklands project for the most part, on the Royal Docks and so on. So it is quite extraordinary how little has happened, and I think it's largely due to having organisations that aren't given enough power to get on with the job, and it's a matter of politics.

Editors: So does this mean you're against the public participation ethos that is presented by the government as fundamental to the modernisation of the planning system?

Peter Hall: I'm all for participation but I think at some point you've got to have an authority that does things, particularly in the most problematic areas, and particularly since in many of those areas there's no one there, or very few people there, and they certainly make a hell of a fuss. In King's Cross, a few people hold up the development for how many months? And they finally lose; of course they were going to lose. No one lives in the King's Cross site except a few people in Stanley Buildings and I think they've been decanted already. And there are a lot of people that like doing 1970s guerrilla warfare and I'm afraid it's about time they actually moved on.

Editors: One characterisation of all this participation is that the way in which New Labour has set it up in London and elsewhere is through decentred forms, all the way down to local strategic partnerships, but, in actual fact, all it seems to be is just another form of top-down centralism, and regeneration essentially is still being driven by the old centralist agendas. Do you think that is a fair comment?

Peter Hall: It depends what you call centralist. There will always be those who argue that you should go completely bottom-up and do it all through local inspiration. I don't really believe that's possible. What is at issue here is the right degree and form of local devolution. Clearly the Manchester model couldn't work for London because London is too big. Nor could a borough-based model in general work well for many developments, because the problems stretch across borough boundaries. But if you take Thames Gateway London, which I do feel needs handling as a whole, it really does extend across – it depends on how you count them – probably five or six boroughs, and you need a different organisation that cross cuts. And that's where it becomes very difficult, because you will, at that point, remove a lot of the power from the boroughs.

A borough like Newham in particular would be very impacted, or a borough like Barking and Dagenham would be impacted by the Barking Riverside being taken out – which it already has, in effect – to the control of the UDC, although the UDC doesn't seem to be doing much either. That's the problem. I used to think, and perhaps it's possibly still true, that you could get something based on the model of the 1970s partnership new towns, Peterborough was an outstanding example, where under a very smart manager who saw it as his job to work with the council hand in glove, the organisations worked together brilliantly. But if you could do that you might be able to create a structure that went across borough boundaries but still involved the boroughs, but it would have to be within a framework of saying we want action within a defined point, rather than just endless talking shops.

Editors: Were you disappointed with the UDCs that were set up in Thurrock and East London? Do you think they have done the job that they were set up to do?

Peter Hall: With Thurrock I would suspend judgement. It's doing some development in West Thurrock, it's done very little in East Thurrock so far, on the other hand you've got to allow for a typical UDC, after all LDDC was in business for seventeen years and it didn't really start to deliver huge regeneration until it had been going about seven or eight years. The New Town Development Corporations took even longer, so you shouldn't pre-judge Thurrock, or indeed London Thames Gateway UDC. The problem is partly the diversion due to the Olympics, which has skewed everything onto the Lower Lea Valley at the expense of Barking, and partly the sheer lack of money for infrastructure.

Editors: Can we just follow up something that you mentioned earlier? You were talking about the consequences of economic growth or Ken Livingstone's agenda for ensuring that London's economic future is secured. What are these consequences, and particularly you hinted that they weren't being handled particularly well by the GLA or by other forms of governments in London.

Peter Hall: I really meant the relative failure of this complex mechanism to handle the physical development of the Gateway. You would just expect to see much more happening over a much wider area. And to me, the failure to develop areas like Barking Riverside after sixteen years is astonishing, because it was a key site from the very beginning when it was identified in the RPG9A as long ago as 1995. And nothing, absolutely nothing, has happened. It's somehow symptomatic of an extraordinary paralysis in the system. What's holding it up now is, of course, the fact that under Ken Livingstone and the whole architecturally led agenda, the densities have been jacked up to something like two to three times the original figures, no one is willing to do this without big investment in public transport, they haven't got the money for the Docklands Light Railway extension. And without that the private sector won't move in.

Editors: Does this reflect a failure of strategic vision, strategic guidance or the absence of a strong strategic plan?

Peter Hall: It marks a change in the strategic plan, and again, it marks a question of powers, as between City Hall and the boroughs. Notoriously the boroughs didn't want density. Barking and Dagenham basically wanted, because they're probably the oldest of Old Labour boroughs, to house their own people, they didn't particularly want a lot of people dumped on them, particularly as they thought they might not be Old Labour voters, so they resisted densification. The mayor and his advisors pushed this agenda on them, and they finally gave way and then the problem was that the plan had to be rewritten, it was actually rewritten about three times. And now it's undeliverable until they can get the infrastructure, it's as simple as that. It will happen eventually, I think, but it's unlikely to happen much before the late teens, which was the point when the whole Gateway project was supposed to be virtually complete. Because we're at that point talking twenty-five years on.

Editors: What are your personal views on densification for London, if you can sweep aside the transport issues? Do you think it's a good thing or problematic?

Peter Hall: I'm doubtful about the degree of densification and the way it's actually happening through the private sector, because it's resulting in a multiplication of these notorious two-bedroom apartments, more like fifty two-storey two-bedroom apartments, because the developers see this as a way to make a quick buck as they sell them off to buy-to-let people. It is simply crazy to concentrate on that market to that degree. There are a lot of people coming into London who form small households, but those newly forming households don't determine the market, it's determined by the whole array of households. What it does is push more and more families with kids out of London, and this is going to be the answer, you know, a sort of childless London.

Editors: What should the policy response be?

Peter Hall: It should be to develop very softly a combination of some pyramids of very high density at very good public transport interchanges, plus provision for moderately high-density family homes. We know that we can do this, because study after study from Llewelyn Davies and others have shown that whole areas of inner London, like Barnsbury and Chelsea, have been built, typically, at densities of around seventy, eighty, even ninety dwellings per hectare, with small gardens, and kids grow up happily in these environments. So it can be done. The devil's always in the detail. Much of the delivery of that agenda goes down to a lower level, whether it's the borough or the UDC or whatever, so it's vital that it is well handled at that level.

Editors: There's been a lot of talk about community as a policy focus and the word community is used a lot in policy documents. What do you feel is new and different about the Blairite understanding of community to previous periods where it has been used?

Peter Hall: I profess to a certain world-weary cynicism when I hear the word community. It's often used by people who are peddling a political agenda, and certainly I'm not quite sure what the government means by sustainable communities up these corridors. I can understand that if, along those transport corridors, you develop expansions of existing towns like Bedford, Wellingborough, Kettering, Corby, up to about a hundred thousand, you're creating typical English county towns, places that a lot of English people seem to like living in and working in, and sending their kids to school in, and then if you design the growth so that you have reasonably coherent suburbs, what we used to call neighbourhood units in the time of the Abercrombie plans, around schools and shops. Upton in Northampton is often quoted in this respect, and the new development of The Hamptons, south of Peterborough. This seems to me old-fashioned neighbourhood planning, which is still okay as long as you don't believe you're going to achieve miracles of social engineering by it, because I don't think you ever did. That's about as far as I would go, because in London itself it's highly desirable to create a stronger sense of community in local neighbourhoods, but you have to deconstruct it a little bit and ask what are these communities, what size are they, what character are they?

The Bengali community in Tower Hamlets has a very strong internal sense of community but at another level it's a very closed-off community, highly segregated from its neighbours and from the rest of London, as we know both from academic work, and also from literary evidence. Whether creating this kind of inward-looking community is a good idea is obviously something that is exercising the government. It's a very, very tricky question in London, given its ethnic and cultural diversity. One would want to suggest that as far as possible you ought to create communities of a different kind, which are not so strongly defined in terms of ethnicity or religion or culture or anything else, that are much more mixed. But doing that's going to require quite a lot of hard thought.

Editors: What do you think of these ideas about the promotion of social mixing, particularly through urban renaissance, and the spread of social capital from middle-class people down to working-class communities?

Peter Hall: I like the idea in principle, and I think that it will happen, in part, because of the insistence of incorporating a certain amount of affordable housing into each major development, as you can see occurring now quite widely. There's going to be a lot of resistance to this, though. I was hearing a developer talking about a week ago at an RTPI South West region conference down in Jersey. He was referring to 'pepper-potting', which was essentially mixing all the social housing into each area, and he was saying this is a total disaster, you'll sink the value of the development and no one is going to do that. And that quite shocked me because it was the first time I'd appreciated that there was that degree of resistance from the developers. Desirable as mixture may be, one can see the fear that people won't buy next to what they could regard as – and they don't even know who these people are – potentially neighbours from hell. So I think the objective at least ought to be to create communities where kids can go to primary school together. This is a test we used long ago; it was used in America in the 1960s. If one can aim for that, given the degree to which kids socialise with each other and also socialise the parents outside the school gates, which might be one way of handling this problem. It would be interesting, in this respect, to see what's happening in a development like the Millennium Village down in

Greenwich, where the earlier, very attractive units on the water have been sold in the market, whereas the affordable housing has been planted at the back. Whether this will create some kind of segregation, 'the other side of the busway', like 'the other side of the tracks', will be interesting to notice, but it will be a bit of a good acid test of the ability to handle this.

Editors: Most of the evidence seems to point to the fact people won't socially mix, and the middle classes will not send their children to the same primary schools as a particular version of the working class anyway, what do you think of this, if that happens?

Peter Hall: Well, here you get into the most difficult territory of all, the territory of school choice. I can't help feeling that we've gone backwards in this regard in London since say the 1960s, because we've given the aspirant middle class every opportunity to take their kids out of what they regard as the second or third best school, which didn't happen under the old Inner London Education Authority policies of the 1960s. Then, you sent your child to the nearest primary school and you had to find a very good reason not to. This, to me, is market choice in the private sector gone mad. And it does raise very interesting questions about what could be called the whole Blairite agenda of multiplying choice in the public sector, because a section of the middle class will always exploit choice to gain privilege for their little son or daughter.

Editors: And of course they have so much more money than they had in the 1960s, they can afford private schools.

Peter Hall: Exactly. They can afford private, that's a real problem.

Editors: This brings us on to the idea espoused by Chris Hamnett that London has become a professionalised city. What do you think about that argument?

Peter Hall: I've always tended to accept this, because it's almost self-evident, empirically. There's the question here of two kinds of gentrification: either the gentrifiers physically move in, or an area gentrifies because the indigenous population lifts itself, and the evidence suggests that the second has been very important in London: basically, almost all of us do service industry jobs, there's been a vast loss of the old manufacturing jobs, which have almost disappeared, and there's been a big contraction in the more junior clerical jobs, because of automation and out-movement of those jobs to lower rent areas. So although it's a little more complex than that, basically the huge affluence of London produced by the growth of a very successful economy is generating this internal gentrification, which, in turn, is pushing lower income people out, because they can't afford to do anything else. That is the same process as the other kind, the physical gentrification of people moving in, it has the same impact, but an increasingly affluent London population produces it. And I don't easily see what you do about this: it is a phenomenon that is being driven by the very nature of the London economy.

Editors: How do you think increased gentrification and professionalisation of the population connects to regeneration pressures?

Peter Hall: It's bound to. Because in other cities like Manchester there is a more partial gentrification, which is especially gentrification of the young in the apartment areas around the city centres. We've still a big question as to what happens to those people when they actually start having kids. Whereas in London, we have a much more continuing process, in that large sections of the middle class want and are able to remain in London, in a way colonising new areas, apart from the fact that there's this internal gentrification process. It is very varied of course, because there are still surviving areas of London which are not subject – at least yet – to the pressures we're talking about, because they've traditionally been very working class and quite low income, they're still not seen as highly attractive to migrating gentrifiers, and they don't seem to be experiencing the same internal gentrification pressures. A very interesting question is whether over time they will also experience both kinds of gentrification, given that the process of gentrification seems to be extending from its original cores into marginal areas, for instance from Wandsworth into Tooting and Earlsfield. Over time it may extend, so it is a real issue in London, a continuing issue that won't go away.

Editors: What ought to be the policy responses in relation to those continuing pressures?

Peter Hall: I go back to the old argument of Alfred Marshall, 1884, in his paper 'The Housing of the London Poor', where he said that it makes no sense for poor people to live badly on high-value land, and so here I'm an unreconstructed Ebenezer Howard person: encourage as many people as possible to move out to places where they'll get better lives for them and their kids. And hopefully the Sustainable Communities strategy will help them do that. It's not producing enough houses at present, but as soon as it does you can do a lot by advertising. I remember the time when Milton Keynes was advertising on the London Underground and the Location of Offices Bureau, now long gone, was saying, 'Live out of London and get more out of life.' We could start doing that again; people will respond.

Editors: Do you think there are problems with decentralisation, that certain people respond, are able to respond and other people who are not able to respond get further left behind?

Peter Hall: Well, yes. That must happen, but the answer is then you redouble the efforts and target those people.

Editors: So if you were to have a vision of London, say 2020 or even 2050, are you saying to us that it's going to be an incredibly middle to upper middle class city, predominantly?

Peter Hall: More than now.

Editors: Relatively childless?

Peter Hall: Yes. I fear it is, and of course it already is and has been. That's been the situation for decades. Way back, in the 1931 census, household sizes were much smaller; there were fewer kids in London, than in the rest of England. I'm sure it goes back even before 1931: London has always been somewhat like that, more like that than the rest of the country, and will get even more like that. We have to find ways of trying to resist the process as far as possible by keeping London family friendly; it's not going to be easy physically.

Editors: One observation might be that urban regeneration over the years has always been physically led, and that urban regeneration is still primarily about property development companies that are interested in bricks and mortar.

Peter Hall: Right now I would have to say that's true. The only way you could alter that would be to reintroduce a much bigger Social Housing component, and I mean capital S, capital H, Social Housing component, than we have dared contemplate for the last twenty-five years. We did it differently in the 1960s, when we were building all those London County Council and Borough tower blocks all over the place, many of which have withstood the test of time and have become very attractive buildings for the middle class, and I think we may have to contemplate something like that again. One of the astonishing stories of the Blair government is its resolute resistance or failure to consider anything like that, despite the evidence in that first Kate Barker report of 2004 which shows this huge decline in the total amount of housing, not just in London but nationally, totally occasioned by the collapse of the local authority build, and no one seems to have followed the obvious conclusion from that.[2]

Editors: When the Urban Task Force reconvened in 2005 why did you not support some of its recommendations on densification?

Peter Hall: The Task Force re-appointed itself and it was obviously driven by an agenda to jack up the densities, which I refused to go along with. I really couldn't and wouldn't, so I had to sign a minority report, but most of the rest I agreed with, particularly the argument that the mechanisms weren't very good.

Editors: And what was your experience of being on the original Urban Task Force?

Peter Hall: On the whole, very good. We had a brilliant secretary and he had a strong agenda, which we all shared, actually, that was rather remarkable given we'd come from very different places. We all agreed to every single one of the 105 recommendations, some more enthusiastically than others, but there was no real serious disagreement with, for instance, the idea of, first, jacking up the brownfield percentage of development to sixty, or, second, jacking up minimum densities to around thirty per hectare, which was a serious agenda ten years ago because there was so much development taking place well below that. Where the split was bound to occur was in that Mark 2 taskforce where the agenda was going crazy. I recall that there were arguments for 100 per cent brownfield, and for jacking densities generally up to fifty, sixty, seventy dwellings per hectare, and I just couldn't go with it, and I don't think anyone in their right senses would do it. But it was very, very ideologically driven, that Mark 2 agenda, I'd have to say.

Editors: And what do you think about the way that the Urban Task Force fed through to the Urban White Paper? Are you pleased with how the Urban White Paper came out?

Peter Hall: By and large, yes, although by that time market forces were achieving many of the recommendations, particularly on brownfield percentages and densities, even without much positive action. There were some failures, and they're continuing failures. Our biggest single failure was to get harmonisation of the VAT on new build and rebuild, where we ran into this incredible Treasury resistance claiming it was contrary to EU policy, and that's never been sorted, and it is continuing to have daft results. As, for instance, if you take what Urban Splash has done so brilliantly up in Salford, in the Langworthy Terraces, that was only possible because they managed to get it classified as new build.

Editors: Could you say one or two things about the Olympic Games and the impact and effects that it may have on the regeneration of that part of London?

Peter Hall: I think in retrospect there's a serious doubt about whether we ever should have ever campaigned for the Games, and of course one version is that the government never ever thought for one minute they were going to get it, that Paris was going to win, but they had to show enthusiasm, and they were absolutely blown apart when they got it. And it's been more or less a disaster ever since.

The physical regeneration of Stratford was going to happen anyway. It didn't need the Games. It will clean up a vast mess of the Lower Lea Valley, between Stratford and Canning Town, which is a good thing and generations in the future will say that's great – as long as they don't mess it up afterwards, but there's now a rumour that they're going to try to develop half of it afterwards and not leave it as a park, which you can well see the Treasury trying to do.

But it has had terrible distorting effects, apart from the cost of it all, direct and indirect. It has skewed all the regeneration of Thames Gateway on to the Lea Valley and to some degree the Royals and away from Barking and other areas, which I think is a negative. And if we wanted to clean up the Lower Lea Valley and get Barking done, we could have got the whole job done much cheaper, than what we'll pay for the Games and the Lea Valley.

Editors: Do you think it is a common problem with London that big flagship projects tend to get prioritised to meet the global city aspirations of policy-makers?

Peter Hall: I think you're bound to get that; it comes with the territory, literally and metaphorically, that schemes like Canary Wharf, King's Cross and Paddington Central are the kinds of things that London does, because the commercial pressures are there to do them, and because you get this unique opportunity, which was of course central to the Thames Gateway vision, of these huge development potentials along the new railway line. And in this sense King's Cross should be regarded as the end of Thames Gateway because it's a kind of once for all realisation of a vision, and you don't build the CTRL, or at least its original line, to anywhere else but central London. So that's it, you know.

Editors: Ken Livingstone talked about London giving the country twenty billion a year. Do you think there is a politics now building up about supporting London more in terms of national policy, or is the argument still, do you think, going the other way towards trying to redistribute?

Peter Hall: I think that London will always continue to subsidise the rest of the country because it's richer. I think probably the big argument for the future is one that is more subtle: will the money go mainly to the growth areas in the Greater South East, will it go to the north of England or will it go to Scotland, which is partly dependent on the devolution agenda, whether Scotland has just cast itself off. But given the number of marginal seats in the Greater South East, I'd say that at the least, any political party has to placate that Greater South East in the run-up to a general election. It's got to see some goodies.

Editors: Wouldn't it make more sense for government policy to invest much more in London, this is what Ken Livingstone was kind of arguing, of course, that you need to feed the golden goose and all that kind of argument.

Peter Hall: Well, the question is how much you need to feed the golden goose. If you take the ultimate argument, which is Crossrail, I personally find this the most extraordinarily hyped argument by a group of self-interested people I've ever heard in my life. Of course they all get together with Gordon Brown at breakfast at Number 10 and say we've got to have Crossrail, because they're not paying for it and they see they're going to make a lot of money through property development. I'd do that if I were a property developer, but whether anyone's going to listen to them is another question.[3]

Editors: Do you think the London Plan is a strategic vision for the future of London, and what kind of London would you like to see by say 2050?

Peter Hall: It is a strategic vision and it's a very clear strategic vision, I think, based on pushing London east. It's not the vision I would have liked in detail, and in fact there's a personal autobiographical story here. There were two London Plans: there was the Nicky Gavron plan and there was the Ken Livingstone plan, and as ever Ken won, and the Gavron plan, which was for a much more polycentric London, got completely beaten out. It will be very interesting to see whether elements of the Gavron plan ever come back, particularly in the priority Ken gives to the completion of Orbirail through the East London Line extension phase two, which is still not funded, because there is even an opposition to that on the part of a key group of people in City Hall, who see the entire strategy as being based on a very strong easterly biased central area, consisting of the City of London, Canary Wharf and Stratford City. I'm not against a strong multi-centred London down there, but I think it needs to be balanced by a stronger growth of the middle ring town centres, and that is what's missing from the London Plan which needs to go back to it.

Editors: About Transport For London, an observation one might make is that it's just chaos, chaotic, in the context of privatisation, that there isn't any real coherence towards providing for a transportation system that works. What do you feel or think about that, and what ought to be done or could be done?

Peter Hall: Well, it's been massively complicated by the incredible backlog in investment in modernising the underground, and the way in which Gordon Brown forced his solution on to a very reluctant Ken Livingstone and Bob Kylie, and then saw the most important part, the Metronet consortium, literally beginning the collapse, physically and financially. I don't know what the outcome will be; I don't know whether with £750 million of debt, they will actually pull out and say enough is enough.[4] In which case certainly Ken Livingstone will be vindicated, but who picks up the pieces? I wouldn't like to say. They've obviously done a very poor job, they're arguing, as they would do, that it's all Transport for London's fault. We'll see when the adjudicator adjudicates; there are already indications as to what way he feels. That needs to be sorted because London's suffered from massive disinvestment in that system over forty or fifty years and now it's got to be done because the thing is literally falling to pieces in places. Once that is done then you could consider, I think, a programme of really new investment, of which for me the most important is the orbital line.

But another big question, which TfL, I think, have massively dodged, is that outer London is different from inner London: it's much more car dependent, for good or ill, and it is very, very difficult to develop an alternative strategy for outer London. Part of the strategy probably has to be bus based, meaning road based, and given TfL's resolute refusal to invest in roads, at least under the present mayor, this is, I think, inhibiting an adequate solution. It goes along with a feature of Ken's strategic vision for London, that it's very centrally based and inner London based. Someone – Mark Kleinman used the phrase while he was still an academic, borrowed from an American academic, I forget who – said, 'All mayors of cities tend to become zone one politicians.' And I think Ken has become a very zone one, or maybe zones one and two, politician.

Editors: That's interesting. And that strikes us in relation to the wider sustainable communities agenda, decentre, decant, take people out, how do you then get them back in? We know from personal experience there's a real crisis, well, it's a crisis in relation to transport affordability. In a context of trying to generate an urban regeneration policy or plans for London, it seems to us that this isn't being addressed. DCLG are thinking of one thing, the Department of Transport are doing something else, the Treasury, of course, are just trying to reduce expenditure; how can those things be resolved?

Peter Hall: My simplistic solution on this is that more money has to be spent on increasing the capacity of the long-distance commuter lines, not because we want to encourage commuting – that would be perverse in a Sustainable Communities strategy – but because, and this does sound a bit perverse, the more you push growth out to the fifty- to eighty-mile ring, the more you will achieve self-containment out there. We know from one critical study, where we measured this, that even there some people will commute long distance, even eighty miles each way. Bad news. But it's better to buy that bad news than have a lot of people commuting shorter distances. So there is a vital need to increase capacity on some of those main lines. The West Coast Main Line has the capacity, but it will run out. The East Coast Main Line has a problem at Welwyn and one or two other places, such as Hitchin. And the Liverpool Street line badly needs four tracking up the Lea Valley. There are all kinds of improvements that need to be made on those lines to prevent the system progressively collapsing. Also, very importantly, Crossrail needs to be refigured so that it is much more like Thameslink, which is a regional metro connecting places up to fifty miles out. Thameslink will, I'm sure, be completed, because there are four hundred people working on it at present and they're confidently expecting to get a solution wrapped around the Olympics.[5] When Thameslink is completed that will be a brilliant solution for north/

south travel, but it needs to be balanced by a similar east/west longer-distance commuter railway, which Crossrail isn't at present but could become.

Editors: We are going to have to go. Thank you very much. We really appreciate the time you have given to us.

Notes

1   And was in fact effectively abolished soon after this interview took place!
2   Subsequently Gordon Brown announced that local councils would be allowed to return to building public housing on a limited scale.
3   Subsequently the private sector was persuaded to play a bigger role in the package announced in October 2007.
4   Metronet in fact went bankrupt after this interview took place, and it continues to do work on an emergency basis as contractor to Transport for London.
5   The government announced soon after the interview that Thameslink would be completed in two stages, the first ready for the Olympics.

Chapter 3

Regenerating a global city

Tim Butler and Chris Hamnett

Introduction

In this chapter, we identify four key 'motors of change' that have driven London's transformation from a declining industrial city to its current status as an iconic centre of global financial and cultural flows. This resurgence, which has been both rapid and recent, contrasts sharply with a period thirty years ago when some saw the decline of cities such as London and New York as terminal (O'Connor, 1973). The four principal motors of change that have driven this transformation in London's fortunes in recent decades have been:

1. the decline of manufacturing industry and allied transportation uses which has produced redundant sites that have subsequently become available for redevelopment
2. the growth of the financial and business services which have always been central to London's economy but which have now become the focus of its growing global role. This has given rise to an associated demand for modern office space
3. the change in the occupational class and income structure of London's population and the associated demand for residential housing
4. the political (and governance) context for both urban boosterism and social inclusion that has fuelled central and local government commitment to large-scale development and regeneration activity.

In examining the overall development of London since the end of the Second World War, it has been the first factor, the decline of manufacturing industry and transport uses (notably Docklands, but also old canal basins, rail yards and riverside land), that has been crucial in making parts of London available for reuse. This has been a necessary, but not sufficient, condition for regeneration. It has been the second factor, the growth of financial and business services and particularly their internationalisation, that has been a major driver of regeneration. The internationalisation of the City of London can – of course – be traced back three hundred years but the origin of its current phase can probably be found in the rise of the 'euro dollar' market in the late 1950s and, more specifically, in the 'big bang' deregulation of financial services in 1986. This has provided the effective demand for new office space that has characterised the redevelopment of London since the 1950s when much of its central area was still manifesting the devastation caused by the wartime bombing.

The early office developments in both the City and the West End were followed in the 1980s by the redevelopment of Canary Wharf, and a host of other smaller schemes in central and inner London. The importance of this property-led redevelopment, for an understanding of both the longer trajectory of post-war trends and their more recent manifestations in central London (where many of the buildings that went up in the post-war decades are themselves now being redeveloped), cannot be overstated. Although the office property market is traditionally highly cyclical, the London office market has been on a rising trend since the mid 1990s until the downturn in late 2007 which has given developers confidence to maintain their investment even when the national and international economy appears to have paused. London's growing international role has ensured a substantial demand from domestic and overseas companies and institutions for high-quality office accommodation as well as a steady flow of investment funds which has forced up prices and driven down yields. The demand has also spilled over into secondary areas, leading to conversion of old industrial and commercial space for offices in the area bordering the City of London known as the City Fringe.

The third factor mentioned above, the changing occupational and income structure, has been linked to the rising demand for *residential* property and has been responsible not just for driving up prices across the board and for the strong construction activity in new apartment buildings in London. It has also driven the conversion of previous land uses such as warehouses and industrial or commercial uses into high-price residential units for the new elite, often in the City Fringe areas into which the secondary office development sector has spread. The huge demand for housing, driven by the growing professional and corporate sector, has not simply resulted in the gentrification of much of inner London, but has been the mechanism which has driven the demand for a wide range of services which have grown up to support both the production and consumption sector of the London economy (Sassen, 2001).

The fourth factor, government commitment to regeneration and development, has manifested itself in two major ways. The first has been to encourage the development of London's infrastructure (including importantly its cultural economy), so as to ensure its continued attractiveness to international businesses and investors. The second has been to mitigate, at least to some extent, the tendency identified by Sassen and others for the process of commercial and residential gentrification to lead to social polarisation and exclusion. At times, government policy has had directly contradictory effects. The most significant example of this policy was the setting-up of the London Docklands Development Corporation (LDDC) in 1981 that was of key importance for the redevelopment of Docklands in the 1980s and 1990s. This was seen as crucial if the City of London was to survive the perceived competition offered by cities such as Frankfurt and Paris. In its early years, it was believed that this was leading to working-class displacement both residentially and from the central London labour market (Brownill 1990; Crilley et al., 1991; Foster 1999). The policy was wound down in 1998 by which time the area had established itself, and gave way to a greater policy focus on social inclusion policies (Brownill et al., 1998). The perceived success of Docklands' regeneration encouraged a similar policy towards the regeneration of the East Thames Corridor (now the 'Thames Gateway').

A further strand of government policy has been witnessed in a clutch of policies for the regeneration of smaller areas of cities and towns nationwide. These policies were brought together in the early 1990s under the Single Regeneration Budget (SRB) which focused in a more holistic manner on particularly deprived areas. This policy continued to be rationalised when New Labour came to power in 1997 with a concept of fighting social exclusion. This included the New Deal for Communities (NDC) initiative that aimed to rehabilitate problem social housing estates through a mix of physical improvements and social engineering – including reducing or demolishing tower blocks and making some housing available for sale or shared ownership. A good example of this in London has been the regeneration of the notorious Holly Street Estate in Hackney (see chapter 15 in this volume). Important though government policies have been in underpinning regeneration in London, Canary Wharf and many subsequent developments, such as Paddington Basin and King's Cross, have been driven by commercial developers in which the state has been a relatively small though crucial player in terms of its role in granting planning consent.

In the remainder of the chapter we look first at the historical context in which these changes have been occurring, and then consider how these drivers have played out in the context of the changes that have occurred in London's economic and social structure over the last twenty-five years. We then briefly look at the key issues of cultural and transport policy that we suggest provide the social glue that links the physical changes to the city's changing demography. In the final section, we note, by way of conclusion, that a key area of policy failure in London's regeneration in recent years has been the inability to create appropriate levels of access to affordable housing.

The historical context: the shift from industrial to post industrial London

As we indicated earlier, the extent and nature of contemporary London's physical regeneration is a function of its nineteenth-century industrial development. London's 'Victorian Manufacturing belt'

> is dominated by the great industrial crescent which runs around the north and east sides of central London, from the western edge of the City and the West End, through the southern parts of St Marylebone

and St Pancras, through Islington, Finsbury, Holborn, Shoreditch, Bethnal Green and Stepney. It extends to Southwark on the south bank of the river; to the north it throws out two great projections, one north and northwest to Kentish Town and Holloway, one northeast to south Hackney and Stoke Newington . . . this crescent lies wholly within that area of London that was fully built up before 1900.

(Hall 1962: 226–7)

In addition to its manufacturing zones, the nature of the transport infrastructure which supported it has been critical to the way its subsequent deindustrialisation, at the end of the twentieth century, has played out – mainly through the provision of land. Notable here were the development of London's docks and the associated growth of port processing industries that were built between 1805 and 1926, extending progressively further downriver. Associated with the docks was the construction of the Regent's Canal that connected the Thames-side docks in the east via an arc around inner London to the Paddington Basin in the west. The third element to London's infrastructure was the construction of the railway network and the major metropolitan terminals, most of which had substantial railway goods yards that have provided the 'redundant' spaces for some of the most recent and large-scale developments (Kellett, 1969).

It is, however, important to note that the heritage of this legacy of industrial infrastructure was not restricted to nineteenth-century developments. The interwar industrialisation of inner north-west London (for example around Park Royal) and the extension of the older manufacturing areas into Tottenham and Edmonton in north London along the River Lee suffered widespread disinvestment during the 1980s as these consumer goods industries fell victim to competition from cheaper producers elsewhere in the UK and worldwide. The physical legacy of these developments has been of great importance, not least because many of the rail yards, docks, gasworks and factories began to fall into disuse from the 1960s onwards, leaving large areas of land derelict and supposedly redundant.

These exindustrial areas were not distributed at random. In an important paper written at the beginning of the 1970s when this disinvestment was at an early stage, Willmott and Young (1973) characterised London as being organised like a 'cross'. As figure 3.1 shows, the four arms of the cross followed the low ground of the river valleys – the Thames running from west to east and the River Lee to the north and the River Wandle to the south. The centre and the suburban quarters on the high ground marked London's relatively affluent areas whilst the low-lying river valleys with their associated railway lines were the industrial zones with their concentrations of working-class housing. The railway marshalling yards located on the low-lying lands in 'the cross' have become the focus of some of the biggest development projects in London (such as Paddington and King's Cross).

Willmott and Young noted that a river could either be repellent or attractive – the former if it was used for commerce but attractive if it was simply for

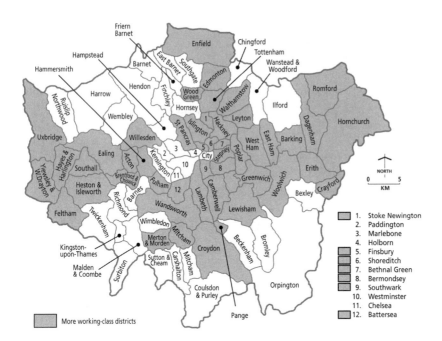

3.1
'The Cross': showing
the interaction of
human and physical
geography on the
distribution of London's
housing (Willmott and
Young, 1973)

1. Stoke Newington
2. Paddington
3. Marlebone
4. Holborn
5. Finsbury
6. Shoreditch
7. Bethnal Green
8. Bermondsey
9. Southwark
10. Westminster
11. Chelsea
12. Battersea

More working-class districts

pleasure. Such was the case for the Thames: to the east of the City of London it was repellent whereas to the west of the Cities of London and Westminster it provided an attractive frontage to some of London's most desirable areas. Willmott and Young made a bold prediction: that, as London's river industries moved downstream to the east, the Thames would become an increasing amenity for the city as a whole and a focus for its residential development (see chapter 10 in this volume). This has proved increasingly true and, more generally, this legacy has provided many of the underpinnings for the transformation that has taken place in London's cultural economy and its residential gentrification. A dramatic example, which is discussed in chapter 13 of this volume, is the 'South Bank' (of the River Thames) between Waterloo and London Bridge that is an area that even ten years ago was very run down. It now forms London's premier cultural quarter, in which a redundant power station, has become one of the city's leading art galleries and been transformed into one of its most iconic buildings.

Developers and urban policy-makers alike have discovered, as Willmott and Young predicted, the benefits of transforming an industrial heritage into a post-industrial urban landscape which immediately provides visual evidence that marks out the city's success in developing a residential, consumption and cultural infrastructure expected of a global city. In so doing, they have often 'imagineered' the motifs of a previous age and use (dockside cranes, old industrial warehousing etc) into the new era (Jager, 1986).

In the 1970s, London, like New York and other major once-industrial cities across the world, was haemorrhaging jobs and people. Approximately three-quarters of a million people left London during the 1970s (Buck et al.,1986).

Inner London boroughs, such as Hackney, lost up to a fifth of their population between 1971 and 1981 as the white working class left, many for a better quality of life in outer London and beyond (Hamnett and Randolph, 1982, 1988). Whilst white working-class decline was a key factor in explaining this, it was, in turn, part of a bigger picture of urban restructuring in which once working-class cities began to be transformed into the staging posts in a new global post-industrial finance-driven economy (Sassen, 2001). While thousands were made redundant in the labour market, many others, as Hamnett and Randolph (1988) have shown, were able to achieve upward mobility by buying houses in London's suburbs and moving into non-manual and managerial occupations.

Thus, as Buck *et al.* (1986) show, there was a dramatic transformation of the London economy as jobs disappeared and the working class that remained in the inner city became concentrated in economic inactivity and in social housing that itself became an increasingly marginalised form of housing tenure. Whilst the 'new economy' had its origins in this period, it was significantly held back by the subsequent recession in financial and housing markets from 1987 that hit London particularly hard (Hamnett, 2003). It was only from the mid 1990s that the stalled growth in the financial services economy and the slow-down in the nascent gentrification of the early to mid 1980s resumed their upward growth (Lees, 2000). It has not slackened since despite minor and – so far – short-lived hiccups in the global and national economies.

Following the dramatic population losses of the 1960s and 1970s, in the last two decades London's population has risen again by approximately half a million (Champion and Coombes 2007: 448). Champion and Coombes demonstrate that, although 100,000 more people left London in 2001 than came in, there are two ways in which London is distinguished from other UK cities. First, unlike every other significant UK city, there has been a net gain in higher managerial and professional occupations. Second, this net domestic outflow of population is more than compensated for by international in-migration. It is this last factor that is particularly striking in the case of London and has accounted for both the scale and nature of its recent growth (Hall, 2007). The best symbol of this initially halting but subsequently apparently unstoppable resurgence in London's growth is Docklands. The Canary Wharf development in Docklands forced the City of London to allow the redevelopment of many of the buildings that had been built in the post-war era and which were subsequently judged 'not fit for purpose'. Despite the early fears that the Docklands redevelopment might undermine the City's pre-eminent position, it has in fact helped to cement its role as the leading European financial centre.

The political context

There has been a remarkable transformation in the governance of London over the last thirty years. In the early 1980s, with the resurgent Conservative government under Mrs Thatcher and the Labour party in disarray, the Greater London

Council (GLC) under Ken Livingstone's leadership was in effect the unofficial political opposition. Installed in County Hall across from the Houses of Parliament, and displaying a huge sign announcing the level of unemployment in London, it promoted an alternative economic regime based on a mix of old- and new-left values. The Livingstone GLC had some success in reducing the unemployment rate in London and laying the basis for an analysis of the new urban economy based around culture and consumption. Unsurprisingly perhaps, Mrs Thatcher's response was to abolish the GLC. With New Labour's return to national government in 1997, it found itself under pressure to honour an election pledge to restore devolved governance to London. The result was the creation of the Greater London Assembly in which the office of mayor had a powerful strategic role. Ken Livingstone offered himself as the Labour Party's candidate but, having fallen out with both Blair and Brown, failed to achieve the Labour Party nomination despite clear polling evidence that he was the strongest candidate with the electorate. He subsequently stood as an independent and convincingly won the first election in 2000 and again in 2004 having by then been restored to Party membership. Despite his disagreements with the Treasury over how to improve London's infrastructure, it soon became obvious there was little substantive difference between his policies for London and those of New Labour for the UK as a whole. Both involved courting international investment and recognising that the fortunes of the nation were largely tied to the success of London, which was emerging as the financial and economic powerhouse for the country as a whole – although see Massey (2007) for a different reading of this claim. Both nationally and in London, New Labour presided over the dismantling of an industrial economy in favour of one based around consumption and the provision of services.

In order to prosper in this new climate, it was necessary for London to make itself attractive to an international elite which demands not only high-quality residential and commercial accommodation but also a similarly high-end provision in terms of a cultural, leisure and shopping infrastructure. Ken Livingstone has also consistently promoted London's diversity as reflecting its global status (Hall, 2007; Massey, 2007). Massey – whilst broadly supportive of this argument – has argued that there are unresolved tensions here between London's various global roles which are both inward and outward looking which place responsibilities on London as a promoter as well as beneficiary of this 'rolled out neo liberalism'.

To what extent has the extensive social, economic and physical reshaping that has occurred in London been for the benefit of the few to the exclusion of the many (Amin *et al.*, 2000)? We argue that, to some extent at least, the answer to this question depends on how we understand the changing social structure of London and the ways in which it absorbs its new citizens from its national and global hinterlands. The dividing lines between winners and losers have been evolving from those associated with the old class divisions between a working-class majority and upper-class elite that characterised old London. Arguably, and we return to this in our concluding remarks, some of the sharpest contemporary divides are around housing tenure rather than occupational class.

The changing economic and land use structure of London

Manufacturing employment accounted for almost a third of London's labour force in 1961 but just 7 per cent today. Conversely, employment in financial and business services and the creative industries has grown dramatically over the same period to account for almost a third of total employment. These changes are of profound importance and have been widely discussed (Buck *et al.*, 1986; Fainstein *et al.*, 1992; Buck *et al.*, 2002; Hamnett, 2003). These changing economic and employment structures have had significant implications for changes in both land use and occupational class. In the remainder of this section, we indicate the main strategic changes in land use that have occurred in London over the last quarter of a century and in the follow-up section we discuss the changes that have occurred in relation to occupational class.

In recent years there has been an increase in the scale and scope of London's business districts. In addition to the development of Docklands, which has been so symbolically important in terms of London's transition to a new global financial centre, there are currently three 'mega schemes' under development around inner London (Paddington Basin, King's Cross and Stratford) (see figure 3.2). These will add significantly to London's office and associated retail/residential/cultural infrastructure. In addition, the plans for the Thames Gateway will add substantially to London's residential housing stock. The main focus of the London economy is now based around the following areas:

- The West End – now the focus for the head offices of hedge funds as well as more traditional property development, advertising and media industries. It also remains the centre for much of London's leisure and night-time economy. The Paddington Basin and King's Cross developments both border on the West End and will therefore consolidate the influence and scope of this area of economic activity.
- The City (of London) – now the focus of considerable physical redevelopment for the major global players in the investment banking and associated industries (notably big law, consultancy and accountancy partnerships).
- Docklands – which has attracted many of the top retail banks (HSBC, Barclays and Citibank for example), leading media players and some of the big legal firms as well as many other major players in the international financial economy.
- Heathrow – a major business centre in its own right for high-tech industries as well as European headquarters for global companies wanting a base near the world's best-connected airport.
- Croydon – a significant back-office location which developed as such during the 1970s and has retained this function because of being near but not in inner London and thus more able to attract highly-skilled middle-range administrative and support workers.

(a) Paddington Basin

(b) St Pancras, Eurostar Terminal

3.2
Development areas in London.
Source: Peter Howard, Department of Geography, King's College London

Subsequent chapters in this book discuss many of these developments, but what we wish to note here is their strategic role in adding to London's provision of high-quality and accessible office/retail/residential/leisure facilities. Such large-scale redevelopment schemes, whereby financial or consumption centres are expanding from their relatively constrained historical centres, are becoming more ubiquitous (a good example of this being the way that Barcelona expanded out of the old city in the early 1990s and Sydney around Darling Harbour ten years later).

In all cases, the trick has been to transform an outmoded (and supposedly redundant) land use into a more modern, prestigious and profitable one with the twin goals of attracting global investors and increasing investment values. Unsurprisingly, they differ in their timing, function and precise locations to the existing centres although often a mega-event such as the Olympic Games can be used to provide political as well as financial leverage (see chapter 8 in this volume).

London first experienced large-scale reconstruction in the decades following the Second World War, as areas of bomb-damaged commercial property in the City and housing in the East End were cleared and redeveloped. However, it was not until the 1960s that this redevelopment of inner London really got underway with, on the one hand, the clearance of old bomb sites and the building of the first round of modern high-rise office buildings and, on the other hand, the redevelopment of large areas of poor-quality private housing into social housing. Examples of such a form of commercial development in this period would be the high-rise offices on London Wall in the City and – a little later – the development of Centre Point by Harry Hyams at the crossing of Tottenham Court Road and Oxford Street in the West End. Both were intended to provide state-of-the-art accommodation for the corporations of the time: such organisations were hierarchically organised into many separate departments, each of which could be allocated a separate floor with prime corner offices being given to departmental managers and their deputies. Many of these commercial buildings are no longer regarded as 'fit for purpose' and are being demolished and the land redeveloped.

New corporate structures and information technologies require a different kind of building with big ceiling voids for cabling and large trading floors with flexible dividers for project-based team working. Corporate fashions have also been changing, reflecting a move away from the rather functional and ascetic modernist style of many early high-rises to a more extravagant architectural style and use of materials that reflects their current occupants' status as contemporary masters of the economic universe. The failure of the residential social housing high-rises is a familiar and similar story, although it is, however, interesting to note that the Barbican estate in the middle of the City is now highly sought after. This demonstrates how, if properly resourced and built to a high standard, high-rise building 'works' – at least for affluent households without children (see also chapter 9 of this volume).

These schemes transformed large areas of inner London in the 1960s and 1970s, and are now the object of much contemporary redevelopment activity. Our interest however, is primarily focused on the large-scale commercial redevelopment schemes which have taken place, or are planned, on the site of old industrial, port or transport activity. These range from luxury residential developments such as Chelsea Harbour, on the Chelsea waterfront, through to the large-scale residential redevelopment of the Surrey Docks in south London and the residential developments in Docklands including Galleons Reach on the site of the Beckton Gasworks (see also chapter 10 of this volume). Other schemes have included Tate Modern (formerly Bankside power station), the planned redevelopment of Battersea power station and a host of others (Newman and Smith, 2000).

Docklands is the largest redevelopment in Europe and Canary Wharf is Europe's largest new financial centre around which there are plans for substantial further expansion (Rossiter, *Times*, 16 July 2007). When this is linked to the Excel Exhibition Centre, London City Airport and the Docklands Light Railway (DLR), it is clear that substantial redevelopment has taken place which has provided tens of thousands of jobs and helped shift London's financial centre of gravity eastwards in the 1990s. The LDDC also initiated plans for construction of thousands of new (private) houses and flats. This emphasis on private, as opposed to public, housing provision has been strongly criticised but the LDDC plan was quite clear that they wished to shift the local housing market away from social renting, which formed 85 per cent of housing in Tower Hamlets in 1981 prior to the redevelopment of Docklands. The LDDC wanted to create a more balanced housing market. It has undoubtedly been a process of state-sanctioned gentrification, in which few of the new homes have gone to local families – although it is worth noting that at the end of the 1980s social landlords buying the otherwise un-saleable flats bailed many of the private developers out. Canary Wharf has become an upmarket dormitory for young City workers (Butler, 2007). Clearly there has been gentrification and displacement, but it would, however, be perverse to see this as a failure in terms of regeneration as some critics are prone to do. If this is a failure, it is the type of failure many cities would be delighted to have.

The King's Cross rail lands scheme is another example of large-scale redevelopment; in this case, of semi-derelict land immediately to the north of King's Cross railway station – which is the best connected of all the London termini to the underground network. The streets immediately around the stations of King's Cross and St Pancras provided one of London's most notorious 'red light' districts whilst the surrounding area was a wasteland occupied by cement factories and waste sorting in the early 1970s. There had been longstanding plans to redevelop the area that fell foul of collapses in the office market of 1974 (in the so-called secondary banking crisis) and then again in the recession of the early 1990s. Consequently, the area remained largely undeveloped except for the much delayed building of the new British Library on a site immediately to the west of St Pancras station. In the mid 1990s, however, plans were announced to make St Pancras the terminus for the Channel Tunnel Rail Link to Brussels, Lille and Paris. The site owners immediately realised the huge commercial potential of the site with its excellent travel links not only to the rest of London but also to the north and Midlands. Their plans for redevelopment, as documented in chapter 6 of this volume, had a substantial office and retail component, and have been vigorously resisted by community pressure groups determined to try to wrest more benefits including housing and open spaces for local residents. At this point in time, however, it looks at though the local residents have lost much of the battle after a series of protracted planning and legal struggles.

Rather similar sets of issues, as outlined in chapter 7 of the book, are at stake in the Paddington Basin redevelopment scheme that abuts the West End to the west as King's Cross does to the east. The developers want to utilise the land primarily for new offices and luxury housing in an area which also has excellent local links to the affluent areas of inner west London as well as Heathrow Airport (15 minutes away through Paddington Station) and, via the high-speed train network, out along the M4 corridor to Reading and Bristol. Like King's Cross, Paddington Basin (as the name suggests) has been able to capitalise on the aesthetic advantages of the canal frontage that runs through the area. The big issue in both developments has been the socially skewed nature of the development favouring upmarket housing and retail developments in addition to commercial and financial sector office developments.

The changing social structure of London

For the last twenty years, there has been considerable debate over the changing social structure of London, and of global cities as a whole (Johnston, 1994). The debate has hinged around whether such cities have become more polarised – this has been defined as the social structure comprising a larger share of higher and lower income groups at the expense of a decline in the share of middle-income groups. Alternative explanations have posited that such cities have become more professionalised (i.e. that they have experienced a growth in the middle and at the top end) or more proletarianised (i.e. primarily with growth at the bottom end). To date, much of the evidence points towards an Atlantic divide in that, despite a growing income inequality, London, Paris and other European cities demonstrate that there is little evidence of the kind of acute social polarisation found in New York and Los Angeles (Hamnett, 1994a, 1994b, 1996a, 1996b; Hamnett and Cross, 1998; Buck *et al.*, 2002; Preteceille, 2004).

More recently, however, these findings have been challenged by May *et al.* (2007) for London in the light of their research on recent and large-scale labour immigration. These findings were based on intensive and (in contrast to Hamnett's approach) qualitative research involving specific communities of migrants. These groups are unlikely – for obvious reasons – to feature in large-scale official statistical surveys such as the Labour Force Survey or the decennial census used by researchers like Hamnett. While there is little doubt that large-scale immigration has satisfied the demand for the large number of construction and service jobs in the last few years and ensured the sector remains poorly paid, evidence from the census for the period 1981-2001 confirms that overall London has become a more middle-class city, with a large growth in the professional and managerial middle classes.

There are thus interesting methodological questions here and the issue remains one of scale. As Butler *et al.* (2008: 73-4) show, in an analysis of London's changing class structure, inner London has a higher proportion of those in the top social groups (higher managerial and professional occupations) and those at the bottom (never worked and long-term unemployed) than elsewhere in the UK. This analysis also shows however that the biggest decline (1981–2001) has been amongst the old manual working-class groups; their decline however has not left a vacuum but they have been replaced by new groups of middle- and lower-middle-class non-manual working households. There is thus continued inequality in London but there is little evidence of social polarisation between the top and bottom of the occupational class structure on the scale implied by Sassen's work.

These findings therefore provide some support for the arguments made by Pahl (1988) and Saunders (1990) at the beginning of the 1990s about a 'middlemass' of society which – they argued – was transforming the traditional social pyramid into one that resembled an onion. What we have therefore seen in the last two inter-censal decades is a reshaping of the geography of social class in London which reflects the transformation of London's industrial structure and the increasing dominance of jobs in finance, business services and creative industries and a renewed premium on proximity and accessibility to central London.

To say this is not to adopt a 'panglossian' position regarding the joys of living in the new middle-class city (Slater, 2006). On the contrary, the changes in occupational class structure have been accompanied by a sharp increase in earnings and income inequality as the salaries and bonuses of the top decile have risen much faster than for other groups, thus widening inequality (Hamnett, 2003). Thus, London has simultaneously become both a more middle-class and a more unequal city in recent decades. New class fractions have opened up with significant divisions within the middle class. This has had profound implications, particularly in terms of the housing market as the size and purchasing power of the new elite has dramatically pushed up property prices since 1995 to the point where average prices now far exceed the possibility of individuals or households even on middle-class incomes to aspire to owner occupation in much of London.

At the other end of the scale, the activity of 'buy-to-let landlords' and the growth of the new upper middle classes linked to a growing demand for central and inner city residence and lifestyles, has been associated with the continued growth of gentrification across large swathes of inner London (Butler and Lees, 2006). It is not too much of an exaggeration to claim that, with the exception of social housing estates, much of inner London has now largely been gentrified. As demand has increased and prices have risen, middle-class residential demand has gradually pushed further outwards, particularly towards the east. What were once working-class areas in the former East End are now seen as desirable residential areas with close links to the City of London. Many of the areas of lower-middle-class and working-class owner occupation in the outer eastern suburbs are now subject to a process of class re/displacement by upwardly mobile middle classes including those from black and minority ethnic groups (Hamnett et al., 2007).

A further manifestation of this process has been the expansion of loft conversions and luxury apartment buildings in central and inner London in former industrial and commercial buildings (Hamnett and Whitelegg, 2007). This process can be seen as a specific form of gentrification and as a result of the revaluation of urban centrality by a cosmopolitan fraction of the middle classes who like living in close proximity to restaurants, bars and entertainment facilities. This process has been of considerable importance in the regeneration of run-down ex-industrial and commercial areas such as Clerkenwell, Spitalfields, Shoreditch and Borough in the City Fringe, not least because of their proximity to both the City of London and the West End which allows residents to avoid a long commuting journey and in many cases to walk to work. In addition, there have been a large number of new residential apartment developments in inner London in recent years, particularly along the river and in Docklands (see Davidson and Lees, 2005, Butler, 2007; and chapter 10 in this volume).

The cultural economy of urban regeneration

Regeneration involves an interaction between the built environment and social policy but it is not always clear what is the goal for this interaction. There has been a longstanding tension between encouraging social inclusion and economic competitiveness. As the regeneration of Docklands has shown, the state has been quite prepared to sponsor gentrification, exclusion and replacement in order, as it saw it, to safeguard the long-term competitiveness of London as an economic centre. On the one hand, some have argued that this is a very dangerous strategy because in being successful it creates social exclusion, division and potentially such a degree of polarisation that it runs the danger of frightening off those very groups who make cities like London an economic success story. On the other hand, others note that unless the state is prepared to restructure London's built and social environment, it will lack the 'cool' that is now deemed a necessary part of any economic strategy (Florida, 2005).

In this respect, New Labour's attempt to engineer a third way of balancing social cohesion and economic competitiveness can be seen as a well-judged policy imperative. This was expressed most clearly by the recently deposed Mayor of London, Ken Livingstone, who has argued that if London is to prosper it has to be a globalising city attracting not just capital but people from all around the world. In order for the London of capital to work, it had to – in his view – be inclusive to the diverse populations who now call it home. This social aspect of London's global status has recently been recognised by Peter Hall (2007) and Doreen Massey (2007) who have previously approached the question of London's regeneration from somewhat different perspectives. Both emphasise that contemporary London is a city of immigration and that this interaction with global factors is now a crucial aspect of London's contemporary development.

Whilst not as dramatic as the call from the Statue of Liberty in New York to 'Give me your tired, your poor, Your huddled masses yearning to breathe free', there is more than a hint in both of these accounts that to function properly London must become the 'city for the many and not the few' – as Amin et al.

(2000) put it. Regeneration policies need to address issues of economic self-interest as well as of social inclusion. Former Mayor Livingstone recognised the central role played here by cultural policy. One of the innovations of the GLC under his stewardship was that cultural policy not only provided a basis for integrating otherwise marginalised social groups but also that the 'cultural economy' is itself a major economic driver (Scott, 2000). In the remainder of this section, we focus on this area of cultural politics and the ways in which – potentially at least – this has brought together the 'holy grail' of social cohesion and economic competitiveness in London by striving to cater for the mass of the population rather than simply providing a cultural experience for the traditional elite of cultural consumers.

Cultural production and the role of the cultural industries have become an increasingly important element of the London economy. Where once it might be argued that the level of cultural provision was a reflection of the strength of the underlying economy, it is now undoubtedly the case that culture is a major component of the economy of cities (Zukin, 1995). In order to be a successful city nowadays there must be a cultural infrastructure and an ongoing programme of constructing significant buildings devoted to culture. This has been demonstrated in London – for example – by the South Bank developments such as Tate Modern, the Globe Theatre and the refurbishment of the Festival Hall (see chapter 13 in this volume) and even more dramatically perhaps by the way in which Frank Gehry's Guggenheim Museum rescued Bilbao from post-industrial decline following the closure of its steel and shipbuilding industries (Vicario and Monje, 2003; Hamnett and Shoval, 2003).

Cultural development is now part of any regeneration strategy and the Department of Culture, Media and Sport demand a cultural regeneration strategy from all local authorities. Consultancies have sprung up to provide help to local authorities in thinking through such strategies and commodifying their historical past into cultural goods for an increasingly omnivorous group of consumers. Culture, however, is not just an economic driver but is also part of the social glue that holds diverse communities together by celebrating aspects of that diversity. There are many examples of this. The UK Treasury recently funded a large 'invest to save' project in the South Bank to investigate the extent to which the cultural providers there were making their output available to the young people of some of London's most fractured and deprived communities. None of this, however, can work unless all groups have access to the city, which means that transport becomes an essential element to urban regeneration.

Transport: glueing the hard to the soft?

Culture provides an instance of the way in which 'soft' regeneration is now a key element of the 'regeneration toolkit' – it also provides an example of how regeneration can be seen as promoting a virtuous circle. Culture acts as a social glue yet the provision of cultural products helps to promote the urban economy and draw in those who might not otherwise be seen as either cultural producers or consumers. For this to happen, however, there is a further crucial element to the regeneration agenda: transport. Transport in a sense ties together the physical and the social aspects of regeneration and it also brings it to a historical full economic circle. As we have argued, much of London's physical regeneration has happened in spaces made redundant by the collapse of old industries and transportation technologies.

As Londoners, we now live and work in a city where the 'failure to arrive' joins house prices and education as the most talked about topics around metropolitan dinner tables and office water coolers. Transport is also, as Mayor Johnson suggests, something that ties the city together not just in terms of getting people to work but also enables diverse groups of different people to make full use of the city's cultural, physical and economic assets. If London is to be the 'city for the many and not for the few' then transport has to be efficient and accessible – in all senses of the word. This perhaps also explains why it is such a tempting target to terrorists wanting to disrupt the city and the relative democracy of its underground network. However, transport in London is not working and has for years suffered from a lack of investment. Most transport lines have been irregular, unreliable and overcrowded; they have also followed a radial pattern making travel across London's communities difficult with very few exceptions – such as the North London Line which runs circumferentially around the north of London from Richmond in the west to Woolwich in the east.

More recently, new infrastructure has been built including extensions to the Jubilee Line (which was critical to the success of Canary Wharf) and to the Docklands Light Railway connecting new parts of the city together across the river Thames in the East. The East London line is now being extended from Croydon in the south to Hackney in the north connecting together areas which had previously been inaccessible to each other. Cross Rail – which has recently been approved – will link the west from Heathrow to the West End and the City and out to the eastern suburbs. Former Mayor, Ken Livingstone, claimed that this huge project, which will have the same effect on London as the RER did for Paris, is vital to London's continued economic viability although others have criticised it for simply linking its suburbs to the centre and to each other.

There is no doubt that such projects have had a dramatic effect on previously deprived areas: when the Victoria Line was first built it transformed the fortunes of Canonbury and Highbury which were run-down declining areas into ones in which merchant bankers were happy to live even before the boom in merchant banking and City incomes. More recently, the extension of the DLR to Greenwich has transformed the area, making it into an inner London gentrifying district which is only twenty-two minutes from the City; the effect on the prices of its terraced housing has been equally dramatic. Some might argue against such projects precisely because they cause gentrification but this would seem to take a view of urban development that might only have found favour with Pol Pot. The continued investment in transport is clearly a vital component of a London regeneration strategy not only for reasons of economic competitiveness and social cohesion but also to replace the reliance on private cars and reduce the pollution and carbon footprint of the city (see chapter 11 in this volume). The imposition and expansion of the central area congestion charge and the investment of the proceeds in an expanded bus network has seen a dramatic increase in journeys throughout the day and increasingly through the night – although it might also be argued that the pricing out of private cars has led to central London becoming more of a premium place to live.

Conclusions

Ruth Glass (1964) brought the word gentrification into the urban dictionary over forty years ago to describe a process of social change that was already well underway in central London. Since then, as we have argued, London has become, at least in terms of occupational classifications, a largely middle-class city. In addition, old land uses and technologies have been replaced by new ones in response to primarily economic developments. This transformation has occurred in the context of London changing from being the national capital at the heart of a declining industrial economy and imperial power to what is arguably now the 'first city' of an emergent global economy. In so doing, it has changed from being a mono-ethnic city primarily divided on class grounds to a diverse, multi-ethnic one whose growth is driven by international migration.

It is this dynamic, we argue, that has driven the changes in its physical, social and cultural infrastructure over the past twenty-five years to a situation in which now approximately 30 per cent of its population was born overseas and a similar proportion is of a non-white heritage. We do not suggest, however, that class is no longer important in understanding the dynamics of London's social structure – see Butler *et al.* (2008) for an analysis of how class remains the prime source of social division. We have suggested that cultural and transport policies are crucial elements of urban regeneration in the potential they have for resolving the tension between economic competitiveness, social cohesion and (increasingly) environmental sustainability – which many argue is now a driving force behind urban regeneration (Raco, 2007a). There does, however, remain one major issue that has been absent from this discussion: that of housing affordability.

Housing has traditionally been the driver of urban regeneration leading, it was argued, to social and health benefits for those unable to bring private assets to the housing market. In recent years, successive Conservative and New Labour governments have actively disinvested in traditional ('council') forms of social housing (see chapter 12 in this volume). There have been many reasons for this but there must be a suspicion that there is a bipartisan desire to disassociate from what has been seen primarily as a working class form of tenure. The consequences of this policy have been beyond doubt: it has led to a highly polarised housing market. This has been particularly the case in London where not only the economically inactive and the working classes but also many of the middle classes are now unable to consider home ownership and continued residence in London. This polarisation of life chances has been far more dramatic than the comparatively benign divisions within the labour market.

Housing inequality remains the most serious issue facing those concerned with social inequality in London. It is one that appears set to get worse despite the recent dramatic decline in house prices in London and beyond. Less dramatic perhaps is the consequence high house prices have for the quality of life of even its high-achieving citizens who can only continue to live near where they work and play by trading accessibility for living space and/or security of tenure in a growing private rented sector. 'Buy to let', as this new curse on London's housing market has come to be known, often offers a maximum of six months' security, a decrease in maintenance and sociability in those streets it blights. There is a danger, unless housing inequality is addressed, that for many Londoners urban regeneration is experienced not so much as gentrification but urban degeneration as they pay more and more of their salaries for less and less accommodation in a situation where they live in private squalor surrounded by public affluence. Whilst it can be argued that successful regeneration policies form a virtuous circle, failed policies can seem like a vicious cycle.

Chapter 4

Governing London: the evolving institutional and planning landscape

Mark Tewdwr-Jones

Introduction

This chapter discusses the recent experience of strategic planning and the governance of growth and development in London, a city that is experiencing many of
the socio-economic and physical problems facing world cities today. It provides
an insight to the unique nature of governance and planning within London, one of
the world's foremost global cities. The institutions of change are constantly undergoing reform and modernisation, in order to set a strategic framework for growth
and investment. But choosing an appropriate governing and institutional framework for London has always been problematic. As Travers (2004: 1) has
remarked

> Governing London is a complex business. The city's vast population, its
> geography and history conspire to make the British capital an unusu-
> ally difficult place to govern . . . The regularity with which London's
> government is reorganised suggests there is something unusual about
> the pressures that affect successive systems.

With the city serving as the economic core of the UK's global position and as
her capital city, London's effects are felt over a much wider territory than the
administrative boundary of London alone (John *et al.*, 2005; Musson *et al.*,
2006). Questions have been addressed continuously as to the nature and form
of the governance of London (Robson, 1939; Davis, 1988; Hall, 1963; Travers *et
al.*, 1991; Pimlott and Rao, 2002; Travers 2004). Should London possess a city-
wide top-level authority? How extant should this authority be and over what
geographical area? What is the relationship between the national government
and London, and between the south-east region within which London is situ-

ated and the city itself? And what is the governing relationship between London and its constituent boroughs?

London's role as the capital city and as the location of central government, global business interests and the financial markets, significant arts and cultural facilities, a place of tourism, and as a renowned worldwide centre for education have all justified successive governments' desire to promote London and its wider region economically, and to protect the city as a world urban power (Hebbert, 1998). A range of interventions by government have demonstrated a commitment to promote and strengthen London further over time in the face of global competition and as the UK's premier city. This is evidenced by decisions to support massive regeneration schemes in and around the capital such as the Thames Gateway; to invest in infrastructure and transportation developments like the Channel Tunnel rail link, the extension of Heathrow Airport, and Crossrail; to lead on the Olympic Games 2012 bid; and to support the city financial hub of London as a focal point for global business.

The provision of highly specialist support systems for international finance and business generates economic growth that is in the interest of the UK's economy. This is London as the world city, a success story that physically is bursting out of the urban core, forming new patterns of growth and pressure around the capital, and causing externalities that Londoners experience through high prices, housing and transport costs, and social polarisation, and makes the city one of the world's most expensive cities to live and work within (Hamnett, 2003). House prices, in early 2008, are now ten times the average London salary and there remain difficulties to house and accommodate key workers essential to deliver London's services. London's population doubles during the working day as millions of people commute into the city from a significantly wide and increasingly extensive catchment area. The infrastructure necessary to support this growth and pressure remains archaic and so delay and frustration have become part of the commuting experience for many. This, in turn, has led to many Londoners to migrate from the city to other less expensive parts of the UK for quality of life reasons.

London has also been a principal gateway for in-migration into the country, a subject politically controversial, and one ever folding to the extent that in 2006 London plays host to 300 different nationalities of people, speaking 200 different languages (Morphet, 2006). The social and ethnic mix of London today is in marked contrast to the London of sixty years ago, when the politicians and planners first attempted to coordinate change and bring about reconstruction. Patrick Abercrombie's Greater London Plan of 1944 talked of the city as comprising a series of separate and readily identifiable communities that survived the war, each with their own spirit that the Plan attempted to build upon rather than diffuse; the programme of new town construction occurred beyond both the urban core and a newly designated Green Belt (Abercrombie, 1944).

Concern with the persistent growth and sprawl of London through urbanisation and development is not a new phenomenon today, anymore than it was in the 1940s. The architect and rural campaigner Clough Williams-Ellis wrote in 1928 of 'England and the octopus', the danger of London sprawling into the surrounding countryside along arterial roads like giant tentacles (Williams-Ellis, 1928). The point Williams-Ellis and others were making here in the interwar years was partly in relation to the continued growth of London out from the centre, but also hinting at how governments could create and control these places as growth proceeded. It was a subject concerned with questioning the ability of government to exercise authority over a significant metropolitan territory, the meaning and extent of London itself, and of those various populations and communities that make up the city. These are exactly the same issues that London is facing today: numerous and overlapping contentions for future direction between competing interest groups.

These tensions are associated with divisions between advocates of continual growth for wider regional and national economic benefit, and proponents of restraint and environmental – and to some extent social – protection. They encompass not simply growth versus protection interests, but also national and local priorities, and inner London and outer London contentions. These arguments are persistent, often hostile, and are played out within a turbulent theatre of governance which itself is often changing. Generating a vision, strategy and plan to coordinate change in London is one that politicians and policy-makers find incredibly difficult to undertake.

Over the last fifty years, successive governments and politicians have attempted to grapple with the governance, institutional structures and planning of London (Pimlott and Rao, 2002; Simmie, 1999). It seems that London, governmentally and institutionally, is in a continual state of flux, searching for an institutional fix to govern and coordinate intervention, while arguing about the delineation of power to strategise the range of ongoing economic, social and environmental problems and bring about change. Since 2000, London has been governed by an elected mayor, within a broader governmental framework provided by: central government; regional governing structures; local municipalities; an elected London-wide Assembly; a range of quasi-autonomous central government bodies; and ad hoc partnerships. There has been little consensus by commentators in the period since on the right relationship and degree of responsibilities between these bodies, even though London's mayor was awarded further additional powers in 2007, particularly in relation to strategic matters. The recent growth of mayoral powers raises significant wider issues concerning democratic accountability across the region, and serves to highlight the ongoing and perhaps historic tensions that exist between the agencies of change on the one hand, and different forms of democracy and claims to democracy that are indecorously present in London on the other.

The need for coherent planning and governance within London, across London and between London and the South-East is arguably more important than ever. London has become increasingly a world-city region, possessing inter- and intra-dependencies and a diverse composition that makes coherent government and intervention problematic (Sassen, 2001). This chapter looks at the efforts to achieve coherent government and planning in London over the last fifty years. It examines the attempt to manage growth and change within and across the London city region area, and goes on to examine the concept of vision and strategy making through new spatial strategies. The chapter discusses developments in the governance of London caused by the election of a mayor of London, and the strange anomaly where the office-holder may possess some of the powers necessary to set a clear vision for the city, but as a result of the fragmentation of power between central and local interests, often lacks many of the implementation roles that are necessary to turn that vision into a practical reality.

The evolution of governance and planning in London

The period 1888–1901 saw the creation of the London County Council (LCC) and then the twenty-eight metropolitan boroughs. This system of government existed for much of the last century but attempts to develop a comprehensive plan for the wider metropolitan area as the city sprawled into neighbouring counties failed to take hold, despite recognition of the need for some means of strategic growth management. Proposals to extend the LCC boundary to match the outward growth patterns of London were resisted, especially in suburban areas outside London that had no desire to be swallowed by 'the octopus' of the metropolitan authority. Boundaries remained tightly drawn and the planning ideas of the first half of the twentieth century followed the prevailing suburban sentiment by attempting to contain growth artificially and permit growth instead in new settlements and garden villages beyond a green wedge that would form a defence barrier between London and its surrounding rural areas. The need for more integrated planning between the LCC and its regional hinterland was acknowledged in 1927 by the formation of the Greater London Regional Planning Committee, bringing together 126 local authorities, but as Thompson (2007) states, the Committee's work was regularly frustrated by the parochialism of the LCC on the one hand and by the conservatism of the surrounding authorities on the other. Even here, there were intractable differences in opinion on meeting the needs and growth of London while protecting outside interests. In 1937, a Standing Conference on London Regional Planning finally replaced the Committee, but even this lacked the powers and resources necessary to deal with metropolitan-wide concerns and boundary issues.

The period just before the outbreak of the Second World War and the era of reconstruction after 1943 pushed the requirement for strategic and regional planning onto the national political agenda. Following the publication of the Barlow Report on the Distribution of the Industrial Population in 1937, it was central government rather than the Standing Conference on Regional Planning that gave the impetus for the preparation of a Greater London Plan by (Sir) Patrick Abercrombie. The plan of 1944 articulated a strong regional policy with a strategy of planned decentralisation into satellite towns some distance from London and a green belt restricting sprawl from the existing built-up area, epitomising the principles of the garden city and planning pioneer Sir Ebenezer Howard in practice. These ideas were taken up by central government and formulated into new towns and green-belt policies in the post-war period by the socialist Labour government.

Thompson (2007), commenting on the merits of the Abercrombie plan and its implications for London, maintains that despite its almost mythological status amongst planners and the rolling out of the new towns programme, the spatial concepts of the Abercrombie plan were frustrated by two factors. First and crucially, Abercrombie made little attempt to engage the local planning authorities in the formation of his plan and proposed a Regional Planning Board, which would be charged with its implementation, but this was thwarted both by the LCC and entrenched local authority interests, both of whom were suspicious of the powers of a regional body. Second, the plan was deterministic, employing a regional design imposed over the existing fabric of government and planning; the problem was that 'the world did not conform to the master-planner's vision'. As with so many plans, the pace of change frequently outstrips the good intentions and forecasts. In London, demographic change and growing economic prosperity generated a much faster rate of decentralisation than the plan had envisaged. Despite this, the Abercrombie plan provided London with an extremely important set of concepts about accommodating growth that has had a legacy.

The Conservative governments of the 1950s mistrusted regional planning even if the problems created by London's growth were difficult to ignore, particularly in relation to protection of the green belt and accommodating housing growth, matters of concern not only for pressurised London boroughs but also for the Conservative-voting shires within the green belt. The government established the Herbert Commission on London Government in 1960, which found an overwhelming deficiency in the lack of an overall authority responsible for strategic planning, including transport planning (HM Government, 1960). The Standing Conference on London Regional Planning, created in 1961, was to prove an enduring body, albeit one whose nature changed. It was only in the years that followed that the government accepted the logic that London had entirely outgrown the boundary of the LCC. The resulting legislation in 1963 saw the replacement in 1965 of the LCC by the Greater London Council (GLC) and the thirty-two London boroughs; the governance of the city of London itself, the historic core and location today of the financial heart of London, has always been controlled by the Corporation of London which has withstood all processes of reorganisation around it over successive overhauls.

Thompson (2007) states that the Conservative government's motives for creating the GLC were less to do with regional planning and more influenced by political influences. The exodus of affluent voters out of the LCC area into the hinterland progressively reduced the prospects of a Conservative majority. The new Greater London boundary captured many of these voters but was still tightly drawn, while the Council actually possessed limited planning powers, with most planning functions remaining a borough responsibility. Arguments over boundaries, the division of responsibilities, and vested interests abounded while the pressure for development continued. And amidst these contentions, it fell to the then Labour Government to manage the scale and location of growth through a 'strategic plan for the south-east', published in 1970.

The plan was developed in association with the Standing Conference and the GLC, but its driving force was central government eager not to allow political infighting to limit growth and create a policy vacuum. It was more extensive than Abercrombie's plan, covering the wider region, and envisaged the majority of the growth being accommodated in growth and expansion areas through a strong spatial framework. But the plan was to suffer the same problems as its predecessors with the deterministic approach ineffective in persuading the various key agencies, particularly elected government, to support its implementation. The GLC resisted the continued loss of people and jobs from London, while the surrounding county councils were recalcitrant about receiving substantial quantities of further development.

The abolition of strategic metropolitan government

The Thatcher government scrapped the GLC (and the six other metropolitan counties in England) in 1986 as it was seen as an unnecessary tier of government between central government and the London boroughs, although in reality the GLC was viewed as a Labour power base (Thornley, 1991). Irrespective of the reasons for abolition, the demise of the GLC meant the loss of formal strategic policy powers over London-wide issues. Young and Garside (1982) state that in earlier reforms of London's government, exactly the same political forces were at work: the Conservatives feared a strong Labour-dominated London government and sought to weaken it by enhancing borough powers.

Peter Hall remarks that the GLC design may have been flawed: 'it did the things it was supposed to do badly or not at all, and it tried to do too many things it should never have tried to do' (Hall, 1989: 170). The GLC had been created as a slim, strategic authority to coordinate, inter alia, land-use planning and transport, in the spirit of the recommendations of the Herbert Commission. But to do that effectively, it would have needed some cessation of powers from the thirty-two London boroughs, possibly with binding directives over their plans and planning decisions, a move that would be unpalatable to all local authorities. The GLC had been set up during 'the heyday of a certain fashion for strategic planning, the confidence in which now appears exaggerated' (HM Government, 1983: 2), with the GLC engaging in 'a natural search for a "strategic" role which may have little basis in real needs' (HM Government, 1983: 2) and one certainly out of place in the New Right thinking of the 1980s (Thornley, 1991).

The Thatcher government had reduced the role and status of local authority planning and effectively stripped away regulatory planning from urban regeneration, the latter increasingly performed by non-democratically-elected Urban Development Corporations and through private sector property-led regeneration. In London, the London Docklands Development Corporation was established in east London boroughs, reducing the role of both the GLC and local planning powers and imposing a centrally led solution (Brownill, 1990). As Thornley illustrates in his quote of the then Secretary of State:

> We took their powers away from them because they were making such a mess of it. They are the people who have got it all wrong. They had advisory committees, planning committees, inter-relating committees and even discussion committees – but nothing happened . . . UDCs do things.
>
> (Heseltine, quoted in Thornley, 1991: 181).

Under the LDDC and with the demise of the GLC, services still functioned locally in much the same way, while major new developments occurred through, for example, major regeneration of London Docklands, particularly at Canary Wharf, the establishment of a Docklands Light Railway, and major road building in east London. The Thatcher Government was deeply adverse to local government, but also to strategic and regional planning, relying instead on market instincts (Young, 1984; Flynn et al., 1985). Although its track record on strategic planning can be questioned, the abolition of the GLC, according to Thompson (2007), represented 'an act of ideological antagonism to the concept of strategic planning and of the re-centralisation of control'. Strategic planning for London and for the South-East now became the responsibility of central government, with advice from the South-East Regional Planning Conference (also known as SERPLAN). This had been re-established in 1983 from the Standing Conference on the South-East and comprised the county councils and representatives of district and London boroughs. SERPLAN's role was to advise government on the issuing of Regional Planning Guidance for the South-East, even though the powers of final approval remained with Whitehall. Strategic planning in this instance was weak, since SERPLAN was a voluntary organisation, relying on consensus between its constituent members, and struggling to engage effectively at reconciling London–South-East issues.

SERPLAN performed its role creditably for twenty years by drawing together a significant politically and geographically diverse set of authorities. One of its principal successes, however, was to generate debate about London's decentralisation, and to encourage local authorities to concentrate on sustainable quality development within London rather than beyond its boundaries, through urban regeneration schemes that had the effect of retaining population and economic growth by the start of the twenty-first century.

In the absence of a formal elected strategic governing body for London in the late 1980s and 1990s, partnerships and networks filled the vacuum, more by necessity than design, including the London Planning Advisory Committee

(Newman and Thornley, 1997). As Travers remarks, 'In the absence of city-wide government, the capital's political and business class indulged in an orgy of power breakfasts, canapé-laden receptions, seminars, conferences and report-launches' (Travers, 2004: 34). The London boroughs grew used to determining their own fate and, through collaboration, came to play a much more strategic but intensely uncoordinated role, leading to a crisis in strategic management of the city (Thornley, 1992). The boroughs increasingly showed divergent styles of govern-ance and even quality of performance. Faced with the absence of a strategic coordinating body, London boroughs began to be engaged in a multitude of government-required partnerships, networks and focused programmes, that made strategic decision-making more difficult to achieve.

Post-2000: the mayor and the GLA

Labour returned to office in 1997 and pledged to reinstate not only directly elected strategic government for London, but also a new directly elected mayor. Since 2000, the UK national government has transferred the responsibility for strategic planning in such important areas as transport, economic development and plan-ning to a new elected position, the mayor of London. The mayor leads a new Greater London Authority, at face value a successor to the GLC but also funda-mentally different (Rydin *et al.*, 2004), while a new directly elected London Assembly comprising of thirty-three members keeps check on the mayor's activi-ties and ensures accountability. Working on behalf of the mayor, new delivery vehicles with dedicated budgets for transport and economic development have also been established, the most important of which are Transport for London and the London Development Agency, to support the implementation of the mayor's policies and strategies.

At the same time, many of the resources required to achieve the objec-tives of the mayor's strategies sit outside the mayor's direct controls with a wide range of national and local government agencies, including thirty-three separate municipal governments across the city. The Mayor coordinates London-wide authorities for policing, fire and emergency services, transport, and economic development, and sets the budget for the GLA and the functional agencies. The office of Mayor of London has been described as one of the least powerful world mayors (McNeill, 2002a), but the London Assembly is even weaker in compar-ison: it scrutinises the mayor's work, considers the budget and investigates issues of importance to London.

The first office-holder of Mayor of London was Ken Livingstone, the former and last Labour Leader of the GLC. In a bitterly fought election campaign, Livingstone won the election as an independent candidate, having failed to secure the Labour Party nomination. His politically left-leaning credentials were a cause of concern for New Labour and of the then Prime Minister Tony Blair in particular, who stated his belief that a Livingstone victory would be 'disastrous' for London (*The Independent*, 2000). But Londoners elected Livingstone, relegating the official

Labour candidate to fourth place, a move seen as a public vote against the Blair premiership as much as faith in Livingstone himself (Rallings and Thrasher, 2000).

Despite the renaissance for strategic governing and planning in London after 2000, there remains institutional complexity, multi-level governance and a diverse range of interests in the governing structure, with a new push in partnerships led by these agencies and encouraged by a New Labour ideological mantle towards collaboration, joined-up governance and consensus-building. Following the way in which London's governance became used to the partnership ethos in the absence of strategic elected government in the 1980s and 1990s, the new partnership ethos under the mayor and the GLA has created a breeding ground for public policy innovation and for unique competitive-advantage responses to the challenge of urban regeneration. This has occurred partly because the mayor has formed strong alliances with business interests in the city (Thornley *et al.*, 2005). London now demonstrates what may be termed responsive partnership working, but with flexibility to respond rapidly to short-term economic opportunities for the benefit of the capital.

London has sought to respond to the challenge of urban renewal and regional competition, but remains occasionally handicapped by a complex London government structure. National, regional and local governmental actors are all, to some degree, concerned with economic growth and development in London. The plethora of institutions and organisations, each with their own objectives, resources and interests, creates a unique institutional environment. It is not only concerned with those organisations that fall within the public sector, but also creates a new platform of governance inclusion for a myriad of voluntary and community organisations concerned with different aspects of London's growth and development, many of whom play an important role in policy and development delivery. Although this governance form engenders a rich strategy and policy-making environment, many of these organisations do not lend themselves to delivery, and so other mechanisms are sought to ensure that things happen.

The main role of the mayor is to set a framework of strategies in order to promote sustainable development, health and equality within London. Central to the mayor's activities is responsibility for the creation of eight inter-connected metropolitan strategies, the most significant of which are:

- the London Plan – which provides the spatial development framework for planning and growth in London
- the Transport Strategy – which sets out a package of policies and proposals designed to significantly improve transport in London
- the Economic Development Strategy – which suggests a programme of action to address London's economic weaknesses, build on its strengths and capitalise on key opportunities.

As these strategies begin to be implemented through the actions and activities of Transport for London and the London Development Agency working in partnership with other levels of government and the private sector, London is increasingly responding to the challenge of renewal. The London Plan is the most important document as something of a strategy of strategies (GLA, 2004a), but the Mayor was in a difficult situation with regard to implementing the plan mainly because – as Abercrombie and the South-East Plan found before – planning also sits as a statutory activity within each borough, and it is the local authority's spatial strategy or local development framework that is implemented by that local authority and delivered through development control decisions locally.

Under the 1999 Greater London Act, most development decisions in London remained with the boroughs and the Corporation of London. Some strategic developments had to obtain the mayor's opinion but the mayor only had any power in the sense that he could direct that an application be refused over the decision of a borough. The mayor could not direct that permission should be granted, and so this meant that while the GLA formulated the London Plan, its implementation remained largely with the London boroughs, many of which were, at the time, opposed politically to the office-holder.

What became clear in the first term of office of the mayor was that the emphasis was on strategy development but not necessarily implementation. A key issue facing the mayor is therefore how he influences the agenda of others to deliver policies. In order to do this, the Mayor therefore must engage with the partnerships, business organisations and other local borough interests through coalition building to bring about change (Sweeting, 2002; Gordon, 2003). The office-holder of Mayor of London 2000–2008, Ken Livingstone, never shirked from expressing forthright views, and his political vision to see more affordable and key worker housing (Raco, 2008), tall buildings in the city (McNeill, 2002b), and his introduction of the congestion charge in central London (Richards, 2005), all emerged as areas of conflict with many of the boroughs themselves.

Some of the innovations that emerged from Ken Livingstone's administration, despite the relatively weak powers and animosity between the mayor and the boroughs, included:

- a 50 per cent affordability target for all new housing development
- a London-wide childcare affordability programme to allow more people to enter the labour market
- a central London congestion charge to reduce travel times and pollution – coupled with an enhanced bus service to encourage public transport usage
- a dedicated Climate Change Agency to foster energy conservation and resource efficiency; and of course
- a successful bid to bring the Olympics to London in 2012 as a major driver of renewal in some of the city's most deprived areas.

In all instances these innovations were driven forward by one or more of the mayor's agencies and the question is whether many of these activities would have been possible without the creation of a new tier of regional government for London. Or would they have occurred without a directly elected mayor, responsible for strategic planning and coordination across London, possessing a clear vision for London's long-term growth and development, as well as responsibility for delivery vehicles such as Transport for London and the London Development Agency?

Extending the mayor's planning powers

Ken Livingstone won his second term of office as Mayor of London, this time as a Labour candidate, in 2004. He had been expelled from the Labour Party for five years for standing as an independent against the official Labour candidate. But forces within Labour wanted him to return, and a series of discussions took place during his first term of office to secure this. It was also recognition on the Blair government's part that Livingstone maintained the popular support of Londoners and would have, most likely, defeated any Labour candidate, a prospect Labour was keen to avoid for a second time. But Livingstone saw an opportunity for a political deal with the Labour government and pressed for an extension of powers to the mayoral office in return for accepting adoption as a Labour Party candidate (Young, 2006). Aside from the personality politics and deals involved in this process, there are grounds to suggest that Livingstone also had a legitimate claim to do something about planning decision-making and to avoid the narrow parochialism caused by the London boroughs determining strategic planning powers. This argument was also timely and chimed with opinions within the Treasury, itself voicing criticisms of local planning for its perceived failure to address economic growth adequately (Barker, 2006).

In July 2006, the government announced that a range of additional powers would be granted in relation to planning, waste and a number of other strategic functions. The new planning powers provide London's mayor with the ability to take over and determine planning applications of strategic importance, vital to ensure the delivery of the London Plan but also addressing a contentious area of London politics for decades – the relationship between strategic policy formulation and implementation within a single governmental agency. The government believes that such a change will enable the mayor to ensure the implementation of strategic planning policy in Greater London as set out in the London Plan and other strategic policy instruments. The new planning powers propose a two-stage test where the mayor will need to consider two issues:

- whether a proposed development raises issues of a nature and scale that would significantly impact on the implementation of specific London Plan policies
- whether the issues raised by the development have a significant effect that go wider than a single borough.

The powers will enable London's mayor to direct an approval and a refusal, for the first time, of significant development issues by taking the planning application away from a borough. As part of the partnership ethos, however, central government still sees the relevant boroughs undertaking the necessary public consultations on development proposals and passing these responses to the mayor in a spirit of cooperation. The uncertainty caused by one tier of government relying on another tier of government is not unique to London. Extending a planning implementation role for the mayor is similar in nature to the powers already in place nationally with the Secretary of State's call-in powers. These powers are used rarely partly because of the unease with which one tier of government may remove the act of decision-making from the democratic level closest to the public. Ken Livingstone, on the other hand, had a reputation for taking a close interest in development proposals across the city and stated his view on schemes on a number of occasions. This raises the potential of the Mayor of London utilising these new powers on a much more regular frequency than the Secretary of State.

A further concern rests on the relationship between the mayor and the boroughs. The new powers are intended to militate against adversarial behaviour but the proposals may enhance tension. Where the mayor has directed refusal of a planning application, until now there has remained a right of appeal for the applicant. Under the new powers, boroughs may only challenge the decision, the conditions on the approval, or the lack of conditions, through the courts since there exists no third-party right of appeal. However, the boroughs can try to persuade the Secretary of State to call in the scheme. Whether the Secretary of State would be minded to do this would depend on the circumstances, and within the context of the devolution of powers from the centre this is probably only going to occur rarely. There is a danger here that if relationships between the boroughs and the mayor breakdown over a planning application, the decision-making and governance processes could grind to a halt.

Furthermore, there will be practical issues to arrange and issues of timing may be paramount, in the context of government proposals to speed up the planning decision and provide more certainty for users of planning. Delays could occur by the mayor in the boroughs' assessment of strategic issues, or more pertinently in the public consultation arrangements that the boroughs will have to undertake on behalf of the mayor where he has taken over an application. We may yet witness a new phase of relationships between the strategic governing body for London and the boroughs.

Conclusions

Devolution – the creation of a new government for London and the office of mayor in 2000 – has created a strong institutional and political structure that returns strategic governance to the capital after an absence of at least fourteen years. But the landscape of the state within London and locally is now fundamentally different; it has become much more crowded with agencies that operate more fluidly and tactically, formally and informally, solo and in partnership, in order to strategise problems and deliver solutions.

The direct powers of London's mayor remain limited, when compared to similar offices in other world cities, but he does perform an essential catalytic and influencing role across agencies, performing an ambassadorial role both outside the UK and inside government, and with the business community (Tomaney, 2001). As was pointed out early in the new process:

> [The] new Mayor will need to be more like a broker, inserting himself into the space that remains between the might of national government on his doorstep and the bloody-minded boroughs that will go on running London's main services. He will be expected to conduct the orchestra, not write the score.
>
> (*The Economist*, 29 April 2000: 25).

This new role has, in turn, created a new form of integrated strategic planning at the London metropolitan scale, with a commitment to planning and a determination for public, private and voluntary actors to enter into partnerships to realise development. If anything, this should have taken some of the political heat out of controversial large-scale development projects. But the fact that both central and decentralised government each operates at the Greater London level (through the Government Office for London and the GLA) exacerbates the landscape of governance and also leads to a confusion of roles at this level. There remain huge questions about London's capacity to deliver and to galvanise political leadership across multiple competing agencies, particularly in relation to issues such as planning, housing, transport and other public investments. Travers (2004: 182) remarks:

> The first three years of the Greater London Authority suggest that London's government remains balkanized and weak . . . the largest city in Europe simply defies all efforts at giving it an effective and consistent system of government. The best that could be said of this fragmentation and change is that the atomized and constantly reformed system of government had much in common with the habits of individualism recognised by urbanists in London's social development.

Peter Hall has remarked that: 'In a huge, complex, polycentric place like London, governance will always be fragmented'. But Ken Livingstone's strategies compounded this by assuming that 'London' ended at the GLA boundary' (Hall, 2006). Those tensions have remained ever present in London for most of the last 120 years, despite government restructuring and questions over the division of power and responsibilities. Despite or perhaps because of this, the surprising point to remark is that London nevertheless seems to have been highly successful in its transition from a manufacturing to a global financial city and remains an attractive place to live and work with new migrants from within and outside the UK. This has been achieved, perhaps in part, because Ken Livingstone was instrumental in circumventing such a tightly defined set of parameters to nevertheless carve out a role for himself that creates achievements. With little in the way of direct responsibility for social services and housing, unlike council leaders and directly elected mayors elsewhere, the London institutional framework forced Livingstone to concentrate specifically on economic development, planning and transport policies while also engaging in the type of networking, brokerage and partnership that New Labour requires in new elite governance structures (Leach and Wilson, 2004).

In his second term of office, Young (2006) maintains that Ken Livingstone consolidated his position and moved the mayoral office away from an enabling role to one that potentially created a strong metropolitan decision-maker. The post-2007 powers vested in the mayor provide a powerful but potentially controversial set of tools over planning. The degree to which they will be utilised will probably vary according to the personal interests of the office-holder. The relationship between the mayor and the boroughs to work the new powers is essential but may lead to further, or perhaps that should be ongoing, friction. For as Young (2006) remarks, a strong strategic metropolitan decision-making model tends to reopen old wounds and conflicts between traditionally elected tiers of government and the new enhanced middle tier. Planning may well be the area of policy that starts to break the fragile partnership consensus between the three levels of government in London. Although the powers should enable the mayor to implement the London Plan more easily, London's elected Assembly could also view an opportunity to become more involved in strategy preparation much earlier as part of their accountability and scrutiny role.

To some degree, the position of the London mayor between national government and local boroughs with a strong strategising and coordinating role but weak implementation role fits the model of directly elected mayors that New Labour had envisaged in the 1990s as part of a commitment towards 'joined-up government' (Rhodes, 2000). The shift from government to governance supposedly reflects the need to get things done in the face of increased complexity (Stoker, 1998; Kearns and Paddison, 2000):

> Mayors deliver a leadership capacity better suited to the new tasks and challenges that face local politics and governance . . . The world has changed and local government now faces new demands. Local politicians need to be champions for service improvement, facilitating the expression of voice in diverse communities and reconciling differences, developing shared visions and supporting partnerships to ensure their achievement. Leadership in these new circumstances is not about seizing control of the state machine: it is about building coalitions, developing networks and steering in a complex environment.
>
> (Stoker, 2000, cited in Tomaney, 2001: 226)

The unique combination of a strong institutional framework of government, with a flexible and responsive form of working, has enabled the bidding of projects (that can benefit the whole of London) to be streamlined, and to be embedded within local municipalities. There is no doubt that London – whether intentionally or not – has been given a competitive edge over other world cities by this institutional structure and flexible responsive and partnership style of working, as the successful Olympic bid illustrates. Between 2000 and 2008, London witnessed a form of government working that owed its style and origins to New Labour ideology, but also to the legacies of working within a strategic vacuum in the 1980s and 1990s. This period saw a new political commitment to strategic enabling, rather than strategic governing, and was the breeding ground for innovation and competitiveness across governance actors in London. Confidence was created in collaborative working but the style of London politics and governance is already changing markedly. Party politics has returned to the centre stage in London political debates, and as the mayoral office gained enhanced powers Ken Livingstone cemented his position within the institutional framework much more prominently, so older tensions and conflicts began to emerge. The key question is whether the legacies from the early twenty-first century experience of governing London will deliver in the long term and provide social as well as economic benefit.

Postscript

In May 2008, Ken Livingstone was defeated in the third mayoral elections by the Conservative candidate Boris Johnson. To date, there has been little substantive policy change although the new mayor in his election campaign pledged to review the proposed extension of the Congestion Charge scheme and publicly stated his opposition to new tall buildings in London. He has, however, taken increasing control of both the London Development Agency and the Metropolitan Police Authority in his first six months in office. We may yet see a new pattern of London governance emerging as the current mayoral office holder attempts to integrate some parts of the wider strategic governance structure with his own enhanced powers. This hints at a possible period of consolidation of London governing agencies under Johnson (the Conservative) and may well be welcomed by the municipalities but could prove problematic for national Labour government.

Part II

Prestige projects and the sustainable city

Chapter 5

Figuring city change: understanding urban regeneration and Britain's Thames Gateway

Michael Keith

Introduction

Is the Thames Gateway urban regeneration project in trouble? Looking at the headlines in the summer of 2007 one might be forgiven for thinking that this grandest of *grands projets*, which claims to be Europe's largest contemporary city transformation programme, might not be faring so well. In the spring of 2007, it appeared that the planning inquiry into the major new landmark Thames River crossing between Greenwich (Thamesmead) and Newham had run into trouble as the final judgement of the planning inquiry failed to give the new build the green light. In May 2007, the National Audit Office (NAO, 2007a) published the results of its investigation into the Gateway, *Thames Gateway: Laying the Foundations*, which was taken to be highly critical. It was accompanied by a companion (NAO, 2007b) on *How European Cities Achieve Renaissance*, a survey of 'good practice' across seven metropolitan centres.

And the political reaction was predictably hostile. The National Audit Office reports are subject to scrutiny by the parliamentary Public Accounts Committee (PAC) and its chair, Edward Leigh, was quoted as suggesting that the Thames Gateway was 'looking more and more like an expensive daydream' (e-politix, 2007). In an acrimonious PAC hearing, Leigh went on to criticise both the leadership and the delivery of the programme (PAC, 2007).

Indeed, the concept of the Thames Gateway itself has met with a considerable degree of scepticism in recent years. The formally designated regeneration area runs both sides of the river Thames for 40 miles, from the Tower and London Docklands to Southend in Essex and Sheerness in Kent (see figure 5.1). About 1.6 million people live in the area, about 500,000 work there. It covers about 200,000

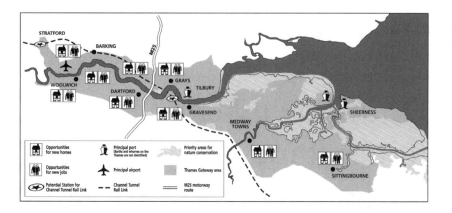

5.1

The Thames Gateway.
Source: The editors

acres, with about 8,500 acres of brownfield sites. Targets have moved up and down through time but it is hoped to generate 160,000 new homes and 180,000 new jobs by 2016. John Prescott, the former Deputy Prime Minister, suggested that it represented 'a huge opportunity to tackle the housing shortage in the South-East'

The Guardian newspaper has variously portrayed the attempt to transform the post-industrial pie slice of London east of Tower Bridge as 'Prescottgrad' (Weaver, 2006) or a Cockney Siberia (Glancey, 2003), whilst the IPPR (Bennett and Morris, 2006) has bemoaned the area's lack of identity or place within the public imagination. Jonathan Glancey (2006) has claimed that the area has become 'a tragic fiction of a non-place . . . the dumping ground of crass new housing for poor people'.

The NAO report was, in reality, slightly more balanced than the headlines. It did suggest that 'the complexity of the decision-making and the delivery chains makes it difficult for potential investors, developers and government itself to understand the programme and integrate investment as a whole' (NAO, 1997a: 5), highlighted weaknesses in leadership of the programme, the lack of a 'programme implementation plan' (NAO, 1997a: 22), uncertainties about the numbers of housing units planned and developed (NAO, 1997a: 32) and identified the need to distinguish long-term programme management from short-term project management.

5.2

New housing in
Thames Gateway.
Source: Laura Keogh

It did also commend the scale of aspiration of the Gateway vision and the high degree of support from local and sub-regional partners. But the point that caused greatest ire at both the Public Accounts Committee hearing, and is at the core of the National Audit Office report, was the lack of a costed delivery programme with commensurable risk register and subsidiary project management for the Gateway as a whole. For Edward Leigh (PAC, 2007):

> the truth is that after twelve years you still do not know what this is all going to cost, do you? One very basic piece of information: after twelve years, you do not know what this is all going to cost.

This might seem to be a quite reasonable, even ostensibly a devastating critique. And yet. The rhetoric of contemporary regeneration looks to flexibilities of the market to provide the driving force of inward investment and the public sector to provide a framework of planning certainty to synthesise public and private interests. But market forces have by definition autonomy of their own and the manner in which *the risk* of state investment is handled creates a tension between public investment and private profit.

In the past the cities and new towns built by state fiat have been seen to be deeply flawed. Equally, the determinants of purely market led city growth have generated – particularly in the USA – urban sprawl that is proving increasingly economically inefficient and ecologically problematic. This chapter argues that we might want to think carefully about the manner in which the contemporary rhetorics of partnership between private and public funding might demand that we think differently about the sorts of 'future thinking' that is appropriate for schemes of contemporary regeneration.

How do we conceptualise the future in the rhetoric and practice of urban regeneration? The languages that we use to describe city change and the practices of land use planning, development control, architecture, social engineering and social science all aspire to capture some sense of the future in their descriptions of the present. In imagining the future of east London, a number of key stakeholders and politicians at national, regional and local levels have shared a sense of the scale of growth that is possible, desirable and sustainable in the largely post-industrial landscapes of the Thames Gateway. But if we unpack the uncertainties of thinking that variously privilege the temporal or the spatial we might begin to unpack alongside this a sense of what we might describe as the Thames Gateway paradox. The paradox highlights a tension between long-term public interest and short-term rational outcomes. But in order to do this it is first worth considering how analysis of historical metropolitan legacies have changed in academic and policy concerns before thinking more generally about the manner in which we conceptualise the future.

The future of the past

How do we think about the ways in which the history of the city occupies the present? Because the urban landscape changes so rapidly there has been a tendency in literatures in several disciplines to emphasise the manner in which the past is obscured, buried or hidden by the pace and the forms of city change. Although this can move rhetorically towards the nostalgic, there is an impressive range of work that unveils, reveals or rediscovers such metropolitan archaeologies. But it is also possible to draw at least a heuristic comparison between two slightly different understandings of city history. *In the first* of these the past is merely that which precedes the present, an authentic vernacular that is at times overcome by an inauthentic commodification. *In the second*, the past actively disrupts the ways in which we think about yesterday, today and tomorrow through the manner in which it infests our understandings of the present day.

In this manner, over the last decade in both urban sociology and cultural geography, engagement with the past has moved beyond the notion of history as sentimental accumulation and towards a more active sense of *the history of the present*, a move from the first to the second historical modes. In the former, the past sits as a parent to the present but frequently as forgotten memory, commonly as redemptive experience. In the latter, the ways in which we speak through languages and values that are historically inflected, the sense that we are embossed, haunted and the assemblages of past constructions, tends to promote a reflection on the forms of urbanism that we take for granted and those we consider more problematic. To illustrate this point we might take as a contrast two pieces of work – both of great value – that have considered the relationship between memory, history and an understanding of the urban landscape. In her pioneering work *The Power of Place*, Dolores Hayden (1995) produced a powerful refiguration of the relationship between modernity, heritage and place, but did so within an essentially linear notion of the historical that exemplifies the first historical mode of address.

Through her explorations of the hidden city landscape of Los Angeles Hayden, in this landmark volume, explored the manner in which community struggles and individual lives can be erased by the turbulence of destruction, regeneration and city transformation. The book explores a number of instances in which the erasure of the past serves particular interests and a powerful exercise in community development, local empowerment and memory work valorises landscape and buildings whose identity has been written out of the story of the neighbourhoods she discusses. Such work is ethically powerful and provides an added spur to local campaigns that value their neighbourhood. This fundamentally redemptive project is similar to work carried out in the UK by groups such as Common Ground who attempt to trace the local histories of particular sites and emphasise and valorise the distinctiveness of the parochial.

In contrast, in Andreas Huyssen's (2003) *Present Pasts*, the historical is the site of the traumatic, an active force in the present, refiguring itself, perennially reconstructing our understanding of the present through new inflections, melancholic legacies and ethical contest. This sense of the haunting of the present has been picked up powerfully in some contemporary cultural geographies. This can lead us to a focus on the nature of psychoanalytic readings of repressed memories as in the work of Steve Pile (1996), or to an understanding of the incommensurabilities of historical commemoration that Karen Till (2005) describes in contemporary Berlin or the forms of sublime that are subsumed in trauma in Huyssen's (2003) own work. But what such approaches share is a sense that we cannot take chronology unproblematically. History can work backwards and forwards; teleology is a product of historiographic rhetoric as much as causal analysis and the history of the present remains a focus of intellectual inquiry.

In part, this might be taken as a reflection of the influence of Foucauldian thinking that returns us to the genealogical. In reality, the notion that the narration of the past makes problematic some aspects of city life and not others does no more than take us back to a sense of critical theory that echoes Max Horkheimer's injunction in his 1930 inaugural lecture at the Institute of Social Research in Frankfurt that there is 'no way of comprehending the structures of reason that does not involve sociohistorical inquiry' (Horkheimer, 1993). Horkheimer's sensibility and the frequently underestimated legacies of Frankfurt School curiosity implied a research commitment to engage in depth with the everyday as well as with the tropes through which the everyday becomes praxis, belief, idealism and enterprise.

But what is no longer challenged is a sense in which the present might bear the contested weight of past narratives and the past might seek to inhabit the quotidian. And so in a directly related manner we might also want to make something problematic that is in some ways banal and is commonly taken as self-evident; the temporalities of the future city, its rhythms and its contingencies. In particular we might want to unpack some of the ways social policy and urban studies alike makes the city that is emerging a subject of study; tells its stories, identifies the contingencies of economic trends and attempts to shape these forms. This is not just about the accuracy or otherwise of such predictions and interventions – although accuracy is clearly important. It is also about the way that 'future thinking' might inhabit the cities of the present in a manner akin to the ways in which the past haunts the present, the way in which such thinking provides a plausible account of the development of the metropolis and how the calculus of the future structures the actions of the present.

Future thinking in the metropolis

David Harvey (1973) once famously suggested that the central question confronting scholars of urbanism was 'in whose image is the city made'. His answer to that question was that largely the city was made in the image of capital and the legacy of thirty years of Marxian scholarship has provided a rich tradition of analytical attempts to deconstruct the manner in which the production of space obeys the logic of capital. And whilst such work has been both influential and impressive I have argued elsewhere (Keith, 2005: chapter 1; 2007) that the consequent juxtaposition between attempts to *deconstruct* the logic of the built form on the one hand and analytical attempts to *promote* the functionality of the city machine on the other creates an essentially two-dimensional scale through which to understand writing about city change. The ethical dilemmas through which some parts of the city come to be subject to governmental intervention (for example in projects of post-industrial transformation) and some collective subjects (for example communities of interest or faith communities) become suddenly visible in the machine of city politics which demands a more thorough analysis of the problem of liberal government and the ethical frames through which city change is rationalised.

In his work *For the City Yet to Come* Maliq Simone (2004: 3) has attempted to focus a study of urbanism on

> the following problematic: in cities where livelihood, mobility and opportunity seem to be produced and enacted through the very agglomeration of different bodies marked and situated in diverse ways, how can permutations in the intersection of bodies in need, and desires in part propelled by the sheer number of them, how can larger numbers of bodies sustain themselves by imposing themselves in critical junctures, whether these junctures are discrete spaces, life events, or sites of consumption or production?

Simone's work is important because it takes as a starting point the creativity of the processes of dwelling in the African city and manages consequently to develop a descriptive understanding of African urbanism that recognises sub-Saharan metropolitan dysfunctionality, respectful of its multitudinous variations and permutations, whilst still framing the urban process within a larger context of transnational restructuring and global inequality. The new normalities of the mega city are acknowledged for their fecundity without being merely celebrated for their novelty in some of the more celebratory tracts of the architect Rem Koolhaas (2007) in his writing about the city of Lagos.

In one way, Simone's work returns us to a take on urban life that is most closely identified with Martin Heidegger, and in particular with the problematic that Heidegger addressed in his famous 1951 essay 'Building, Dwelling, Thinking' around the 'place-making' involved in what it means to inhabit and to build in the city (Heidegger, 1971). The juxtaposition of pastoral and counter-pastoral renditions of modernity are central to the debates in contemporary architecture that draw their inspiration from Heidegger's Building, Dwelling, Thinking and address the cultures of urbanism from starkly different starting points that consider whether it is more cultural or natural to live in the city (Heynen, 2000).

There is both a moral seriousness and – in some eyes – a deeply conservative sense that emerges from Heidegger's injunction that

> the real plight of dwelling is indeed older than the world wars with their destruction, older also than the increase of the earth's population and the condition of the industrial workers. The real dwelling plight lies in this, that mortals ever search anew for the nature of dwelling, that they *must ever learn to dwell.*
>
> (Heidegger, 1971: 161)

There is also though a real sense that we should question the self-evident, think about the manner in which changing forms of bare life reconfigure, appropriate and reshape the built form through their relationship to time as much as their relationship to space. Our sense of *becoming* structures our sense of urbanism as much as our sense of *being.* Hence Simone's work attempts to address 'how Africans make cities they feel they can belong to, whilst at the same time open up multiple possibilities of becoming' (Simone, 2004: 136).

In a similar fashion the urbanist Richard Sennett has become increasingly interested in his more recent work in the manner in which the temporalisation of contemporary capitalism restructures the city dweller's sense of a job, a career, a risk or a collective identity (Sennett, 2000, 2007). This feeds through at levels that are both deeply ethnographic and powerfully policy oriented. If we are to understand the cultures of ghetto urbanism in south London, New York or Rio we need to understand how the temporal horizons of the 'burbs differ from those of the ghetto (Keith, 2005).

Equally, if we are to think through the restructuring of the temporalities of urbanism we begin to unpack the manner in which in many places the conventional city life path and 'housing career' begin to fall apart in the early twenty-first century. The normative life-cycle that takes the heterosexual family unit as the defining patterning driver of the residential space of the twentieth-century city produces a characteristic formation of suburbs and gentrification. Until the insecurities of the new labour markets and the securitisation of future risk that is turned into stock market calculus in the commodification of sub-prime mortgage loans begins to unwind and the residential property market collapses in the mainland USA with significant impacts on the reshaping of city space. Until we begin to think slightly more carefully about the chances of children graduating from university in twenty-first-century Britain buying their own homes. Until, like Kate Barker (2004, 2006), we begin to think about the relative macroeconomic importance of mortgage debt in an equation that figures the future through stock market interests of pension funds generating one sense of the future, house builders and property developers' profit horizons generating another sense of the future and the technologies of land use planning, architecture, urban design and infrastructure construction constructing different senses of the future once again.

And, in turn, these senses of the future must be placed within a political context; within the regimes of both *the government* of places and regions and *the governance* of fiscal regimes of social, private residential and commercial property development and regulatory regimes (of development control and planning) of the built environment. In governance terms, there is a very real sense in which the roughly assembled sets of skills, technologies and aspiration that are involved in this process – that Bruno Latour (2005) might characterise as assemblages but most people would understand as the loosely convened discipline of 'city building' – has waxed and waned over the last five decades. In the immediate post-war years the governance regime and received wisdoms that Bob Jessop (2002) and many other political scientists have characterised as the Keynesian Welfare State fostered a notion of the potential to engineer the future. It promoted a sense of culture's domination of city nature. The notion that the future could be built, that dwelling in the city could be mass produced, led to a scale of urban planning, development and control that made juxtapositions between either side of the Iron Curtain less striking than a shared growing confidence in state machinery to control, configure and deliver the built form.

It is striking to compare the minutiae of the Abercrombie Plan's identification of tiny land plots for London with the sort of regional generalisations evident in the nearest equivalents of the early twenty-first century (Keith, 2005: chapter 10). And although the interface of land use planning with national political culture and the temporalities of economic change is rarely the subject of academic scrutiny the waning of the social role of planners and social engineers of the urban in the late twentieth century is striking.

And it is in Heidegger's fourfold, where the twentieth century begins to unpack the tension between property development and the mass production of housing, that tensions between the sense of the future and the confidence of modernism reaches its crisis point first. Post-war housing estates on both sides of the Atlantic assume an iconic status. In the United Kingdom, Ronan Point, situated in today's Thames Gateway in the London borough of Newham and built in 1966, was subject to catastrophic collapse in 1968, killing five and injuring seventeen. Repaired in the short term but eventually demolished in 1986, Ronan Point assumes a paradigmatic status in the critique of both system-built estates in the 1980s and the hubris implied in systems of mass provision of housing (see chapter 9 in this volume). Across the Atlantic, Minoru Yamasaki, second generation Japanese American architect, later responsible for the architecture of the twin towers of the World Trade Center creates the Pruitt Igoe housing project in St Louis Missouri. The project's demolition in 1972 prompts architectural theorist Charles Jencks (1989) to suggest that this represents 'the end of modernism'.

What Ronan Point and Pruitt Igoe share is that they precipitate a crisis of faith not just in the built form that they exemplified but also in the forms of social engineering implicated in the projects in the USA, the major council estates in the United Kingdom and the attempts to provide mass housing across the world. The roots of architecture's engagement with a social democratic recognition of the need for the majority to dwell in the city can be traced from the City Beautiful Movement through the Werkbund in Weimar Germany to the post-war imperatives across the world to sustain the right to live in the city. It is challenged simultaneously in terms of its built form and accompanying structure of provision and governance (Heynen, 2000; Frisby, 2001). The point here is that the manner in which public housing specifically and the mass production of homes generally comes to be problematic is about both architectural design and particular trade-offs between state and market that structure supply. A focus on the former comes to be the currency of certain strands of architectural debate in the 1980s (Jencks, 1989; HRH Prince Charles, 1993; Wright, 1985). A focus on the latter becomes less explicitly linked to the fiscal retrenchment identified with 1980s restraints on public sector spending and the ascendancy of macro-economic monetarism globally.

A separation of one from the other either aestheticises the social problems of need in the city (frequently in a debate about the social pathologies of public sector housing) or detaches the built form from the ideological consensus of macro-economic political economy (by ignoring the opportunity costs of diminished investment in public sector housing from the 1980s onwards across the globe).

The connection is important to sustain for two reasons. The first of these is that conceptually we need to understand that how the built environment comes to be problematic within studies of the city can too easily detach the macro-economic from the cultural, built form from inhabitation, lego building from community building. We might want to reconsider this sense of 'making problematic' in ways that challenge the conventions of the past in urban studies and the present in social policy received wisdom.

Theoretically, though not the central focus of this chapter, this might make us think critically about the ways the objects of academic scrutiny become visible in both mainstream academic debate and in social policy intervention. This chapter draws on – but does not expand – some of the influences in this strand of thought that can be traced to the rejection of conventional nature/culture oppositions associated with the work of Bruno Latour (1993) and a critical examination of the histories of subjects of the city that can be traced to the *biopolitcs* of the late Michel Foucault. The virtue of such an approach is that it might be helpful in sustaining some of the links that tend to be broken in studies of urbanism that tend to detach architecture from planning, from development control, from political economy, from politics, from community development. Indeed for Rabinow and Rose (2003),

> Whilst Foucault is imprecise in his use of the terms, it might be helpful to suggest that, within the field of biopower, 'biopolitics' designates the specific strategies and contestations over the forms of knowledge, regimes of authority, and practices of intervention that are desirable, legitimate and efficacious.

In short we might wish to think about the ways in which certain kinds of 'future thinking' become legitimate, heard and acceptable in the early twenty-first century and others that are unheard, silenced or scoffed.

The second reason is that in broad-brush terms the governance forms that Jessop identifies as the Keynesian Welfare state in the post-war era were displaced in his terms by the Schumpeterian Workfare state of the Reagan–Thatcher years, commonly identified with putatively 'neo-liberal' macro-economic orthodoxy (Jessop, 2002) but in other theorists' less pejorative vocabulary the advocacy of 'small government', market-based reforms and a diminishing role for the grand ambitions of state controlled city building. Importantly, whilst the hubris of the city builders was challenged by the successive spectacles of demolished tower blocks from Pruitt Igoe and Ronan Point onwards, the whole project (along with some of its social democratic redistributive ethics) of state sponsored housing supply was seen to be discredited as a direct corollary of the discrediting of other forms of social engineering: in the welfare state, the labour market and the fields of both production and consumption.

Practically, there is something much more simple at stake here, a recognition that there is a need to 'join up' not only the institutional forms of local governance through placing them in a single Department of State (in turn the Office of the Deputy Prime Minister or the Department of Communities and Local Government) but also reconcile the incommensurable logics of governance policy. In short we need to think of the logical drivers and the temporalities of different policy programmes and initiatives that may share laudable social motives but appeal to distinct economic logics.

So when we extrapolate development projections for some of the post-industrial areas of contemporary London there needs to be an understanding that we synthesise a combination of public expenditure subsidies (on physical and social infrastructure and in forms of housing subsidy) and private sector investments (in the supply and demand side of the housing market). And yet the former subsumes normative understandings of the right to dwell in the city (in subsidies of key groups – the 'most deprived', the key worker, the recipient of mortgage tax relief). And the latter assumes trends of disposable income, social polarisation/equalisation, household configuration, that collectively configure the demand not only for the quantum of future homes but also their size, their commodification as 'buy-to-let' investments and the opportunity costs of invest-ment in the built environment.

The former is the product of an ethical debate about the definitions of social need, the prioritisation of public expenditure and is properly subject to a moral and political debate today and tomorrow. The latter is the function of micro and macroeconomic variables, whose future risks reside quite properly in the dynamics of market equilibrium and disequilibrium. The calculus of the future determines actions in the present. In short we are at times putting together quite different sorts of things, responsibly so. But what is less helpful is to fail to recog-nise such incommensurability in making sense of the future city.

This can be seen in two extensive and academically rigorous pieces of work that sit at the heart of contemporary British government housing policy which help us to understand the nature of the Thames Gateway paradox. The first of these is the extensive body of work carried out by Treasury economist Kate Barker in considering the nature of housing supply and her subsequent review of the planning system in Britain. The second is the review of the future roles of social housing in England by John Hills. There is neither space nor intention to summarise or critique these pieces of work, both of which are strongly rooted in empirical detail and theoretical sophistication. However, it is important to draw out a significant contrast between the two.

Housing supply and the Barker report

Kate Barker (2004) figures the supply of housing in Britain in broadly neo-classical terms of market failure and the obstacles to market optimisation of supply. Working within an assumption that steadily rising prices of the commodity of housing would be expected to generate a greater response in build-out rates, Barker effectively focuses on the inelasticites of housing supply. The analysis consequently focuses principally on the barriers to sustaining development of greater numbers of housing units in the United Kingdom.

In short at the heart of Barker's comprehensive, scholarly (if econo-mistic) analysis is a sense that housing matters because of the macroeconomic dynamics of the effects of mass home ownership and the potential challenges to this in the longer term. Barker is sanguine about the long-term power of the market to correct itself, less optimistic about the short-term obstacles in it so doing. The latter are identified with the structures of the state that regulate the supply and governance of land through processes of conservation (such as green belts, historic preservation) and most strongly in terms of an asserted sense of barriers within the planning and development control process. And whilst it is fair to say that the report demonstrates a strong sense of the macroeconomics of housing and the implica-tions for the national economy – not least in distorting the value of sterling – it is less strong on the detail, the process and the ethnographic understanding of the institutions of the state that interface with the housing market.

Ends and Means: the Hills report

In contrast the Hills report provides a fascinating account of both the moral taxon-omies of contemporary Britain and the sorts of future thinking that are implicit in these constructions of need and eligibility. The report focuses on three questions;:

1. What can social housing do in helping create genuinely mixed communities?

2.   Can the way we run it encourage social mobility and opportunities, including in the labour market, for people to get on in their lives?

3.   Can social housing and other support be more responsive to changing needs and enable greater geographical mobility?

(Hills, 2007: 1)

It is striking for the ways in which it demonstrates systematically that the switch over recent decades has been from supply side to demand side (Hills, 2007, 3); that in 2007 approximately one-third of the £16 billion annual public expenditure targets supply (principally through grants to housing associations to build homes) and almost two-thirds is focused on demand (principally through payment of housing benefit that pays the rents of those deemed in sufficient need of state support). The cumulative effect of this is to focus the beneficiaries of social housing increasingly on those people on welfare benefits, arguably residualising public sector housing.

The argument of the report, that such a trend will not generate 'mixed' communities – in fact it promotes polarisation almost as much as the gated communities brought forward by the private market – has been contentious in some quarters. But for the purposes of this chapter what is interesting is that the analysis of each of the key questions in the report – a sense of *creating* communities, social *mobility*, *changing* needs and spatial *mobility* – all imply a sense of a normative future based on state intervention. Barker's work is acknowledged, if only fleetingly in two substantive references in the body of the report.

Both are scholarly documents. Both address candidly the problematisations that are constructed for them in their commission; housing supply on the one hand, social need on the other. They exemplify two different ways of conceptualising the future city. And what is striking in the social democratic moment of the British present is that whilst their logics are explicitly articulated, their incommensurabilities are not. The calculi of the future that provide drivers of the actions of the present in Barker are those of the market, those in Hills are the proper (politically contested) moral taxonomies of the state. They imply different logics of governance and the compromise between these logics remains implicit within contemporary policy pronouncement.

What is perhaps the most powerful answer to the critics of the Thames Gateway project emerges from the interstices that separate these two pieces of work, that structure the legitimate ways of future thinking, address head on the sorts of compromise between state and market that might be fit for purpose in the twenty-first century and take as their heart the problem of liberal government to structure what it means to dwell in the city.

Again some parts of this relate to the specificities of the National Audit Office investigation of the Thames Gateway. The institutional architecture of regeneration agencies and institutions is Byzantine, the priorities are unclear and the scale is daunting. But what is equally true is the level of consensus about the desired outcome. There is a sense that the more just city, a socially inclusive sense of urbanism that appeals to a notion of the urban renaissance and a high quality of city life, might be both desirable and economically efficient for the east of London in a manner that both redresses the spatial injustices of London's geography and restores economic activity to its post-industrial landscape (Cohen and Rustin, 2007).

And the reason for the asymmetry between the consensus about desired outcome and the contest around proper means is at heart about the failure to consider the contradictory strands of future thinking that are at the heart of policy interventions. So in the rest of this chapter the intention is to outline firstly the sense of the paradoxical understandings of the Gateway that emerge from these tensions and tentatively suggest that we might want to reconsider the sorts of future thinking that might be more appropriate for the sorts of compromise or stand-off between state and market that the logics of partnership based urban regeneration imply.

The dynamics of change: the background to growth numbers in London

There are three reasons that all point towards an increased need to provide housing numbers in the Thames Gateway area of London.

Economic production

The year 2003 saw a collapse in the commercial office market in London. The landmark Swiss Re building designed by Norman Foster struggled to let its new space. There was considerable turbulence around the future of the Canary Wharf Group, which was once an FT100 listed company on the basis of a single property portfolio on the Isle of Dogs. By 2004 London was witnessing a levelling in London's job growth. Despite all this, the potential for continued employment growth in the east of London appears widely in the forecasts of the financial and business services sectors and in the investment decisions of major corporates such as Citigroup, Clifford Chance, Barclays and HSBC that have located on the Canary Wharf Group estate in recent years. The numbers of jobs on this estate itself will exceed 100,000 in the near future on the basis of buildings coming through the ground at the moment.

The cyclical trend of oversupply and depression of commercial office markets should not distract us from the scale of the change. In the early drafts of the various national Sustainable Communities Plans the ODPM recognised the new financial and business services sectors on the Isle of Dogs as having the medium-term potential to drive the employment base on the estate up to 200,000. The impact of such change on housing demand is considerable and is mediated through the uneven impacts of poor transport infrastructure and the emerging new travel to work areas and geographies that respond to this economic engine.

Social reproduction

Following the 1990s boom and related population growth, the south-east in general and London in particular faces labour shortages in key public sector job markets. In essence the city faces a problem of producing affluence whilst effectively reproducing itself. The need to provide affordable housing for such a labour force is in part about the production of affordable dormitory space within plausible travel to work distances of the new areas of growth.

Household demographics

A third reason for the growth in households is cultural rather a direct result of commercial demand. Long-term reductions in household size and increasing household numbers have generated demand for increasing numbers of residential units. Many of the estates in the inner part of the Gateway demonstrate mass overcrowding and suppressed residential demand. Meanwhile areas of gentrification often service a demand for smaller family sizes at rental and purchase prices beyond the range of most households.

These three sources of demand generate different dynamics of spatial preference. The Barker housing review (2004) highlighted supply side constraints in bringing land forward; cited the rational tendency for private developers to protect profits by deliberately limiting supply in some contexts; and put a spotlight on the relationship between housing subsidy and the role of both developers and registered social landlords. The review has three consequences. It makes it essential to reconsider the appropriate mediation of public interest and private profit. It demands a reconsideration of the institutional architecture of regeneration agencies and social housing provision. Perhaps most significantly, it raises a question about the trade-offs between quality development in specific places and achieving housing numbers quickly in large tracts of lands.

It is clearly the case that the vast majority of the housing numbers in the Gateway will need to be developed by the private sector, even in models that maximise the proportion of social housing. A series of institutional changes might restructure the relationship between the public interest, the market and the way such a relationship translates into housing outcomes. Post-Barker, housing subsidies may be paid to property developers and Registered Social Landlords are increasingly likely to become developers in their own right. Planning law might facilitate value capture through hypothecating future tax revenues in areas of physical infrastructure change and the principles of 'polluter pays' could be compromised by brownfield subsidy. Such changes suggest thinking carefully about the spaces of the Thames Gateway that will be developed in the coming years. They logically demand a politics that accepts the role of the market but reintroduces a much stronger sense of the potential to plan the city.

Thinking spatially and Mulgan's London

In an important piece of research, led by Geoff Mulgan and produced by the Prime Minister's Strategy Unit, a diagnosis of London's present and prognosis of its future was produced in the London Analytical Report of 2003 (Prime Minister's Strategy Unit, 2003). The report covers a wide range of material but in considering the growth agenda for London it is worth making two points.

Mulgan's London has no explanation of where London's economic growth will be realised. It extrapolates exponentially from trends, which is a reasonable exercise. However, it neither analyses the dynamics behind these trends nor develops an understanding of where the jobs growth will be located. The report envisages putatively an additional 300,000 skilled jobs by 2010. Given that there are approximately 300,000 daily commuters to the geographical area of the City Corporation we could be talking about a 'new square mile' of jobs added to the London economy in the next six years. Where will they be located and where will the employees live?

Mulgan's London did not recognise the Thames Gateway at all as a possible spatial answer to either housing growth or job growth. The housing sections of the report (Prime Minister's Strategy Unit, 2003: 48–71 and particularly 70) highlight the limited potential for London housing growth eastwards and suggest instead that the resolution of the housing supply problems are to be found in the inner suburban and central rings of London. This is a result of using extrapolated trends rather than thinking through the dynamics. The current numbers of 10–15 thousand new builds a year in London that the report describes reinforces Barker's complaint of supply-side problems and underplays the possibilities of intervention by regeneration agencies. By 'making places' such as Docklands it was possible to create a new market for housing expansion in a part of London where previously there was secular long-term low demand. The London Analytical Report's silence highlights the need for policy intervention both to transform current housing supply trends and to think spatially about how this might be translated into brownfield rather than greenfield city growth.

Temporality and the Gateway investment paradox

Consecutive updates of the Sustainable Communities Plan has population growth numbers for Thames Gateway that are possibly too high over the short term and too low over the long term. This arises because:

1. *Of the understandable need* to deliver a vision that is financially realistic and not over-ambitious on the longer term supply side. With current trends of new house build at 10–15 thousand units p.a. a very large proportion of London's annual build would need to take place in the Gateway to meet even the modest targets for housing new build given in the Sustainable Communities summer 2003 update, let alone

the more ambitious numbers outlined in plans for the Gateway publicised by the Department of Communities and Local Government in 2006.

2. *Of the understandable manner* in which there is a desire to be seen to deliver over the electoral cycle.

3. *Of the understandable manner* in which the model in the Sustainable Communities update is driven by the historically low numbers of new build rather than by the regional employment potential of the Gateway.

A paradox thus arises: the current model of growth in the Gateway aims at financial modesty and limited demands on the Treasury but because of its modesty is fiscally wasteful and economically sub-optimal. However, lower aspirations could translate into suburbanised low-quality development at below 'urban renaissance' densities. At lower densities physical infrastructure becomes more expensive because of higher per capita costs for each public sector infrastructure decision. For example, in public transport investment decisions the numerator (population growth) diminishes and the denominator (investment costs for any specific public transport project such as Crossrail) remains fixed. Already at least one consultant has attempted to claim that if population targets are set at the levels in the summer 2003 targets then there is no need for some of the major physical infrastructure projects that are so central to the future of the Gateway.

5.3
New residential developments, Royal Arsenal, Woolwich (above) and Chatham Docks (below). Source: Laura Keogh

Consequently the worries must be:

1. As a housing driven model the planning framework of the Sustainable Communities Plan will not cater for the economic drivers which would demand greater transport infrastructure investment. It would be possible to realise modest housing targets in east London without infrastructure spend but not possible to realise a jobs-driven economic model on this basis. South-eastern economic growth is potentially jeopardised if places such as the new business district of the Isle of Dogs and growth sites such as a post-Olympics Stratford cannot be made to work.

2. The buy-in at regional governmental level to the London Gateway will potentially dissipate as the 'Global City' thrust of the London Plan is jeopardised.

3. The buy-in at local government level will be jeopardised if boroughs to the east of London that are the subject of medium-term continued patterns of de-industrialisation see the future they are offered in terms of low-quality suburbanisation that will bring few new jobs, limited social infrastructure and the 'export' of the overcrowded inner East End to the less densely populated outer London boroughs. A caricature of these arguments generated the council by-election victory for the British National Party in Thurrock and the strength of the BNP in the 2006 local elections in Barking and Dagenham.

Conclusion

In considering the future of the eastern pie slice of London that maps the Thames Gateway, higher housing numbers and densities are not only possible, they are imperative if we are to deliver both high-quality urban change and social inclusion. High numbers can be achieved. In an institutional maze that might confuse Theseus, they depend on achieving an institutional architecture that is congruent between the new London Housing Board, two Urban Development Corporations, the developing role of the Housing Corporation as it merges with English Partnerships, the London Development Agency, the big spending departments and regional and local government.

There is a default model. The concentrations of brownfield land within the perimeter of the M25 have the potential to provide plentiful housing land and serious residential growth if the lessons of the Barker review are read principally in terms of planning-induced supply constraints. Although density can become a fetish it is the case that high density costs more in the short term whilst yielding financial and social returns in the long term. Managing this temporality is essential. Relatively low-cost intervention could produce low density numbers in East London that created residential numbers in some post-industrial areas. It would be a future of low-cost mixed estates of low quality. It is not quite the post-1945 nightmare of social engineering gone wrong. The default is a model of low quality, economically sub-optimal suburbanisation. But this would be a waste of the opportunity of a generation.

But there is a more interesting and hopeful alternative. Experiments in governance are creating hybrid forms of trade-off between state and market, such as the new Registered Social Landlord/developers, as some of the major housing associations become increasingly involved in the regeneration of major sites and some of the private developers construct special purpose joint ventures with RSLs. The development of the entity out of the merger of Housing Corporation and English Partnerships that has been variously described as Communities England and the 'new homes agency' will be a novel social engineer of considerable budget and contested mission. There is recognition of the need to synthesise design obligations and economic imperatives (Williams, 2007).

In practical terms this demands a more honest debate about the sort of hybrids of state and market that are already emerging and will continue to do so. There are emerging examples of good and bad practice but the debates about land trusts, ecological sustainability, carbon footprint, mixed communities, community cohesion and urban renaissance all share an *implicit* pay off between forms of market completion and forms of social engineering that needs to be rendered *explicit*. It also might open up thinking around fiscal risk that could lead to the development of experiments in city bonds, securitised rental revenues and uplift associated with infrastructure investment, that recognises the potential for innovation in instruments of regeneration, that can accommodate the paradox of the Thames Gateway rather than guarantee its failure.

Theoretically, this might imply a consideration of such hybrid forms that focus thinking on the city yet to come that is neither the functional outcome of capital's imperatives in the Marxian tradition of urbanism nor the technocratic functionality of mainstream paradigms of urban studies. But such a theoretical focus itself demands a more sophisticated understanding of the pluralities of the future that already inhabit the present, the sense that the production of space assembles around a multiplicity of temporal horizons that might place 'future thinking' at the heart of a contemporary urban studies.

Chapter 6

'An exemplar for a sustainable world city': progressive urban change and the redevelopment of King's Cross

Rob Imrie

Introduction

> We and our peers have to work harder to demonstrate that we are well
> intentioned and that we understand our responsibilities. We know that
> there are commercial and social advantages in building long term rela-
> tionships in the communities in which we operate.
>
> (Chairman's statement, Grosvenor plc, 2003)

Government publications and statements reinforce the message that cities are
undergoing a major transformation, with significant investment and redevelopment of inner city areas (DCLG, 2006). At the launch of the English 'State of the
Cities' report, David Miliband declared that 'our cities have made a successful
recovery after years of decline' (ODPM, 2006b: 2). This recovery is being led by
new waves of property-led investment. One example is the redevelopment of a
significant portion of land immediately north of King's Cross (KX) station in London
that is presented by government as exemplifying the best of urban policy and
practice (ODPM, 2006b). The redevelopment is based, so it is alleged, on sustainable development principles. These include the recycling of waste materials
generated by construction activity, the design of eco-friendly buildings and the
incorporation of local community views into development proposals, policies and
processes.

Argent Group plc (hereafter 'Argent'), the developer of the KX site, claims to be part of the process of best (urban) policy and practice, with its declared commitment to inclusive, mixed-use, sustainable development. In a publication entitled *Our Principles for a Human City*, the company defines sustainable development as comprising three strands, economy, equality and environment and, for Argent (Arup, 2001: 2), 'each supports and reinforces the other'. Argent appears to be part of a new, progressive movement in the development and construction industry, in which commercial objectives are being aligned with non-commercial possibilities and outcomes. This is especially evident amongst a 'new wave' of property companies, such as The Maghull Group and Urban Splash. The latter, for instance, has declared 'that any urban redevelopment is about more than bricks and mortar. It's about using enlightened design, creating new communities, enhancing people's lifestyles' (Urban Splash, 2006).

This echoes government policy that, since the early 1990s, has encouraged developers, and other agents, to promote inclusive urban regeneration, in which local community values and viewpoints are expected to be part of the development process. The Urban White Paper (DETR, 2000a: 4) made the point forcibly; urban regeneration must be inclusive and communities 'must be fully engaged in the process from the start and . . . everyone must be included'. This directive has been reaffirmed in subsequent policy pronouncements, most notably in the Sustainable Communities Plan (ODPM, 2003a), and by members of Gordon Brown's first cabinet. Thus, Hazel Blears (2008), in a speech about rebuilding communities, has suggested that 'governments on their own cannot regenerate communities . . . the answer lies in a progressive partnership between a community, with activists and leaders who are emboldened and empowered, and a government which is on their side'.

The government's focus on community involvement is part of a broader agenda to construct an active public sphere by targeting areas deemed to be disadvantaged, and containing populations considered to lack the skills and resources to engage in what Amin (2005: 614) refers to as 'the principles of market freedom'. These principles are particularly to the fore in regeneration schemes in London, in which policy is seeking to create new urban land markets that appeal to global and international investors. This is the case with KX, a locale with a history of vigorous community activism, and characterised by a distinctive lack of (the community's) engagement with 'market freedom'. Into this has stepped Argent, with a brief to re-capitalise local land markets, and into a development context characterised by institutional and political complexity, and a plurality of, often divergent, community interests.

This chapter considers a neglected part of the debate about community, inclusion and urban policy, by investigating the attitudes and approaches of a property developer, Argent, to the government's agenda about the activation of place-based groups and organisations. While Argent's interactions with, and inclusion of, local community groups and organisations in the development process at KX can be interpreted as part of a broader (governmental) socio-political project, this interpretation, in and of itself, is insufficient. Rather, in this chapter, I view Argent, and the actions of its agents, as situated and reflexive, and not reducible to an 'agent rationality' or an economic calculus, as suggested by much of the literature about property development (see, for example, Cadman and Austin-Crowe, 1983; DiPasquale and Wheaton, 1992). As the next part of the chapter outlines, developers' actions are related to a complexity of social, institutional, governance and political relationships that reveal the development process to be 'dynamic, deeply contextual, and contingent' (Guy and Henneberry, 2000: 2410; also, see Keogh and D'Arcy, 1999).

I relate such ideas to recent rounds of regeneration in KX, and I evaluate Argent's approach to the process, with a focus on the developer's visions for, and approaches to, community involvement and participation. Referring to testimonials from a range of actors, including the Chief Executive (CE) of Argent, officers from the London borough of Camden and local activists and residents, I develop the point that community engagement poses significant challenges for developers, especially in relation to sites of national and international significance. Community engagement is neither a straightforward nor an easy process for developers. As the data suggest, it is characterised by tensions and difficulties relating to defining who or what the community is that ought to be consulted, and how best to facilitate engagement that avoids either the propagation of 'single-issue' politics or the views of activist experts that may not necessarily represent much more than the view being presented.

However, notwithstanding this, the evidence of Argent's involvement in community engagement in KX seems to herald less a brave new world of progressive consultative and participative processes, and much more the propagation of a rhetoric about the sensitivity of the development process to the viewpoints and wishes of (some) place-based groups. The data suggests that community engagement in KX has been partial and piecemeal and is akin to what Amin (2005: 614) refers to as 'a conformist civic particularism'. Despite the language of participation, or the good intentions expressed by Argent and other actors, the organisation of the project's key components, including the developer's approach to community engagement, has not challenged or changed power inequalities or the (hierarchical) social relations of the development process. In this respect, I conclude that community engagement in KX falls far short of the inclusive policy agenda that the Urban White Paper originally outlined as integral to urban regeneration.

Inclusive property development – a new urban entrepreneurialism?

Much of the debate about urban regeneration is characterised by caricatures of the process, actors and outcomes. Some of the key caricatures relate to the property developer, often portrayed in the literature as a semi-mythical figure, a purveyor of destruction and despoliation, or, perhaps, a positive force, as a creator of urban environments. Some of the classic texts, such as Oliver Marriott's (1969) *The Property Boom*, conceive of the property development process as one led by pioneers, in which strong-willed individuals trail-blaze through the urban environment (see also Ambrose, 1994; Cadman and Austin-Crowe, 1983; Ambrose and Colenutt, 1975). More recent renditions celebrate the cult of the developer as celebrity or personality. In one characterisation, of Tony Bloxham, the owner of Urban Splash, it is suggested that he has a reputation as a 'restorer' and 'a one-man regeneration machine' (Alexander and Burdekin, 2002: 8).

This caricature of the developer is usually offset by the more dominant portrayal as a self-seeking, profit oriented, individual (see figure 6.1). The chairman of Grosvenor (2003: 2) captures this in an annual report: 'the perception (remains) of sharp-suited men imposing unappealing architecture and land uses on communities with whom they have no sympathy or commitment and making large profits in the process. There is still distrust of developers'. The property boom in the 1980s particularly heightened this image, in which developers were seen, by some, to be cashing in at the expense of local community views, failing to consult with local people and producing places characterised by bland architecture and lacking social facilities and uses. The redevelopment of Canary Wharf in London's Docklands was emblematic of much of a period characterised by excess, often fuelled by the use of public subsidies to provide developers with development windfalls (Brownill, 1999).

Not surprisingly, the property sector became the subject of much negative comment by both academics and government organisations, such as the Audit Commission (1989) and the National Audit Office (see Cochrane, 2007; Imrie and Thomas, 1999). In 1988, the former noted that the flagships of regeneration, the Urban Development Corporations, were spending too much money on physical infrastructure, and were failing to respond to local community needs

6.1
A caricature of property developers.
Source: CartoonStock, 2008

(see also Imrie and Raco, 2003: 11). Commentators, such as Turok (1992), characterised the period as one of 'property-led' regeneration, in which construction and building activities dominated inner-city policy, at the expense of responding appropriately to social and economic needs (see also Imrie and Thomas, 1993, 1999). Later on, the Social Exclusion Unit (1998: 5) reaffirmed such views: 'there has been too much emphasis on physical renewal instead of better opportunities for local people'.

Throughout the 1990s, a different emphasis emerged, in which issues about social and corporate responsibility were part of an attitude relating to the sustainability of the built environment, and the inclusion of communities in the development process. Government programmes, such as City Challenge and the Single Regeneration Budget (SRB), encouraged community involvement in regeneration. By 1997, New Labour's urban policies were committing to a raft of policy measures to ensure partnerships in regeneration, including New Deal for Communities (1998), the National Strategy for Neighbourhood Renewal (2001), and Local Strategic Partnerships (2003) (see Holden and Iveson, 2003; Imrie and Raco, 2003; Tiesdell and Allmendinger, 2003). Later on, the Egan report (ODPM, 2004: 9) was important in highlighting the need for developers to 'raise their game', to go beyond the 'financial bottom line' and to contribute to sustainable community building 'by delivering high quality attractive places for people to live'.

Property companies have responded to the changing context by adopting a language of social inclusion, partnership and community focus. For instance, Land Securities plc (2006: 80), in their 2006 annual report, note that 'urban community development' is a priority that requires 'innovation, commitment, and partnership with stakeholders'. Likewise, Countryside Properties (2007) claims on its website to be 'recognised as an innovative, responsible developer'. It declares that 'we encourage local people to participate in the development process and in the management of community facilities to help promote social inclusion'. A similar tone and emphasis is apparent amongst other property companies with Development Securities plc (2005: 2), a major player in the redevelopment of Paddington Basin, suggesting that 'we want to ensure our developments enrich local communities'. This point is also made by Grosvenor plc (2003: 2): 'developers must ensure that development is, in effect, initiated, inspired and delivered locally'.

Similar sentiments are part of Argent's approach to the redevelopment of KX, outlined in a regeneration strategy document (Arup, 2001; see also Arup, 2004). This situates the proposed development in the context of a plethora of government policy documents, quoting, for example, the Commission for Architecture and the Built Environment (CABE, 2003: 3): 'it is crucial to understand the local geography of the community, the social and economic fabric of the neighbourhoods'. The document describes the (re) development of KX as a part of New Labour's sustainable communities agenda (ODPM, 2003a), suggesting that the regeneration will deliver 'benefits to local communities' (Arup, 2001: 10). For Argent, critical to the process is to create 'community ownership of the place', for communities 'to be involved in decisions' and to develop 'stronger social capital, across existing community boundaries'. All of this is suggestive of a developer sensitive to the inclusion of people in the policy processes that shape places.

The political context and relations underpinning regeneration in London shape this sensitivity. For instance, directives from the mayor's office provide a steer about the importance of the inclusion of community organisations in urban regeneration. The London Plan (Greater London Authority, 2004a), as the strategic-wide document for the metropole, says that developers should support the government's neighbourhood renewal agenda and provide community benefits. It is suggested that 'the mayor is particularly keen that communities adjacent to development . . . secure benefits that are most appropriate to them'. For the Greater London Authority (GLA, 2004a: 83), social and economic impact assessments of regeneration schemes require developers to enable 'local communities to articulate their own interpretations of the impacts of development'. The sentiments are broadly echoed, and reproduced by the London boroughs. Thus, in Camden's (LBC, 2006: 9) unitary development plan, the council state that they are committed to an inclusive regeneration process, 'through innovative processes of community involvement'.

These directives place significant responsibilities on developers to work in and through identifiable entities called 'communities' as part of the regeneration of areas. There is much onus on the development industry to demonstrate that community engagement is core to the process. However, with few exceptions, literature about property development and regeneration rarely identifies, or documents, the challenges and issues of community engagement for developers. It is too readily assumed that the process is a given, of a type, often characterised by developers' tokenism and by an inequality of power that favours development interests (that are seen as different from those of community groups and organisations). These formulations are reductive, and potentially unhelpful, because they present both developers and community groups as opposites, while reducing each to a singular when, in fact, there is much complexity that surrounds the entwined, and messy, ways in which developers interact with those that are deemed to constitute the community.

As much is suggested by Ball (2004) who, in one of the more sensitised writings about property development, suggests that there are difficulties for developers in creating appropriate conditions for successful community engagement (see also Defilippis and North, 2004). The difficulties, and challenges, of engagement for developers are manifold and include: developing an understanding of the government's community engagement agenda and translating this into practice; defining who the object/subject of engagement is or ought to be; seeking to cultivate representative voices and opinions; tapping into often unheard voices; responding to many viewpoints, including 'non community' or extra local interests that have a future stake in the regeneration; and developing the skills and approaches to interlink engagement with project objectives and outcomes. As Ball (2004) intimates, none of these tasks is easy, and none of them is pre-given or can be read off from a structural logic. Rather, they are situated within, and responsive to, the particularities of specific development contexts and opportunities.[1]

There is, however, little evidence or investigation into how precisely such opportunities shape developers' approaches to community engagement. This suggests certain lines of investigation. Thus, how do developers, such as Argent, seek to overcome some of the difficulties involved in engaging with place-based communities, and how far, and in what ways, are property companies following through the claims that they are making about being responsive to the political agenda in relation to socially inclusive regeneration? How far are developers 'opening up' the development process, and providing the tools and mechanisms for community voices not only to be heard but also to be active in shaping and influencing project outcomes? Conversely, is it the case of 'more of the same', in which place-based groups are marginal players in the process, part of legitimating exercises and provided with tokens instead of substantial gains for them and their memberships?

Dialogue, consensus and community

In addressing some of these issues relating to developers' interactions with placed-based communities, I focus on the redevelopment of KX, a 67-acre brownfield site primarily to the north of King's Cross and St Pancras stations in central London (see figure 6.2). The developer, Argent (Arup, 2001: 1), has characterised the site as 'the largest plot of derelict and underused land in Central London'. This was probably an accurate description as far back as the early 1970s, in that much of the railway infrastructure around the two stations was either under-utilised or abandoned (Fainstein, 1994). The site comprised a mixture of semi-derelict and derelict Victorian infrastructure, including railway sidings, loading depots, warehouses and a number of fine listed buildings, such as the Granary and the Stanley Buildings (see figure 6.3). The area was not without economic activity or vitality, and a number of small businesses operated on the site, taking advantage of the central location and low rents.

The development potential of KX came to the fore in 1987, after the identification of the area as the terminus for a high-speed train link to Europe. An outline planning application for comprehensive redevelopment was submitted by a newly formed development organisation, London Regeneration Consortium (LRC), in April 1989. The application was for 6.9 million square feet of office space that Camden Council objected to on the grounds that it was 'unrealistic' and out of step with their strategy to regenerate the area for mixed uses. A re-submission of the application, in October 1989, scaled down the proposed office space to 5.3 million square feet, but it never came to fruition. This was due to a mixture of local community opposition, Camden Council's dissatisfaction with the lack of community consultation by LRC in drawing up the application and a down-turn in the

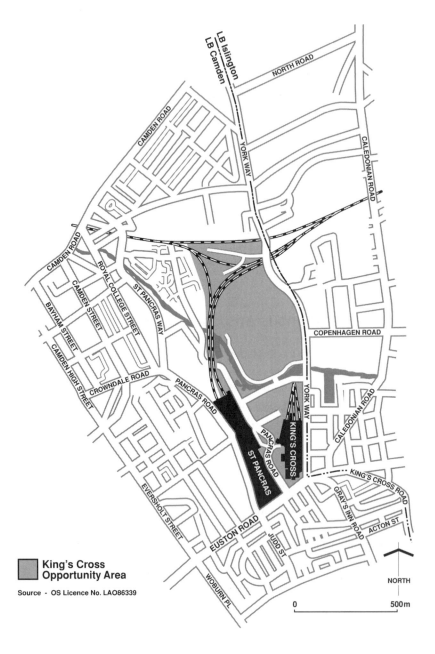

King's Cross
Opportunity Area

Source - OS Licence No. LAO86339

NORTH

0   500m

property market in the early 1990s that made the construction of new office space an unviable proposition.

A feature of the process was local community groups opposing LRC, in particular the King's Cross Railway Lands Community Development Group that was set up in 1987. This organisation produced a document entitled 'Towards a People's Plan' in 1990, that fed into two alternative planning applica-

6.3
Images of King's Cross.
Source: Rob Imrie, 2008

tions submitted to Camden Council in 1992, based on retaining local housing, and comprising mixed uses, including community and leisure facilities. This application failed, like the previous ones by LRC, although it provided a challenge to the development orthodoxy of property-led regeneration. However, in 2000, with the government trying to secure deals for a Channel Tunnel rail link, Argent were appointed as project partners with LRC, and they proceeded to outline a mixed-use development proposal.[2] An energetic, and targeted, community consultation process was also set up, in conjunction with Camden and Islington Councils.

The planning application for the site, given final approval in November 2006, spans two local authorities, the London Borough of Camden (LBC) and the London Borough of Islington. Most of the redevelopment site falls within the jurisdiction of LBC, and this authority has been one of the major players in influencing the regeneration of KX. Some activist groups see LBC as part of the problem in pushing KX as a focal point for international investment, and because of its willingness, so it is alleged, to concede too readily to Argent's demands (see, for example, Railways Lands Group, 2006). Thus, LBC's vision for KX, outlined in 2001, is not dissimilar to Argent's articulation of an international future for the locale: 'a development that has international stature and contributes to London as a world city' (LBC, 2001: 5). LBC has, however, been important in pushing Argent for community engagement, and providing a context through the setting-up, in 2002, of the King's Cross Development Forum, an umbrella organisation that has sought to represent the broadcloth of place-based community views about the future of KX.

In evaluating Argent's approach to community engagement, this chapter refers to data gathered as part of a two-year project investigating community involvement in urban regeneration in London, Shanghai, and Taipei. The project's objectives were, first, to evaluate the contrasting forms of community involvement in processes of urban plan making and implementation, and, secondly, to consider the factors that limit or inhibit active community involvement in the governance of the study cities, and possibilities for remedy. The London focus was KX, and multi research methods were used to generate data. These comprised scoping interviews with key actors, the collection of documents, such as local planning statements, interviews with a representative of the developer, local planners, and community activists, including members of King's Cross Community Forum and the Railway Lands Group. Interviews were also conducted with local residents, and use was made of two focus groups.

The rest of this chapter outlines and evaluates tensions and difficulties for Argent in defining who or what the community is that they ought to be engaging with. The subjects of engagement are, at best, ambiguous and, in the KX context, revolve around two competing conceptions. One is a global or 'outward' view that conceives of the area as a context for supporting London's global city status. This is a cosmopolitan outlook that defines community as extra-local, a trans-national flow of people who are transitory and, perhaps, only fleetingly a presence in KX. It also conceives of an 'imagined' community of individuals and groups, or those regarded by Argent as the future users and consumers of the regeneration of KX. While Argent, and other actors, have been keen to push this global line, they are mindful of an alternate conception of community, stemming from the place-based demands by local groups for a share in the regeneration outcomes of KX. In particular, much of Argent's effort to engage community has been directed at this, prompted, in part, by the government steering developers towards an 'inward' or area focus and basis for community engagement.

I consider how Argent has responded to this agenda, and outline some of its approaches in seeking to resolve tensions surrounding the establishment of dialogue and interaction with some of the pre-existing KX place-based groups and individuals with stakes in the regeneration. As the data show, Argent, and other actors, have adopted a stance premised on the propagation of, broadly, consumerist views of the public. While appearing to be far-reaching, even innovative, the forms of engagement used have rendered much consultation a series of technical and procedural issues, and neutered, effectively, political opposition and dissent (see Ball, 2004). Indeed, testimonials from interviewees suggest that, despite a vigorous and proactive campaign by Argent to engage with local organisations, there has been a failure of the process to 'break out' from formal political institutions, or spaces of governance that many residents, and others, regard as state-centred and biased. This means that inclusive urban regeneration, featuring community participation, is likely to be weakly developed or peripheral to the process.

Cosmopolitan communities and defining the community

Mega projects, such as KX, are usually characterised by political debates and struggles over development objectives, and bring to the fore the interrelationships between rationality and power (Flyvbjerg, 1998). The articulation of what KX is or should be, by Argent, the GLA, the London Development Agency (LDA), Camden Council, and others, is part of Flyvbjerg's (1998) understanding of 'power defining reality', in which what are presented as rational options and outcomes become the focus of debate and struggles over the definition and understanding of 'the rational'. In the KX context, the rationality of urban regeneration is dominated by a pre-existing planning framework and discourse that, for years, had identified KX as a site of national and international significance. The importance of KX goes well beyond the area itself, so the argument goes, and this is particularly evident given the designation, by the GLA, of KX as one of twenty-eight 'opportunity areas' in London.

Such areas are to be foci of intensive mixed-use development, to cater for needs at the London scale and beyond. This resonates with other pronouncements about the redevelopment of KX, as articulated by the main protagonists through the context of London as a world city. For instance, Argent has suggested that KX 'has an important role to play, within London as a world city' (Arup, 2001). Likewise, the Director of Culture and Environment at the London Borough of Camden, said: 'by defining a collective vision for the area we can transform King's Cross into a world-class visitor and business destination'. The Chief Executive of Central London Partnership further notes that 'King's Cross is on the brink of becoming one of Europe's most exciting areas in which to live, work or visit'. She suggests that the development 'will ensure that the area develops in its own right as a major international gateway for the 2012 Olympic Games'.

The (subsequent) development of community engagement in KX might be conceived of as the cultivation (of such) rational argument and outcome, by use of specific procedural and political mechanisms. This is reflected in Argent's emphasis of the cosmopolitan character of the area, and the significance of responding to the needs not only of people living in KX, but also of prospective users of the regeneration, or individuals and groups who are yet to develop an attachment to KX. Argent has articulated what it presents as an outwardly looking perspective: 'King's Cross Central should have links into a much wider geographic area than the development site alone' (Arup, 2001: 2). A respondent from the LDA reinforced this view: 'we are aware of where it sits in a wider setting . . . in terms of the global position of London'. He amplified by noting that community engagement had to respond to the extra-local scale: 'I think this is common throughout any major development, between someone's very local personal issue and someone's wider regional or international issue.'

Such emphasis is not surprising given that the scale of mega projects, such as KX, means that they are conjoined to places and events beyond the locale, and this influences the understanding of who or what the community is in relation to KX. The regeneration of KX is part of the place marketing of London, and it is also contributing to labour market and economic change that transcends the immediate area. The permeability of mega projects, in this way, has focused part of Argent's efforts in seeking to influence local community groups of the legitimacy of 'looking outwards', responding to the extra-local ties, and socio-spatial flows and connections that tie the area to other places. One respondent summarised this approach to community involvement:

> KX is an international communication centre in the only extending capital city in Europe . . . it behoves the government . . . to realise that and balance it against the so-called local community . . . the local community, if you look at it, it's a very self-contained package.

Argent was aware, however, that the global and cosmopolitan outlook that it was espousing had potential to be unhinged by operating in the London context. The CE of the company felt that the socio-demographic and political profiles of parts of London created a context in which resistance to development is, in his opinion, high. As he suggested, 'in most of the south-east of England, most of London . . . people see change as bad, you know, one more house is one more car on the road, one more office is even more people'. He also felt that local politicians and officers were more likely to make life harder for them in London than elsewhere. As the CE argued:

> It's a lot better in the Manchesters and Birminghams of this world . . . basically, if you're someone that wants to invest in Birmingham or Manchester, generally you're greeted, not with a red carpet, but the first question you get is, 'How can we help? You want to come and invest in our city or in our town, how can we help?' And that is a totally different approach to London.

The sensitivities of Argent to the KX local context were particularly evident in relation to issues of place-based community engagement in the KX regeneration process. The recent history of community activism and opposition to redevelopment plans, coupled with the GLA and Camden Council highlighting community engagement as integral to change, meant that Argent felt it was left with little option but to pursue particular strategies and tactics of engagement with different community groups in KX. This brought to the fore a significant, practical, difficulty for Argent, and other actors in the redevelopment, in defining who or what the community is or ought to be for the purposes of engagement. The Head of Planning at Camden articulated the difficulty in defining 'the community' in KX: 'it's almost gestalt-like, in the sense you're doing it in the negative. What is it not? Because the way they define themselves . . . is really quite complicated'.

Argent was entering into a 'crowded field' of community groups and activists, some of them long established, but most of recent origin, relating to SRB, neighbourhood renewal and other New Labour initiatives. Such groups included the King's Cross Business Forum; a neighbourhood renewal funded organisation called the King's Cross Community Development Trust; a mini local strategic partnership, the Construction Impact Group; a Community Safety Partnership; the King's Cross Public Arts Partnership; and, perhaps most significantly, the King's Cross Community Development Forum (CDF). These are a few of the hundreds of organisations in KX that, potentially, fit into the government's understanding of who ought to be engaged as part of consultation. A community representative, in interview, noted that refugee communities in KX have 'set up their own support systems . . . and now in Camden you've got 1500 different organisations . . . the Somali community probably has about 140 organisations'.

This highlights the numbers of potential consultees that developers may have to engage with, and a problem for them in not only deciding who to consult with, but how, in practical terms, it can be done. The situation is one that, as Ball (2004) suggests, 'makes the idea of community participation difficult in practice'. This is usually compounded by difficulties in generating representative viewpoints, although, as the CE of Argent said: 'the first commitment we made was I would go anywhere, any place, to talk, discuss, listen, understand, with anyone'. The rationale of the CE was to develop a consultative approach that went beyond the tried-and-tested, but limited, methods of leafleting or disseminating newsletters. The head of regeneration at Camden explained the approach: 'instead of just dumping an occasional newsletter on people's doormats, particularly when you have communities that don't respond very well to that kind of communication, we said . . . we'll go and talk to every community group'.

This took shape through an intensive, and still ongoing, series of discussions, meetings, and debates. As the CE of Argent said: 'the first thing we did was to phone up. I got a list of thirty odd community organisations in the local area, from Camden and other sources, and I wrote to them and then I phoned them up . . . whether it was the Vietnamese organisation or whether it was the local mosque'. This initial 'stocktaking' was part of a process of introducing the company to local people, and going to talk about the proposed development: 'We built up a database . . . and we started to expand our network . . . we would always go to anyone who invited us and we were always made welcome, most people were very grateful and surprised to be there. One of the biggest questions was, "Why are you here so early?"' Argent's approach has been seen as positive and, as a local community activist said: 'I'd have to credit Argent that they've turned up to every tiny meeting in every tiny place, on every occasion, rain, snow, the rest of it.'

Other interviewees, including members of different community groups, noted the focus on consensus building by Argent, and, in particular, the attempt to co-opt individuals and groups to the dominant, global-outlook, vision of regeneration. One suggested that the whole style of engagement between developers and local people had changed. As he recalled, 'It was a different style, it was the 1980s, it was much more confrontational, you know, we didn't get to talk to developers.' Others concurred, with another person characterising Argent as 'quite socially aware and responsible and . . . (they) sit around and talk for hours'. Some saw it as part of a charm offensive: 'you know, it's a style, isn't it, it's a sort of New Labour style compared to, you know, the old developers wouldn't let us in the door'. Others felt that it was not necessarily for the good: 'these days Argent would bore you to death at a thousand meetings, it's a different tactic.'

This consensus seeking approach by Argent, in conjunction with Camden Council, has focused the developer's attention on managing the potentially disruptive costs associated with community engagement. One potential disruption for Argent relates to what it perceives to be local groups' lack of clarity of what they want from the proposed regeneration. As the CE of Argent said: 'local groups haven't been able to define what it is that would be most useful to them, and they keep going off in weird directions'. Argent are mindful of weaving in between extreme viewpoints or opinions or what Ball (2004) characterises as 'extreme or intransigent' strategies and tactics sometimes adopted by local (community) personalities. The company, with Camden Council, has also identified a need to develop mechanisms for groups and individuals in the area to articulate diverse viewpoints, partly as a way of deflecting what the CE of Argent regards as the possibilities of 'unrepresentative voices' dominating debate.

Managing plural publics

Subsequently, a number of approaches have evolved as part of these entwined processes of (the management of) community engagement. One is the attempt by Argent, and partners, to manage 'activist experts' or individuals and organisations that the company regards as unrepresentative of the majority opinion. As the CE of Argent observed: 'we're fed up with the same half dozen people spreading misinformation'. He amplified by noting that

> it's half a dozen people . . . who've been around for a long time, who, for whatever reason, do not think what we are proposing is good enough . . .

> they made their mind up before we even came on the scene they were going to resist, and they use everything in their power to communicate the facts that make their case look better.

For Argent, the activist expert is usually an opponent of large-scale regeneration, and does not understand the development process. As the CE observed: 'it's so important . . . to understand the developer, to make links with the developer, otherwise, I think if you just stand aside sniping, my term, then ultimately I don't think that's to the benefit of the community'.

The process of managing 'activist experts' has been aligned to Argent's management and deflection of 'single issue' groups and comments, and the exercise of what some, in the area, see as 'democratic closure' (see Cruikshank, 1999; Dean, 1999). As the CE said: 'we find criticism very helpful, healthy and helpful, providing it's well informed, not kind of single issue stuff'. The solution, for Argent, was in the form of the CDF, set up by Camden Council in 2002. For the CE, the CDF was a major innovation: 'The Forum was Camden's very good attempt to say, "Well, hang on a minute, we're fed up with the same half dozen people spreading misinformation, let's get a much broader group". Paradoxically, though, the CDF appears to be operating as part of a system of closure, or the control of dissent. A community leader suggested that 'I think a lot of us spend hours going to those Forum meetings and actually what we get out of it we should just have boycotted it from the beginning, it just has been a complete farce.'

Not surprisingly, the CDF has met with mixed opinion, and, for some, it is a consumerist approach to consultation, in which the public are asked to choose from a series of pre-selected (regeneration) choices (see Clarke and Newman, 1997; Dolton, 2006). A local community representative argued: 'it's primarily an information exchange, which has its uses, between the planning officers of the local authority and already active members of the local community'. For others, the CDF seems to be no more than what Amin (2005: 621) characterises as 'an instrument of political conformity and control', or a mechanism to channel, and manage, opinion, so redolent of previous periods of property development. As a leader of a local community organisation commented about the CDF: 'The attitude I perceive in the King's Cross team is the public are a great nuisance, community groups are a great nuisance, unless they can be corralled and controlled . . . into the forum and the forum does what it's told.'

Some issues have been regarded as the remit of the planners, not community groups, and were decreed to be not up for discussion. One respondent characterised the CDF as restricting scope for community involvement:

> it's been officer led; we haven't been allowed to meet without officers present, although it's supposed to be an independent forum. I mean I think it's worked quite well in terms of them telling us what's happening, it hasn't worked very well in terms of feeding back.

'Consultation' appears to have focused on the wants and needs of special interest groups, to be either accepted or rejected. Round-table discussion of the proposed plans does not appear to have been an option. Groups have been constrained in their attempts at involvement by lack of resources. There does not appear to be a shortage of well-informed and tireless individuals willing and able to participate but shortage of money and time has been a block to more effective involvement.

In seeking to develop a greater level of community involvement, Argent, with Camden Council, has set up mechanisms of participation through a rescaling of representation. The developer has used teams of private consultants to meet up with people in the local community, and Camden Council have trained up, and deployed, advocate planners as intermediaries to convey messages about the regeneration plans. However, there are real tensions, and contradictions, between, on the one hand, Argent and Camden Council's modernising agenda, based on participative democratic fora, and, on the other hand, the solution that appears to be a centralising approach through the context of advocates or professional experts who are not necessarily sensitised to, or seeking to propagate, 'community views'. As a local resident cynically put it: 'community empowerment means exactly the opposite . . . all these words have been taken and used and are now being used against us all. It's not about empowerment . . . it's about consultants getting jobs and privatising things'.

This reflects the views of others in the area that suggest that Argent's approach to community involvement in regeneration is based on developing (a manufactured) civic consensus and community cohesion around pre-set agendas. While the company recognises a plurality of groups and individuals with a stake in the regeneration of KX, its approach to consultation seems to revolve around the cultivation of a 'singular politics' or one voice that represents the 'community view'. There is the understanding that contested claims, and different understandings, of regeneration ought to be parcelled into a collective view or, otherwise, ignored. One community activist described Argent's approach: 'they've done a good job at working out what the major issues were going to be that they have to meet'. Others reaffirmed this, with a community leader noting that talking with Argent had been frustrating: 'we've spent hundreds of hours at meetings with Argent and got nowhere'.

How far, then, can the claim be sustained that Argent's approach reflects a new politics of consultative and participative processes? The answer to this depends, in part, on what Argent has done that is radically different to traditional, top-down consultative forms of engagement, and how far the regeneration plans have been altered in line with some of the views of place-based organisations. The evidence on both counts suggests that little has changed. With regards to the former, Argent has seemed intent on controlling who is involved and how, primarily through judicious management of activists and the channelling of opinion through the local authority-run CDF. With regards to the latter, evidence suggests that its proposed plans for KX, first mooted in 2001, have changed little or only in minor forms or matters of detail and not substance.[3] While this might reflect local organisations' satisfaction with the developer's original proposals, the evidence is equivocal with one respondent noting Argent's refusal to incorporate leading edge green technologies: 'it's not going to be anything like a zero energy development, which it could be . . . it's cosmetic, they've got a few wind turbines, they've got a few solar panels'.

The frustration evident here is borne out by hours spent in meetings that seem to lead to no change. A community leader recounted one example of local traders asking Argent for the provision of low rental accommodation for their businesses. He recalled the views of a trader: 'we don't see anything here for us. We don't think that ten affordable business premises across the whole of this scheme is really anything that's adequate for us, how does that help us?' Despite a year or more of negotiations between Argent and small businesses, the revised plans for KX, that subsequently received planning permission in November 2006, show few concessions to local traders. An extract, from an interview with a local community representative, highlights Argent's approach:

> nothing's changed, they (Argent) haven't gone to the traders and said, 'we've listened, we can do a bit more for you on this. Let's try, what can we do that would help us win you over?' I mean that hasn't happened, so from where some of us in the community are standing it seems cosmetic, it seems a show . . . we know Argent's been meeting various community groups but what has come out of that, what changes have been made as a result of meetings?

Where concessions to the original plans have occurred, these appear to have been through pressure exerted by Camden Council and not local place-based groups. A local community worker noted that

> Argent has had to compromise, in order to gain Camden's support . . . but they haven't gone anywhere near what most of the community want . . . they've made compromises with Camden, with the GLA, like renewable energy . . . I would like to know from Argent where do they feel they've made the compromise with the community? I can't see the evidence of that.

This was a view held by most interviewees, especially in relation to the provision of social housing. As an interviewee said:

> even Camden are saying fifty per cent affordable, they're only providing forty-four, we want more than that, and the number of housing they've come up with is a total of eighteen hundred, we wanted twenty-five hundred, you know . . . it's all kind of degrees of what they are providing but it always seems to be the minimum, you know, the minimum thing that they can afford.

Conclusions

Pronouncements by developers about commitment to community engagement appear to be part of a 'new wave' of property development, characterised by companies claiming to be sensitised to, and willing to work with, place-based groups in regeneration areas. Argent is no different and it entered the KX context with a declared intent to pursue community engagement as part of its broader commitment to sustainable development (Arup, 2001). This intent was influenced by much of the development context, and especially the locale's pre-existing community politics and history of active involvement of local groups in seeking to shape the area's regeneration. Argent could not afford to ignore, or work against, the prevalent political climate, characterised by Camden Council's commitment to the engagement of local groups, and the various pronouncements of New Labour and the GLA encouraging developers to work much more closely with place-based community organisations.

To this extent, Argent's behaviour was constrained and conditioned by its operational context, including local expectations by community groups, and by local officers and politicians regarding community engagement as integral to the regeneration of KX. However, Argent's approach to engagement, although appearing to be far-reaching and sensitive to the range of views, has revolved around tried-and-tested methods that have not challenged the underlying tenets of the proposal regeneration. While Argent's initial proposal for KX was a mixed-use redevelopment, with an emphasis on commercial office, retail, leisure and residential spaces, aimed at national and international markets, the amended proposal, presented to Camden's planning committee in November 2006, was more or less the same, leading a spokesperson for a local group to conclude that 'I look back on it now, it really amazes me how they (Argent) tried to pull the hood over the community.'

This view suggests that Argent's approach to community engagement is 'lip service', and falls short of meeting New Labour's encouragement of, and visions for, inclusive participation in urban regeneration. It highlights a 'shallow approach' to engaging with place-based groups. It is also revealing of an organisation that, unsurprisingly, was seeking to ensure minimum disruption to its plans as originally envisaged in 2001 (see Arup, 2001). The terms of debate have been couched within a specific set of parameters that can be thought of, following Flyvbjerg (1998), as part of a 'project of control', or a process of securing the power of rationality. Such rationality has revolved around a variety of issues and struggles to legitimate the trajectory of development in KX, including those between organisations, such as Argent, the LDA and GLA, intent on emphasising the non-local use of the regeneration, and others, such as place-based organisations, intent on securing significant benefits for pre-existing, local groups.

That place-based views and opinions have done little to influence or change the underlying principles and content of Argent's plans for KX is testimony, in part, to the propagation of what Newman (2001: 137) refers to as the 'rule bound rational discourse of liberal democracy'. New Labour's rhetoric about sustainable communities, including the importance of developers engaging with place-based groups, is not based on sophisticated conceptions about democracy and, instead, revolves around what St Pierre (1997: 1) refers to as 'the liberal logic of self-interest as well as liberalism's emphasis on competition'. This conception tends to conceive of relationships as stable, unified, and seeking to progress 'through the right use of reason' (St Pierre, 1997: 2). Argent's attempts to create consensus, manage dissent and deflect opinion bear the hallmarks of the rationality of liberalism in propagating the primacy of the autonomous and responsible self that, in the KX context, has led to some foreclosure of views stemming from the multiple and intersecting identities that make up the place.

Acknowledgements

My thanks to the Chiang Ching-kuo Foundation, Taiwan (grant number, RG 005-U-04), who provided the funding to carry out the research reported in the chapter. My thanks also to Marion Kumar who conducted many of the interviews that I draw on here, and who also read an earlier version of the chapter. The chapter also benefited from the comments of Sarah Fielder, Marian Hawkesworth, Loretta Lees, Mike Raco, and Emma Street.

Notes

1   Such attitudes suggest that processes of property development cannot be reduced to economic relations, or understood as (just) responding to economic stimuli, such as profit motive. Instead, recent research on the property industry reveals it to be embedded in complex social, institutional, and political networks, in which property developers, and their agents, are conceived of as knowledgeable social actors, and not, as Wharf (1994: 328) puts it, 'some passive actor in the construction of landscapes'.

2   The landowners are London and Continental Railways and Exel and the plans, which were submitted to Camden Council in September 2005, comprise 7.9 million square feet of mixed-use development. The proposals include business and employment space; new homes (up to 1946 in total); student housing; hotels and serviced apartments; shopping, food and drink; visitor, cultural and community uses, including a primary school, children's centre, pool and gym facilities, an indoor sports hall and two health centres. It is likely that 40 per cent will be public space, including three new parks and five squares. The proposals also include: a new entrance to the London Underground; a bicycle interchange facility; options for Cross River Tram; space for a new western concourse for King's Cross Station; 3 new bridges over Regent's Canal; the refurbishment of 20 historic buildings/structures, including 4 listed gas holder frames; 14 wind turbines, and other renewable energy methods; 20 new streets and 10 new public spaces; and streetscape improvements in the surrounding area.

3   The KX plan sets out the redevelopment of a derelict site in tandem with the arrival of the Continental Rail Link. As the plans have evolved, it is noticeable that a number of amendments have only been achieved under pressure from activists. Schemes for 24-hour working on some parts of the site had to be fought on the grounds of a threat to the health of residents. Road closures threatening the livelihood of small traders have similarly been fought. Further battles have focused on the height of buildings, preserving green spaces and heritage buildings, the incorporation of renewable energy and the inclusion of a mix of accessible, family, social and affordable housing. It is no coincidence that informant discourses use the language of war!

Chapter 7

Local government and the politics of flagship regeneration in London: the development of Paddington

Mike Raco and Steven Henderson

Introduction

The politics of flagship development in London has been dominated by the experiences of the London Docklands in the 1980s and more recently by major projects such as the regeneration of the South Bank and the London 2012 Olympic Games. Much of the academic and policy focus has been on the ways in which government quangos, such as the LDDC and the ODA, and London-wide agencies, including the LDA and the mayor, have taken responsibility for such developments (see Brownill, 1999; Florio and Brownill, 2000). And yet, within these broader discussions, the role of sub-metropolitan local government has been rather overlooked. There has been a tendency to see London as a prime example of the broader shift from local government to local governance or a context in which the power of elected local authorities has been eroded and redistributed to a range of public and private sector actors (see Imrie and Raco, 1999; Rhodes, 2003; Taylor, 2007). This is particularly true in relation to flagship regeneration projects in which it is commonly accepted that local authorities acting alone are unwilling and/or unable to take a lead in developing and implementing agendas. Indeed, as Gordon and Buck (2005) argue, one key aspect of the new conventional wisdoms that now dominate discourses of governance is the perception that local authorities lack the capability and imagination to act in an entrepreneurial and proactive manner.

This chapter examines the regeneration of Paddington in London to explore broader questions over the governance and delivery of flagship regeneration projects in the capital. Paddington has been promoted as a model example of sustainable urban brownfield regeneration as it has attracted significant national and international private sector investment, has been constructed in and around a major public transportation hub, and has generated new jobs and economic activity alongside some of the most deprived wards in London. It represents exactly the type of development that Ken Livingstone sought to emulate in the London Plan. However, as we argue, the evolution of this project is not a consequence of the actions and agendas of London-wide agencies, seeking to create new development spaces that will support London's wider, global ambitions. Its roots, instead, are to be found primarily in the politics and contexts of the borough of Westminster City and the actions of the local authority in shaping and structuring development processes and priorities. The chapter demonstrates that no understanding of the development would be complete without an examination of its emergence in, and through, the local, sub-metropolitan politics of development in Westminster and it calls for a broader conceptualisation of the governance of urban regeneration in the capital. It begins by discussing the role of local authorities in the politics and governance of flagship initiatives before looking at development imaginations, partnership-building processes and community engagement in Paddington.

The politics of flagship developments in London and the role of local government

The rise of the 'global city' thesis in the 1990s and its subsequent adoption by Ken Livingstone and London-wide agencies has shifted much of the academic and political scale of attention to the metropolitan city-level (see Massey, 2004). London has increasingly become a site of action – a space that is imagined as an object that can be controlled, shaped and worked on as an integrated and bounded unit (see chapter 1). Flagship projects have primarily been conceptualised in terms of what they can contribute to the wider development of London, rather than what they can provide for local communities and neighbourhoods. As Budd (2006) argues, the emphasis is increasingly on the provision of infrastructure for London's global hubs, such as the City of London and the expansion of Heathrow airport. The effect of this re-scaling in policy imaginations is that borough-level, sub-metropolitan politics seem to have become increasingly irrelevant to flagship projects. What takes place at this scale is increasingly understood in and through the contribution that it makes to London's broader global competitiveness.

It is for this reason that the period between the abolition of the GLC (1985) and the creation of the Mayor of London (1999), in which planning powers were devolved to the London boroughs and the cross-borough London Planning Advisory Committee (LPAC), is often characterised as a time of fragmentation and indecision (see Buck *et al.*, 2002; Travers, 2004). Others equate the decline of effective strategic planning in London with the 1960s decentralisation of power to parochial, unimaginative and short-sighted London boroughs (see Ackroyd, 2000;

Collins, 1999). The expectation that local authorities are unable and/or unwilling to plan for flagship developments for the wider benefit of London was reinforced by the creation of the London Docklands Development Corporation in the 1980s and the emergence of the London Development Agency, the Olympic Delivery Authority, the London Urban Development Corporation and other London-wide bodies in the 2000s (see Raco, 2005; Young, 2006). Indeed, in the LDA's early Corporate Plans for London's growth, local authorities are barely mentioned at all.

This negative characterisation of local government is increasingly reflected in wider government policy reforms to the planning system in England. The implementation of a new, powerful Infrastructure Planning Committee, for example, is being introduced on the assumption that local authorities and their electorates tend to be defensive in outlook and will oppose, rather than support, flagship developments. The IPC is designed to override such local opposition if developments are seen to be in the 'national interest' (see DCLG, 2008a). Similar changes have been introduced in London (in January 2008) in which the mayor and the London Development Agency have been given enhanced planning powers to deliver on major projects, even if local communities and authorities are opposed to schemes (DCLG, 2007b). Such measures are being rolled out, in large part, as a response to wider pressure from private sector interests. They have become increasingly critical of the planning system's perceived 'failure' to deliver the infra-structure for new growth and development, particularly in and around London (see Jones, 2005; While *et al.*, 2004). The planning powers and perceived anti-development biases of local authorities have been a particular target for criticism.

And yet, this characterisation underestimates the role that local authorities may play in flagship regeneration projects in London and elsewhere. Rather than being marginal players we argue that there are at least four inter-related roles that they can play in the development, governance and implementation of policy programmes. First, local authorities often provide a much-needed sense of *continuity* to governance arrangements unmatched by other agencies. The current boundaries of the London boroughs were established in 1965, making them the most stable and long-lasting governance institutions in the city and providing a focus for other communities and development interests. Even though, outside the capital, local government boundaries have been the subject of reviews in the 1970s and 1990s, they still provide a sense of fixity, or what Taylor (1999) terms place-space congruence, in many areas. Second, local authorities continue to play an important *representational* role within local development politics and partnerships. Despite the erosion in local government's powers and resources since the mid 1980s, local authorities, as we will see in the Paddington example, are often cautious about their electoral support and this can influence their attitudes towards key planning issues such as conservation and heritage planning, and community engagement. Moreover, the introduction of the Local Government Act 2003 and its requirement for local councils to draw up community strategies and local strategic partnerships have, in many cases, given local authorities a new political impetus, albeit in a context where central government still plays an important role in shaping local policy outcomes (see Geddes, 2006; Raco, *et al.*, 2006).

Third, local authorities can also provide an important *coordinating* role in what are becoming increasingly complex, fragmented and confusing development contexts. With more agencies now involved in policy development and delivery, particularly in London, local government's position may, paradoxically, be becoming more significant in terms of policy-making, rather than less. Ball and Maginn (2005), for example, show that where local authority involvement is marginalised, development projects become prone to failure as community and development interests are unable to reach compromises. In many cases local authorities, therefore, play a key role in providing 'confidence' in the regeneration process for potential investors and developers, particularly as property markets, even in London, are notoriously fickle and unpredictable.

Fourth, some local authorities have also been *proactive in developing policy networks and partnerships*. As Jones and Evans (2006: 1506) argue in some cases local activities 'run ahead of central government policy' and influence subsequent rounds of reform at higher scales. In the King's Cross development, for example, the boroughs of Camden and Islington have been instrumental in shaping local development partnerships and policy priorities (see chapter 6 in this volume). Similarly, in the former LDDC-area, local authorities have taken a proactive role in initiating major projects, such as Stratford City and Barking Reach, both of which have featured heavily in the government's plans for the Thames Gateway. In some parts of London the boroughs have also been active in developing cross-authority networks. The Thames Gateway London Partnership, for instance, has been a key player in shaping development agendas in east London and local authorities have had a significant influence on other development initiatives such as the implementation of new UDCs and the London Olympics (see chapter 8 in this volume; Raco, 2005). In such cases the local authorities are playing a vital mediating role between new developments and local communities by, for instance, setting up local training and/or welfare programmes and legitimating projects to local communities.

The remainder of the chapter now draws on the example of the flagship Paddington development to examine and assess the influence that sub-metropolitan institutions and politics has had on the form and character of development programmes. The discussion draws on a two-year investigation into the redevelopment of land around Paddington Central. During 2003–4 information was collected through archival work, 2 community focus groups and 40 interviews with a wide range of stakeholders including 6 with Westminster City Council (WCC) representatives, 15 developers and landowners, 3 with higher levels of government and 17 with local and community organisations. The chapter begins by situating the project in a longer term development context before turning to a discussion of development imaginations, partnerships, strategies and community engagement in relation to the Paddington development. The analytical focus is particularly on the role and influence of the local authority, WCC and the complex and tangled relationships between local political relations, economic changes and broader development rationalities and practices.

The redevelopment of Paddington – from a problem place to an opportunity space

'Neither one thing nor the other' – physical legacies and development histories in Paddington

In the nineteenth century what is now Paddington Central was an important spur on the London canal network (see figure 7.1). The area's role as a transport node was expanded in the 1840s with the building of the London terminus of the Great Western Railway and these developments have had important socio-economic legacies. Their construction involved significant infrastructure development and generated a range of heavy-use economic activities. As with other British indus-trial urban areas the existence of heavy rail tracks came to represent an important social as well as physical divide (see Imrie and Thomas, 1999). Neighbourhoods to the north of the railway lines became working-class housing, characterised by close-knit communities and a well-developed social infrastructure of churches, public spaces and civic amenities. In the districts to the south, however, increas-ingly exclusive and expensive developments were constructed between the new station and Hyde Park. These, in turn, became some of the most desirable prop-erties in and around the capital and have traditionally supported the local Conserv-ative party. This is particularly significant as WCC, since its formation in 1965, has remained a Conservative party stronghold, with members currently holding forty-eight of the available sixty seats. The Labour party that has historically repre-sented wards to the north of Paddington holds the remaining twelve seats.

Modernist, post-war development projects continued to divide the area. In the 1960s the construction of the Westway motorway cut a swathe through the communities of north Paddington. The Westway was one of the only parts of the notorious London Motorway Box to be constructed before a combi-nation of public opposition and rising costs forced the project to be abandoned (see Gyford, 1999; Hall, 1989). Its construction led to the demolition of many of the urban and civic spaces around which communities had formed and cleared the way for major slum clearance and modernist housing development programmes. In the words of one long-term Westway community interviewee: 'we lost the whole of the town centre . . . we lost the Police Station, we lost the Town Hall, we lost shops, we lost cinemas, we lost churches, you know we were messed over'. There was little in the way of planning for the impacts of the devel-opment on local communities or any real effort to identify and address local prob-lems (see Duncan, 1992; Porter, 1989). These physical changes also coincided with the arrival of new waves of national and international immigration during the 1950s and 1960s, particularly from the Caribbean. The net effect of the new devel-opments was an increase in the socio-economic differences between the north

7.1
Paddington.
Source: Mike Raco, 2008

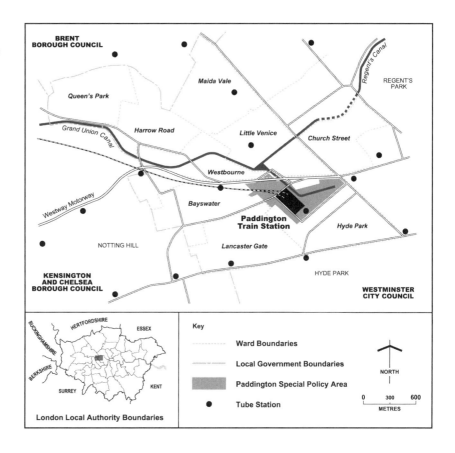

and south of the area and the physical imposition of divisive new infrastructure in the urban environment.

This physical separation was further reinforced by the land uses on the sites alongside Paddington Station. During the 1960s and 1970s most of the land around Paddington Canal was owned by public sector organisations such as British Waterways, the National Health Service and the National Freight Corporation. There was little incentive for these organisations to actively develop the land and as de-industrialisation took hold throughout the 1970s and 1980s, less intensive land uses emerged including car parking and industrial storage. By the mid 1970s the area's wholesale redevelopment seemed a distant prospect. In the words of one WCC Planner, 'Paddington always had the problem of being, you know, on the edge . . . neither one thing nor the other' and was 'right up there as one of the infamous blighted sites of London' (Sadek, 2002: 233).

It was in this context that plans for the area's widespread redevelopment emerged. There have been two principal development phases to the regeneration. The first took place during the property boom of the late 1980s when new development proposals emerged including the redevelopment of Paddington train station and the expansion of a major local hospital (St Mary's) and the commercially oriented Metropole Hotel. This initial period of development interest was subdued in the early 1990s by a national economic recession, but a second, more substantial phase of development took place from the mid 1990s onwards. This renewed activity was fostered by a different set of property developers, encouraged by the announcement and eventual completion of the Heathrow Express rail link in 1998. Since then the Paddington area has been physically transformed with massive changes in its economic structure and use. By the mid 2000s, as figure 7.2 shows, approximately a third of the planned development had been completed on two key sites (Paddington Basin and Paddington Central) including more than 7 hectares of office development, over 900 new homes and 1.5 hectares of retail/leisure use. Additional achievements include the creation of 1 km of new towpath, the construction of five new pedestrian bridges across the canal, the attraction of thirty resident businesses and employment opportunities for over 7,000 workers.

The remainder of the chapter now discusses the rationalities, politics, and practices embedded in the area's re-development. It divides the discussion into three inter-related parts. The first examines the rationalities underpinning the development. The second assesses local development partnerships and governance processes, and the third explores the relationships between the development and local communities.

Development rationalities and the emergence of Paddington as a development space

Much of the early impetus for development came from a combination of the growing importance of urban policy in the late 1970s and the realisation that Paddington represented a significant development opportunity. With plans to infill the canal and extend St Mary's hospital shelved in the mid 1970s, other possibilities came to the fore. In 1976 Paddington station was identified in the Greater London Plan as a preferred office location. At this point such plans were strongly opposed by the local authority, WCC, who argued that Paddington was

7.2
Redevelopment
outcomes in
Paddington.
Source: Mike Raco, 2008

outside of London's central commercial area, and its largely residential status should be protected.

During the 1980s attitudes towards the site began to change. Building on a major community consultation exercise undertaken by WCC, British Waterways looked to develop a waterside regeneration project involving low-density private sector housing and recreational uses of the canal. Before such a scheme could proceed, the privatisation of public corporations in the late 1980s introduced a different set of drivers. Land was increasingly seen as an asset that could and should be sold for development both to facilitate new forms of regeneration and to generate resources for increasingly stretched public organisations. Local landowners, such as British Waterways, came under direct pressure from the Treasury to supplement their incomes through the sale of land at top market value. The abolition of the National Freight Corporation in 1981, a major local landowner, had also opened up new development opportunities as it brought potential investment sites onto the property market.

At the same time, the national government's focus on the London Docklands and the perceived lack of significant development opportunities in central London were having a significant impact on development thinking. Development pressures continued to strengthen. For WCC the absorption of rising development pressure was becoming increasingly difficult. Over 75 per cent of the land within the local authority's boundary is (and has been) protected by heritage conservation regulations. In contrast to the City of London, height restrictions have been rigorously enforced, particularly in the central and southern parts of the borough where strong residents' groups have vociferously opposed development proposals on heritage and conservation grounds (see below). The identification of suitable development sites in the 1980s therefore took on an added priority.

It was in this context that WCC played a key role in identifying Paddington as a potential 'opportunity space'. As one experienced WCC planner noted in interview, the original rationality for development

> envisaged Paddington as being a growth area for commercial office space. The constraints of the West End and their projections for the amount of space that you required within Westminster led WCC to identify Paddington as an area for larger scale developments that couldn't be accommodated in the core West End . . . WCC saw Paddington as being an area where larger office buildings could be built to accommodate the more private sector occupier base that they wanted to encourage to stay in Westminster but couldn't otherwise accommodate them in a modern large-scale office development.

Or, as the current leader of WCC noted in interview,

> planning policies got tighter, as a result commercial landowners were feeling the pinch . . . so the two came neatly together, there was this

underdeveloped derelict land out at Paddington, it was blighting the area, it was a poor area anyway, and there was this demand for commercial space.

This re-definition of land around Paddington Central as an office expansion zone allowed new development to take place and enabled the formation of a development network to emerge in which, in the words of one developer (Development Securities),

both WCC and we as developers saw Paddington as being, if you like, the safety valve for the West End, [that could] relieve the development pressures in the West End which are terribly constrained by a whole host of things.

The metaphor of the safety valve was used in relation to two particular types of pressure on WCC and local developers. First, WCC was coming under significant criticism from the private sector for its relatively tight planning regulations from developers keen to expand in Central London. During the 1970s and early 1980s the area around Victoria Station further south had been prioritised for new office developments but it was clear that there was a lack of capacity for growing demand. With some developers explicitly threatening to relocate, a re-evaluation of policies became a matter of priority. One interviewee recalled that,

basically, we and others [developers] were saying in the 1980s you must let us knock down swathes of the West End in order to provide modern buildings otherwise one contract is going to go to Frankfurt or Amsterdam or New York or whatever, and if London is going to survive in the modern world it has got to provide accommodation.

Property developers and businesses were arguing that London and Westminster's long-term competitiveness was being directly threatened by the limitations on building.

Second, the focus on Paddington enabled major development to proceed in ways that would not inflame political sensitivities amongst its core Conservative party voters. The development of a 'peripheral' and underused site enabled local planners and policy-makers to effectively bypass opposition from community groups. It was argued that there was little 'ownership' of the site amongst local communities and little direct opposition to the principle of development. As a chief planner noted in interview, 'because the Westway had wiped out any sense of inherent community in Paddington, they were physically gone, all the communities that had existed, those that remained were on the edge and didn't see this as part of their territory'.

Local politicians expressed similar sentiments. A councillor, for instance, noted that 'because the site has been locked in by the station and the motorway it has never been seen as part of the community . . . it was always a sort of a no-go area'. Not that the communities surrounding the development area were themselves completely disinterested in what was being proposed. In particular, residents living in Conservative-voting wards immediately to the south of Paddington Canal were quick to protest about the noise and the congestion produced by the regeneration. In general, off-site impacts dominated local concerns to a greater extent than what was being proposed on the development site itself.

For WCC it was nevertheless felt that there would be political dividends in developing a site on the cusp between Labour-voting areas to the north and Conservative-voting wards to the south. Local community representatives recalled, in interview, that there was local political support in the early days of the development. For example, one commented in interview that,

> it had become a dislocated part of London with the canal and the railway and the Westway carving through the area and there was an opportunity to knit it together again in some way, albeit with a scale that was clearly different from the scale of things around it.

This process of 'knitting together' was presented as an important rationale for re-development. The dominant message was one of reconnecting the area in a physical sense through improved 'permeability', thus helping to overcome the legacy left by the multiple layers of infrastructure history. This local politics of legitimation was particularly important at an early stage as the ripple effects of negative publicity from the Docklands emerged through the 1980s. The leader of WCC, for example, argued that 'everyone was conscious of the need not to create another London Docklands where it was sort of hermetically sealed off from the immediate adjacent communities and neighbourhoods, that it should be more permeable'.

In summary, the emergence of Paddington as a development opportunity owes less to major central government initiatives or the agendas of London-wide delivery agencies than it does to a coming together of sub-metropolitan development priorities. It fulfilled a number of local political and economic criteria and enabled new forms of less controversial development to take place. Much of the impetus has come from the local authority, WCC, working in and through specific sets of local social, economic and political relations. The development needs to be understood as being as much about the circumstances of Westminster as it is about the broader property and development markets and spatial development priorities of London. It is also a reflection of particular geographical and historical imaginations over the site and the relationships between re-development, local politics and the stated objective to create new and better places within Westminster.

Coordination across the development and partnership working

The actual development of Paddington Central was, in practice, much more diffi-cult than the 'opportunity' discourses described above would suggest and had, what one developer described as a 'chequered history'. There was nothing inevi-table about the development of the site and this section discusses the develop-ment process and the ways in which relationships between the planning authority and developers have evolved.

In 1988 WCC designated the area around the Canal Basin as the Paddington Special Policy Area (PSPA). The purpose of the PSPA was to 'secure the development of the PSPA in a balanced manner, which establishes an identity for the area as a place of interest with its own character where people can live and work' (paragraph 4.3, cited in WCC, 2002: 23). The PSPA represented a crit-ical step in realising future development. It gave investors confidence that WCC had a 'pro-investment' perspective towards the area's development, and the anticipation that the planning process would be relatively 'fast-tracked'. As one interviewee noted, the PSPA

> tells the developer that he [sic.] has got a very good chance of getting planning permission and planning is such a huge risk in London, you have all the other criteria to deal with – the consultation, impact, stra-tegic reviews, local authority housing, social housing, road closures etc. When you have a Special Policy Area to develop you find a condu-cive, encouraging environment offered to you by the local authority as opposed to the relatively confrontational approach you get when you are trying to develop in a traditional location.

The PSPA designation also indicated that the area was being treated as an inte-grated object of development, what one developer referred to as a 'blank slate' approach that gave them

> the opportunity to contribute to a whole area of redevelopment . . . and that gives you control of the masterplan, it helps you improve the environment, the security and enhance the destination for people you are trying to encourage to occupy your building.

In line with development thinking and practice elsewhere there were seen to be development advantages in treating the development zone as a blank canvas, something to be shaped and worked on (see English Heritage, 2004). In drafting the PSPA, WCC made the key decision not to create an overall master plan but instead to establish a framework based on a set of underlying principles. Site-specific development briefs would, in turn, supplement this. It was a decision that reflected the fragmentation of land ownership in the PSPA and the low possibility that sites would come forward at the same time. It was further argued by a planning officer at WCC that 'the reality is that a master plan would have become very quickly out of date'. It was thus a decision that reflected WCC's perceived role as being one of responding to, and if possible influencing, prevailing development pressures, rather than adopting a more active role in establishing detailed planning briefs. Inevitably it would have an important bearing on what would be achieved within the development area.

Key WCC priorities included delivering a more balanced mixed-use scheme rather than the office-dominated proposal that many developers would have otherwise preferred. Other objectives included improving accessibility throughout the site thereby improving the physical connections between north and south Paddington. The PSPA also represented an innovative attempt to coordinate the extraction of financial resources from the development process. From the perspective of one officer from the Government Office for London,

> one interesting dimension to us was the relatively open Section 106 [developer contributions] negotiations that WCC held. In our experience it was relatively unusual to get representatives of all development organisations round the table and say we want this out of section 106, you can decide between yourselves who's going to give us what.

Through pooling contributions, larger scale priority projects could be tackled such as traffic, pedestrian and public transport improvements. The approach had the added advantage that it set a standardised rate of contribution, which provided prospective developers with a clearer estimation of development costs. The PSPA also made mention of a proposed Social and Community Fund through which development contributions would be collected and redistributed to surrounding communities.

One additional local factor that helped facilitate development activity was continuity in key personnel within WCC. Authors such as Groth and Corijn (2005) have highlighted the ways in which 'indeterminate spaces' exist in relation to urban policy-making in and through which actors are able to develop and prioritise agendas (see also Larner and Craig, 2005). In Paddington, the same leading figures have been involved in negotiations during both the first and second development phases and developers noted in interview that this has been an essential component of its wider attractiveness. As one indicated, 'without them none of this would have ever happened I don't think'. Another indicated that WCC was 'much more used to dealing with conservation . . . that's their sort of mindset . . . someone like [Planner named] they've given him responsibility and he thought outside of that framework'. The current leader of WCC reiterated such credits

> We've had extremely good continuity at our end . . . [Planners x and y named] have been doing this really since the beginning, so that's helpful to the development industry because they get consistency and

they also get to build relationships which will have helped them straighten their own thinking out, because they know they can go to X and say, we're thinking of doing this, and they'll get a very honest and reliable reply as to how the council would be likely to view that.

For this key individual in WCC, the objective was less about vision and more about getting 'other people to realise its [Paddington's] advantages, to turn those issues and advantages into some kind of policy context, so that others who have the money, and who have the means, can do something'. Thus rather than creating a new future vision, the dominant approach was driven by protecting and building on what was already there, such as the canal, safeguarding St Mary's as the last hospital in the City of Westminster, and protecting a Grade I listed railway station.

WCC also had other influences over the development of the site. Early plans from the developer Trafalgar House for a commercially dominated develop-ment were rejected and WCC turned to a smaller developer Chelsfield to, in the words of a WCC Planner, 'unlock some of the things that Trafalgar House had failed to do'. Their proposal for the site gained support from WCC as it involved reducing the office element, and increasing the amount of land devoted to resi-dential apartments and ground floor retail. Chelsfield's approach also differed in that they were willing to invest upfront in site infrastructure, were more aware of the need to negotiate with individual leaseholders, and engaged in both pre-lets and the sale of individual plots to attract confidence and to obtain capital returns. The shake-up of development interests was not limited to Paddington Basin, with the owners of the PSPA's other major commercial property development scheme selling out to London-based Development Securities in 2000. Outstanding matters attached to the outline approval were quickly negotiated including an affordable housing contribution that allowed Development Securities to begin a mixed-use scheme that incorporated speculative office buildings, residential apartments, and a limited leisure and retail element (see figure 7.3).

Underpinning this renewed development interest was the introduction of major London-wide transport infrastructure projects. In the late 1980s it was announced that Paddington Station was to become the London terminus of the new Heathrow Airport Express Rail Link. The designation was not without protest. Responding to local concerns, WCC was adamant that the decision was made without serious consideration of the transport implications or need for substantial investment. The Link was strongly advocated by the British Airports Authority (BAA) who was required to expand public transport connections as part of the planning approval process for the building of Terminal 5. As a result WCC brought BAA into PSPA discussions, with BAA becoming a major part-funder of exten-sions to a road bridge crossing the development site. As a BAA representative noted in interview, before the Link

Paddington was seen as a bit of a backwater because it wasn't as close in as some of the other London termini so we were quite keen . . . to

7.3
**Residential apartments
in Paddington.**
Source: Mike Raco, 2008

use the railway as a big catalyst . . . Paddington demonstrates that if you have good links to a major airport then it is a good economic regenerator . . . the development was good for London.

Paddington being earmarked as a major transport node on the London Cross-rail scheme has stimulated further development interest.

The need for coordination was integral in the formation of the Paddington Regeneration Partnership in 1998, later renamed the Paddington Waterside Partnership, and to the introduction of a more comprehensive regeneration approach, including the creation of an organisation known as Paddington First to act as a local job brokerage.[1] Thus from its inception the Partnership provided a forum within which developers and landowners could negotiate a set of bottom line principles, not just in terms of land within the PSPA, but in terms of how development would relate to surrounding communities.

However, changing commercial perceptions of the area has not been a straightforward process and even with Paddington's flagship status, development

practices and perceptions in London have proved to be relatively fickle and difficult to predict. There has been what one developer termed 'significant viability
issues' not least because of the high cost of land in and around Paddington. The
implication for profit-seeking developers was the need for high-value end uses,
including expensive office developments and residential apartments. Other developers accused WCC of 'turning a blind eye' to quality issues in the development
and admitted that for them 'it is frankly what a developer can get away with – the
development is soulless'. Whilst WCC has been minded to limit the height of
buildings, critics have argued that this has also restricted the emergence of iconic,
area-defining buildings that might have otherwise attracted visitors or investors.
The corporate-orientated or 'soulless' character of the new spaces was seen by
many respondents as a barrier to the longer term commercial sustainability of the
site. In one developer's terms 'at the moment there is a series of private office
buildings supporting an office population but it needs to re-orientate the public
spaces for people who want to dwell there'.

 The low rate of occupation of 'investment' apartments and the slow
uptake of designated retail establishments has not helped. Breaking out of the
cycle of low-value investments is going to be difficult as the area is already
acquiring a reputation for being an 'edge' location within Central London – the
very aspect of the site that was originally presented by WCC and others as its
main advantage. Development constraints within the PSPA are also continuing.
There have been significant delays to some of the proposals on public sector
land. The St Mary's hospital site and the barrier of the Westway motorway are
limiting the opportunities for further re-development. Phase II redevelopment
plans for Paddington railway station, including plans to open the station towards
the canal and to enhance area connectivity, have faced significant protest from
English Heritage. The longer term commercial sustainability and viability of the
site is increasingly being questioned.

 In summary on-site development activity at Paddington received a
major impetus from Westminster's designation of the PSPA, and its creation of
a development framework that stressed a mixed-use scheme, improved area
permeability and managed transport impacts. Not only did the PSPA send a
positive signal to developers, but it also demonstrated WCC's commitment to
the site and its willingness to provide a strategic framework within which
prevailing concerns could be addressed. Yet whilst it stimulated developer
activity, it did not in itself lead to the commencement of development. Wider
property-market cycles and strategic London-wide decisions about future transport investment were influential in determining the speed of construction. As
development has proceeded more critical perspectives have concluded that
WCC's approach was more about coordinating and directing prevailing development pressure than constructing a detailed area-based future vision. From one
perspective it would simply take more residential development and more people
living in the area to enliven the emerging urban space. An alternative perspective is more critical, suggesting that the Paddington re-development has not

sufficiently integrated with surrounding communities and it is to this issue that the chapter now turns.

Community engagement and benefit

The relationships between residential communities and the development process in Paddington reveal much about the rationalities, priorities and practices of urban development in London and elsewhere. There have been keenly contested arguments over the definition and identification of 'communities', how they should be represented in decision-making structures, the extent to which existing representatives reflect broader concerns, and the benefits and negative impacts that developments have had for different groups (see Cochrane, 2007). However, as this section will demonstrate, the form and character of community politics in Paddington reflects and reproduces a specific set of local authority dominated politics enmeshed within a wider London context.

First, as noted above, the perceived *lack* of community ownership of brownfield land around Paddington Canal was seen to be a major advantage by developers and planners. Rather than being seen as an essential well-spring of local knowledge and political legitimacy, community engagement was seen as an obstacle and a barrier to investment, reflecting Ball *et al.'s* (2003) findings that many developers possess a 'sense of frustration at the . . . potentially unrealistic expectations of local authorities and community groups'. In Paddington, interviewees saw the absence of development 'expectations', barring the need to mitigate transport effects, as a key reason for the site's growing popularity with the investment community. WCC and developer respondents talked openly about the advantages of 'de-politicised' urban development in an area where 'the community doesn't yet exist'. As a chief planner noted in interview,

> in the local context we've never actually had to argue our case . . . Paddington has never been to a public enquiry, our policies have never been challenged by anyone at the Urban Development Plan [level], we've never had an appeal on the major development site so . . . we've never been tested.

Areas such as Paddington present particular difficulties for development agencies for which bureaucratic-instrumental definitions of identifiable community groups lie at the heart of policy processes. WCC officers argued, in interview, that in terms of the planning process the area was dominated by 'terminally hard to reach communities' that are, according to the leader of WCC,

> reception areas for people newly arriving in the country or into London, so what you get is a turnover of people who will always start at the bottom, who will then improve a move out to be replaced by further people starting at the bottom.

The consequence, it was argued, was that community residents had little or no interest in local development processes – an attitude that has had a significant influence on local authority–community relations.

In practice, far from being 'dis-interested' in the development, a significant local community politics has emerged to challenge the development on a number of fronts. There have been heated discussions, for example, over the meaning of 'regeneration' and who should have responsibility for ensuring that the 'benefits' of development are spread beyond the immediate site. In our research there was a clear mismatch between the concerns expressed by residents in focus groups and surveys and those of policy-makers, planners and developers. For the former, the area's regeneration should primarily be concerned with the provision of suitable new job opportunities, crime prevention and protecting existing green spaces from housing development. Far from being dis-interested in the process of regeneration, alternative visions and imaginations were readily put forward. However, such views were of relatively little concern to the latter for whom the regeneration was primarily about meeting the needs of London property market investors and, as discussed earlier, borough-wide priorities. Moreover, in line with wider New Labour thinking, the emphasis has been on changing depressed local aspirations (WCC, 2005). It was argued new forms of active, responsibilised citizenship would emerge locally in and through which 'problem' communities and individuals would change their ways of thinking and acting.

The absence of community-orientated infrastructure within the PSPA has proved a notable limitation of the development thus far. WCC officers openly celebrated smaller scale achievements and argued that some financial investment might follow and that this would be a positive outcome in its own right. Yet there was also the feeling that WCC lacked direction in terms of how to use the funds that would be raised and as one critical WCC Labour councillor commented,

> [the] Social and Community Fund was basically . . . a cop out, it saved the council having to do all the planning before hand . . . we'll get £10 million off the developers and we'll spend it over the next 10 years but we haven't really got any ideas for what we're going to spend it on yet, but we'll ask people what they want to spent it on and we'll let council departments bid for this money.

The lack of positive direction on the part of WCC in part reflects internal political protests about who should benefit from urban re-development projects. Thus, as one WCC planning officer acknowledged in interview,

> There's still a debate between the two groups of residents and when I go to a Paddington Steering Group meeting . . . this lot are asking well why are we spending money up there . . . we've managed to [demonstrate] that there's been quite substantial levels of investment and

> involvement and it hasn't all been through Section 106. I mean . . .
> Chelsfield have spent a lot of time and energy in contributing to the
> Education Action zone voluntarily.

However, rather than engaging with the community in an attempt to identify and address local needs, what followed was more instrumental on the part of developers as they attempted to gain community support through off-site measures. As one noted,

> the first thing we did was to get the community on our side because if they are against us from the very beginning, as they generally are, they're a bit cynical and say 'what's in it for us?' . . . that's why the Paddington Trust was set up to give money to good causes . . . you got brownie points for that. So we get to understand how the community works and what, what is demanded of us.

In doing so the Paddington Regeneration Partnership has constructively engaged in many urban regeneration initiatives, including in some cases formalising ideas that were contained in the PSPA, such as the Social and Community Fund and Paddington First. Other schemes include investing in local education, realising a Business Improvement District on adjoining Praed Street and encouraging both business leaders and new employees working in Paddington to embrace the wider area.

In summary, responses to local community inclusion have, therefore, been relatively bureaucratic and instrumental in a process-orientated sense. Bottom-up forms of inclusion are, it is argued, relatively difficult, not least because of the transient nature of the deprived North Paddington community. The commercially oriented nature of the regeneration, and WCC's active role in directing development pressure, ensured that less initial consideration was given to how the needs of deprived community residents might be best met, or how the local community could be given new ownership of the Paddington Canal redevelopment area. Instead discussion focused on delivering off-site benefits, including a Social and Community Fund, enhanced area permeability and local employment linkages. Whilst there has clearly been an attempt to move away from the politics of conflict that characterised the London Docklands regeneration in the 1980s, the practices of engagement have still been fraught with difficulties and a mismatch between the commercial needs of investors and in-coming firms and a broader focus on place-making and the creation of a 'new', inclusive Paddington.

Conclusions

The redevelopment of Paddington provides a London-based example of an area-wide, local-authority-driven redevelopment scheme that has successfully moved from proposal to construction. As the discussion has shown there were significant limitations in terms of what WCC could achieve, in large part because of London's property cycles and the preferred geographies of property investors. However, WCC moved beyond a more traditional, regulatory approach to planning and adopted a more proactive role by designating Paddington as a key development space and then creating a framework that could address prevailing concerns and area-based needs. The development's outcomes reflect a combination of changing investment markets and imaginations and also, crucially, the ways in which the development suited WCC's own political priorities as it promoted regeneration in a neighbourhood between Conservative and Labour returning councillor wards.

The Paddington example, therefore, highlights the significant role that sub-metropolitan politics plays in shaping the form and character of flagship projects, even in a fast-growing and increasingly globalised city such as London. We have demonstrated that local government, and borough-level politics, continue to play a key role in such developments. With the emergence of the London mayor, the broader acceptance of the global thesis by policy-makers and many academics, and the wider reforms to the planning and local government system, it is tempting to focus attention elsewhere. In this chapter we have argued that one of the ironies of these wider shifts in local governance is that the need for a coordinating, representative institution such as a local authority has, in many ways, become greater than ever. WCC has acted as the institutional anchor around which development strategies and plans for Paddington have been developed. It has been the focus for community politics and the wider legitimation of the development. For developers, local authority support has been pivotal in underpinning their investment decisions and creating market confidence. The introduction of a Special Planning Area, for example, was a critical (and innovative) step in directing the progress of the regeneration.

In addition, the case study has also demonstrated that local-authority-led flagship projects do not necessarily prioritise more inclusive, community-focused agendas than those pursued by quangos and other development agencies. Whilst WCC involvement has had some progressive impacts for local communities in and around Paddington, the overall programmes have not sought to tackle wider problems such as levels of affordable housing for local people and crime and disorder. Indeed, the Government Office for London have recently criticised the Paddington development for its lack of affordable housing provision and WCC's failure to obtain significant social benefits through developer contributions. To date only 165 affordable housing units, out of a total of 919 apartments (i.e. 14.6 per cent), have been delivered through commercial projects (Edwards, 2002). The extent to which the inclusion of democratically elected local authorities actually leads to more inclusive forms of governance and regeneration has, therefore, to be questioned. If, as the chapter has shown, the contours of regeneration policy are shaped by local power relations and politics then there is significant scope for relatively powerful and well-represented communities and development interests to dominate agendas in new but legitimate ways.

And finally, the chapter's findings have implications for the broader politics of flagship urban regeneration in a context where central government, development agencies and city authorities are increasingly thinking in terms of polycentric 'city-regions' (see Allen and Cochrane, 2007; Morgan, 2007). The role of local authorities within these new development spaces is potentially significant, even though the discourse of the city-region implies a broader 'strategic' and cross-boundary approach to the governance of cities that ostensibly downplays the role of local authorities. We have shown in this chapter that site-specific knowledge is critical to the effective planning of flagship development projects and that local authorities can be well placed to carry out the key role of facilitating development and defining the contours of political engagement and debate.

Acknowledgements

The research carried out for this chapter was funded by the Engineering and Physical Sciences Research Council's Sustainable Urban Brownfields: Integrated Management (SUBR:IM) Research Consortium (Grant Number: GR/S148809/01). The views expressed here are those of the authors alone and do not necessarily reflect the views of the SUBR:IM Consortium as a whole. Thanks also to Rob Imrie and Loretta Lees for their comments on an earlier draft.

Note

1   Paddington First was established to help connect residents to emerging job opportunities in construction, the service industries and the commercial sector. By 2005 approximately 4,000 people had been placed into employment. The jobs brokerage has received positive support from government agencies, including the London Development Agency, and as a model has been adopted in other areas of London.

Chapter 8

The 2012 Olympic Games and the reshaping of East London

Gavin Poynter

Introduction

After twenty-five years of 'regeneration', East London has entered the twenty-first century at the centre of the largest urban renewal scheme in Europe – the Thames Gateway, a government designated regeneration area that stretches from the City of London to the mouth of the Thames Estuary. In this latest and most expansive phase, the area has become a laboratory, a site of social experiments in community development that incorporate a mix of wealth and poverty, high and low rise and social inclusion and exclusion. It was in this context that London's bid for the 2012 Olympic and Paralympic Games was conceived and Stratford, in the borough of Newham, identified as the main location for the Olympic Park (see figure 8.1). The International Olympic Committee's (IOC) support for London arose from the city's focus on regeneration in an area of cultural diversity and social deprivation that incorporated five designated 'Olympic boroughs' – Greenwich, Hackney, Newham, Tower Hamlets and Waltham Forest. The IOC's concern with 'legacy' – a concern arising in large part from the necessity to legitimise the huge expenditure involved in hosting the Games – was addressed directly by the London bid. The 2012 Games, according to the bid's authors, will provide a major catalyst that accelerates an existing and ambitious plan for urban renewal.

This chapter explains why the Olympic Games have become an important catalyst for programmes of urban regeneration and economic development over recent decades. It then considers three main themes. First, it places the 2012 project in the context of East London's renewal since 1980. Second, it outlines the governance structures designed to deliver the Games and their legacy in East London. It is argued that the governance approach to urban regeneration in East London has significantly changed since the first

8.1
The location of the 2012
Olympic Games.
Source: By permission
of Karina Berzins,
London East Research
Institute

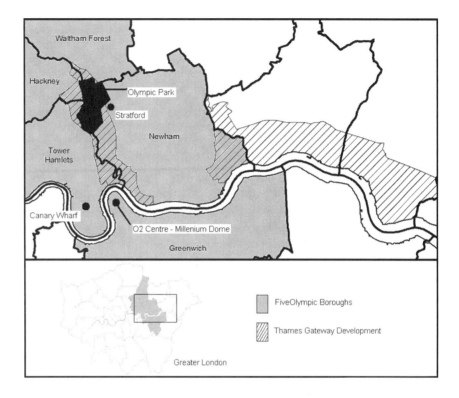

8.1
The location of the 2012
Olympic Games.
Source: By permission
of Karina Berzins,
London East Research
Institute

phase of renewal focused upon Docklands in the 1980s. Third, the catalytic role of the Games is explored, in particular focusing upon how such a role may be reconciled with considerations of the sustainability of the project and public engagement with it. Finally, the chapter concludes with an evaluation of the Games' impact upon social development in East London and the process of urban regeneration in the city.

Mega-events, Olympic cities and urban regeneration

The mega-event is by its nature large scale, organised via a social elite in the host nation or city and projects secular values and principles through the creation of an official version of the city or nation's history and contemporary identity. Performance mega-events are typified in the twentieth century by the Olympics and represent a populist cultural expression of the achievements of the host city or nation (Roche, 2000: 8–9). The organisers attempt to project to the world an image of the city or nation that seeks to affirm or catalyse its economic, cultural and social development or renewal.

The potential provided by festivals, exhibitions and mega-events to catalyse programmes of urban regeneration arose in the USA in the 1970s. In America, federal aid for cities significantly diminished and local governments had to seek new sources of finance for their development plans (Castells, 1980: 200–14). City planners had a series of complex problems to tackle. First, the decline of urban industrial complexes as a focus for local employment and city identities was accelerated by recession in manufacturing and production-based industries. Second, reductions in federal aid meant that city governments had to seek new ways of raising funds beyond their traditional reliance on hard-pressed capital budgets and established forms of local taxation (Chalkley and Essex, 1999). Finally, urban centres in cities like Chicago, Los Angeles and Atlanta had large areas of social deprivation and decay that required urgent action if they were to avoid repeated experiences of race riots and social unrest (Sanders, 1992).

The more entrepreneurial US cities, often located in regions most affected by de-industrialisation and economic restructuring, adopted a policy of consumption-based economic development which focused on the post-industrial service-based industries (Andranovich et al., 2001: 114). Cities such as New York and San Francisco built arts and entertainment complexes, convention centres, museums and shopping malls as well as providing retail, professional and government office spaces (Zukin, 1991). Others, such as Miami and Orlando, created what Hannigan (1998) has referred to as fragments of an urban landscape in which Fantasy Cities emerged that were 'theme-centred, aggressively branded, in constant operation, modular in design, separate from existing neighbourhoods, and postmodern' (Andranovich et al., 2001: 115).

The construction of the 'Fantasy City' focuses on visitor attractions, prestigious events and themed festivals. Its construction is primarily designed to conform to the images and expectations of the visitor rather than the practical needs of those living in it. Financing their construction often generated local political problems, in part because of the complex public/private financial arrangements upon which their development depended. The creation of the Fantasy City often rested upon the dilution of the role of local government in planning processes and the removal of public scrutiny over the financing arrangements required to construct them. In this way, consumption-based urban regeneration programmes have often been accompanied by a restructuring of local politics in order to accommodate the role of special purpose quasi-governmental agencies and the public-private partnerships that are required to create the financial framework for their implementation (Sanders, 1992).

By the mid 1980s, in the wake of the economic crises that signalled the end of the post-war boom, hosting the Olympics seemingly provided a compelling prize for the entrepreneurial city that sought a little 'fantasy' in the not too distant future. Los Angeles (1984) captured this trend by hosting Games that were privately funded with high revenues realised from selling promotion and broadcast rights to television networks and other commercial sponsors (Preuss, 2004: 16). The surplus achieved by Los Angeles revealed the potential offered by using a mega-event and a globalised media to brand a city on an international scale.

In the post-cold-war twenty-first century, this projection of a city or host nation's identity has become a more complex affair. As the old certainties of 'empires' and 'isms' have disappeared, performance events have been utilised by hosts in part to offset domestic disintegrative and fragmentary social tendencies that have accompanied the transition of city and national economies toward more flexible, service-oriented activities operating in a global market economy (Roche, 2000: 220–1) or, as with the case of the recent Beijing Olympics, to contain the social disruption arising from rapid urbanisation and economic expansion (Perry and Selden, 2000; Nolan, 2004). Recent host cities have also sought to use mega-events to re-present themselves in various ways to the wider world through 'place marketing' – revealing, for example, their capacities for innovation and the clustering of high value-added service activities and enhancing their competitive advantage over other cities as a result (Buck *et al.*, 2002: 2–5; see also Rutheiser, 1996).

Each host city and nation has utilised the event to achieve specific local and national goals. The 1992 Barcelona Olympic Games represented an opportunity to redevelop the city using a mix of public and private sector funding that balanced commercial and social aims. The aggressive commercialism of Los Angeles and the tourist orientation of the Fantasy City model were modified and the Barcelona approach emerged as an alternative to obtaining a post-Games regeneration legacy (LERI, 2007). Since 1992, 'Legacy' has assumed a considerable significance to the IOC – as its evaluation process has incorporated environmental and other social dimensions – and is now firmly focused upon non-sport-related outcomes as a source of legitimation for hosting the Games. The Barcelona-inspired modification of the 'commercial' approach to hosting the Games was replicated by London – with the 2012 bid creating a combination of public and private funding and partnerships to deliver the event and an ambitious social, cultural and economic legacy.

Transforming East London

The 2012 Games are focused upon East London and are designed to achieve a programme of urban regeneration, especially in Stratford and the borough of Newham. Newham, like its neighbours Hackney and Tower Hamlets, has significant areas of social deprivation and brownfield sites that were once the scene of traditional manufacturing industries, docks and railroad yards. The area is at the centre of the Thames Gateway development and is near to Canary Wharf. Canary Wharf represented an ambitious 1980s scheme set up to expand the city's financial centre eastwards, emulating the success of the Manhattan development in New York, undertaken in the 1960s (Poynter, 1989). The scheme, overseen by the London Docklands Development Corporation (LDDC), circumvented local authorities and established planning frameworks to afford developers opportunities to invest in extensive high-rise office development and upmarket housing. Peter Hall has argued that the Local Government, Planning and Land Act of 1980 that provided the legal basis for urban development corporations, such as the LDDC, represented:

> The most extraordinary set of powers ever given to a set of quangos, and by the same token the most extraordinary incursion into local authority powers ever authorised by a British government.
>
> (Hall, 1999: 912–13)

This 'market-driven' pro-business initiative, designed to provide 'leverage' through which initial public investment gave the impetus for subsequent large-scale investment from the private sector, eventually succeeded in attracting major companies to relocate to Canary Wharf but not until several financial crises were overcome. While Canary Wharf was undergoing development in the 1990s, the Conservative government responded to pressures, mainly from the business community, to establish a London-wide or metropolitan authority. The Conservatives set up a Government Office and a cabinet sub-committee for London in recognition of the need to establish a more planned and integrated approach to running the capital. On Labour's return to government in 1997, it took this approach much further by creating the Greater London Authority (GLA), establishing the elected office of Mayor of London and introducing a London Development Agency (LDA) (see chapter 4 in this volume). It was the mayor (Ken Livingstone), in conjunction with these new agencies, who provided strong political support for London's Olympic Bid.

The Thames Gateway scheme was initiated in 1990 by the South-East Regional Policy Guidance Plan and was championed by the then Secretary of State for the Environment, Michael Heseltine. The decision in 1991 to route the Channel Tunnel rail link through north Kent and into central London via Stratford provided an important catalyst for improvements in road and rail infrastructure and by 1995 the Thames Gateway Task Force drew up plans for 30,000 new homes and 50,000 new jobs to be established in the Thames Corridor by 2021 (Buck *et al.*, 2002: 84–5). Since 1997 successive Labour governments have provided vigorous support for the Thames Gateway through the Department of Communities and Local Government (DCLG, formerly the Office of the Deputy Prime Minister, ODPM) and a variety of partnership agencies, including the Mayor's Office, the Greater London Authority (GLA), the London Development Agency (LDA) and the local authorities located within the region. The ambitions for the development of the Thames Gateway have correspondingly risen with, for example, the proposal to develop a new bridge crossing the Thames and an expansion of plans for house building and the development of new townships along the Thames corridor. These plans were incorporated into the Labour government's 'Creating Sustainable Communities' (2003) in which the number of new houses to be built increased to 120,000, with many of these located in fourteen 'zones of change'.

The prospect of East London hosting the 2012 Games, and the imminent arrival of the high-speed domestic services offered by the Channel Tunnel rail link in 2009, prompted a government-inspired review of the Gateway Plan in 2006. The DCLG commissioned consultants Hornigold and Hills to review the

Thames Gateway 'vision'. The consultants' report was highly critical of the fragmented and unfocused leadership of the Gateway development, and its association with increased housing supply and little else. In response, a new strategic framework was developed for publication in November 2006. The framework shifted the emphasis of the Gateway away from housing and toward higher targets for employment creation, with a renewed focus on attracting inward private sector investment to facilitate the generation of 180,000 new jobs. The framework also recommended a change of name, with Thames Gateway being replaced by a 'greener' vision encapsulated in the title 'Thames Estuary Parklands'. Estimation of the potential for the successful implementation of this new 'vision' is a complex affair. The Olympics would not have come to East London if it had not been part of an existing and ambitious regional regeneration plan. Equally, the development of the Olympic Park and the Lower Lea Valley rests upon significant infrastructure investment in a relatively small area of the Gateway, creating the likelihood of a displacement effect with the Olympics sucking in investment that could otherwise have taken place elsewhere.

The impetus for a London bid to host the 2012 Games arose, in part, from the agencies that were created to address the inadequacies of the commercially driven model of regeneration that was typified by the Canary Wharf development. The regeneration plans for the Thames Gateway provided a compelling context for the bid. The bid's success has ironically created significant issues in relation to the viability of the wider regeneration project by concentrating investment on 2012, focusing attention on the financial or commercial viability of the Games and shifting the mode of governance further toward a state-centred model that greatly modifies the roles of regeneration professionals, especially those at local authority level. As a consequence, the Games may be the catalyst that pulls apart rather than facilitates the implementation of the integrated vision of the 2006 Thames Gateway Strategic Framework.

The state, governance and the 2012 Games

Here three dimensions of the state's role in utilising the 2012 Games to catalyse urban regeneration in East London are examined. First, the forms of institutional governance of the London 2012 and Thames Gateway projects are outlined. Second, the relationship between the state and agencies established to deliver the Games, and how these interface with existing political structures, is explored. Lastly, it is suggested that the current form of disconnected institutional governance faces significant challenges in attempting to reconcile an ambitious 'local' social regeneration agenda with the 'national' commercial imperative to deliver a mega-event such as the 2012 Games on time and on budget.

The concept of governance has arisen in policy circles from recognition of the potential of 'market failure' and an unwillingness of policy-makers to return to forms of direct state intervention that typically occurred in the 1960s and appeared to be a primary cause of UK economic weakness in the 1970s (Bacon and Eltis, 1976). Governance refers to ways of bringing institutions representing the state and market into forms of public/private partnership to deliver regeneration projects. The concepts of governance and partnership are fluid, contested terms in the academic literature (Jones and Evans, 2006). Partnerships between the state and private sector may vary according to the levels of cooperation and interdependence of the public and private institutions engaged in specific projects (Davies, 2001). The network of institutional relations – national, local, public, private – may assume the character of 'self-organisation' in implementing mutually agreed goals or remain largely 'state centred' with control firmly in the hands of national government. The self-organised form involves institutions engaging directly with the communities in which renewal takes place; while the state-centred approach tends to focus upon using quasi-state agencies to develop and deliver regeneration programmes, with community involvement confined to often tokenistic forms of consultation (Raco and Henderson, 2005: 2–3).

London 2012 and the wider Thames Gateway project bring together a complex network of agencies and institutions from across the public and private sector. Government, the Mayor of London and the British Olympics Association oversee the Games. The agency acting on their behalf is LOCOG (the London Organising Committee of the Olympic Games – whose composition reflects this coalition) and their delivery, via the Olympic Development Authority (ODA), is trusted to a private sector consortium. Despite the outward attributes of partnership, London 2012 and the wider Thames Gateway project reflect the 'state-centred' rather than 'self-organising' mode of urban regeneration. State-centred urban regeneration is controlled by state or quasi-state agencies and decision-making is dominated by executive officers with relatively little downward accountability to local institutions or the local community. Such characteristics tend to be reinforced when regeneration projects – particularly those catalysed by a mega-event – are required to be completed to tight time-scales and budgets.

London 2012 relies heavily upon state investment in infrastructure and a mix of public and private investment in meeting the operational costs of putting on the Games. The Olympic Delivery Authority Board consists of representatives from the public and private sectors and works with the London Development Agency (LDA), Transport for London (TfL), Thames Gateway and five designated Olympic local authorities. The ODA acts as the client to the 'delivery partner' responsible for the construction of the whole Olympic project, including all the sites. Following a tendering process, a consortia 'G3' (consisting of AMEC, Balfour Beatty and Jacobs) won the contract to be the delivery partner to the ODA. Parliamentary legislation (the London Olympic and Paralympic Games Act 2007) underpins the legal powers of the ODA to be the local planning authority for the Olympic Park though such legislation does not guarantee clear distinctions between the powers of the LDA and local authorities concerning, for example, planning and transport infrastructure development. Jack Lemley's resignation in October 2006 as chair of the ODA revealed the potential for tensions as he alleged that local politics and government interference got in the way of project delivery.

The oversight for the development of the Thames Gateway rested, until November 2006, with over forty regeneration agencies, central government ministries, the Mayor of London and the LDA as well as numerous local authorities. The complexity of this system of governance was widely criticised in the media as contributing to a lack of focus or vision (Sherwood, 2006: 12). In response, the Labour government, following the Hornigold and Hill report, launched, in November 2006, a new Strategic Framework that was to be overseen by an integrated grouping of agencies working with the private and public sectors; a reformed system of governance that relied upon improved coordination to deliver ambitious plans for the Thames Gateway. The ODA and its various sub-groupings, with its primary focus on 2012, sit alongside this reformed structure.

The modified Thames Gateway governance structure may improve coordination across the quasi-state agencies but little more; the necessities arising from preparations for 2012 place considerable pressures on the coalition of interests and stakeholders engaged in the Gateway development. As the costs of 2012 rise and project completion dates draw closer, so the competition for resources required for infrastructure development become an increasingly contested terrain; the national/local rhetoric of partnership, arising from the presentational demands of the 2012 bid, being sorely tested as national concerns dominate the local. The unfolding of the Olympics project and wider Thames Gateway scheme appear to support Jessop's contention that 'markets, states and governance all fail' (Jessop, 1999: 11); both developments, but particularly the former, involve complex networks of institutions operating within tightly determined temporal and spatial conditions. Under such conditions it is not possible to fulfil the expectations of all stakeholders, nor is it possible to effectively integrate or embed these institutions in the local community. The achievement of a 'successful' Games appears to rest upon the capacity to sustain the public rhetoric of partnership while the national increasingly dominates local interests. Inevitably, such an outcome defines the regeneration legacy. Weak local or civic voices may well result in a local legacy that primarily favours commercial viability rather than addressing the deep-seated and long-term social, housing, employment and education issues facing East London.

Such an outcome is likely to further consolidate London as a 'divided knowledge capital' (Hepworth et al., 2006: 39–43) with a significant proportion of the working population to the east providing an unskilled workforce primarily for the services sector, a service 'underclass', whose growth, ironically, will have been ensured by what Lovering has called a 'regional service class' whose professional existence rests with the responsibility for implementing nationally defined regeneration projects (Lovering, 2003). Such an 'underclass' expands in the entrepreneurial, global city because of the market orientation of public/private sector partnerships and the market related distribution of resources, including housing and employment opportunities. This expansion is reinforced by the accelerated development afforded by urban regeneration projects (Sassen, 1994).

The capacity to reduce rather than reinforce the tendencies toward a divided capital relies heavily upon the public response in the period leading up to the Games and the extent to which that response generates new forms of civic engagement that serve to moderate market pressures and the state-centred form of governance that currently prevails. Without this moderating impulse, the regeneration process afforded by hosting the Games is likely to focus upon the short-term pre-event and event phases rather than addressing the underlying socio-economic issues facing East London. This short termism undermines the sustainability of the regeneration project and the prospects for it to become firmly rooted, or embedded, in the local community. Despite the public rhetoric of partnership and commitment to a transformative socio-economic legacy, the current mode of centrally directed governance of 2012 may reinforce rather than reduce existing social divisions within the city. Ironically, the state-centred mode of governance of 2012 may lead to a similar pattern of urban renewal as to that achieved by the commercially driven Docklands development initiated in 1980s. The potential for such an outcome is explored in more detail below.

The London 2012 bid

The London bid was well crafted within the IOC guidelines. The process commenced in 1997 when the British Olympics Association (BOA) commissioned a feasibility study into a London bid to host the 2012 Games. The failures of the Birmingham and Manchester bids for the 1992, 1996 and 2000 Olympic and Paralympic Games convinced the BOA that only a London–based bid was likely to taken seriously by the IOC. In 2001, the feasibility study was submitted to the government and the Mayor of London, and it was the latter (Ken Livingstone) that insisted that the Games bid was focused upon East London, with the sporting benefits complemented by a firm commitment to enhancing an existing regeneration agenda. This shift in focus, the positive public support revealed in a 2001 ICM poll – with 81 per cent of UK respondents supporting a bid – the success of the Manchester Commonwealth Games in 2002, the positive global images of the Sydney Games (2000) and the desire to address the failure of projects such as the Millennium Dome and Picketts Lock (an aborted attempt to construct a new national athletics stadium in north London) were factors that prompted the government to finally support a bid following a cabinet meeting on 15 May 2003 (BOA, 2007).

The London bid was considered to be second or third favourite behind Paris and Madrid when, in July 2005, the final presentations were made to the IOC in Singapore. London's success was attributed to its focus on urban regeneration and the importance attached to the sporting legacy to be provided for generations of young people as Jack Straw (then Secretary of State, Foreign and Commonwealth Office) commented in Parliament on the day following the announcement in Singapore:

London's bid was built on a special Olympic vision. That vision of an Olympic games that would not only be a celebration of sport but a force for regeneration. The Games will transform one of the poorest and most deprived areas of London. They will create thousands of jobs and homes. They will offer new opportunities for business in the immediate area and throughout London . . . One of the things that made the bid successful is the way in which it reaches out to all young people in two important respects: it will encourage many more to get fit and to be involved in sport and, whatever their physical prowess, to offer their services as volunteers for the Olympic cause.

(Hansard, 2005)

Straw's statement provides a compelling interpretation of why London's bid was successful with its emphasis on non-sports-related regeneration outcomes and its focus on using the Games as a vehicle for the pursuit of non-elite participation in sport and exercise. These values struck a cord with the IOC in its post-commercialisation phase and were consistent with the prevailing values of the UK government's health policies and its appropriation of sport as a vehicle for the articulation of 'new' Labour's social policies, including its commitment to social inclusion. The government's attachment to the Olympic event as a vehicle for expressing and legitimating its own political and social policies presents a significant challenge to those implementing the regeneration agenda in east London. The achievement of 'a successful Games' has become closely associated with the effective construction, preparation and holding of the event and the attainment of a transformative legacy that has a sustained impact upon east London and its communities.

Sustainability and legacy

Sustainable social regeneration schemes involve, for example, the improvement of public services and infrastructure, the enhancement of public spaces, the reduction of social disadvantage and changes in the public perception or image of an area (ODPM, 2006c; Colomb, 2007). The proposed legacy of London 2012 strongly reflects these aspirations. The early phases of 2012 development, however, provide some evidence of the difficulties in achieving such aspirations as cost pressures have increased and social legacy plans modified.

Within the first year of 2012 preparations, concerns over costs emerged. The infrastructure developments planned for East London have tight time limits for completion and include, for example, new road and rail links, the construction of forty bridges and the placing of overhead power lines underground. The costs of providing the main sports facilities – the Olympic stadium and aquatics centre – and the media centre were initially budgeted at £690 million, a relatively modest sum (IOC, 2006; Arup, 2002). In tacit acknowledgement of this, LOCOG sought to 'value engineer' the Olympic site, bringing the aquatics and media centres into closer proximity to the new Stratford City development.

8.2
**The emerging Olympics
stadium site.
Source: By permission
of London East
Research Institute**

Despite this exercise, by early 2007 it became clear that the initial £2.4 billion operational budget had to be revised upwards to around £3.3 billion. Equally, the LDA ran into difficulties in relation to the purchasing of the land for the Olympic Park, with compulsory purchase orders on local businesses attracting adverse publicity. The reconfiguration of the Olympic site has assisted the LDA to reduce the number of compulsory purchase orders and thereby modify the disruption to local businesses. In completing the purchases in summer 2007 which enabled the LDA to secure access to the whole Olympic site, LOCOG and Ken Livingstone had to acknowledge that cost overruns would be met by the sale of parts of the Olympic Park land to developers on the completion of the Games in 2012 rather than allowing it to remain as part of the open and green space that had been part of the original design (DCMS, 2007).

The problem of sustainability is not confined to the design of open spaces; it is also illustrated in relation to housing. The Olympics regeneration programme increases the housing stock by 9,000 units – 4,500 affordable houses and 4,500 others to be sold on the open market. For the three London boroughs in closest proximity to the Olympic village – Tower Hamlets, Hackney and Newham – the affordable housing provided by the Olympics will represent 6.6 per cent of all local authority stock. In turn, the Thames Gateway development as a whole will facilitate the construction of a total of 33,000 new houses in the three boroughs in the period 2007–2012, with Olympic-related construction providing 27 per cent of the total stock (GLA, 2004c). The Olympic effect will be felt in two further ways: first, through environmental improvement, and second, through the overall improvement in existing housing stock, social amenities, retail and public facilities that such a development entails – particularly around the Stratford City project.

Improvements in housing and social infrastructure change the dynamics of the relative value of living in a particular area. The relative value of living in East London is measured by comparing the area to the London average. In Newham, for example, in 2006 the borough had average house prices below the London average and a higher proportion of 'unfit' stock compared to the London-wide average. The Olympic effect may significantly improve existing stock and change the dynamics of the quality of housing, especially around the Stratford City and Olympic Park areas. It is here that a micro 'Barcelona effect' may occur. Barcelona witnessed a significant rise in the market value of housing within the city leading up to and following the 1992 Games, as did the Homebush area of Sydney following the 2000 Games.

Such an effect, however, in East London is likely to ensure that whilst Stratford remains a socially mixed community there is also a reinforcement of the trend toward a greater level of separation and segregation at the micro-community level, as the Olympic Park attracts residential units that serve the needs of young professionals and those who shop in Stratford City – a public-private partnership development designed to host upmarket retailers such as John Lewis. This pattern of separation and segregation at the local neighbourhood level has been a feature of regeneration and gentrification schemes in East London over recent years – with stark divisions emerging in the same street between the 'gated' and those without. The Olympic effect is likely to accelerate this trend as concerns over costs in the lead-up to the Games helps to deliver large parts of the responsibility for the post-2012 legacy into the hands of private developers for whom rapid gentrification may be a desirable outcome for parts of the Olympic Park and its environs. Such a trend tends to displace lower income groups who move to other, often nearby, parts of the local area. The boundaries of social segregation shift but the underlying problem of social disadvantage remains, especially for lower income groups working in London's service economy (Hamnett, 2003).

The Olympics provide temporary employment opportunities in transport, media, health, education, cultural industries and in leisure, tourism, hotels and food and catering. These sectors have diverse structures ranging from the relatively integrated and large scale – health and education sectors – to those dominated by small businesses and sole traders – restaurants and food outlets. Establishing an effective framework for the development of training and education opportunities for local residents is a significant task and one that is not served well by the diversity of industry structures and agencies with responsibilities for education and training in East London (Learning and Skills Council, 2005). Equally, what constitutes an East London labour market is a complex affair with the inner London boroughs containing variations in economic activity, worklessness and skills profile.

Those boroughs in closest proximity to the Olympic development site – Hackney, Newham and Tower Hamlets – have a higher proportion of the workforce with no qualifications than the London-wide and national averages. The boroughs, and East London as a whole, have a relatively lower proportion of the workforce in knowledge-based occupations and a higher proportion of these knowledge workers concentrated in the public sector by comparison to the city as a whole. Equally, East London has a higher concentration of workers in elementary or unskilled occupations by comparison to most other areas of the city. The potential for the polarisation of temporary and permanent employment opportunities arising from the Olympic Games to be divided with local people taking low-skill jobs and specialist skilled labour being recruited from outside the region is considerable (Donovan, 2006). The issues surrounding land sales, housing and employment illustrate the difficulties in attaining a sustainable legacy that reduces rather than reproduces existing patterns of social division in East London.

London 2012 and community engagement

Whilst the ghosts of Montreal (1976) with its cost overrun of $1.2 billion being met by taxpayers over subsequent decades and Athens (estimated cost overrun of $0.5 billion) haunts the London 2012 organisers, there is evidence that Londoners and people in other UK cities are prepared to support the Games through taxation. A study published in January 2006 indicated that UK taxpayers were willing to pay a total sum of around £2 billion for London to host the 2012 games. For London residents a proportion of this sum will be derived from the mayor's precept on council tax bills (Atkinson *et al.*, 2006). This show of popular support for the 2012 Games provided its organisers with a positive starting point for managing the interface between LOCOG and the agencies responsible for delivering the event and its legacy and the various interests groups, or stakeholders, who seek to benefit from the significant investment required to host the Games. A broadly supportive public opinion within East London was also demonstrated by Newham Community Partnership's 'Big Sunday' event held at the ExCel London exhibition centre in February 2006. A largely promotional event, organised by Newham, LOCOG and the ODA, was extremely well attended by over 32,000 people. 'Big Sunday' represented a public demonstration of partnership between Olympic organisers and the key local authority and was clearly aimed at enhancing local support for hosting the Games.

Since 'Big Sunday', Newham and other East London boroughs have provided Olympic forums and public events for their respective communities at which a range of specific and typically 'sectional' concerns have emerged, about, for example, the relocation of businesses from the Olympic Park, opportunities for local businesses to benefit from 2012, planning permission for a new mosque in Newham and the impact of the Olympic preparations on the environment. A broader-based citizens group, the East London Communities Organisation (TELCO), secured an 'ethical statement' from LOCOG and Ken Livingstone, concerning guarantees to ensure, for example, that a London living wage would be paid to those employed by contractors of the ODA in the lead-up to the Games and a commitment to the provision of social housing as a component of regeneration plans (GLA, 2006; London Civic Forum, 2007).

In early 2007, such forms of political participation appear not to have seriously challenged or disturbed the prevailing discourse of partnership between national and local agencies; and in the absence of such fissures the public space for debate is unlikely to be occupied by voices expressing broader social or political objectives that challenge the prevailing rhetoric of partnership, modify central government influence or, locally, go beyond the expression of 'single issue' or sectional interests of particular ethnic, residential or business communities. In this sense, public engagement is confined to a process of 'consultation' rather than a form of public mobilisation that engages communities in defining and developing their own local regeneration schemes. The state-centred mode of governance is synonymous with the domination of the regeneration agenda by state-sponsored agencies, which in the Olympics setting includes the co-option of the British Olympics Association and other sporting bodies, and the involvement of city-wide partners such as the mayor and LDA. The special legal powers afforded by Parliament and the time constraints imposed by the 2012 event reinforces this centralising tendency and makes difficult any efforts to connect the Olympic development with the aspirations underpinning the wider Thames Gateway scheme. A wider public debate that might question the legitimacy of the current coalition configured around a state-centred 'partnership' would have to challenge the authority of the governance structures established to deliver the Games and their legacy in East London and the Thames Gateway. It would have to reject the 'satisficing approach' inherent in such structures (Jessop, 1999: 11). Such a scenario would require a political challenge to prevailing orthodoxies concerning the respective roles of the market and state in coalescing to provide public/private partnerships to implement national policies for urban regeneration. This scenario is explored in the concluding examination of the influence of the Games on public attitudes to urban development in London.

Conclusion

Cities that host the Olympic and Paralympic Games push urban regeneration at a more rapid pace than 'normal' development. As the Games-related planning process removes local control and accountability, so it is possible to achieve infrastructure developments, relocate people and create new centres of housing, commerce and cultural activity within an accelerated timescale. Seoul, Atlanta and Beijing demonstrate that large areas of a city may be rejuvenated though this is at the expense of those least able to protect their own interests; with, for example, poorer communities being moved to make way for the Games (Preuss, 2004: 79). The accelerated process of urban renewal, and the social 're-engineering' that accompanies it, raises important issues about governance, sustainability and the public perception of the role of high-profile mega projects in promoting urban renewal.

The London 2012 project is already having a major direct and indirect impact upon urban renewal in the city and beyond. The famous West End is undertaking the regeneration of shopping areas in order to offset the potential threat posed by the development of a new upmarket shopping centre at Stratford City, adjacent to the Olympic Park. The Thames Gateway development has attracted greater attention as a result of London's successful bid but much of this has been critical in relation to governance structures and the lack of clarity over its objectives and its capacity to deliver given the likely displacement effect of investment in infrastructure development arising from hosting the Games (Poynter, 2006). In this context, London 2012 is undoubtedly a 'catalyst' for a major programme of urban renewal whose effects, direct and indirect, positive and negative, are not confined to a brownfield site to the east of the city.

The development is taking place under the guidance of the state in accordance with a state-centred paradigm that is quite different to that which prevailed at the time of the Canary Wharf development. The Canary Wharf project eschewed direct state interference, removed local authority controls and favoured the private sector as the major catalyst of renewal. By contrast, the Olympics project is state-centred with a strong supporting role played by London's mayor (Ken Livingstone and now Boris Johnson) and city-wide agencies such as the LDA, with local authorities exercising influence 'at the margins' by, for example, using the leverage of the Games to develop public-private partnerships to deliver complementary projects, such as Stratford City. London 2012 serves to legitimise the role of the state in exercising control over the regeneration project and its legacy via a variety of agencies whose 'partnership' working tends to, paradoxically, reinforce rather than modify state control.

The complex, hierarchical governance structures for 2012 reflect the adaptive capacities of the state in contemporary capitalism; rather than weakening its influence it has strengthened its capacity to define and determine the social, economic and cultural agenda of the 2012 legacy. This is not simply a product of astute political management, it is more a reflection of the transient nature of private capital's attachment to the neo-liberal ethos that prevailed in the 1980s and, more specifically, evidence of that sector's increasing reliance upon state-led regeneration projects to provide the framework for speculative investment (Woodhuysen and Abley, 2004: 292–4, 298–9). Perhaps, most importantly, the evidence to date suggests that the state-led Olympic project is, ironically, increasingly likely to achieve outcomes that are focused upon forms of commercial viability and patterns of regeneration that have similar social consequences to those that accompanied the market-driven development of Docklands in the 1980s and 1990s. Such a trajectory has significant consequences for the public perception of major urban regeneration projects in the city and throughout the UK, particularly in relation to their capacity to reduce social division.

2012 is the latest flagship project in London. Earlier projects in the capital have produced mixed results. The Dome, a relatively small-scale project compared to 2012, was an economic failure that adversely effected the reputation of the government but did not create a deeper questioning of the strategy to regenerate derelict, once industrial, land for service-oriented leisure purposes (Hamnett, 2003: 218). Equally, the Docklands development, though subject to boom–bust–boom, eventually achieved its stated goals. It shifted the financial centre of the city eastwards and provided a boost to mainly private sector housing development with many luxury homes attracting the relocation of professional dwellers. The future of London as a global centre for financial services was secured. The development, initiated in the neo-liberal climate of the 1980s, did little, however, to address the underlying social problems of East London. Indeed, critics have rightly argued that the Docklands development has served to reinforce the polarisation between rich and poor communities (Foster, 1999).

It is precisely this divide that the organisers of 2012 claim to address; with the legacy of the Games being linked to challenging the underlying social and economic problems of East London – the skills deficit, worklessness and the lack of available and affordable housing for local people. This is an ambitious agenda that far exceeds the aims of earlier projects and creates, therefore, a higher risk, in Jessop's terms, of 'failure'; failure in at least four dimensions. First, the complex system of governance for 2012 assumes a shared purpose between stakeholders that will be difficult to sustain as the competition for finance and resources sharpens the potential for conflicts between the goal of delivering the event and securing its ambitious longer term social legacy. Second, the reconciliation of these conflicting ambitions is likely to strengthen the state-centred character of governance, thus underlining the experience for local communities that mega-events bring a form of urban regeneration that happens to them rather than being influenced by them; with tokenistic forms of community consultation being the predominant mode of local participation. Third, and linked to the previous point, while a major sporting event may serve to catalyse a form of post-industrial urban renewal, the contemporary popularity afforded sport culture is an inadequate and passive substitute for the loss of personal and human agency that underlies the often fatalistic response of local people to such patterns of social change. Finally, in the absence of community building measures that address underlying structural and social issues, 2012 will fail to provide a platform for sustainable patterns of urban renewal that aspire to reduce social disadvantage. As a result, public perceptions of large-scale regeneration programmes, or flagship projects, in London will tend to reinforce the view that they are primarily designed to facilitate gentrification – addressing primarily the housing and consumption needs of the expanding middle classes, whose own position and growth has been secured in recent years by, amongst other factors, the consolidation of London's role as a leading global centre for financial services (Hamnett, 2003: 184–5).

The current discourse of regeneration driven by mega-events tends to create formulaic models of community building that breeds close physical proximity of rich and poor but reinforces the social distance between them; and promotes forms of economic activity that take place in 'imperial compounds' from which little of the wealth seeps out to the surrounding districts (Sennett, 2001: 118). The 2012 Games may reinforce and reconfigure this pattern in East London, reproducing the social divisions that arose from the Docklands development that commenced in the 1980s, even though the 'neo-liberal' model of regeneration has been displaced by a 'state-centred' mode of governance. To challenge these trends, public debate about 2012 and its legacy should focus less on cost and commercial viability and more upon the type of good city building that seeks to achieve outcomes whose aspirations exceed 'merely the reproduction of the economic and political conditions of their time' (Sennett, 2001: 119).

Part III

Sustainability, inclusion and social mixing

Chapter 9

The rebirth of high-rise living in London: towards a sustainable, inclusive, and liveable urban form

Richard Baxter and Loretta Lees

Introduction.

> When I was first told I was going to live in a high-rise block I thought I
> was going to have a heart attack.
>
> (Interview, Corrine, Edrich House, 2005)

The residential high-rise has seen something of a renaissance in London of late amidst renewed interest in its potential for delivering a more sustainable form of urban living. Though eye-catching 'blow-downs' of system-built tower blocks still continue from time to time across London (Kerr, 2003; see figure 9.1), for the first time in a generation, residential high-rises are being built. The return of the residential high-rise to London has been driven, in no small part, by Mayor Ken Livingstone (see McNeill, 2002a, and Charney, 2007, on Ken Livingstone and tall buildings). Drawing on the Urban Task Force report (DETR, 1999), Livingstone and his advisors believed that an increased density of new housing on a single footprint would contribute to environmental sustainability by increasing energy efficiency and public transit use, and – when combined with mixed-use and mixed-tenure developments – contribute to the social regeneration of inner-city sites. In the absence of many taxation or regulatory powers, the mayor sought to drive London's regeneration forward by exploiting his authority over planning and development control (McNeill, 2002b). By the time the London Plan was formally approved in 2004, Livingstone and his officers were not simply promoting but indeed actively pushing local boroughs to accept high-rise residential buildings as one of the centrepieces of London's 'sustainable' brownfield regeneration policy.

9.1
**The end of the high
rise?
The tower blocks
Antrim House and
Cavan House in Tower
Hamlets were
dramatically demol-
ished by controlled
explosion on Sunday 20
January 2002 (www.
towerhamlets.gov.uk/
data/housing/data/
housing-choice /
downloads/oh-06.pdf).
Photo by Dave Sinclair,
London Borough of
Tower Hamlets**

This policy turn dovetails with increasing commercial and architectural interest in building residential high-rises. In London's super-charged residential property market, there is now considerable demand for high-end high-rises, especially in areas near the City of London. Poverty-stricken inner London boroughs are cashing in on their proximity to the Square Mile by selling off undesirable council tower blocks to private developers as the recent BBC1 documentary *The Tower* charts. This documentary focuses on the sale, by the cash-strapped Lewisham Council, of a council tower block – Aragon Tower – on the Pepys Estate in Deptford to the private developer Berkeley Homes. Berkeley Homes has regenerated the high-rise and added five extra floors of penthouse flats on the top, making it, at least for the moment, the tallest privately owned residential tower block in London. Their market is young professionals, whom Lewisham Council hope will regenerate the area.

Aiming squarely at that market, a number of iconic designer towers have been built and more than forty are now being planned across London, including the London Bridge Tower – popularly known as the 'shard of glass' – which will, at sixty-six storeys, be the tallest building in Europe and provide a mix of office, retail, hotel and residential accommodation, advertised as 'first-class sky-high living' (see www.londonbridgetower.com). At the same time, other, more publically minded architects and social housing providers are also looking with renewed interest at the residential high-rise. There are a number of 'sustainable' proposals already on 'drawing boards', such as Marks Barfield's Skyhouse (see figure 9.2; also www.marksbarfield.com/project.php?projectid=8) and Bill Dunster's thirty-five-storey SkyZED flower tower (see www.zedfactory.com/prj_skyz1.htm), aimed at meeting the demand for key worker housing, though none have yet come to fruition.

9.2
**Marks Barfield's Skyhouse.
Printed with permission of
Marks Barfield Architects**

This reversal in fortunes for the residential high-rise has provoked something of a popular backlash. For instance, proposals by St George's Plc to build a forty-nine-storey tower at Vauxhall were initially rejected by Lambeth Council in the face of stiff local opposition, and only given planning permission when Ken Livingstone intervened to override the local decision (GLA, 2003a). With London's skyline reaching ever higher, the House of Commons Select Committee on Urban Affairs (2002) conducted a public inquiry into Tall Buildings. Many of those submitting memoranda to it rejected the Urban Task Force's (DETR 1999: 60) celebration of high-rise living as utopian elitism out of touch both with English heritage and with the legacy of alienation, social exclusion and anti-social behaviour left by the 1960s Tower Block 'experiment'.

Such conceptions of the high-rise, however, are not backed up by much systematic research into the actual experience of high-rise living in London or the UK more generally. Almost all of the research to date has focused on council tower block tenants and public housing estates (Jephcott and Robinson, 1971; Saegert, 1976; Coleman 1985; Power 1997; Towers 2000; Green *et al.* 2002; Jacobs 2006), rather than on the rising number of inner London purpose-built flat dwellers in other tenures. Thus Towers (2000: xiv) notes, 'the experience of multi-story living has been little studied, and largely subsumed within the broader question of the future of 'council estates'.

In this chapter, we address that research gap through empirical exploration of the contemporary experience of high-rise living in London. Drawing on a questionnaire survey of, and interviews with, a representative sample of high-rise residents across all tenures in inner London,[1] conducted as part of a larger ESRC-ODPM funded project,[2] we seek to draw out the major factors influencing residents' perceptions of the liveability and sustainability of London's high-rises. Such knowledge is key to regenerating existing high-rise social housing (see chapter 15 in this volume) and ensuring that the new generation of high-rises sprouting up along the riverside (see chapter 9 in this volume), and elsewhere in London, are liveable, inclusive, sustainable and successful components in the regeneration of their local areas.

The research project

The research focused on forty-five residential high-rises, across all tenures, selected randomly out of 340 such buildings in inner London. The random sampling procedure used means that the study is based on a representative sample. There were four stages involved in the sampling, the first being the creation of the sample frame. Three software programmes, Cities Revealed Building Class, Ordinance Survey (OS) Mastermap and ArcView GIS were utilised. Cities Revealed Building Class is a GIS ready dataset that classifies all residential buildings by type. It has thirty-two classifications including two high-rise categories, buildings six stories and above and ten stories and above. We focused on those ten stories and above. OS Mastermap is a comprehensive GIS dataset that is compatible with Cities Revealed Building Class and, importantly, contains postal address data. ArcView

GIS is a utility that allows GIS datasets to be displayed on screen spatially and, importantly, manipulated. Cities Revealed Building Class and OS Mastermap were merged in ArcView and the sample frame was then created by locating all the high-rises in the fourteen inner London boroughs using ArcView's search function.

The second stage concerned the decision over how many high-rises should be in the final sample. Overall, there were 340 high-rises in the sample frame of the fourteen inner London boroughs. Given a limited research budget yet also a requirement to be representative we decided to include forty-five of these high-rises in the final sample. The third stage involved the random sampling of these forty-five high-rises. The sample frame was stratified into four geographical areas or quadrants – north-east, south-east, north-west and south-west. Importantly, this ensured that the final sample was distributed across inner London, rather than being concentrated in one or two geographical areas. The number of high-rises that needed to be in each quadrant was then calculated. For example, the north-east segment had eighty high-rises out of a total of 340, or 28 per cent of the total number of high-rises in inner London. It was, therefore, allocated thirteen high-rises in the final sample, which is 28 per cent of forty-five. Each of these high-rises was then designated a number and a random number generator was used to create a random sequence of numbers and the first thirteen numbers of this sequence were recorded.

The fourth stage involved the extraction of postal address data for the forty-five high-rises from OS Mastermap into ArcView. A total of 2,500 postal questionnaires were then sent to the residents of the forty-five high-rises in the sample. Although response rates were low (18.4 per cent), there were 459 responses in total with at least ten responses for each building except for two, which were subsequently dropped from the research. As well as basic demographic and tenure information, the eight-page survey asked residents a number of open and closed questions about their neighbours and neighbourhood, the cleanliness, safety, design and management of their building, its sense of community and their overall experience of high-rise living. The survey was also used to recruit fifty-seven residents from half of the buildings to participate in a further round of qualitative research involving in-depth semi-structured interviews.

These interviews brought out more fully the resident's experiences, encounters, thoughts, attitudes and emotions with regards to high-rise living. In addition fifteen residents volunteered to keep photo-diaries to document their everyday experiences of high-rise living. These were written accounts of residents' experiences that included photographs. The qualitative data from the in-depth interviews and photo-diaries was triangulated against the findings of the questionnaire survey to provide a rich understanding of the diversity and specificity (cr. Jacobs, 2003) of high-rise living across inner London.

Using a Latourian approach to address the 'problem' of high-rise design

In the research we sought to problematise two alternate explanations often given for the success or failure of high-rise housing. First, there is a long-standing tradition of seeing social behaviour and the character and quality of social life as heavily shaped, if not altogether determined, by the design of the built environment. Whereas those opposed to the expansion of residential high-rises insist that 'vertical living has in fact resulted in . . . the break-up of traditional communities and patterns of life' (Save Britain's Heritage, 2001), proponents often point to the Barbican in London as proof that these problems can be eliminated through good design and management (e.g. Church and Gale, 2000; Brown, 2003). Though their assessments of high-rise living are diametrically opposed, they agree about the power of design in determining the high-rise's success or failure. Significant in cementing this first policy narrative about the centrality of design to the quality of high-rise housing in Britain has been the work of Alice Coleman (1985).

Drawing on Oscar Newman's (1972) ideas of defensible space, Coleman conducted a series of government-funded research projects on high-rise public housing estates in London during the late 1970s and early 1980s.[3] She concluded that there was a causal relationship between the particularities of the high-rise design (e.g. its height, secluded internal corridors, lifts and fire-stairwells) and anti-social behaviour. Her research provided the basis for multi-million-pound programmes of estate renovation to put those design flaws right (see Price Waterhouse, 1999). But the case for design determinism was unproven and Dicken (1994:127) scolded Alice Coleman (and Oscar Newman) for 'engaging in the very type of architectural determinism which they took modernist architects to task for'.

Second, critics of Coleman and her influential brand of design-determinism have offered an alternative explanation for the social problems popularly associated with high-rise public housing estates (Spiker 1987). Reviewing the legacy of the regeneration programme Coleman inspired, Hill (1997: 13) concluded, 'The real lesson of all these interventionist remedial programmes is that some estates will fail, however they are designed if they are full of poor people, with no capacity or opportunity for making real choices about their lives.' Likewise in her study of Les Minguettes and the Broadwater Farm Estate in London, Anne Power (1997) pointed to social factors such as poverty and the concentration of socially marginal or excluded tenants in them as the underlying cause of the problems on those notorious public housing estates. In their own way such sociological explanations can often be just as determinist and mono-causal as the design determinism they challenge.

By contrast, in this research we challenge both these explanations. In so doing we go a step further than van Kempen (1994:176) who argued: 'high-rise design is neither a sufficient nor a necessary condition for the emergence of social problems on housing estates. The crucial element is the combination of design with a heterogeneous, transient and poor population'. Drawing on the Actor Network Theory (ANT) of Bruno Latour (2005), we follow Jane Jacobs (2006)[4] in questioning any absolute distinction between the social and technical in architecture and its experience. As Jacobs et al. (2007:613) explain: 'Actor network theory does not simply place the categories "society" and "technology" as equal "actors" or equivalent "determiners", but reconceives the world as an assemblage of heterogeneous "objects" that cannot, a priori, be categorised as technological or social.'

ANT critiques the modern practice of social science for separating society from nature. Latour (1993) argues that with its focus on society and social forces social science omits non-humans such as animals and technology from its analyses. Such a practice is related to the hegemony of humanism in social science and the commonly held conception of actors and agency in social science as involving ideas of intention and cause which animals and technology are seen not to have:

> The main reason why objects had no chance to play any role before was not only due to the definition of the social used by sociologists, but also to the very definition of actors and agencies most often chosen. If action is limited a priori to what 'intentional', 'meaningful', humans do, it is hard to see how a hammer, a basket, a door closer, a cat, a rug, a mug, a list, or a tag could act.
>
> (Latour, 2005: 71)

The inclusion of non-humans significantly expands the number of participants involved in social analysis. Latour (2005:71) considers the examples of a person hitting a nail with a hammer, walking in the street with clothes, and boiling water with a kettle. He argues that the non-human technologies, the hammer, clothes, and kettle, should be documented in any social study because these events could not have been carried out the way they were without their assistance. Non-humans can also influence how humans behave. He uses the example of doors and their hinges (Latour, 1997) arguing that doors can cause changes in our behaviour, for example, a door that is closing quickly may force humans to move faster. Non-humans are particularly relevant to this study because of the modernist architects, like Le Corbusier, who intended that the technology of the high-rises would influence human behaviour and shape a new society.

Jacobs (2006), writing about high-rise building 'events', including the collapse of Ronan Point in 1969, and Jacobs *et al.* (2007), writing about the Red Road high-rise estate in Glasgow, utilise ANT well but the discussions seem strangely disassociated from the high-rises under investigation. The latter article for example, tells us little about the social life of Red Road, its atmosphere or the residents who live there. This research, therefore, seeks to extend Jacobs' work on residential high-rises by using ANT in the context of a study that examines residents' *lived experiences* of their buildings and surrounding neighbourhood. In keeping with an ANT theoretical framework our analysis focuses on interaction and on the ways in which the quality of life and experience of London's high-rise residents are shaped through practical and material engagements and through the interaction of factors that cannot be understood as either exclusively social or technological, but instead as hybrid assemblages of both.

Careful analysis of our survey and qualitative data has indicated four factors key to determining the quality of life experienced by high-rise residents in inner London:

1.   The material condition of the building and its maintenance,
2.   Its physical design and security,

3. The prevalence of anti-social behaviour;
4. Residents' feelings about their neighbours and neighbourhood.

Conventionally, these four factors might be said to lie along a continuum from the technical to the social. But in keeping with our ANT approach, we understand each of them as hybrid and heterogeneous assemblages of both human and non-human elements. But before turning to discuss these key factors in detail we provide a general characterisation, drawn from our survey, of the lived experience of high-rise living in inner London.

Characterising the lived experience of high-rise living in inner London

Contrary to the popular stereotype of the tower block as a symbol of misery and urban anomie, the majority (63.4 per cent) of the high-rise residents reported being satisfied (41.1 per cent) or very satisfied (23.3 per cent) with living in their high-rise. This tallies with the National Tower Block Network (1992) who found that significant numbers of the tenants in their study of tower blocks were satisfied with their homes. In response to open-ended questions they offered generally positive assessments such as 'Lovely, everyone is very friendly and welcoming', 'It's great' (anonymous authors, questionnaires, Edrich House, May 2005), 'I enjoy the peace and quiet, being high above street level and the great views', and, 'Excellent' (Anonymous authors, questionnaires, Landmark Heights, May 2005). Only a small minority of just over 20 per cent reported being dissatisfied (8.6 per cent) or very dissatisfied (11.6 per cent) with high-rise living. It was possible to aggregate the residents' survey responses so as to give each building an overall liveability index score, which was then used to rank and classify the forty-three buildings included in the study (see figure 9.3; for further details about the aggregation methodology, see Baxter, 2005).

The aggregate liveability scores ranged from 13.63 to 28.41. Since the numbers themselves are arbitrary, what is important is the range and diversity of scores. The average liveability score for the top quartile of buildings was over 150 per cent higher than that of the bottom quartile. Though it is always possible to quibble around the edges of any classification, closer inspection of the scores suggests the buildings fall into three broad classes. At the top there are eight high scoring buildings in which residents consistently report high levels of satisfaction. Although the highest scoring building in the study was, not surprisingly, Lauderdale Tower in the Barbican, where privately owned flats regularly sell for more than half a million pounds, that top grouping of buildings also included a number of local authority or Registered Social Landlord (RSL)-managed high-rises, such as Edrich House, Bowsprit Point, and Seaton Point in which, right to buy notwithstanding, 75 per cent, 30 per cent and 91 per cent of respondents respectively were council or RSL tenants. Bowsprit Point, for example, was ranked sixth on the liveability index. Its residents liked the newly refurbished building, the park adjacent to the high-rise

Rank	High-Rise	Liveability Score	% in class
1	Lauderdale Tower	28.41	
2	Horizon Building	27.34	
3	Edrich House	26.98	
4	Landmark Heights	25.88	
5	Osprey Heights	25.65	19%
6	Bowsprit Point	24.96	
7	William Harvey House	24.91	
8	Totteridge House	24.80	
9	Blair Court	23.98	
10	Seaton Point	23.86	
11	Bacton	23.64	
12	Oatfield House	23.10	
13	Stangate	22.49	
14	Brinklow House	22.49	
15	Tatchbury House	22.39	
16	Rundell Tower	21.90	
17	Snowman House	21.88	
18	Angrave Court	21.71	
19	Wayman Court	21.05	
20	Farnborough House	20.67	
21	Penge House	20.65	
22	Clinger Court	20.34	60%
23	Bannerman House	20.31	
24	Pope House	20.29	
25	Bedford House	20.03	
26	Edgecombe House	20.02	
27	Barton House	19.80	
28	Park View House	19.73	
29	Columbia Point	19.60	
30	Castlemaine	19.56	
31	Kelson House	19.02	
32	Granville Court	18.80	
33	Denning Point	18.60	
34	Stanway Court	18.38	
35	Overton House	17.68	
36	Kenley	17.34	
37	Babington Court	17.13	
38	Taplow	17.01	
39	Brawne House	16.65	21%
40	Charles House	15.56	
41	Tissington Court	14.58	
42	Wendover	14.58	
43	Chillingford House	13.63	

and its location near to Canary Wharf. The tenants were well behaved, they tended to know their neighbours on their floor, and the Tenants Association was quite active. The residents especially enjoyed the peace and tranquillity and the views across London offered by their building. Although there was a strong correlation in our survey data between reported levels of satisfaction and both tenure and employment status, the high levels of satisfaction offered by these buildings puts paid to simplistic sociological explanations that look to class or levels of social inclusion as the sole determinates of high-rise quality of life.

At the other extreme there were a small number of buildings, almost all in local authority ownership, at the bottom of the Liveability Index where residents consistently reported being dissatisfied with their building. Taplow Tower, on Camden's Chalcot Estate in Swiss Cottage, was one of the lowest ranking buildings in the study (see figure 9.4). Though elderly tenants recall how it used to be different – one respondent even stated that when it first opened, there was a long waiting list to get in – it now epitomises all of the worst stereotypes about public sector tower blocks. Many of its exterior windows are broken or covered over with cardboard, its once gleaming interior is now covered in graffiti, and the lifts, when they work at all, smell of urine. As one resident reported:

> I am very unhappy with living in a high-rise block and the walls are very thin. I come home with the lifts unbearable or broken. The entry-phone system is always broken down, for the past 3 months it's not working and the entrance door is not closed at all . . . I am ashamed to ask people to visit.
>
> (Anonymous, questionnaire, June 2005)

9.4
Taplow, Swiss Cottage.
Source: Richard Baxter, 2008

However, the largest group of buildings fell somewhere between these two extremes. Although most residents in this broad middle category were basically satisfied, they were not uncritical either and many expressed specific concerns with various aspects of their buildings. Taking Columbia Point, in Docklands, as an example, 64 per cent of the residents who responded were satisfied and 7 per cent were very satisfied with living in their high-rise. They praised their relatively large flats whose broad windows maximised natural light and offered expansive views across London. The building was regarded as safe, with one resident commenting during interview 'I do like living in a high-rise . . . You're safe, I do feel safe in my flat, and we've got this community you see, and the park, there's always people coming through from the tube all the time' (interview, Columbia Point, July 2005), but then several minutes later they complained about the dark interior corridors and a mattress that had been left in the lobby for weeks by an indifferent management. Several other residents also complained about the management of this local-authority-run building, variously calling them, in open-ended responses, rude, evasive or inept. No survey respondents reported being satisfied with the service they provided, with half neither satisfied nor dissatisfied and the rest either dissatisfied or very dissatisfied. Residents complained about the lack of proper cleaning and maintenance and the difficulties of getting the local authority to respond to problems with a building that otherwise they greatly valued. Such ambivalent experiences exemplify the varying combinations of positive and negative encounters faced by residents in high-rises in this broad middle category.

For the most part, however, academic research has tended to ignore such ordinary experiences. Instead it has focused upon trying to explain the bad or failed high-rise, frequently drawing on one of two kinds of determinism – technical (the high-rise is bad because of its design/construction) or social (the high-rise is bad because it is a sink estate for the socially marginal or because it is badly managed by an incompetent or cash-strapped local authority). By contrast our research highlights the ordinary experience of high-rise living. We show this now in our discussion of the four factors we found to be key to determining the quality of life experienced by high-rise residents in inner London.

Material condition of the building and its maintenance

For the social scientist, the physical fabric of a building is easy to overlook, but as Jenkins (2002: 229–30) notes, it is important to consider the materiality of the structure itself. The unreliability of basic services such as heat, water and power was a common complaint for residents of our lowest ranked buildings. For example, residents at Denning Point regularly lost their water supply because of burst water pipes in the building. There were also frequent black-outs due to power surges in the old electrical wiring.

One design flaw with many early modernist high-rises was that their flat roofs and concrete panel construction were prone to leakage and moisture ingress and to damp patches on residents' interior walls:

> My Mum and Dad's bedroom that's where all the leak came in. It's continuously damp even in the summer . . . I mean my Dad, god bless him, died of chest cancer, and I mean we were living in a damp flat at the time, and at the end of the day it couldn't have done him any good. The last four weeks of his life he slept in a chair in the living room.
>
> (Jimmy, interview, Pope House, September 2005)

Even high scoring buildings were not immune to these problems. Both Lauderdale Tower and Bowsprit Point, the first and sixth ranked high rises in figure 9.3, had to undergo extensive repair programmes to rectify such structural deficiencies.

The quality of such repairs and the failures of management to carry out proper maintenance were problems consistently raised by residents of low scoring buildings. Right-to-buy leaseholders in local-authority-managed buildings experienced particular difficulties because of policies to separate out service provision for council tenants from that for leaseholders expected to pay their own way. Residents at Denning Point were dismayed to see Tower Hamlets spend thousands replacing the doors of council tenants, but not leaseholders, leaving the interior corridors with a garish mixture of doors in different styles and colours. More serious problems were experienced by a Tissington Court leaseholder whose bathroom flooded. Her privately contracted plumber could not stop the leak because it originated from an area of the building that could only be accessed by council employees. She complained to the neighbourhood office, but they refused to fix it because she was a leaseholder: 'In the end I went to the Environmental Health people, and they said this is ridiculous, they've got to think about the structural integrity of the building' (interview, Tissington Court, July 2005).

For high-rise buildings, the lift is perhaps the element of infrastructure most crucial to residents' quality of life. Architectural historian Tom Peters (1987) has argued that along with the steel frame it was the invention of the electrical elevator that made high-rises possible. In their analysis of the experience of Glasgow's first generation of high-rise residents, Jephcott and Robinson (1971) found troubles with the lifts to be among their most frequent concerns. They frequently failed, and when they worked properly waiting times were long, especially during peak periods. In our survey there was a statistically significant correlation between overall levels of satisfaction with high-rise living and the reliability of the lifts. The centrality of the lift to high-rise living was graphically demonstrated in the diary kept for us by one elderly Tissington Court resident for whom a broken lift meant she was a virtual prisoner in her fifteenth-storey flat, because of her difficulty walking up and down stairs. Older buildings had particular problems with the reliability of their lifts, not simply because of the age of the equipment itself, but also because of the difficulty of sourcing spare parts. When the lifts failed at Taplow it could take several weeks to get them running again because the parts were no longer in production and so replacement parts had to be custom made. But as this example demonstrates, the lift, like other building technologies, depends upon wider social networks, and when those networks breakdown, because of vandalism or poor maintenance, technical failure was often the result. As one Park View House resident explained:

> If people drop food on the floor, food gets caught on the doors. All it takes is that to stop a lift on a floor and then it's out of action. And you've got to find it and kick out the can or whatever and get it started again. It is annoying.
>
> (Interview, Park View House, August 2005)

Even well-maintained and technically sound lifts could become spaces of fear and loathing if in the wrong social context. One Edgecombe House resident described how after a disturbing incident in the lift, she now preferred to walk rather than risk being trapped in the confined space of the lift with her antagonist:

> earlier this year I walked into the communal area of the block, the same girl appeared. She kept pressing the lift button so that I couldn't go upstairs. I decided to go up the stairs instead, and she called me a 'fucking cunt' and continued to verbally abuse me as I walked away. I find her nasty and intimidating.
>
> (Photo diary, 17 September 2005)

Physical design and security

Such distressing experiences were often indicative of wider problems with physical security in the building. Security was a persistent theme in our qualitative data. Residents of buildings with high liveability scores felt safe and secure in the buildings, while those in low liveability scoring buildings frequently did not.

The high-rise residents in the sample emphasised the importance of design and of security systems in sealing off their high-rises and filtering who enters and leaves the building. In general those managing high-rises have sought to make them more secure by introducing secure entry, concierge and closed-circuit television (Farr and Osborn, 1997). The best security systems, however, did not just involve 'security technology' like intercoms, CCTV and secured entrance doors, but also involved other factors such as defensible spaces and a good concierge. Recent renovations at Seaton Point in Hackney introduced all these features. There is an intermediary zone in front of the building created by steps and an access ramp that separates the entrance to the building from the street (see figure 9.5). Access to the building is then through a secured entrance door, opened either with a fob key or through an audiobased intercom. The entrance hall is visible from both the outside through a glass façade and from inside over a glass partition to the lift lobby, which creates another intermediary zone and allows for high surveillance of both the internal and external spaces. Within the entrance hall there is a concierge and a CCTV camera watching all visitors and making it physically and psychologically difficult for potential intruders to enter the building.

9.5
The first intermediary zone at Seaton Point (also notice the glass). Source: Richard Baxter, 2008

Most of the high-rises in the sample, however, did not have such comprehensive security. A few high-rises had a CCTV camera in the lift or lobby, but residents were often unsure whether they were actually connected. More commonly, there was a secured entrance door accessed by fob key and either audio- or video-based intercom systems through which residents could allow their guests to enter the building. The problem with such systems is that they are easy to bypass. Intruders simply follow immediately behind residents or bona fide guests or call on flats through the intercom claiming to have lost their keys and asking to be let in, as one Pope House resident explained:

> The intercom, you have to put a tag up to it . . . but the kids are going to get in. Someone will come in the building and they'll all come in after, or they'll wedge things in the lock. During the week it's a bloody nuisance because they go on the stairs and leave all their rubbish, and drink, and smoke, and that.
>
> (Lisa, interview, Pope House, June 2005)

Despite these limitations, secured entrances and intercoms were better than having no security at all, as was the case at three of the twenty-one high-rises visited where it was possible to gain entrance to the upper storeys of the building directly from the street. One resident of Tissington Court explained how difficult it had been to get the council to retrofit the building with security doors:

> All the tenants living in Tissington Court have in the past signed three petitions to get security doors on the entrance door, and my friend and myself wrote to our local MP Simon Hughes in 1976 requesting security doors. Thirty years later we're finally going to get them!
>
> (Photo diary, Tissington Court, 28 June 2005)

In some high-rises such as Denning Point and Taplow, what appeared at first glance to be basic security proved, on closer inspection, to be defective or broken (see figure 9.6). For example, residents at Taplow complained that the steel entrance door to their building was left open all the time because it was often broken and the intercom system never worked, while the shiny CCTV camera pointed at the entrance was not even connected, as could be plainly seen from the frayed wires dangling down from its wall mounting:

> It's not effective at all. It packs up quite regular because of its age. Mine rings, sometimes you push a button and it will ring three or four different floors, and there's no security as such at all. Those CCTV cameras have never worked since they were put in.
>
> (Interview, Taplow, September 2005)

But again security was not simply a function of technology or design. Human factors count too. The effectiveness of concierges, for example, depended on having 'good' ones as this resident complained:

> They're there 9 am to about 12 midnight, but sometimes they're not there and you know they don't ask you any questions, you just walk in and out. Sometimes they're just reading and not looking, you know it's just a token presence.
>
> (Interview, Denning Point, September 2005)

Similarly the effectiveness of defensible space designs also depended on social context, as illustrated by the contrast between Lauderdale Tower in the Barbican, the highest ranking building in our study, and Park View House in south London. At Lauderdale Tower there was a concierge's desk, high ceilings and glass panels separating the interior from the exterior to allow full surveillance from passers-by. Partly as a result all Lauderdale Tower respondents (n=36) reported feeling safe (60 per cent) or very safe (40 per cent). Although Park View House was also designed according to the principles of defensible space, the results there were very different. The building's entrance was

9.6
Taplow appears to be secure from a distance.
Source: Richard Baxter, 2008

secured by two intermediary zones: a ramped walkway setting off the front door from the street, an entrance lobby with glass doors to provide visibility to and from the street, as well as an open stairwell from which residents waiting for lifts could see people on the stairs and vice versa (see figure 9.7). This was a particularly unique feature that addressed one of the main indefensible spaces associated with high-rises: the enclosed stairwell. Similar defensible space designs were also apparent on the upper storeys where the arrangement of the flats relative to the lift and the landings allowed residents to survey their landings and the front doors of two other flats through their spy holes:

> If someone's trying to fiddle with your lock and trying to get into your flat they'd be conscious that three doors behind them there could be someone spying on them or people could walk out at any time . . . I can stand here [in the floor landing] and just keep an eye on them so that I can see who it is from here as they come round the corner. From the hallway here I can actually see what is happening over there [in the small corridor] through the glass.
>
> (Interview, Park View House, July 2005)

Overall, this sophisticated transition from the lifts to flats improved the intimacy of floors, the territoriality of residents and the security of the buildings, much as defensible space theorists predicted. Nevertheless Park View House still experienced multiple difficulties with anti-social and criminal behaviour. Shared spaces were covered in urine, there was rubbish and litter everywhere, and flats and the underground car park were being used for drugs and prostitution, as the above informant explained:

> Sometimes you don't know what you're about to step into when the lift door opens and who's going to be there. Um . . . I was going out of the block quite late at night and I stepped into the lift. There was a guy smoking a pipe, a little pipe, and I realised after a while standing there

9.7
The stairs at Park View House are in the lift lobby and open.
Source: Richard Baxter, 2008

that it was a crack pipe and he offered me it! No thanks. Perfectly friendly you know, but it's a recurring problem.

(Interview, Park View House, July 2005)

Anti-social behaviour

As the above comment suggests, the prevalence of crime and anti-social behaviour was an important factor shaping residents' experiences of high-rise living. There was a strong statistical correlation between residents' overall levels of satisfaction and their feeling safe in the common areas. High-rises near the top of the Liveability Index were characterised by 'good' resident behaviour. Residents reported that the common areas were generally kept clean and that there was never graffiti. In interviews and open-ended survey responses, residents of highly ranked buildings made little or no reference to anti-social behaviour by other residents. By contrast, the frequency and severity of such problems was much higher in lower ranking high-rises. The occurrence of criminal behaviour, such as assaults, robbery, prostitution and drug dealing or taking, was only mentioned by residents of Park View House, Denning Point, Wendover and Taplow, high-rises all near the bottom of our Liveability Index.

Resident anti-social behaviour is a problem for any street or neighbourhood, but it is particularly problematic for high-rises because the effects of such behaviour can be exacerbated by the high-rises' design, the close proximity of flats and the fact all residents pass through contained shared spaces with small spatial areas. Importantly, this means that a very small proportion of problem flats can significantly impact upon the lived experience of many households that have to share those common areas with them. A good example of this is Park View House, which was disadvantaged by only two or three flats that were primarily responsible for the anti-social and criminal behaviour in the building. Had these residents not lived there, Park View House would have scored much higher on liveability:

> Yeah I would definitely say it's a minority of people, say about four or five people in individual flats who have, you know, an issue with the loud music and like I said the dogs. The graffiti, the weeing in the communal areas and actually vomiting . . . I mean certain people I can pinpoint and say it's x who lives at number yeah.

(Interview, Park View House, July 2005)

A key factor in controlling such behaviour was the effectiveness of informal mechanisms for enforcing social norms of decency, civility and appropriate conduct. At Edrich House, for example, one resident related how a new tenant once held a late-night party with loud music, only to be bombarded the next day with complaints from neighbours. Since then she has never held another party without first clearing it with her neighbours first. The high-rise also had a strict no-smoking policy, and another resident talked about how her friends used to be told off for smoking in the lifts:

> When I first moved in, my friends used to complain that in the lift someone told them off for smoking. But it's basically good and like you can approach someone and say you're not supposed to smoke in the lift . . . Everybody wants to live in this block the same way I want to live. Peacefully and with some order basically.
>
> (Interview, Edrich House, July 2005)

Such mechanisms of informal social control were much less effective at lower ranking buildings. One Taplow resident related a particularly graphic example of the breakdown of ordinary norms of polite conduct:

> Now this is absolutely true. Four of us in the lift one day going down and then she couldn't speak a word of English. She gets in the lift and she does no more than squats on the floor. She just got out of her flat opposite and then into the lift. She squats on the floor and then uses it as a toilet. We's in the, in the, and we're all going [pause]. We're all in the lift, and we're all shouting at her, and she took not a blind bit of notice.
>
> (Interview, Taplow, August 2005)

It is not uncommon to attribute such breakdowns in social norms to a lack of social capital (e.g. Putnam, 2000). In our survey residents of high-ranking buildings were much more likely to report feeling strong ties to their neighbours than those of lower ranking buildings. But just as we argued that the physical condition and security of the high-rise depends on a wider social network of actors, so too do social interactions within high-rises depend on their material context. One of the major contributors to the anti-social behaviour experienced in the very worst buildings was the breakdown of the security systems that allowed criminals and other intruders easy access to buildings. At Taplow, for example, rough sleepers sometimes used the internal corridors and stairwells:

> Once [laughs] I opened the door. I thought I'm not walking down there it's full of 10 people, on the stairs between 17 and 18. There are all drunken men sleeping on the floor at about 10 o'clock in the morning.
>
> (Interview, Taplow, August 2005)

Design was also a factor in the levels of noise and disturbance from neighbours experienced by high-rise residents. One reason that the residents of Lauderdale Tower, our top-ranked high-rise, so rarely reported being disturbed by their neighbours was because of its design:

> This is one of the nice things . . . The design is such that on the point of each of those triangles is an escape stairwell. So no flat touches another flat, so acoustically it's fantastic. Above and below obviously they're tough because it is a concrete floor slab and there are two metres of concrete between us.
>
> (Interview, Lauderdale Tower, July 2005)

By contrast, several residents of Brinklow House and Taplow complained they could regularly hear their neighbours, or other loud noises around the building such as drilling or banging, because, as the GLA's (2003b: 11) *Interim Strategic Planning Guidance on Tall Buildings* warns, poorly designed flats using cheap materials are vulnerable to noise transference from elsewhere in the building. By comparison the Lauderdale Tower flats were extremely quiet not simply because its residents were more considerate of their neighbours, but also because its design made them less likely to be disturbed.

Neighbourhood and community

The final factor influencing residents' satisfaction with high-rise living was their perceptions of their wider neighbourhood. Although the literature on what makes neighbourhoods good is limited (Parkes *et al.*, 2002), residents discussed a number of aspects. One was the feeling of community:

> I have nice neighbours like and this is one of the most tranquil floors. Uh it's been very stable for a long time and we all get on they're all nice people. We're neighbourly I suppose. If Georgina or Jackie my other two neighbours on this floor. If they leave a little bag of rubbish out outside the front door and I'm going out of the block anyway I'll take their rubbish down for them.
>
> (Interview, Park View House, July 2005)

While critics of high-rise living often depict them as soulless places of anomie, our informants often found the elevators and other common spaces to be pleasant meeting points for unscripted encounters with neighbours and friends. The diary of a Brinklow House resident contained many entries about positive encounters and conversations with neighbours in the corridors and lifts:

> On my way to do food shopping I meet three neighbours who all talked . . . On the way out meet other tenants in block who I know to say hello to. There is a nice lot of tenants in this block.
>
> (Photo diary, Brinklow House, September 2005)

In addition to these feelings of community, residents of successful high-rises also felt positive about its location and wider neighbourhood. CABE and English Heritage (2007) argue that one of the reasons why high-rises failed was because of their poor locations. Accordingly the *London Plan* (GLA, 2004a) and *Interim Strategic Planning Guidance on Tall Buildings* (GLA, 2003b) both recommend locating high-rises near to public transport and other amenities, such as parks. This was supported by our research and residents stated that their high-rises' central locations were important to their overall satisfaction. For example, one of the main reasons Nicola stated she liked living at Park View House was due to the people on the nearby streets, and the adjacent park, shops, coffee shops, restaurants and bars. She contrasted this with her previous place of residence in the Dock-lands, which she described as 'soulless'.

Access to outside space was important for many of our informants. Some residents made good use of their balconies:

> My balcony is like a small garden area, with plants and flowers . . . We are very lucky to have lots of wild life, mixture of birds and on the odd occasion bats. On my balcony I'm happy to have lots of insects which come to visit my plants and sometimes a robin, blackbird or once a wagtail to use my bird feeders.
>
> (Photo diary, Brinklow House, 2005)

But many more felt access to park space was particularly important. For instance, several residents of that building mentioned the attractions of Brockwell Park adjacent to Park View House. Likewise, the mid-sized park near to Edrich House was also a favourite, used by residents for park activities such as walking, sitting on the benches and playing basketball. Every year a festival was held in the park called the Stockwell Project with fairground stalls, food and live music. This meant the park was not just somewhere residents could see trees and stretch their legs, but also a social place to encounter other people in the neighbourhood and deepen the feeling of being part of a wider community:

> The Stockwell Project where the whole of Stockwell basically come out. They have a little carnival and they have five-a-side football, they have a live stage, and they have classical music. They have dancing and they do it on a Saturday and Sunday every year. It's all to do with the people from Stockwell.
>
> (Interview, Edrich House, July 2005)

Conclusions: towards a sustainable, inclusive and liveable high-rise living

> Public sector high-rises include some of the most stigmatised housing in British society, yet its counterparts in the private sector, not least the modern blocks of high-density London, symbolise the most affluent urban lifestyles. Such contradictions are a constant accompaniment to the story of high-rise housing in Britain.
>
> (Turkington, 2004: 147)

The rebirth of the residential high-rise in London is associated with a new era of urban regeneration, one that has turned its back on functionalist mass housing. The majority of the high-rises being constructed and indeed renovated in London today are by private developers or public/private partnerships; the public sector no longer has the money for such endeavours (although some housing associa-tions have undertaken this role – see chapter 15 in this volume). Wassenberg,

Turkington and van Kempen (2004: 271) argue that the residential high-rise 'has an important role in the high demand markets of London and the south-east', This is reinforced by the massive population pressures on an already overheated housing market, which also means reduced access to owner-occupation and increased demand for social and affordable housing. As such there is demand for *both* private sector luxury high-rises and public sector high-rise housing.

The luxurious high-rise blocks appearing along London's watersides and in other attractive locations have helped to create a more positive image for high-rise housing and to turn people's minds away from the legacy of the mass housing period. There is, however, a significant mismatch between the number of high-design, high-income, high-rises being built in inner London and the difficulties that those architects who have designed the sustainable and mixed-use Skyhouse and Flowertower have had in getting clients for their affordable high-rises for low-income people. This is something that the GLA needs to address if we are to have an equitable, socially inclusive policy for the rebirth of the residential high-rise in London.

The research presented here provides evidence to back up ODPM's (2001) claim that if well designed and managed then the residential high-rise can make an important contribution to developing more sustainable urban environments. It also provides evidence that public sector high-rises can be as successful as privately owned high-rises but that certain elements have to be in place for this to occur. The residents of the pricey private flats in the Barbican had some of the highest levels of satisfaction, but so too did the council tenants in Edrich House. As Jacobs (2006: 13) has argued: 'the residential high-rise – is always at the same time situated and specific'. The lesson from this is that it might be time now to look more seriously at the residential high-rise as the solution to London's key worker, social housing and other sustainability problems.

We found that four major factors influence the liveability of residential high-rises in inner London: the material condition of the building and its maintenance; physical design and security; anti-social behaviour; and neighbourhood and community. We argue that these four factors cannot be understood simply as either technical or social issues. What counts is interaction between the social and the technical and context. In this we follow Latour (2005) who is critical of 'cause' being found in one or a small number of factors and then being used to explain – in this case the success or failure of the residential high-rise:

> to explain is not a mysterious cognitive feat, but a very practical world-building enterprise that consists in connecting entities with other entities, this is, in tracing a network. So ANT cannot share the philosophy of causality used in social sciences.
>
> (Latour, 2005: 103)

Indeed, in the vein of Latour we would like to emphasise the complexity, multiplicity and hybridity of the residential high-rise with respect to its success or failure as a liveable residential environment. The argument made here is that the success or failure of residential high-rises is due to multiple potential causes that are complex and non-linear. This is a difficult message for policy-makers. The residential high-rise is a complicated socio-technical system. This is not a satisfactory answer but that is the reality. The challenge now is to develop a more detailed understanding of these empirical relationships and to communicate this complexity to policy-makers.

Acknowledgements

We would especially like to thank Donald McNeill for his input on an earlier paper that we draw on in the introduction to this chapter and David Demeritt for his help in developing the Latourian framework. Thanks also to Sarah Fielder and Rob Imrie.

Notes

1   For the purposes of this study, Inner London was defined as the fourteen boroughs of The City of London, Westminster, Tower Hamlets, Camden, Southwark, Islington, Lambeth, Hackney, Wandsworth, Haringey, Hammersmith and Fulham, Lewisham, Kensington and Chelsea, and Newham.

2   ESRC-ODPM 2003-2006 'High Rise Living in London: Towards an Urban Renaissance'. Loretta Lees designed the project, applied to the ESRC-ODPM scheme for funding and was the primary academic supervisor on the project. Richard Baxter was the PhD student awarded the project, Sarah Fielder the ODPM supervisor on the project, and Donald McNeill the second academic supervisor.

3   Alice Coleman led the Land Use Research Unit in the Geography Department at King's College London.

4   Drawing on Jenkins (2002) Jacobs extends Lees's (2001) call for a 'critical geography of architecture' into what she calls a 'new geography of architecture'.

Chapter 10

London's Blue Ribbon Network: riverside renaissance along the Thames

Mark Davidson

Introduction

London's riverside renaissance dates back to 1981, when Michael Heseltine, then Secretary of State for the Environment under Margaret Thatcher, declared London's docklands a space without local democracy by replacing local government with the highly autonomous and non-elected London Docklands Development Corporation (LDDC) (Brownill, 1990). This body was charged with using public funds to attract real-estate capital into the economic vacuum created by the migration of London's dock activities to the east of the city. The urban development process initiated at this point continues today, even though the LDDC was dismantled in 1998, as the collection of corporate skyscrapers clustered around the initial One Canada Square building continues to grow (see figure 10.1). This transformation of ex-industrial waterfront spaces into gleaming beacons of post-industrial urbanism was replicated elsewhere, in places such as Baltimore's Inner Harbor, USA, and Melbourne's docklands, Australia, using London docklands'-style entrepreneurial approaches to bring about renewal (Dovey, 2005; Harvey, 2000).

The riverside redevelopment that has taken place in London over the past ten years should be distinguished from earlier phases. The Thatcherite policies implemented in, and subsequently symbolised by, London Docklands are no longer rigidly adhered to. A New Labour government states it has taken heed of the failure of policies inspired by liberal economic theory to produce trickle-down benefits for the poor (NAO, 1988). Consequently, it has designed a national urban policy framework that looks to learn from the mistakes made in places such as

10.1
The cluster around
Canada Square, Canary
Wharf.
Source: Peter Howard,
Department of
Geography, King's
College London

Docklands (DETR, 2000a). Add to this context the reestablishment of metropolitan government – the Greater London Authority (GLA) – in London, and subsequently the election of a socialist mayor, Ken Livingstone, and the creation of its
own urban policies, and it is clear that the context surrounding the most recent
riverside redevelopment is distinct from earlier phases.

This chapter examines this latest phase of London's riverside redevelopment. It begins by examining the urban policies developed by the new metropolitan government since 2001, specifically focusing upon the waterfront renewal
vision formulated by the GLA. Following this, the type of urban development that
has taken place in three Thames-side neighbourhoods under this policy framework is explored, with the intention of identifying whether or not the GLA's riverside vision is being realised. The chapter concludes with a reflection on the current
situation along the Thames, and some thoughts about the prospects for communities affected by redevelopment.

Livingstone's London Plan and the Blue Ribbon Network

The formulation of London's urban policy – under the rubric of a 'Spatial Development Strategy' – began in May 2001 when the mayor released the *Towards a
London Plan* (GLA, 2001a). This served as a basis from which the mayor could
develop consultatively the city's long-term vision. In this document, the mayor
identified the key challenge facing the city: 'London needs a strategic plan to set
out policies and proposals for change to meet the many complex demands
created by such growth and to ensure that all Londoners can share in the city's

success' (GLA, 2001a: vii). Here Livingstone pointed to the overwhelming tension associated with London's global city stature: how to manage London's growth in such a way that the social polarisation and inequity, that had deepened over the past 25 years, were reduced to manageable proportions (see Buck *et al.*, 2002; Hamnett 2003)?

The *Draft London Plan* (GLA, 2002b) followed. This provisional document aimed to incorporate input from the consultation process and the mayor's appointed advisory team. The most notable advisors were the 'Chief Advisor to the Mayor on Architecture and Urbanism' architect Richard Rogers and Nicky Gavron, 'Cabinet Advisor on Strategic Planning'. In the document's foreword, Rogers and Gavron set out their key concerns and objectives. These highlight the close dovetailing of national and metropolitan urban policy in terms of the rhetoric of New Labour's urban renaissance (see Imrie and Raco, 2003). As is stated in the *Draft London Plan*:

> Urban renaissance is about making the city a place where people want to live, rather than a place from which they want to escape. A successful and sustainable city needs to be both beautiful and environmentally responsible, both compact and polycentric, with distinctive communities and neighbourhoods. But above all, it must be a fair city, respecting and celebrating the diversity of its people.
>
> (GLA, 2002b: ix)

Livingstone, as some feared he would, did not therefore develop his vision for London in conflict with national government. The final *London Plan* (GLA, 2004a), published in February 2004, adhered closely to national urban policy and adopted all of the main policy directions set out in the *Draft London Plan*. The *London Plan's* principal goals are to continue the city's economic growth and global city prosperity along with reinvesting in the city's infrastructure, increasing social inclusion and, fundamentally, improving London's environmental sustainability.

The mayor therefore found few contradictions between pursuing current trajectories of economic growth and a desire for greater social inclusion. Questions about whether greater inequities are endemic to global cities are not addressed (Harvey, 2005). The challenge for the mayor has, therefore, been how to make significant inroads into social inequalities within an unchanged economic context. The *London Plan* ambitiously sets out to do what few cities have done and balance economic growth with sustainability and equity. It is within this context that the GLA's plans for redeveloping London's waterfront spaces – a policy programme named 'the Blue Ribbon Network' – have been formulated.

The Blue Ribbon Network first appears in the *Towards a London Plan* (GLA, 2004a: 84), where the objective of the policy is set out as: 'to recognise the special character of river and canal corridors as both a strategic and a scarce resource, and address the competing needs, uses and demands that are placed on them'. This initial proposal was substantially developed and expanded upon in the *Draft London Plan* where mayoral advisor Richard Rogers looked towards the River Thames as a physical feature which could be developed to bring about social inclusion:

> The real heart of London is the river. Look at any satellite image and it is the Thames that dominates . . . It is this huge and beautiful waterway that holds the key to revitalizing the metropolis. It must once again become a cohesive element linking communities.
>
> (GLA, 2002b: iii)

This statement represents a shift in the *Draft London Plan* where the Blue Ribbon Network vision moves from being purely concerned with the particularities of waterfront development and towards a wider vision where the 'Blue Ribbon Network has an essential role to play in delivering all the key elements of the mayor's vision of an exemplary sustainable world city' (GLA, 2002b: 302).

These policies remain largely the same in the final *London Plan*. Now adopted, they serve two primary purposes. First, they replace pre-existing planning guidance for Thames-side development (RPG3b/9b Strategic Planning Guidance for the River Thames [Department of Environment, 1997]), helping to ensure that the particularities and strategic importance of the Thames-side are recognised in planning decisions. Second, and distinctively, waterfront spaces have been given strategic importance in the effort to deliver the entire *London Plan* vision through being recognised as under-utilised resources and spaces which can help synthesise the various elements of the mayor's vision. The Blue Ribbon Network is therefore positioned as a strategically important synergistic tool, combining environmental, economic, planning and social policy objectives.

The Blue Ribbon Network Principles (figure 10.2) provide an overview of the many policy elements that are incorporated within Ken Livingstone's vision. They include the identification of water spaces as natural resources with important ecological functions that require protection and enhancement. Implementing the Blue Ribbon Network therefore involves 'resisting development that results in a net loss of biodiversity' and 'designing new waterside developments in ways that increase habitat value' (GLA, 2004a: 197). They identify bodies of water as key open spaces, alongside parks and green spaces, vital for urban liveability and flood defence. The mayor included an urban design strategy within the programme where London's planning authorities were instructed to 'seek a high quality of design for all waterside development' and ensure that all developments 'integrate successfully with the water space in terms of use, appearance and physical impact' (GLA, 2004a: 209). Mirroring the national government's emphasis on 'good' urban design, the policy also emphasises mixed usage, the creation of accessible and inviting public spaces along the river, and appropriate building scales.

Collectively, these objectives formed an important part of the mayor's sustainable growth programme. In order to achieve sustainable growth, the

10.2

**The Blue Ribbon
Network Principles
Source: GLA, 2004a:
193–4**

To accommodate London's growth within its boundaries without encroaching on green spaces, policies should make the most sustainable and efficient use of space in London, by protecting and enhancing the multi-functional nature of the Blue Ribbon Network so that it enables and supports those uses and activities that require a water or waterside location.

To make London a better city for people to live in, policies should protect and enhance the Blue Ribbon Network as part of the public realm contributing to London's open space network. Opportunities for sport, leisure and education should be promoted. The Blue Ribbon Network should be safe and healthy and offer a mixture of vibrant and calm places.

To make London a more prosperous city with strong and diverse economic growth, policies should exploit the potential for water-borne transport, leisure, tourism and waterway support industries. The attractiveness of the Blue Ribbon Network for investment should be captured by appropriate waterside development and regeneration. This will include the restoration of the network and creation of new links.

To promote social inclusion and tackle deprivation and discrimination, policies should ensure that the Blue Ribbon Network is accessible for everyone as part of London's public realm and that its cultural and environmental assets are used to stimulate appropriate development in areas of regeneration and need.

To improve London's accessibility, use of the Blue Ribbon Network for water-borne transport of people and goods (including waste and aggregates) should be increased. Alongside the Blue Ribbon Network there are also opportunities for pedestrian and cycling routes.

To make London a more attractive, well-designed and green city, policies should protect and enhance the biodiversity and landscape value of the Blue Ribbon Network. The network should also be respected as the location of a rich variety of heritage that contributes to the vitality and distinctiveness of many parts of London. London must also have reliable and sustainable supplies of water and methods of sewage disposal and a precautionary approach must be taken to the risks created by global warming and the potential for flooding.

mayor identified twenty-eight Opportunity Areas. These are defined as areas of under-utilisation, deprivation and strategic importance, and

> have been identified on the basis that they are capable of accommo-
> dating substantial new jobs or homes and their potential should be
> maximised. Typically, each can accommodate at least 5,000 jobs or
> 2,500 homes or a mix of the two, together with appropriate provision of
> other uses such as local shops, leisure facilities and schools. These areas
> generally include major brownfield sites with capacity for new develop-
> ment and places with potential for significant increases in density.
>
> (GLA, 2004a: 41)

Riverside sites account for twenty-two of the total twenty-eight Opportunity Areas, demonstrating the amount of development earmarked for London's riverside, and the important riverside development will play in achieving the *London Plan's* primary objectives.

Mirroring the national government's policies, the mayor's objectives of sustainable growth and design-led regeneration were paired with social policies framed in terms of social exclusion/inclusion (Powell, 2000). In the fourth Blue Ribbon Network Principle, the mayor identified an accessible, regenerated and enriched waterfront as an important element in the effort to 'promote social inclusion and tackle deprivation and discrimination' (GLA, 2004a: 194). Through a combination of directing urban development to Opportunity Areas, well-designed spaces and enriched waterfront environments, the mayor saw the Blue Ribbon Network as an important tool in dealing with London's social problems. Although these objectives are praiseworthy, they do stop short of providing direct benefits – excluding limited affordable housing – to London's socially excluded residents. The Blue Ribbon Network proposals therefore continue with programmes that foresee indirect benefits – such as those provided through localised economic growth, planning gains and improved urban environments – as the principal means of alleviating social exclusion.

This may reflect the fact that the mayor's most powerful redistributive tool continues to be his ability to negotiate planning gains beyond those recommended by central government (McNeill, 2002b). Livingstone's goal, at the time, of 35 per cent affordable housing for all new developments exceeded the national government figure of 25 per cent (on leaving office Livingstone's 'strategic' target was 50 per cent affordable housing). As such, given his limited fiscal powers, the promotion of continued economic growth and urban development alongside the increased numbers of affordable housing units offered Livingstone one of the few means of providing direct benefits to London's poorest residents. Taking into account the amount of development earmarked for waterfront spaces in Opportunity Areas, the riverside will therefore be central in any future attempts to combat social exclusion.

This intent is evident in the *London Plan* where the mayor set out his ambition to see the city's waterfronts developed for all Londoners, not just the city's growing legion of high-earners:

> The Blue Ribbon Network should not continue to be developed as a private resource or backdrop, which only privileged people can afford to be near to or enjoy. It provides many different opportunities for enjoyment, some actively involving the water and others simply benefiting from the calm and reflective feeling of being near water. Both active and passive activities can contribute towards improving the health of Londoners.
>
> (GLA, 2004a: 207)

This commitment to stop the Blue Ribbon Network becoming purely the preserve of the wealthy came after the London Assembly, the body elected to oversee the mayor, published a report entitled *Access to the Thames: Scrutiny of the Thames Foreshore and Path* (London Assembly, 2003). In this, they heavily criticised the exclusive forms of urban development that had continued to take place since 2000. In particular, the committee was alarmed at the manner and pace with which developers have privatised waterfront spaces and limited access to Thames-side pathways:

> The Committee is concerned that the Thames is being barricaded from the rest of London by riverside developments that fail to consider how they relate to the river and its immediate hinterland. New riverside developments do normally make provision for a riverside path but such provision is compromised if the path is only a part of a river frontage made up of identikit apartment blocks.
>
> (GLA, 2004a: 1)

The committee urged Livingstone to ensure all future riverside developments make adequate riverside access provisions in order to have the riverside become a space that all Londoners can enjoy.

Recently, riverside redevelopment has therefore taken place under an ambitious urban policy vision that sees the city's waterways and waterfronts becoming integral to Londoners' lives, and a significant part of the effort to maintain economic growth and reduce social exclusion. The remainder of this chapter critically examines some of the redevelopment that has taken place. It analyses the urban spaces created by riverside residential developments and finds the benefits of reduced spatial segregation have been mitigated by an excluding architecture. Following this, interviews with riverside residents are used to show how those living in new residential developments have largely failed to become incorporated into local communities, therefore posing questions over the ability of current policies to bring Londoners 'together' and provide social benefits beyond those received by the few lucky enough to access affordable housing.

The Blue Ribbon Network realised?

This section draws upon research conducted in three riverside neighbourhoods – Wandsworth (south-west London), Brentford (west London) and Thamesmead West (south-east London) – situated across London (see figure 10.3). Each of them has experienced a significant amount of redevelopment over the past ten years. In Wandsworth, a number of riverside sites, including a derelict gas works, flour mill and power station, have been remediated and redeveloped into prime residential space. A similar story of redevelopment has occurred in Brentford, where a large gas works and dock facilities have been replaced by a string of apartment complexes. Over in south-east London, a vast swath of riverside land once used as a naval arsenal is being transformed into a residential and commercial space. This has involved both the renovation of old arms-storage houses and the construction of new residential apartments. Corporate real-estate developers along the Thames have built all the new residential spaces that have replaced brownfield and industrial facilities. These spaces have all taken the form of high-density, multi-storey apartment complexes. Whilst each of the neighbourhoods has witnessed multiple residential developments, this study selected one particular development from each: 517-unit Riverside West (Berkeley Homes plc.) in Wandsworth, 234-unit Capital West (Barratt Homes plc.) in Brentford, and 414-unit Royal Artillery Quays (Barratt Homes plc.) in Thamesmead West (see figure 10.4).

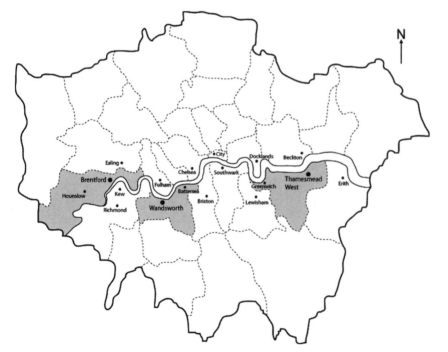

10.3
Location of study sites in the context of London.
Source: Mark Davidson, 2008

10.4
Images of the Thames-side Developments Studied.
From top clockwise:
Riverside West (Wandsworth), Royal Artillery Quays (Thamesmead West) and Capital West (Brentford).
Source: Mark Davidson, 2008

Riverside development

Corporate developers, such as Berkeley Homes plc., St George plc. and Barratt Homes plc, have been central to the riverside's reinvention for a number of reasons. The scale of ex-industrial brownfield sites along the riverside and the amount of remediation often needed to make these spaces safe for inhabitation requires significant capital expenditures and an expertise in large project construction which only they possess. In addition, since national and metropolitan urban policy requires compact, high-density development, the amount of housing earmarked for riverside sites naturally positions them towards those capable of constructing large apartment complexes. Finally, corporate developers have been almost completely responsible for recent riverside development because prospective investment returns mean demand for sites is high, and as a result, these actors use their capital resources to outbid smaller actors.

At both Capital West (Brentford) and Royal Artillery Quays (Thamesmead West), affordable housing has been provided. Riverside West (Wandsworth) does not contain any affordable housing due to initial planning permission being granted before legislation became enacted and a local authority resistant to any form of social housing (Dowding *et al.*, 1999), and a series of subsequent planning decisions that have seen Riverside West expand without affordable housing being made required. In Capital West, 27 per cent of all housing units (sixty-four) are affordable, whilst at Royal Artillery Quays 21 per cent of the development (eighty-two units) is affordable. However, the social composition of affordable units varies between the developments. The Department for Environment, Transport and the Regions defined affordable housing as: 'both low cost market housing, and subsidised housing (irrespective of tenure, ownership or financial arrangements) that will be available to people who cannot afford to occupy houses generally available on the local market' (DETR, 1998b).

This definition has allowed a significant amount of flexibility over what comprises affordable housing (Pawson and Kintrea, 2002), and who is eligible for it, something that was highlighted as a problem in the ODPM's review of affordable housing provision in the South East of England (ODPM, 2003b) because it allows local governments to excessively manipulate the urban renaissance vision (DETR, 1999) of socially mixed neighbourhood communities. At Capital West, eligibility for affordable housing has been limited to key workers and social housing applicants, and therefore is mainly inhabited by public sector workers and extremely low-income groups. In contrast, Moat Housing, the housing association responsible for affordable housing at Royal Artillery Quays, has been given an 'open' eligibility criteria from Greenwich Borough Council. This has meant a wide array of income groups have been granted access to affordable housing under shared ownership agreements.

Despite affordable housing requirements, recent redevelopment has had an overwhelming upgrading effect on the social composition of the riverside, gentrifying much of the waterfront (Davidson and Lees, 2005). Using survey data collected in the three study areas, together with occupational data from the 2001 census,[1] the total upgrading effect of riverside development can be estimated. In Brentford, Capital West alone has increased the ward's population of managers and senior officials by 20 per cent and professionals by 15 per cent. Presuming other newly built riverside developments in Brentford (e.g. Ferry Quays/Brentford Lock/The Island) have similar occupational profiles, riverside development will have increased the ward's population of managers and senior officials by 70 per cent and professionals by 52 per cent. In the Wandsworth borough ward of Fairfield, Riverside West has increased the population of managers and senior officials by 13 per cent and professionals by 27 per cent. Once completely inhabited, the neighbouring development Battersea Reach will increase these figures to 24 per cent and 50 per cent respectively. Finally, in the Glyndon ward of Greenwich, Royal Artillery Quays has increased the population of professionals by 59 per cent and associate and technical professionals by 12 per cent. When completed, the neighbouring 1,223-unit Royal Arsenal development will likely increase this upgrading threefold.

This movement of middle-class people into working-class neighbourhoods, such as Brentford and Thamesmead West, has certainly brought some of London's different social groups into closer proximity. Yet, whilst affordable housing provisions have addressed the needs of some, it is unclear whether the redevelopment has accrued further benefits, reduced social exclusion, or created the kinds of urban spaces and inclusive communities envisaged in the Blue Ribbon Network. In the following sections, two elements of riverside redevelopment relevant to these queries will be examined: (i) the types of urban spaces created, and (ii) the types of communities that are developing. These two elements are focused upon not only due to their significance in national and metropolitan policy agendas, but also because the creation of inclusive spaces and communities is pivotal to the avoidance of displacement due to gentrification along the riverside. If riverside redevelopment simply achieves the gentrification of the riverside without any significant benefits for the existing resident low-income communities, the Blue Ribbon Network may become an unfulfilled policy vision which, at best fails to address London's social inequity and exclusion, and, at worst exacerbates pressing social problems through imposing the unjust negative consequences of gentrification (see Lees *et al.*, 2008) upon the very same communities targeted by social inclusion programmes.

The physical transformation of the riverside

> They can play tennis on the all weather court, relax in the sauna and order theatre tickets, limousines and even maids through the porter's lodge. Best of all, they don't have to share any of these luxuries with their neighbours: a security barrier at the entrance to the grounds ensures that the hoi polloi in the council estates across the road will stay where they belong. This is, in other words, the antithesis of the development the government's Urban Task Force wants to promote.
>
> (Monbiot, 1999)

The journalist George Monbiot, describing the Richard Rogers-designed Montevetro riverside development in Battersea, south-west London, provides an account of the types of urban spaces that have been constructed along the Thames, and indeed the stark contrast between them and the urban policy objectives of national government. It raises the question of how the façade of renewal generated by riverside redevelopment and the attraction of capital-rich groups to working class neighbourhoods may *not* result in new forms of community and reduced social exclusion. This section examines the architectures employed at recently constructed riverside developments to show how this has stifled the ability of affordable housing legislation to do anything beyond serving the immediate housing needs of those granted access to it. It argues that if the Blue Ribbon Network programme is to use the development opportunities along the riverside to either create attractive and accessible public spaces and/or help reduce inequities and poverty, current approaches have to be changed.

Gated communities have become a particularly symbolic part of the post-industrial urban landscape (Low, 2003). They are continually criticised by community activists for having damaging social effects and contributing to the introversion of urban life. Yet, at the same time, demand for them appears unabated as developers continue to incorporate all manner of security features into developments. London's riverside is no exception to this. Although current

planning legislation controls against the most extreme forms of gated developments seen elsewhere (Álvarez-Rivadulla, 2007), segregating architectural
designs and security technologies are constant features along the riverside. The
result is segregation between those living in privately owned, market housing in
riverside developments and both affordable housing residents and surrounding
neighbourhood residents.

At Capital West, the separation of affordable housing from privately
owned housing is stark and has contributed to class-based divisions within the
development. Affordable housing has been provided in the form of a stand-alone
apartment block of sixty-four units on a site close to the riverside. It stands just
ten metres from market apartment blocks, yet interviews with affordable housing
residents show they feel almost completely segregated from the community
opposite. One reason consistently referred to by affordable housing residents
was the physical segregation within the development. The most visible symbol of
this segregation is an eight-foot steel fence and gate that encloses the market
housing, separating it both from the surrounding neighbourhood and the block of
affordable housing adjacent (see figure 10.5). This dividing mechanism is accompanied by a speakerphone security system, an onsite security patrol, numerous
warning signs, private fenced garden spaces, and CCTV cameras.

An affordable housing resident at Capital West explained how the
fencing and gates within the development had the effect of dividing space and
consequently communities:

> I just tend to drive in and come up to the flat . . . I mean, why would I
> go through the front gates? You can't walk through or anything and I
> don't feel like it is my space. I guess I just never run into anyone over
> there, so I never end up having a chat . . . It is the opposite of what it
> is like in these flats. I have gotten to know people going up and down
> in the lifts.

Whilst residents of the privately owned housing were not unsurprisingly less critical of the security features at Capital West given their housing choice, interviews
did reveal mixed feelings over them. In particular, the use of gates and restricted
entry systems were viewed with ambiguity by some:

> I have mixed feelings about the security features onsite. I like the
> speakers, patrol and gates because I know my girlfriend is more safe,
> but I also think it is not very good socially. You know, it separates out
> people and definitely produces a 'them and us' feeling.

The reference made here to 'them and us' was a distinction also fostered by
the onsite facilities offered only to residents of the privately owned housing in
Capital West. This situation was repeated in all developments. The most
common of these facilities was the fitness centre, but they also included life-

style management services, dry cleaning services, crèches and beauticians. The affordable housing residents interviewed consistently talked about not being able to access these facilities and they were critical of the ways in which onsite concierge/security guards policed entry to them.

The public spaces constructed in and around the riverside developments have also caused segregation between the new developments and surrounding communities. In direct contrast to the Blue Ribbon Network vision, riverside developers have tended not to provide the kinds of spaces along the riverside which either contribute to the city's stock of public spaces or provide somewhere people want to visit. At Capital West, the immediate area surrounding the apartment complex is gated, and therefore the direct contribution to public space is negligible. However, as part of Section 106 planning gain, the developer Barratt Homes plc was required to contribute to the renovation of a public park on the neighbouring riverside. Although interviews in the community suggested usage of the area is limited by fear of crime, this development has therefore contributed to a marginal improvement, if not addition, to riverside public space. At the other two developments, contributions to the Blue Ribbon Network spatial vision are less tangible.

Riverside West consists of four large apartment complexes that face onto the Thames. Access to the development is not restricted by large gates and fencing as at Capital West. Indeed, people are free to walk into the development's public spaces without hindrance. However, architectural design and security features severely restrict Riverside West's contribution to the Blue Ribbon Network. Access to the development, and as a result the riverside, involves bypassing a security guard office at the main entrance area or using uninviting narrow alleyways (figure 10.5) that lack footpaths. Highly visible CCTV cameras positioned around these areas ensure a panoptican effect and give the riverside space in front of apartment buildings a distinctly private character, something furthered by the fact there has been no pedestrian throughway provided along the riverside. At Royal Artillery Quays, explicit types replace subtle forms of exclusionary architecture. Here, steel gates are used to completely restrict access to the riverside spaces in front of the development (figure 10.5). Paired with more CCTV cameras and security patrols, this development is an archetypal gated community.

The most explicit example of architectural segregation observed occurred in Brentford, where a developer had gone to significant lengths to separate privately owned properties from affordable housing and public spaces. The developer acquired derelict docks abutting the Grand Union Canal where it meets the Thames. As with all new developments at the time approximately 25 per cent of the units were required to be 'affordable' (that central government figure, with many caveats, is now 40 per cent, for example, 2006 PPS3 Housing Green Paper), and therefore it promised a mixed community. Yet, the developer sub-contracted some site construction, notably including affordable housing provisions, to another developer and reserved a small section of land for its own development.

10.5
Gated Architectures along the Thames.
From top right clockwise: Security gates separating housing tenures at Capital West; Eastern alleyway entrance to Riverside West; locked gates restricting access to riverside areas at Royal Artillery Quays; and the Grand Union Canal dividing 'The Island' development from the sub-contracted affordable housing development.
Source: Mark Davidson, 2008

The site they chose was a former-dock area that is separated by the Grand Union Canal from the rest of the purchased land and the wider neighbourhood (see figure 10.5). The effect of this has been to completely segregate the central development from affordable housing and the adjacent communities. It therefore negates any benefits that might have been accrued from incorporating a range of tenure types within the same development. Indeed, the developer marketed its exclusive collection of private housing as 'The Island'!

Riverside development has therefore segregated tenure types and produced riverside spaces that rarely bring the Thames into London's collection of open spaces. Developers have sought to colonise and privatise the riverside, and therefore have not contributed to Livingstone's Blue Ribbon Network vision. They have also built a collection of gated communities to ease concerns over the suitability of some working-class riverside neighbourhoods for the market of young professionals they have targeted with one- and two-bedroom apartments. Yet despite this, recent riverside development has undoubtedly brought different social classes together in close spatial proximity. It is therefore important to examine the types of neighbourhood communities that are beginning to form along the Thames and consider whether the social inclusion agendas of both national and metropolitan governments are being served by these recent urban changes.

Mixing between communities: is the neighbourhood vision being realised?

The promise of Opportunity Areas and socially mixed neighbourhoods lies in the prospect that targeted redevelopment and reduced spatial segregation might allow greater numbers of Londoners to share in the benefits of London's economic growth. Riverside development has certainly changed class propinquity in London, bringing a number of social groups together along the Thames. It can therefore be claimed that recent Thames-side development is achieving Richard Rogers' vision of 'bringing London's communities together' and helping bring about growth in the mayor's Opportunity Areas. However, if current policies are to significantly reduce social exclusion, these developments should be generating a host of indirect benefits, such as employment opportunities, better jobs, reinvestment in public services and neighbourhood improvements. If socially excluded groups are to 'receive' these benefits, then the class divisions that generate exclusion will have to be reduced. This may take the form of, for example, expanded social networks that grant better access to economic opportunities or re-balanced and politically empowered neighbourhood communities. Yet, if class divisions remain and the benefits of reduced spatial segregation and local development are not spread to low-income groups, then the riverside will likely only feature spatially juxtaposed, 'socially tectonic' (Butler and Robson, 2003) communities.

In the three case study areas, a series of interviews with residents of both riverside developments and the surrounding communities revealed that in both Brentford and Thamesmead West riverside development had resulted in almost no social mixing between new and existing residents. Wandsworth had a slightly different pattern of social interaction, with some neighbourhood residents having developed relationships with those Riverside West residents who had become users of neighbourhood amenities. However, this interaction had not taken place across class lines and had been focused in a small section of gentrified space within the surrounding neighbourhood. The riverside developments have not led to the formation of a socially mixed community. Rather, the life-worlds of many new residents simply bear little relation to those in the surrounding areas. The differing perception of the utility of the local neighbourhood between these two groups was a striking example of this.

The privately owned housing residents within the new riverside developments did not see the local area as offering appropriate or desirable retail, public, social and leisure facilities. Instead, they often gravitated towards central London and beyond the city. This meant most residents of Capital West and Royal Artillery Quays had very little knowledge of their surrounding neighbourhood beyond occasionally using convenience shops and restaurants. In developments where these amenities had been provided onsite, such as at Riverside West, residents barely used local shops and restaurants at all. This provided a curious example of where the mixed-usage planning agendas of national and metropolitan governments were serving to mitigate their social policy goals, since the commercial premises within the development were removing the requirement of new residents to use neighbourhood facilities, therefore reducing neighbourhood-based social interactions.

Riverside West was the exception to this scene of mismatched lifeworlds. Here, some residents had become incorporated into the Wandsworth area, albeit within a small geographical space. A collection of Victorian housing, known locally as The Tonsley's, had undergone significant gentrification over the past twenty years and as a result has developed a strip of high-end retail services. These were frequented by both neighbourhood and Riverside West residents, representing a point of social and spatial confluence. This led to both social relations developing between the two communities and feelings of separation being much less than in the other study areas. Indeed, it was possible to identify a shared sense of place between these two groups, especially so when they both made reference to the wider Wandsworth area, which both thought largely rundown and unsuitable for their needs. But this hardly represents a success for urban policy – the Blue Ribbon Network achieved – given these neighbouring gentrifiers are not forming a socially mixed community; rather, newly arrived gentrifiers in riverside developments are maintaining and enhancing processes of gentrification which will continue to erode the area's social diversity.

Interview data suggested a number of reasons as to why spatial proximity has not led to new neighbourhood communities. Although all of these reasons cannot be covered here (see Davidson, 2008) it is important to briefly note a major point of distinction between the two counterpoised communities. The pre-existing neighbourhood residents explained that their common points of interactions, such as local schools, public amenities and public spaces, had not become frequented by the new residents. Although interviews with some development residents refuted assertions of a complete disregard for such local affairs, many did have limited local interests. Most of the interviewees living in the private units in riverside developments did not have children, were single or couples aged twenty-five to thirty-five, and worked in professional jobs outside of the immediate area. They spent much of their leisure time socialising in central London or outside London, and expected to have relatively short-term residency within the development (three to five years). The consequence of this was a dramatically different perception about the utility of the local neighbourhood between development and neighbourhood residents. For many residents of the surrounding neighbourhood, their lives were intricately bound with local spaces. Their children used local schools; they bought at local shops; they ate at local restaurants; some were involved in local politics. This is not to say that they only had local social networks; they also had many other diffuse associations. Rather, it is the distinct absence of local associations for many of the development residents that distinguished the two populations. The life-stages and lifestyles of new riverside residents therefore meant that they had no reason to form relationships within the wider neighbourhood.

However, the type of built environment constructed along the Thames also contributed in large measure to the creation of these 'social tectonics' (Butler and Robson, 2003). The vast majority of new housing units along the Thames are luxury one- and two-bedroom flats. This has meant that riverside developments have been particularly attractive to a demographic that tends not to look towards neighbourhood-based resources. For example, development residents would often make reference to the impetus that having children might have in encouraging them to be more interested and concerned with local affairs and to use local amenities. Yet their current residencies are perceived to be highly unsuitable for children:

> I don't think you could have kids here [Riverside West]. I mean, I could not see us have them here. You need a garden and that stuff . . . We rent here. Probably will for a year or so yet, but once we decide to have kids, we will have to move . . . Knowing you are likely to shift somewhere does mean you're less concerned with the area. Some people are, but local issues . . . are not really worth the bother.

The distinctive building type (one to two bed apartment complexes) along the Thames has therefore contributed to the juxtaposed lifeworlds described above.

Conclusions

The research conducted in these three Thames-side neighbourhoods has shown that the inclusive spaces and society envisaged in the Blue Ribbon Network policy are not being realised. This stated, it is important to insert two caveats. First, the Blue Ribbon Network vision embodies a whole set of other objectives, such as biodiversity protection and transit development, which are being implemented independently of the developments examined here. The criticisms here are therefore not a condemnation of the entire programme. Second, it should be recognised that the research presented here can only offer a snapshot of these new developments. Most riverside developments have only been inhabited for around five to ten years, and the types of redevelopment, indirect social benefits and communities envisioned in policy documents will almost certainly take longer to develop. In this concluding section, I therefore want to offer some thoughts on the future prospects for London's riverside.

The redevelopment of brownfield riverside space into desirable residential space has certainly brought new life to areas of blight along the Thames. In addition, an influx of affluent residents to riverside neighbourhoods also offers a boost for local economies. For some riverside communities, the long-term effects of riverside renaissance may be positive, even if they do not substantially readdress social inequities. However, the influx of high earners and capital reinvestment to previously working-class neighbourhoods carries with it a significant threat of gentrification and subsequently displacement. There are already signs of this occurring as the social composition of riverside areas has become progressively more middle class over the past fifteen years (see Davidson and Lees, 2005). With the exception of Thamesmead West, where Royal Artillery Quays was surrounded by aesthetically unpleasing social housing, many development residents stated they had become more open to the idea of moving into the local neighbourhood as their lifestage changed. Indeed, many owner-occupiers stated an important consideration for buying their apartment was the fact they, and others, considered the riverside neighbourhood 'up-and-coming'. This is certainly an idea embraced by real-estate agents. Brentford is in the process of being re-branded 'Brentford-upon-Thames', mimicking nearby bourgeois Kingston-upon-Thames. Wandsworth's infamous downtown shopping centre has also been subject to re-branding and tenancy by the upmarket grocery store Waitrose, providing a stark juxtaposition with neighbouring discount retailers.

If gentrification continues along the Thames, then many low-income residents are likely to experience greater and greater displacement pressures as housing costs rise, friends and neighbours disperse, local shops reorient to new clients and local politics shift. Of course, all of this relies upon the continuation of class disparities that exist along the Thames-side. Gentrification, and consequential (indirect) displacement, could be halted or mitigated if the class-based differences that drive these processes are reduced. If socially excluded and low-income groups do receive benefits from current policy initiatives – such as better paid and more secure jobs, and political empowerment – then they will be better able to absorb rising housing costs, support their preferred commercial facilities and control political change. The onus is therefore upon the social inclusion agenda enshrined in the Greater London Plan. If detrimental changes are not to occur and the Blue Ribbon Network is not to become the reserve of London's bourgeois professionals, the GLA must adequately address London's growing social inequities.

Since the GLA's urban policy programmes are largely reliant upon the indirect benefits of economic growth – the same type of economic growth that has significantly contributed to current problems (see Harvey, 2005) – this issue will be a difficult one to deal with. Beyond affordable housing provision, metropolitan urban policy has not attempted to make direct interventions to reduce social exclusion. This is reflected along the Thames. Redevelopment and growth has been generated in many riverside neighbourhoods, yet this shows few signs of alleviating social exclusion or providing benefits for marginalised groups. Furthermore, the widespread gentrification that has resulted along the Thames may deepen social exclusion. If the Blue Ribbon Network is therefore to become a space which unites London's communities, plays a part in addressing the city's disgraceful social inequities and develops into an attractive public space, then a significantly greater commitment to dealing with the causes of social exclusion has to be made. Surely then, London would truly be able to claim itself to be an exemplary 'sustainable world city'.

Note

1   The main occupational categories used in the UK census are: managers and senior officials, professional, associate professional and technical, administrative and secretarial, skilled trades, personal service, sales and customer service, process, plant and machine, and elementary.

Chapter 11

The promotion of London as a 'walkable city' and overlapping walks of life

Jennie Middleton

Introduction

On 26 April 2007 a group of early morning London commuters dressed up in Dolly Parton wigs and walked over London Bridge to City Hall. This 'Walking 9–5' message was part of the official launch of the 'Walking Works' campaign, a three-year Transport for London (TfL) funded initiative being run by Living Streets (formerly known as the Pedestrian Association) with the aim of promoting the benefits of walking to Londoners. This Greater London Authority (GLA) backed campaign formed a part of Ken Livingstone's strategy to make London 'one of the world's most walking friendly cities by 2015' (TfL, 2004: 4). In conjunction with this walking strategy for the capital, TfL has produced several documents including *The Walking Plan for London* (TfL, 2004) and *Improving Walkability* (TfL, 2005), within which walking is promoted as providing a range of benefits that include reducing traffic congestion and pollution, encouraging people to exercise, boosting the local economy, and promoting social interaction. However, despite this increasing policy interest in walking, there is in fact 'almost no reliable local data' on pedestrian movement, particularly in terms of the social outcomes of moving on foot (Select Committee on ETRA, 2001). For as Kellerman (2006: 90) observes: 'it has been questionable, whether walking on the street, being directly exposed to fellow walkers, encourages or discourages any kind of social contact'.

This chapter begins by discussing the role of walking in London's regeneration strategies, particularly in terms of the 'social benefits' of walking as cited in pedestrian policy documents. It is argued that terms such as 'social mixing', 'community cohesion' and 'social interaction' are rarely unpacked so it is unclear as to what they actually mean, or the specific role walking has in facilitating them. The chapter moves on to examine these 'social benefits' in light of empirical data collected in inner London in 2005/6. The local data reveals how walking does not facilitate social interactions and exchanges in straightforward ways. Acknowledging debates that assert there is an over-privileging of face-to-face interaction in constructions of 'community', the chapter illustrates the significance of walking in maintaining existing social relations as opposed to creating new ones (see Young, 1990; Larsen *et al.*, 2006). The chapter concludes by discussing the implications of these findings in relation to the promotion of walking for engendering social mixing in London.

Research context

The research being discussed here formed part of an ESRC-CASE funded project on urban walking in London (see Middleton, 2008). As stated above, despite a growing policy and public interest in walking, to date there has been very little in-depth research on pedestrian movement in the policy arena. Existing studies and research on walking are primarily characterised by the collection of statistical data such as travel surveys, pedestrian counts or local pedestrian audits (see DfT, 2005, 2006; TfL, 2007a). There is a wider, theoretical, literature relating to urban walking, yet this is characterised by a lack of any systematic empirical exploration of the actual practice of walking (see Amin and Thrift, 2002; Benjamin, 1983; de Certeau, 1984; Rossiter and Gibson, 2003). As such, an overall aim of this chapter is to contribute to the current lack of research on walking in both the policy and academic arenas. The research reported here had three principal aims; first, to explore the relationship between walking and the built environment; second, to examine the different types, forms and characters of walking; and, finally, to engage with the social dimensions of urban pedestrian movements.

These research aims were interrogated across a transect that runs through the inner London boroughs of Islington and Hackney. The transect started with Barnsbury in the west moving eastwards through Canonbury, De Beauvoir Town and then London Fields (see figures 11.1 and 11.2). Part of the rationale for selecting this transect was due to the variation it displayed in terms of the built environment, access to public transport, and social factors such as levels of wealth and social deprivation. This variation was required so as issues could be explored concerning what walking means to different groups of people and, more specifically, its role in facilitating social interaction. The study drew upon a mixed-method approach, including a postal survey, experiential walking photo diaries, and in-depth interviews. A total of 1,000 postal surveys were sent out across the transect using a stratified random sampling framework, with a response rate of 21.1 per cent

The rationale for using a postal survey was threefold. First, the survey was used to obtain a broad picture of the walking patterns of residents across the transect, particularly in terms of travel choices or difficulties, and the significance of different dimensions of the built environment as they moved on foot. Second, it provided information on the social characteristics of residents such as age, gender and ethnicity that enabled the potential relationships between these

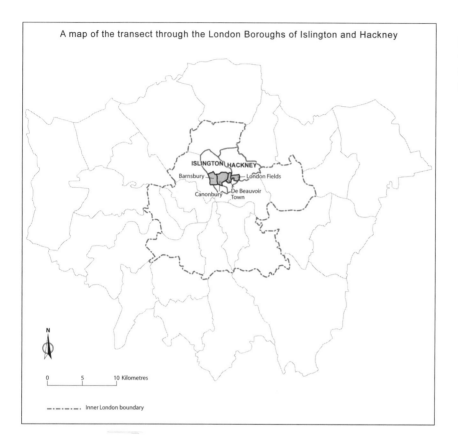

11.1
Map of research areas within Greater London. Source: J. Middleton, 2008

11.2
Images of transect through the inner London boroughs of Islington and Hackney. (*From top right clockwise*: Barnsbury (Islington), Canonbury (Islington), London Fields (Hackney) and De Beauvoir Town (Hackney) (source: study participants)

independent variables, and where, why and when people walked to be explored. However, despite ensuring the sample of postal survey addresses was randomly selected, it was notable that a high proportion of respondents were in 'professional' occupations. A similar situation emerged with respect to the ethnic mix of respondents. Ninety per cent of respondents classified themselves as 'White British', 'White Irish' or 'Other White Group' and only 9 per cent responded across all other ethnic groups. Although this meant that the social variations across the transect could not be explicitly explored in terms of potential issues associated with pedestrian movement, levels of wealth, social deprivation or ethnicity, it did not mean that the social dimensions of walking could not be addressed throughout the research, as this chapter will subsequently reveal.

Third, the postal survey served as a tool for recruiting participants for twenty walking photo diaries and forty in-depth interviews. The purpose of both of these methods was to explore in greater detail participants' spatio-temporal, embodied and social experiences of moving on foot. The diary task involved participants providing details of their individual walking patterns by noting down the date, time, how long and where they walked, for one consecutive week. In other words, they spatialised their experience of time whilst on foot by producing personalised time-space budgets in the diaries. It was then up to the individual what else they recorded but some things were suggested including: why were they walking, was it choice or necessity; what was it like where they were walking and how did they feel; who were they walking with or who did they encounter whilst walking; and how were they walking?

Each diary participant was given a disposable camera to take photographs of anything that struck him or her as significant or interesting. These were then used as a discussion prompt in the follow-up interviews, a method referred to by Zimmerman and Wieder (1977) as the 'diary, diary-interview method'. Of the forty interviews conducted across the transect, twenty were follow-up diary interviews and twenty were stand-alone interviews. The overall aim of the interviews was to engage with all three of the principal research objectives. However, more specifically, they enabled access to more in-depth detailed data on issues raised in the postal survey, provided an opportunity for further issues associated with walking to emerge, and were used as a means to discuss specific details with respect to the completed walking photo diaries. The data generated from these research methods demonstrated that in order to understand fully the complexity and multiplicity of pedestrian movement, it is necessary to engage with walking as an everyday urban practice in the context of its relational dimensions.

Pedestrian policy in London

Since the early 1990s there has been a general shift nationally to re-orientate transport plans from private to more sustainable modes of transport such as walking and cycling (see DETR, 1998a, 2000a; DfT, 1996). These modes of sustainable transport are an integral part of the current government's plans in promoting an urban renaissance. The Urban Task Force (UTF), established by the then Deputy Prime Minister John Prescott, to identify causes and make recommendations to reverse urban decline, advised that:

> One of the best ways to attract and absorb more people into urban areas is to reduce the need for car travel. This requires policies that discriminate in favour of walking, cycling and public transport . . . We want to see further encouragement for walking by reclaiming space for pedestrians and encouraging street facilities that make walking attractive.
>
> (DETR, 1999: 9)

The government's formal response to the UTF report, and the subsequent Urban White Paper (UWP) *Our Towns and Cities* (DETR, 2000b), echoes these recommendations as it proposes 'better integration of transport and planning policies so that jobs, services and other facilities will be more accessible to public transport, cycling and walking' (DETR, 2000b: 45). These recommendations are mirrored in London policy documents, particularly in terms of the role of walking in the capital's wider regeneration strategy. For example, The *Mayor's Transport Strategy* (GLA, 2001b: 61) proposes to make 'London a prosperous city by: supporting sustainable economic growth by tackling congestion and unreliability, providing improved access by public transport, walking and cycling'. In addition, the Central London Partnership (2001) outline in their *Walking Strategy for Central London* what they consider to be the principal benefits of moving on foot. These include it being a healthy and sustainable mode of transport that benefits 'the community' and is 'good' for 'business'.

In 2004 a series of policy documents were published that coincided with the launch of the first national *Walking and Cycling Action Plan* (DfT, 2004) and firmly positioned walking as a mode of transport considered 'crucial for urban regeneration and economic vitality' in London (Transport 2000, 2003: 3). In addition to studies commissioned by the Central London Partnership on both public space (Gehl Architects, 2004) and pedestrian accessibility (Intelligent Space, 2004) in central London, the GLA produced the *London Plan* and TfL launched *The Walking Plan for London*. As other chapters in this volume highlight, the London Plan was the culmination of several draft documents concerning a 'Spatial Development Strategy for Greater London' (GLA, 2001a, 2002b, 2004a). Promoting sustainable development is one of the key goals of the plan, with part of that remit being the promotion of sustainable transport by 'ensuring that development occurs in locations that are currently, or are planned to be, accessible by public transport, walking and cycling' (GLA, 2004a: 38). A whole range of points are set out for 'improving conditions for walking' that include improving pedestrian access to new developments, promoting six strategic walking routes, and taking 'account of measures set out in the TfL Walking Plan for London' (GLA, 2004a:

123). Yet how did the *Walking Plan for London* evolve and what measures does it deem appropriate for the promotion of pedestrian activity in the capital?

The London walking plan was a product of Ken Livingstone's 'vision' to make London one of the world's most walking friendly cities by 2015. The plan details the benefits of, and potential barriers to, walking. Its stated aim is to encourage walking and in so doing provide benefits which include 'a greater use of public transport; a better environment; social inclusion; healthier lifestyles; an improved economy' (TfL, 2004: 15). Deterrents to walking which were identified in the development of the plan include 'institutional issues; traffic volume; air quality; the walking environment; safety; security; information; mobility and access' (TfL, 2004: 20). The document moves on to set out a six-point action plan 'to improve conditions for pedestrians and encourage people to walk more' (GLA, 2004a: 4) thus addressing these issues. The *London Walking Plan* stems from a consultation draft that was published by TfL in January 2003. The consultation draft was generally very well received, with Living Streets (2003) producing a comprehensive set of complimentary comments.

They stated that Transport for London (2004: 1) 'have treated the subject [walking] with a seriousness seldom seen before from policy-makers' and are 'showing the way on the delivery of the urban renaissance agenda and the implementation of the Prime Minister's liveability agenda'. They went on to highlight how 'the plan makes a strong case for the needs to both promote walking and improve the walking environment' and represents 'the first attempt at combining both a strategic approach and an action plan for meeting this vision' (TfL, 2004: 2 and 5). Despite this praise, Living Streets did make several recommendations to the proposed walking plan as they considered it to have 'some shortcomings'. However, upon the official release of the plan they were 'pleased to see that many of our views have been represented' and the 'shortcomings' had been addressed. In a press release (February 2004) they heralded the plan 'ground-breaking' and 'a triumph for Londoners'.

However, the initial praise of the *Walking Plan for London* has been short-lived as two and a half years on from its launch concerns were raised. 'Walkable London' was a public event held in September 2006, organised by London Living Streets, with the principal aim of reviewing the *Walking Plan for London*. At the event calls were made to rewrite the *Walking Plan* as there were concerns that 'the targets need to be more ambitious', 'the measurement of walking needs to be fast tracked', 'hard targets must be adopted', 'a step change in funding must be invoked' and 'missed opportunities must be capitalised on' (Living Streets, 2006). At the time of writing, there is little further detail of how London Living Streets considers these concerns should be addressed. However, they are planning to highlight the significance of each concern via a campaign focused on the importance of having green men crossings on every junction in London that has traffic lights and a campaign that calls for improved links over the Thames bridges with reallocation of space to pedestrians. The recently launched 'Walking Works' campaign mentioned in the introduction to this chapter can also be seen as a response to these concerns in its focus on the benefits of walking for commuters. These include:

> You get time to yourself to clear your head, and leave your worries behind. It's a really easy way to fit some exercise into a busy day, which makes you feel good. It's good for everyone – with less congestion or emissions.
>
> (Living Streets, 2007)

May 2007 also saw TfL launch a high profile advertising campaign 'Why Not Walk It?', with the aim of encouraging more walking for everyday journeys. The campaign consisted of posters with cartoons by Simone Lai (see figure 11.3) and radio ads with the voice of actor Timothy Spall. The target group for the ads was people under 45 who are habitual car users for short journeys to work or school (TfL, 2007b).

Further initiatives include the TfL-funded Legible London project which aims to promote and make walking easier in the capital through a range of consistent information including street signage and maps (see AIG, 2006). At the time of writing the scheme is running on a trial basis on Oxford Street in London's West End near Bond Street tube station. The aim of the coordinated street signs is to show pedestrians where to walk, how long it will take and significant landmarks along the way. The long-term plan is to roll out the scheme across all thirty-three London boroughs. Discussion up until this point has focused on London-wide pedestrian policy, yet with London boroughs being 'responsible for 95 per cent of London's streets, for developing and implementing the majority of initiatives associated with these, such as bus priority, walking, cycling and parking schemes' (GLA, 2001b: 355), how is walking framed and promoted at the borough level?

11.3
'Why not walk it?' campaign (Transport for London).
Copyright © 2007
Simone Lia

Pedestrian policy in local London boroughs

In March 2007, 'The Walking Advisory Panel, set up to steer and monitor the delivery of the London Walking Plan, commissioned a survey of local authority officers' (TfL, 2007b: 4). The aim of the survey was to benchmark walking by reviewing 'the effectiveness of the current Walking Plan to help officers [in local authorities] establish what further support is required to deliver the Mayor's vision of London being one of the most walkable cities in the world by 2015' (TfL, 2007b: 4). A series of issues emerged from the results surrounding local authorities' achievements, priorities for the future and barriers to walking. The promotion of walking in terms of promoting particular routes and way-finding were both cited as achievements and priorities for the future, with lack of promotion and poor mapping also being raised as barriers to encouraging pedestrian movement (Walker, 2007). A further significant issue was related to the lack of resources directly allocated to walking, with budgets often being hard to find and 'rarely explicit' (Walker, 2007). However, despite this data engaging with the promotion of walking at the local authority level, there is little information available to date as to how these issues play out across the different boroughs. As such, specific attention will now turn to the promotion and barriers to walking in the context of the inner London boroughs of Islington and Hackney in which the transect was located.

Islington Council has been particularly active in taking forward the mayor's vision for walking in London. They have dedicated walking officers who are concerned with the promotion of pedestrian activity in the area in addition to wayfinding. There is also a walking for health officer who organises walks for people who have been referred via their GP, in addition to an engineering team who are responsible for improving the built environment for pedestrians. Walking forms a significant part of Islington's promotion of 'Green Travel' in the local area and is a major focus of a 'Green Travel Map' which has been produced to guide residents in making sustainable transport choices in their local area and beyond. In terms of the promotion of walking, the focus of recent initiatives has very much been on the concept of wayfinding and the ways that increased knowledge of an area can encourage pedestrian movement. For example, the Islington Wayfinding Project is focused on improving the pedestrian environment so that people can find their way better around the borough. The principal aims include:

> street clutter removal – items such as bollards, sign posts, redundant or illegal signage, disused phone boxes and pedestrian guard railing; production of 3D, area-based pocket maps; installation of on-street wayfinding boards in key strategic locations.
>
> (Islington Council, 2007a)

A further example is the recently produced *Walk Islington: Explore the Unexpected* (see figure 11.4). This walking guide details six walking routes through the borough with 'tips to motivate you to get to know your borough better' (Islington

Council, 2007b). According to the Senior Transport Planner who designed the guide, it is aimed at 'young professional women' as they are considered to be the group most likely to adjust their travel behaviour to walking. However, as she moves on to explain:

> One of the major barriers to them [women] walking more was their lack of knowledge of the local walking environment, they were afraid to walk into unknown areas and didn't know the routes through their local area. I therefore sought to create a guide that was targeted to women, and that would give them motivation to walk more- identifying routes through the borough and places of interest along the way.
>
> (Interview – Senior Transport Planner, Islington Council, June 2007)

These 'places of interest along the way' include cafes, shops and galleries within a design that is considered 'female sensitive'. It is interesting to note that there are currently plans afoot for a similar guide to cycling in the local area that is more 'masculine' in its content and design due to males being considered by the council as more likely to cycle than females. Five thousand copies of the walking guide have been distributed around local shops, libraries, and leisure facilities and it is available to download from the council website (www.islington.gov.uk).

By way of contrast, the promotion of walking in Hackney has had much less prominence. This reflects what the Islington Transport Planner described as a *'lack of continuity across the borough'* and how *'Hackney for a very long time*

11.4
**'Walk Islington: Explore the Unexpected'
(Islington Council).
Copyright © 2007
Composite Projects**

have not had an officer [walking officer] and not done very much'. As part of this wider research project on urban walking, several attempts were made to contact Hackney Council to discuss the promotion of walking in the borough. However, on each occasion no one seemed to know whose responsibility walking was. This can be argued to reflect Walker's (2007) concerns relating to the lack of resources at local authority level directed to walking initiatives. This is obviously a resource issue that the mayor, and the boroughs themselves, will need to address in a systematic way across all London boroughs if walking policy and plans are to succeed.

The conviviality of walking: social interaction and pedestrian movement

In addition to the benefits of walking discussed above, in current UK urban and pedestrian policy, the 'social' dimensions of walking are also cited as a significant reason for encouraging pedestrian activity. Explicit links are being made between the social aspects of walking and how this can facilitate forms of regeneration, particularly in urban areas. For example:

> Ensuring that there is a safe and convenient way to get to jobs, education, health care and other services for people without a car is an essential part of promoting social equality. Walking is a cost-free means of getting around which is available to almost all ages . . . Walking helps support local facilities and reinforces community cohesion.
>
> (DfT, 2003: 3)

> Increasing walking and cycling levels will also improve our public space and the social interactions we have. Both modes allow us to stop and chat or just say 'hello' in a way that it is difficult to do when closeted in the car. As such, they improve our sense of community.
>
> (DfT, 2004: 3)

The policy focus on the relationship between walking and social interaction, 'community cohesion' and 'sense of community' is comparative with new urbanist thinking where 'any increase in pedestrian activity is thought to strengthen community bonds and promote sense of place' (Talen, 1999: 1364). These North American new urbanist planning approaches are becoming increasingly visible in UK urban policy whereby the built environment is considered to 'increase the likelihood of community-orientated behaviours, such as walking, and these behaviours will in turn enhance community-orientated attitudes, such as neighbourhood attachment' (Lund, 2002: 303; see also Lees, 2003a; Raco, 2007b). Lees (2003a: 78) states how New Labour's urban renaissance agenda promotes an ideal that communities 'will be created "naturally" through the sustainable compact urban form that will densify people cheek by jowl' yet argues that the concepts of community and diversity are taken for granted and not questioned in the UTF or UWP reports. The sustainable communities agenda has continued as a key feature of UK urban policy, though with less emphasis on the design of the built environment and a greater focus on 'socially inclusive environments' (see Raco, 2007b). However, there is little to suggest that the concept of community and diversity are any less taken for granted. Attention will now turn to how the same argument holds in relation to pedestrian policy and the unsubstantiated claims that walking provides this range of socially desirable outcomes.

The social benefits of walking also feature in London pedestrian policy. For example, both *The Walking Plan for London* (2004) and the *Improving Walkability* (2005) guide refer to the '5C's of Good Walking Networks'. One of these 'C's' is 'convivial' which is described as 'walking routes and public spaces [that are] pleasant to use, allowing social interaction between people, including other road users' (TfL, 2005: 20). Particular reference is also made to 'walking improvements to life in public spaces' that include 'circulation and social exchange, involving a range of activities on foot including window shopping, meeting people' (TfL, 2005: 8). However, what exactly do these 'social interactions' and 'social exchanges' mean, and how are they facilitated by walking? *The Walking Plan for London* (TfL, 2004: 19) does move on to elaborate why these 'social interactions' are important and how they relate to moving on foot:

> If residents are to overcome the anonymity of many neighbourhoods and know the people living close by, it is necessary for them to share time and space with each other. This is what happens when people walk their local streets rather than drive from one door to another.

Nevertheless, TfL say little about the actual nature of these interactions and how they unfold. In addition to this ambiguous relationship between walking and its 'social' aspects within pedestrian policy, it is also argued that the 'benefits' of walking for 'social interaction' are 'proven' (TfL, 2004: 30), yet where, how and in what way these 'benefits' are proven is again quite unclear. However, it is not only in the policy arena that walking is suggested to facilitate social interaction (DfT, 2004; TfL, 2004, 2005). The significance of urban social encounters and the interaction of strangers as they negotiate the city on foot has long been emphasised within urban and social theoretical writings (Jacobs, 1972; Merry, 1981; Sennett, 1977; Zukin, 1995). Given that both urban walking policy and the urban and social theoretical writings are characterised by a lack of empirical data, it is therefore interesting to examine how the empirical data collected as part of the research being discussed here reflects these policy and theoretical understandings of 'social' interaction in the city.

This diary entry from a Canonbury resident describes a particular journey into work one morning:

8.10am: walking to tube station; rather gingerly because not feeling terribly well. Perky young mums are taking children to the local primary school on Canonbury Road. I wonder if they notice how hung-over I am. I decide probably not because (a) I persuade myself I don't look as bad as I feel and (b) no one takes any notice of people when they walk past in the morning rush-hour in London.

Having said that, I'm walking down the escalator in the tube station and a young professional looking man is holding his head in his hands. He definitely looks worse than I feel. Despite my better judgement, I ask him if he's ok. He tells me he has just realised he left his laptop in the train. I tell him where the control room is and he thanks me profusely.

(Diary – Lucy, Canonbury resident, Islington)

Lucy starts her diary entry by describing how she is walking ('rather gingerly') and the reason why she is walking in such a way ('not feeling terribly well'). Lucy attends to this further by contrasting how she is walking with the 'perky young mums'. As she moves onto 'wonder' whether the 'young mums' 'notice' her 'hung-over' appearance, Lucy answers her own question in an interesting way. The conclusion she reaches, that they have not, is framed around the visual ('I don't look'; 'no one takes any notice'). In other words, what it is to look, see and notice other people (or not) resource Lucy's account of her walking patterns in relation to social interactions on foot. Furthermore, Lucy's claim that 'no one takes any notice of people when they walk past in the morning rush-hour in London' is derivative of an understanding of urban disengagement between strangers. For Simmel (1971: 329), this type of indifference is a coping strategy for negotiating the sensory overload of the city:

> There is perhaps no psychic phenomenon which is so unconditionally reserved to the city as the blasé outlook. It is at first the consequence of those rapidly shifting stimulations of the nerves which are thrown together in all their contrasts and from which it seems to us the intensification of metropolitan intellectuality seems to be derived.

However, Lucy does not display complete indifference as she has noticed the mothers to a degree that their presence is a momentary concern significant enough to record in her diary. Goffman (1963) refers to this as 'civil inattention' whereby strangers are registered but not recognised or acknowledged. Goffman (1963: 84) argues that;

> Where the courtesy is performed between two persons passing on the street, civil inattention may take the special form of eyeing the other up to approximately eight feet, during which time sides of the street are apportioned by gesture, and then casting the eyes down as

the other passes – a kind of dimming of lights. In any case, we have here what is perhaps the slightest of interpersonal rituals, yet one that constantly regulates the social intercourse of persons in our society.

Lucy has visually registered the mothers to an extent that she can describe them as 'perky'. However, there is more to be said in relation to Lucy's diary entry beyond the visual. In the second part of the diary extract, Lucy's actions can be understood as breaking from this 'urban indifference' and 'civil inattention' as she addresses a distressed looking 'professional' young male to ask him 'if he's ok'. Yet despite initiating the interaction, Lucy presents this as not 'normal' urban behaviour as she points out that she did so despite her 'better judgement'. As such, Lucy's construction of the exchange still falls in line with the behaviour of the urban dwellers documented by Simmel and Goffman in relation to the visual dimensions of urban social disengagement. Thus, contrasting with pedestrian policy whereby walking is positioned as allowing 'us to stop and chat or just say "hello"' (DfT, 2004: 3). However, are there perhaps other ways in which the inter-actions that occur between strangers whilst on foot can be understood?

This London Fields resident responds to the question of what she likes about walking in her local area:

> I really love walking, I don't understand why more people don't do it, I just think it's nice to, I mean the whole interaction thing with people on the street, I think is just, it's nice to kind of be amongst it all, you know, it's just nice to be in the city and see I think..
>
> (Interview – Alice, London Fields resident, Hackney)

Alice's account is framed around why she 'really love[s] walking'. This claim is strengthened in relation to others as Alice states how she does not 'understand why more people don't do it'. Although Alice makes visual references ('it's just nice to be in the city and see I think'), the salience of her account lies elsewhere. Alice orientates her 'love' of walking to the 'whole interaction thing with people on the street', in other words how pedestrian movement affords physical prox-imity to strangers. This is something that Alice constructs as a positive aspect of urban living, as does Sennett (1977: 40); '[the city] should be the forum in which it becomes meaningful to join with other persons without the compulsion to know them as persons'. In her work, Jane Jacobs (1972) also focused on, and celebrated, the unplanned interaction of strangers on the street as a positive urban phenomenon. However, in explaining her 'love' of walking Alice moves beyond a primary concern with interacting 'with people on the street' to how 'it's nice to kind of be amongst it all'. Alice moves on to qualify and position this 'amongst it all' with respect to how 'it's just nice to be in the city'. Thus, this 'city' is taken as, and beyond, the sum of its human relations.

This Canonbury resident was also asked about what she liked about walking in her local area:

> I like walking because you meet people, you see new shops, you see new things and because I don't shop regularly when I go out I think 'oh this is very interesting'. I like the variety of people and things that you can see. You see a lot of young people like yourself. I like to look at them, how they dress, it makes me feel, it cheers me up.
>
> (Interview – Patricia, Canonbury resident, Islington)

Like Alice, Patricia also draws attention to how interacting with people is one of the key things she likes about walking ('I like walking because you meet people'). Furthermore, Patricia's account highlights the visual dimensions of these interactions ('I like the variety of people and things that you can see'; 'you see a lot of young people like yourself'; 'I like to look at them') and in so doing extends her account, in similar terms to Alice, beyond an exclusive concern with interactions with people to the 'new shops' and 'new things' that she 'sees'. However, there is more at stake in Patricia's account as she reflects upon how and why she likes to interact with people on foot.

Patricia works for a successful finance company in the City of London and although she did not disclose her salary, her high status and position within the company became quite clear during the interview as various PAs and secretaries seemed to be continuously knocking on the door of her luxurious boardroom requiring her urgent attention. In Butler and Lees's (2006: 467) research on 'super-gentrification' in Barnsbury they describe how 'a new group of super wealthy professionals working in the City of London is slowly imposing its mark on this [Barnsbury] inner London housing market in a way that differentiates it and them both from traditional gentrifiers and from the traditional urban upper classes'. With Patricia's high status City job and substantial property she owns with her husband on the Barnsbury/Canonbury borders, could it be argued that she is representative of this new breed of super-gentrifiers? Perhaps. However, it is one particular characteristic of what Butler and Lees (2006: 470) argue to be 'super-gentrifiers' that is of particular significance to Patricia's account:

> Super-gentrifiers work in a 'contact-intensive sub-culture' (Ley, 2004: 157) where co-location in the City and face-to-face meetings are very important. For super-gentrifiers this has influenced their choice of residence too – they want quick and easy access to the City and to be able to easily meet up and socialise with their cohort in Barnsbury (on their doorstep) or the West End (10–15 minutes away).

At one level Patricia's account can be read in terms of how she likes to interact with 'strangers' as she makes reference to the 'variety of people' she sees. However, she moves on to qualify what she means by 'variety of people' when she states that she sees 'young people like yourself'. This is reflective of the significance of 'face-to-face meetings . . . with their cohort' that Butler and Lees (2006) draw specific attention to. It also suggests that the encounters Patricia is referring to are not with completely unknown and anonymous urban others as they are people 'like her'. The writings of Merry (1981), Young (1990) and Zukin (1995) all suggest that the reality of whether, and how, urban social exchanges unfold differ greatly from the positive associations of interactions with urban strangers. Patricia's account not only reflects this but calls into question the extent to which walking can be said to make these encounters the positive ones framed within pedestrian policy documents. As discussed, pedestrian policy and the urban and social theory on interaction in urban spaces tends to focus on the interaction of strangers, with the data discussed thus far emphasising these forms of social encounters. However, pedestrian policy also suggests that inter-actions on foot 'improve our sense of community' (DfT, 2004: 5) yet how this facilitates a 'sense of community' remains unclear. What is the link between walking and having a 'sense of community'?

The potential of walking: the constitution of 'community' in London?

Within walking policy direct links are made between pedestrian movement and the potential it has to foster community involvement and belonging. Putnam (2000: 407–8), in his book *Bowling Alone* details the demise of American 'commu-nities', and makes a case for walking as a means of encouraging social exchange;

> Let us act to ensure that by 2010 Americans will spend less time trav-elling and more time connecting with our neighbours than we do today, that we will live in more integrated and pedestrian friendly areas and that the design of our communities and the availability of public space will encourage more casual socializing with friends and neighbours.

Putnam's plea is a strong reflection of New Urbanist thinking in terms of the built environment influencing community orientated behaviours and attitudes (Lund, 2002). Although Putnam makes specific reference to interactions with 'friends and neighbours', it can also be argued that the assumption within pedestrian policy and urban policy in general is that walking facilitates social interaction between strangers which in time develops into a familiarity that creates this 'sense of community'. Walking is understood as a means to break down the 'social barriers' that make 'strangers' no longer 'strangers', thus resolving a whole host of urban and social problems. For, as previously mentioned, walking is considered in policy terms as something that 'improve [s] our sense of commu-nity' (DfT, 2004: 3). The diary extract from this London Fields resident draws particular attention to her and her partner's Saturday routine:

> This Saturday ritual is very satisfying because it starts the weekend officially for us. We take the walk slowly, enjoying the park + making

the best use of the neighbourhood, sometimes adding Broadway Market or Hackney Central High St. to our journey (also usually the library). Things are reasonably close to each other and there are also a lot of other people out enjoying the morning + making it a neighbour-hood feeling. We recognise a lot of people and/or dogs on this weekly trip.

(Diary – Lindsey, London Fields resident, Hackney)

Lindsey starts her diary entry by explaining the significance of 'this Saturday ritual' in terms of how it 'officially' marks the start of the weekend for her and her partner. However, the salience of the extract lies in relation to how Lindsey moves on to qualify why this 'ritual is very satisfying' to them. Lindsey not only highlights the 'things' that feature in their 'Saturday ritual' on foot ('the park'; 'Broadway Market'; Hackney Central High Street'; 'the library'), but in line with new urbanist thinking, pedestrian policy and the sustainable communities discourse previously mentioned, her diary extract draws attention to the significance of these ameni-ties to a neighbourhood, how 'walking helps support local facilities' (DfT, 2003: 3), and the importance of them being 'reasonably close to each other'. Lindsey moves on to point out how 'a lot of other people [are] out enjoying the morning' and explains how the people they encounter are no longer complete strangers but familiar strangers who they now recognises due to routinised face-to-face contact. As Lindsey details this weekly pedestrian ritual, she makes an explicit association between the amenities they use, the people they encounter, and the 'neighbourhood feeling' they experience, that can be argued to typify the links being made by urban and pedestrian policy between walking and community.

The diary entry from this De Beauvoir Town resident also describes a local journey on foot:

11.15 am

To chemist to collect some pills. Talked to Jay, the pharmacist. Also there is a woman in the shop waiting for a prescription for her child.

On the way back, rang Leah's bell – to get my garden tools back. Rupert, son of a friend on some committee, came across road to pay me for some food for him + his girlfriend that he had picked up the previous week. Also told him about Thursday evenings meeting.

Leah looked out of window + asked if OK if she came down in 10 mins – not yet dressed. I said that was fine.

Ria, who lives across street, drove back. We had a word. I had rang her earlier to check how Simon, her son, was getting on. He has recently joined the Transport Police and was involved in the bombings.

Paul came out of his house – a neighbour across the street. We called over Marcia, who lives directly opposite. She said she was feeling hungover.

> Philip + Mark, next door, off on bicycles. Exchanged stuff as to how
> we were + where we had been. They were cycling down to the canal.
>
> (Diary – Margaret, De Beauvoir Town resident, Hackney)

Margaret's diary entry is framed around the various people she encounters as
she visits and walks back from the local chemist. At one level, like Lindsey, this
extract illustrates the links that walking and urban policy makes between pedestrian movement and social interaction. For example, Margaret details the
numerous verbal exchanges she has on the short walk back from the chemist
('talked to Jay'; 'told him about'; 'asked if OK'; 'we had a word'; 'we called over';
'she said'; 'exchanged stuff as to how we were + where we had been'). Furthermore, although not explicit, Margaret's detailed account of these social interactions can be argued as highlighting this 'sense of community' and neighbourhood
belonging that walking is said to facilitate. Margaret refers to the majority of
people by their forename, qualifies how she knows them ('Jay, the pharmacist';
'Rupert, son of a friend'; 'Ria, who lives across the street'; 'Simon, her son';
'Paul . . . a neighbour'; 'Marcia, who lives directly opposite': 'Philip + Mark, next
door') and then provides details of the content of their conversations, thus situating their relationships as pre-existing.

At one level, this again reflects pedestrian policy which positions
walking as a means of residents overcoming 'the anonymity of many neighbourhoods' and a means of 'know[ing] the people living close by' (TfL, 2004: 19).
However, the social encounters Margaret describes in the diary extract are not as
a direct result of walking per se but as social exchanges between neighbours. In
other words, it is the resident's physical proximity as neighbours that facilitates
these interactions, not pedestrian movement ('Leah looked out of window +
asked if ok'; 'Ria who lives across the street, drove back. We had a word'; 'Paul
came out of his house – a neighbour across the street. We called over Marica,
who lives directly opposite'). Yet that is not to say walking is not an important
aspect of knowing a neighbourhood and providing a sense of neighbourhood
belonging. For example, Lucy also reflects upon the significance of walking in her
local area:

> Our street looks nice in summer because there are trees on both
> sides. Leafy and quiet. I like walking down my own street. I've been
> here for nearly two years now, so I feel very comfortable and at ease.
> Also I'm with my partner – it's nice to walk round with someone else
> at the weekend; because of my job, I tend to rush round on my own
> during the week.
>
> (Diary – Lucy, Canonbury resident, Islington)

Lucy describes how 'nice' her street looks in summer in relation to the trees and
how it is 'leafy and quiet'. Lucy makes the association between walking down her
street over a period of time ('nearly 2 years now') to her feeling 'very comfortable
and at ease' in her local area. Thus walking has provided Lucy with a means of

overcoming 'the anonymity' of her 'neighbourhood' (TfL, 2004: 19). Yet as Lucy moves on to describe how she is walking with her partner, the diary extract has particular resonance in relation to the social dimensions of pedestrian movement. Lucy has not framed her diary entry with respect to any social exchanges she might have with urban strangers. For example, in her own words; 'I tend to rush round on my own during the week.' Rather, for Lucy, the significance of her social interactions on foot lie with whether, and who, she is walking with, not who she encounters as she walks ('it's nice to walk round with someone else at the weekend'). Given that urban policy and much social science literature focuses on social exchanges between strangers as they walk to promote a 'sense of community', how is the significance of walking with someone, particularly where there is some form of existing social relation, best understood?

Allen (2000: 55) problematises this focus of urban policy on face-to-face interaction and the familiarisation of strangers as a means of creating community cohesion. He makes specific reference to the work of Simmel to illustrate 'today's complex networks of social interaction' and draws attention to the contradictory figure of the stranger in Simmel's writings as 'someone who is both near in a spatial sense, yet remote in a social sense' (Allen, 2000: 57). Allen argues that 'in the cases of social community, the tension between nearness and distance is something that may be lived rather than necessarily resolved. It is something that is experienced as a fact of city life, not something that presents itself as an interminable problem which has to be confronted and dispelled' (Allen, 2000: 58). Allen's point is to question the extent to which it is necessary to create a form of community cohesion through the social interaction of urban strangers. In the context of the data being discussed here, are there other ways in which the social dimensions of walking can be understood and promoted? For example, this Barnsbury resident describes walking back from work with his young daughter:

> 5.35 – 6.05 – Rather much slower walk home . . . Tilly insists on walking much of the way, and often turns and toddles off in another direction. But these walks are very significant to me as they are a simple way for us to spend some time outside with each other despite my working. She loves watching the kids playing soccer in the park.
>
> (Diary – Ken, Barnsbury resident, Islington)

Ken's diary entry starts by describing how his walk home was 'much slower' in contrast to the other days he recorded in his diary due to walking with his daughter who 'often turns and toddles off in another direction'. Ken moves on to explain why this 'much slower walk home' is not a temporal or spatial restraint to him (see Harris et al., 2004, and Lyons and Urry, 2005 on transport policy focus on speed and efficiency) but is 'significant' in relation to spending time with his daughter ('a simple way for us to spend some time outside with each other despite my working'). In other words, the social benefits of walking to Ken are the ways this mode of transport facilitates the social interactions he is able to have with his daughter. Furthermore, as Ken makes reference to how Tilly 'loves watching the kids playing soccer in the park', attention is drawn again to the significance of visual interactions on foot discussed in the previous section, as opposed to the focus on verbal exchanges within pedestrian policy documents.

Concluding remarks

The research conducted on urban walking detailed in this chapter has illustrated that moving on foot does not facilitate social interaction in the straightforward way that it is framed within pedestrian policy documents. However, this is not to say that the social dimensions of pedestrian movement should be over-looked. In light of the findings discussed here, two significant issues emerge that have implications for how walking is promoted as part of London's wider regeneration strategy.

The first is in relation to how terms such as 'social mixing', 'social inter-action' and 'social exchange' are understood and conceptualised. As discussed above, it is unclear in London's policy for walking what these terms actually mean and what it actually is about walking that facilitates them. In addition, despite TfL (2004: 19) drawing attention to the importance of people sharing 'time and space with each other', it can be argued that there is an implicit assumption in pedestrian policy that these social interactions are characterised by verbal exchanges that are far from fleeting. However, what this examination of the local pedestrian experiences of residents in Islington and Hackney has shown is the need for a more nuanced understanding of the relationship between walking and social interaction that recognises the significance of other forms of social exchange.

For example, Jacobs placed great emphasis on how the physical proximity of strangers facilitates visual interactions. In her book, *The Death and Life of the Great American Cities* (1972), Jacobs argues that a well-used street is a safe street and how successful city neighbourhoods are those that use the presence of strangers as a safety measure in increasing the 'number of eyes' on the street. As Goffman (1963: 90) describes verbal exchanges as 'face engagements', he also notes 'that while many face engagements seem to be made up largely of the exchange of verbal statements, so that conversational encounters can in fact be used as the model, there are still other kinds of encounters where no word is spoken'. The significance of visual encounters such as these is something that emerged throughout the research, thus raising the question as to whether these kinds of interactions are enough for the community formation that policy-makers desire.

The second implication is in terms of how the focus within pedestrian policy and urban social theory is on how walking facilitates the social mixing of strangers. What the research has made apparent is the key role walking has in maintaining existing social relations as opposed to creating new ones. In relation to London's wider regeneration strategy, policy-makers should be wary of placing too much emphasis on the social interactions between strangers that pedestrian movement is considered to encourage. Rather, in promoting the 'social' benefits of walking, attention should be drawn to the significant role it plays in boosting existing social relations, particularly with respect to how it 'resources' people's day-to-day lives. This nuanced understanding of the social dimensions of pedestrian movement is important for policy-makers as they promote 'social mixing' and 'community cohesion' as a key aspect of London's regeneration. It is by recognising these 'overlapping walks of life' that will assist in the promotion of walking in London.

Acknowledgements

Thanks to Loretta Lees for valuable comments on previous drafts and to Juan Alayo for his input into earlier stages of this collaborative PhD research supported by the Economic and Social Research Council and Arup Transport Planning (award no. PTA-033-2003-00014).

Chapter 12

Social housing and regeneration in London

Paul Watt

Introduction

In *Outcast London*, Gareth Stedman Jones (1984) documents how the 'housing problem', the shortage of decent housing at an affordable cost for the working class and especially the 'casual poor', was a key strand in social and political discourse in late nineteenth-century London. As this chapter demonstrates, London still has a pronounced housing problem despite its twenty-first-century global city status. 'Affordable housing' was Londoners' top priority in terms of improving the capital as a place to live (Mayor of London, 2005a: 7). 'Affordable housing' is usually taken to mean housing below full market price or rent.[1] As such it covers both 'social housing' (local authority and housing association rental property), the subject of this chapter, and 'intermediate housing'. The latter was defined by the Mayor of London (2006b: 28) as encompassing 'a range of housing options that help fill the gap between social renting and full home ownership or market renting', for example shared ownership.

In focusing on social housing in London, the chapter does not attempt to provide a comprehensive account of the complex layers of policy that have impacted upon this topic. Instead, it firstly discusses aspects of urban policy under New Labour in relation to social housing and social exclusion, and secondly it outlines some of the main parameters of change within social housing in London. The chapter moves on to provide an account of how social housing in London is distinctive relative to the rest of England. This distinctiveness provides the framework within which urban regeneration 'area-based initiatives' (ABIs) have to operate. The chapter then goes on to examine how ABIs have addressed council-built housing estates in London with particular reference to New Labour's flagship ABI, the New Deal for Communities (NDC). Finally, some comments are offered regarding future regeneration challenges vis-à-vis social housing in London both in relation to meeting housing needs and enhancing community participation.

Social housing, urban policy and social exclusion

Urban policy embraces programmes that aim to regenerate urban areas at a variety of spatial scales ranging from the whole city to the neighbourhood (Colomb, 2007). Neighbourhood ABIs are by no means always directed at social housing or even on housing at all, since they can focus on health, education, employment, etc., as well as generic programmes such as the NDC (Lupton, 2003). New Labour's brand of what Peck and Tickell (2002) have called 'roll-out neo-liberalism' has resulted in a confusing proliferation of ABIs, several of which can even be found in the same geographical area, designed to 'reconnect' excluded or poor neighbourhoods with what is routinely referred to as the 'mainstream' of economic and social life (Colomb, 2007; Kintrea, 2007). As well as urban policy, social housing is also the subject of specific housing policies concerned with affordability, supply and demand (Mullins and Murie, 2006; Whitehead, 2006).

Although not all ABIs are housing based, many are located in neighbourhoods which contain large tracts of social housing, often in the form of council-built estates, and a great deal of policy attention has been given to the regeneration of such 'poor neighbourhoods' (Lupton, 2003; Kintrea, 2007). Under New Labour such regeneration has been framed in terms of 'tackling social exclusion', even though the identification of problems and solutions in achieving this seductive if opaque goal diverge markedly. Social exclusion incorporates notions of poverty and deprivation, but also includes social relational/ participation issues, for example, being politically disengaged by not joining campaigns (Butler and Watt, 2007: 106–34). Tackling social exclusion in poor neighbourhoods is a key element in New Labour's vision for Britain's 'urban renaissance' (Colomb, 2007). In particular, the emphasis is placed on creating 'communities' which are 'active', 'engaged', 'involved' and 'sustainable' (Imrie and Raco, 2003; Raco, 2007b).

The importance of social housing vis-à-vis social exclusion was highlighted in the Social Exclusion Unit report, *Bringing Britain Together* (SEU, 1998) published by the incoming Labour government. In setting out the failures of previous urban policies and the framework for New Labour's own initiatives, this report highlighted the role played by social housing in generating exclusionary processes in Britain's 'poorest neighbourhoods'. In attempting to promote social *inclusion*, the report emphasised the importance of local community participation. This emphasis can be seen in the New Deal for Communities programme that we discuss below, as well as the broader National Strategy for Neighbourhood Renewal (Lupton, 2003).

In their analysis of the SEU report, Watt and Jacobs (2000) draw upon the work of Ruth Levitas (1998) in suggesting that the report ingeniously conflated distinctive, in many ways contradictory 'discourses of social exclusion'. Levitas (1998) identifies three separate discourses of social exclusion within British political and social policy debates that inform New Labour thinking and practices:

- RED – a redistributionist discourse that emphasises poverty and material inequality.
- MUD – a moral underclass discourse whose main concern is with the morality and behaviour of the excluded themselves.
- SID – a social integrationist discourse that emphasises the significance of paid work for social inclusion.

As Levitas (2005) demonstrates, the contours of New Labour thinking are fuzzy and draw variously upon different aspects of RED, MUD and SID depending upon which policy arena is being considered. In those policy arenas relevant to social housing, concerns over MUD and SID tend to dominate New Labour thinking (Cowan and McDermont, 2006; Cole, 2007). Thus exclusion in areas dominated by social housing is blamed upon MUD cultures of worklessness and anti-social behaviour, and/or SID and tenants' lack of inclusion in the labour market (Watt and Jacobs, 2000; Levitas, 2005). This approach can be identified in the simplistic equation made between social renting, worklessness and poverty in a recent paper by the Mayor of London (2006b). From a RED perspective, however, poor quality housing conditions (overcrowding, damp, disrepair) and homelessness are problems for which the *provision* of good quality social rented housing is the solution in London and elsewhere (Watt and Jacobs, 2000; Ambrose, 2002; Shelter, 2005). A RED perspective on social exclusion also emphasises the poverty wages and insecurity that characterise the bottom end of the labour market including in London where many social tenants undertake low-grade jobs (Watt, 2003; Smith, 2005). Let us now turn our attention to the changing nature of social housing in London.

The changing size and composition of the social housing stock

Before examining the main trends within 'social housing', we need to clarify what this term means. One standard definition is 'housing run by not-for-profit or public landlords for rent, normally at below-market rents' (Hills, 2007: 16). However, this seemingly straightforward definition conceals as much as it reveals. Social housing consists of not one but two main forms of housing tenure. The first is council housing rented from local authorities, and the second is property rented from housing associations, most of which are now 'Registered Social Landlords' (RSLs) following the 1996 Housing Act. Although both tenures are nominally 'social housing', they have quite distinctive histories, modes of governance, organisation and finance, and they also offer different sets of rights for tenants and would-be tenants (Malpass, 2000; Cowan and McDermont, 2006). Housing associations are defined as 'independent, non-profit-distributing organisations governed by voluntary boards to provide mainly rented housing at below market rents' (Mullins and Murie, 2006: 178). They vary not only in size, but also in terms of their organisational structures and remits with some larger associations, in particular, moving away from the voluntary ethos. Housing associations are hybrid organisations encompassing private, public and voluntary sector elements. The balance of such elements has shifted over time although the private has become increasingly important in the contemporary period (Malpass, 2000; Cowan and McDermont, 2006; Mullins and Murie, 2006).

From 1981 to 2001, London has been distinctive relative to the rest of England having consistently had higher proportions of social and private renting households even though these have shrunk over the period, as seen in table 12.1. By 2001, less than one in five households (17.6 per cent) in London were council tenants, down from nearly one in three in 1981. In contrast, the housing association tenure has more than doubled in size, up from only 4.1 per cent of households in 1981 to 9.4 per cent in 2001. Despite this, the proportion of London households renting from social housing landlords has declined quite markedly, down from just under 35 per cent in 1981 to 27 per cent in 2001. The tenure pattern also has an important geographical distribution in the sense that inner London has had a much higher proportion of social rental housing compared to outer London (Hamnett, 2003).

In terms of dwellings, the local authority (LA) sector in London shrank by a third from 703,000 in 1991 to 468,000 dwellings in 2005 (figure 12.1). Over the same period, the RSL sector doubled in size to nearly 300,000 dwellings. Figure 12.1 demonstrates that not only has there been a relative decline in the size of social housing, as seen in table 12.1, but the last fifteen years have also witnessed an absolute decline (10 per cent) in the number of social rental properties, down from a total of 851,000 in 1991 to 766,000 in 2005. Several trends can help account for the changes in the size and shape of the social rental sector as we now discuss.

Table 12.1 Tenure of households in London and England, 1981-2001 (%)

Housing tenure	1981	1991	2001
London			
Rented from local authority	30.7	23.4	17.6
Rented from housing association	4.1	5.6	9.4
Rented from private landlord	16.6	13.8	14.8
Owner occupied	48.6	57.2	57.2
England			
Rented from local authority	28.9	19.9	13.7
Rented from housing association	2.1	3.2	6.3
Rented from private landlord	11.1	9.3	9.1
Owner occupied	57.9	67.6	70.3

Source: Census 1981, 1991, 2001 (adapted from Housing Corporation, 2007, Table 4)

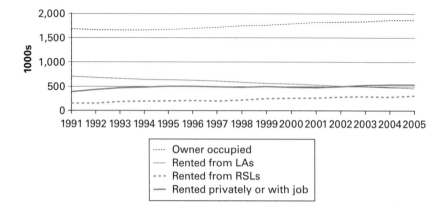

12.1
**Dwelling stock in
London, by tenure,
1991–2005.**
Source: DCLG, 2007c,
Table 109

New building provision

There has been a marked reduction in the building of social rental properties both in London and the UK during the last thirty years as a direct result of national governmental policy, first by the Conservatives and then by New Labour. The post-war peak of new homes built in London was 37,000 in 1970 of which 28,000 were for social renting, very largely local authority (Holmes, 2006: 141). The number and proportion of new social housing declined throughout the 1980s. As figure 12.2 shows, only 1,745 LA and 2,279 RSL units were built in 1990–1, together representing 23 per cent of the annual total. By the time New Labour gained power in 1997, the annual number of completed LA units was down to double figures (52 in 1997/98; see figure 12.2). Since 2004 this already negligible amount has shrunk even further to single figures; in 2006-07 just two LA dwellings were built in London (DCLG, 2007c: table 232). Figure 12.2 also shows that RSL building increased over the 1990–2007 period by nearly four times to over 8,000, raising social housing to 38 per cent of all house building completions in London in 2006–7. Although seemingly impressive, the 1990–2007 social house-building expansion halves once we factor in the collapse of LA building. As figure 12.2 also indicates, the annual number of RSL units built in London during the first years of New Labour government was lower than during the Conservatives' later years. The number of new social housing units in 2006–7 still only represents 30 per cent of the 1970 London total.

The sale of local authority properties

Although a few London councils had sold houses on a discretionary basis prior to the right-to-buy (RTB) introduced in the 1980 Housing Act, it was the RTB that made such a drastic impact on London's available LA stock during the 1980s and 1990s (Forrest and Murie, 1991). This can be seen in table 12.2 which shows total sales in London and England from 1980–2006. The table highlights the way that sales in London were relatively modest in comparison to the rest of England

12.2
**Housebuilding in
London: permanent
dwellings completed, by
tenure, 1990-2007.**
Source: DCLG, 2007c,
Table 232

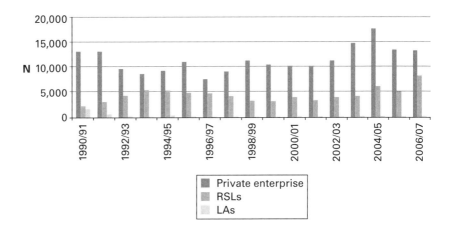

during the first half of the 1980s. During this early period, RTB sales were concentrated in the rural and suburban areas of England where houses predominate, rather than in urban areas such as inner London where flats predominate (Forrest and Murie, 1991). However, after a slow start sales picked up dramatically in London by the late 1980s and early 1990s. The depletion of the LA stock in London and also the total social housing stock (figure 12.1) can be significantly attributed to RTB sales. Furthermore, the social impact of the RTB has meant that the generally more affluent tenants, often in the 'better' properties, have tended to buy. This has helped to 'residualise' council renting since it has shifted from 'general needs' housing catering for a broad mass of the working class to a residual tenure for the poorer working class with the direst housing needs (Forrest and Murie, 1991; Watt, 2003; Malpass, 2005). RTB sales have also contributed towards the expansion in owner occupation (table 12.1 and figure 12.1).

Housing associations and stock transfer

Housing associations have a long history in London, but they expanded dramatically since the 1960s (Malpass, 2000). During the 1970s and 1980s they became an important vehicle for meeting the housing needs of the black and minority ethnic (BME) population at a time when local authority housing policies and practices in London were routinely found to be institutionally racist (Ginsburg and Watson, 1992). Thus the history of housing association provision in London has contained progressive inclusionary elements.[2] At present, however, the RSL sector performs a somewhat different function since over the last two decades both Conservative and New Labour governments have promoted it as *the main* legitimate provider of social rental housing *instead of* local authorities.

The direction of change is towards housing associations, especially the larger ones, becoming more market-oriented organisations (Malpass, 2000; Ginsburg, 2005). This process was given particular impetus by the changes introduced to housing associations' funding regimes in the 1988 Housing Act

Table 12.2 Local authority stock sold through the right-to-buy scheme in London and England, 1980-2006.

Year	London N	England N	London/England %
1980/81	330	2,328	14.2
1981/82	6,833	105,199	6.5
1982/83	17,307	167,123	10.4
1983/84	12,685	106,262	11.9
1984/85	11,420	77,522	14.7
1985/86	10,801	72,142	15.0
1986/87	12,297	76,748	16.0
1987/88	16,491	93,729	17.6
1988/89	24,918	135,701	18.4
1989/90	26,258	133,804	19.6
1990/91	18,060	76,332	23.7
1991/92	10,570	48,290	21.9
1992/93	7,325	37,686	19.4
1993/94	7,321	44,678	16.4
1994/95	6,363	43,336	14.7
1995/96	4,641	31,512	14.7
1996/97	5,220	33,206	15.7
1997/98	7,123	41,329	17.2
1998/99	8,045	40,272	20.0
1999/2000	11,331	54,251	20.9
2000/01	11,439	52,380	21.8
2001/02	9,817	51,968	18.9
2002/03	11,608	63,394	18.3
2003/04	12,778	69,577	18.4
2004/05	10,691	49,983	21.4
2005/06	4,042	26,655	15.2

Source: DCLG, 2007c, Table 670 (percentage, author's calculation)

which meant they had to increasingly rely upon private sector loans to finance new building (Malpass, 2000: 183). The 1988 Housing Act also introduced various schemes such as Tenants Choice and Housing Action Trusts (HATs) designed to promote de-municipalisation via the transfer of ownership and management of council housing into other bodies including housing associations. HATs were tied to estate regeneration and although some London council tenants welcomed them, for example in Brent (Stewart and Rhoden, 2003), in other cases there was vigorous tenant opposition to HATs as in Tower Hamlets

(Woodward, 1991). In the end, only six HATs were introduced, three of which were in London.

The large-scale voluntary transfer (LSVT) of council stock into housing association ownership has proved a far more extensive policy than that of HATs. By June 2007, a total of 251 transfers had taken place in 174 English LAs covering over one million dwellings (DCLG, 2007d). Emerging from initially localised rural and suburban beginnings, LSVT only became part of national housing policy in 1992 (Malpass and Mullins, 2002). LSVT has been enhanced under New Labour. In order to meet the standards set in the Decent Homes initiative introduced in 2000, councils have one of three options: first, transfer their stock to a RSL, second, set up an Arms Length Management Organisation (ALMO) and third, aim for Private Finance Initiative (PFI) contracts.

There is considerable disagreement amongst housing academics as to whether stock transfer equals the 'privatisation of council housing' and also whether it benefits tenants (see *inter alia* Malpass and Mullins, 2002; Stewart and Rhoden, 2003; Ginsburg, 2005; Daly *et al.*, 2005). Irrespective of the nuances of academic debate, LSVT has resulted in a decade-long, nationwide council tenants' campaign of opposition to stock transfer, Defend Council Housing (DCH, 2006). DCH has gained support from trade unions and some Labour MPs who share a sense of dismay at the way that New Labour government housing policy has continued many elements of previous Conservative policy notably in relation to the marginalisation, if not annihilation, of council housing. DCH aims for a 'fourth option' for council housing, i.e. direct investment in stock improvement and enlargement.

The growth in London's housing association stock since 1991 (table 12.1 and figure 12.1) can partly be attributed to new building (figure 12.2), but the LSVT programme also accounts for a major part of the expansion. Table 12.3 shows that fifty-two stock transfers into RSL ownership took place in London until summer 2007, involving nearly 68,000 dwellings. With the sole exception of the outer borough of Bromley in 1992, LSVTs have only occurred in London during New Labour's period of government since 1997 (DCLG, 2007d). Table 12.3 also highlights the fact that the transfer process has been far from smooth in the capital, as indicated by the twenty-six 'no votes' in which council tenants rejected transfer. This means that around one-third of London transfer ballots have resulted in a 'no vote', a higher rate than nationally (DCLG, 2007e; author's calculations; Malpass and Mullins, 2002). The geography of transfers in London has been highly uneven, as table 12.3 indicates, with the majority of successful transfers occurring in only a few boroughs. Even in Tower Hamlets, the borough that accounts for two-fifths of all the successful transfers in London, over 40 per cent of the ballots have resulted in a 'no vote'. The 'no vote' in Southwark occurred at the Aylesbury estate in 2001, an NDC area. Seventy-three per cent of Aylesbury tenants voted against transfer on a 75.8 per cent turnout (DCLG, 2007e). Such 'no votes' can have dramatic consequences for estate regeneration, as we discuss below.

Table 12.3 Successful LSVTs and 'no vote' ballots in London by borough, 1992–2007

Borough	Successful LSVTs	Dwellings transferred	'No vote' ballots	Dwellings in 'no vote'
Inner London	41	31,919	20	45,139
Hackney	7	6,986	0	-
Hammersmith and Fulham	1	668	0	-
Islington	6	2,503	1	1,314
Lambeth	7	7,660	0	-
Lewisham	0	0	2	31,212
Southwark	0	0	1	2,500
Tower Hamlets	20	14,102	15	9,613
Westminster	0	0	1	500
Outer London	11	36,004	6	30,245
Bexley	2	8,215	0	-
Brent	1	1,481	0	-
Bromley	1	12,393	0	-
Ealing	0	0	1	534
Enfield	1	1,194	0	-
Greenwich	1	1,280	0	-
Harrow	1	518	0	-
Hillingdon	0	0	1	11,816
Kingston upon Thames[1]	0	0	2	5,010
Merton	1	1,018	1	7,548
Redbridge	0	0	1	5,337
Richmond upon Thames	1	7,139	0	-
Sutton	1	524	0	-
Waltham Forest	1	2,242	0	-
London total	52	67,923	26	75,384

Note: 1. Two 'no votes' in Kingston; dwellings based on 2nd vote, May 2004
Source: DCLG (2007d, 2007e)

'No votes' occur for a variety of reasons including the prior quality of the stock, tenants' perceptions of the council, as well as the nature of any 'no vote' campaign (Daly *et al.*, 2005). DCH has been active in anti-stock transfer campaigns throughout London. DCH campaigns would not be successful, however, unless they were tapping into genuine tenants' concerns. In one sense, LSVT 'no votes' are quite remarkable given that transfer is 'sold' by councils on the basis of bringing real improvements in housing conditions, which council tenants sorely need in London after decades of under-funding. Watt's (2001, 2003, 2005) research on local authority tenants in Camden identified a profound sense of ambivalence towards 'the council' as landlord. On the one hand, the council was a source of frustration, for example in delays over repairs, but it also provided a sense of security as well as genuinely affordable rents. The prospect of switching landlords to housing associations, with their quasi-private identities, filled many Camden tenants with understandable anxiety about rent hikes, security of tenure and what plans any new landlord might have in prime land value areas such as theirs, as one tenant made clear: 'You can pretty well know what the council's plans are, but you don't know what a property developer's ideas could be' (Watt, 2001: 193)

Camden Council aborted an early attempt at partial stock transfer entitled 'New Opportunities' in January 1998 following a vigorous anti-transfer campaign by tenants (Watt, 2001). In 2004 Camden tenants rejected an ALMO by a large majority. Camden council tenants are not unique in London in relation to their concerns regarding de-municipalisation (Woodward, 1991), although social housing in London is different in various ways from the rest of the country, as we now discuss.

What's different about social housing in London?

The national housing system is characterised by increasing differentiation and fragmentation, not least in geographic terms (Hickman and Robinson, 2006). As Bennington *et al.* (2004) discuss, the policy challenges facing social housing in London are therefore quite different from those in other parts of the country. These differences are underpinned by two trends associated with London's global city status. The first is the transformation of the housing market during the last thirty years, notably in relation to the large-scale property development associated with gentrification and the role of the dominant financial services sector (Hamnett, 2003). Up-market gentrification has contributed to a growing affordability crisis that has seen many middle-income households priced out of home ownership and/or out of the city (Watt, 2008a). The second trend is London's accelerating ethnic diversity (Massey, 2007). In addition to the post-war BME population, London is now also the major destination for new waves of migrants, partly from the European Union A8 countries, but also including asylum seekers and refugees. As a result of these two trends, issues of social exclusion and inclusion, community integration and social mixing are rendered more contested in the capital than elsewhere in England. In the rest of this section, we provide an overview as to how social housing in London differs from the rest of England.

First, the social rented sector in London constitutes a large but also diverse part of the housing stock. Whereas social housing nationally accounts for one-fifth of all households (table 12.1), this is over one-third in inner London, although only 18 per cent in outer London (2001 census). In Hackney, Southwark and Tower Hamlets, over half of all households rent from either a local authority or RSL. Not only is social housing on a large scale in London, but it is also diverse in terms of tenure, landlords and dwelling types.

Second, high house prices mean that for many low-middle income Londoners renting is the only realistic option with social renting providing a very major source of affordable housing (Watt, 2003, 2005; Bennington *et al.*, 2004; Hickman and Robinson, 2006). Demand for social rented tenancies is consequently high in London as indicated in table 12.4 which shows the number of households on local authority waiting lists in England for 1997–2006. Over this period, the numbers on the waiting lists increased by 60 per cent in England, but by 82.9 per cent in London. In the early part of the period from 1997–2001, there was only a very small increase in the numbers on the waiting lists and in several parts of the North and Midlands there were even net reductions. From 2001 onwards, there was a very rapid expansion in the size of the LA waiting list in all parts of the country. This was undoubtedly a response to the national crisis of housing affordability (Ambrose, 2006). By 2006, a total of one in ten households were on LA waiting lists in London, and one in eight in inner London (table 12.4). Report after report highlights the unmet housing needs in the capital and the importance of providing more affordable housing units including social renting (GLA, 2004a; Mayor of London, 2006b; ORS, 2004; Shelter, 2005). Given the difficulties that Londoners have in accessing social housing, it is unsurprising that Bennington *et al.* (2004: 6) describe it as 'more than a stepping stone tenure, being also a tenure of choice and destination'. As they say, it also contains many 'committed tenants' (Bennington *et al.* 2004: 6), as for example in Camden discussed above.

Third, there are extensive and intensive problems of housing stress and need in London in terms of homelessness, overcrowding and the condition of the housing stock (Whitehead, 2006). At the end of the third quarter (Q3) 2006, 62,190 homeless households were living in temporary accommodation in London (DCLG, 2007b: table 634). This is two-and-a-half times the 1997 Q3 figure (24,920), i.e. just after New Labour came to power, as well as two-thirds the 2006 Q3 England total. London households are also three times more likely to be overcrowded than most other regions of England (Shelter, 2004: 11). Overcrowding is highest nationally in the three east London authorities of Newham, Tower Hamlets and Hackney and much of this affects BME groups, especially the South Asian population (Shelter, 2004: 12). Such stress indicators are not monopolised by social housing, however, since they are also prevalent within the private rental sector.

Fourth, London's social housing population is more ethnically diverse than elsewhere (Hickman and Robinson, 2006). Fifthly, despite the stereotype regarding excluded, politically disengaged social housing tenants, there are networks of tenant activists, tenants associations and DCH groups in many London boroughs (Watt, 2001; DCH, 2006; Holmes, 2006). In addition, long-leaseholders on council estates can be vocal and well-organised as seen for example by their lobbying of councils over estate services (Watt and Finn, 2000).

Table 12.4 Number of households on local authorities' housing waiting lists in England, by region, 1997–2006 (thousands)

Region	1997	2001	2006	Change 1997–2001 (000s)	Change 2001–2006 (000s)	Change 1997–2006 (000s)	Change 1997–2006 (%)	% of all households in 2006
North East	74	57	95	-17	38	22	29.2	8.8
North West	125	112	217	-12	105	93	74.4	7.6
Yorkshire & the Humber	174	150	247	-23	97	74	42.4	11.8
East Midlands	103	101	134	-2	33	31	30.1	7.6
West Midlands	92	93	127	1	34	35	37.5	5.8
South West	84	90	151	5	62	67	79.1	7.1
East	86	95	135	8	41	49	56.7	5.9
South East	103	130	196	27	66	93	90.8	5.8
London	181	211	331	30	120	150	82.9	10.3
Inner London	98	109	170	11	61	72	73.6	12.7
Outer London	83	103	162	19	59	78	93.8	8.6
England	1022	1039	1634	18	595	613	60.0	7.8

Source: DCLG, 2007c: Table 600 (subject to rounding errors)

The New Deal for Communities

Kintrea (2007: 267) has identified 'at least a dozen significant housing related policies and programmes in operation that were relevant to the improvement of area quality' in England between 1975 and 2000. These ABIs have varied considerably in their aims, size, funding, geographical scale and scope (Lupton, 2003; Kintrea, 2007). London has been a prominent site for ABIs, mainly in its council-built housing estates. Many research studies have been undertaken on these initiatives in London focusing on various combinations of neighbourhoods and schemes (see *inter alia* Jacobs, 1999; Ambrose, 2002; Lupton, 2003; Stewart and Rhoden, 2003). The 'success' or 'failure' of these ABIs is a matter of considerable debate. Even in schemes which have brought some improvements, structural factors related to material inequality (i.e. RED social exclusion) hamper the ability of ABIs to do more than contribute to what Lupton (2003: 212) terms 'managing deprivation' (see Ambrose, 2002).

New Labour's flagship ABI is the New Deal for Communities (NDC) that covers thirty-nine of the most deprived areas across England, including ten in London (CRESR, 2005). It concentrates on five policy issues: housing and the physical environment, health, education, crime and worklessness. The NDC differs from previous regeneration schemes, such as the Single Regeneration Budget (SRB), in several ways:

- longer-term – ten-year period
- greater funding – each scheme has around £50 million
- covers fewer areas – the six rounds of SRB covered over 1,000 areas
- enhanced notion of community participation – the local community has to be extensively consulted including substantial neighbourhood representation on NDC partnership boards.

Survey evidence from the evaluation of the national NDC programme is summarised by Lawless (2006, 2007). His analysis suggests that the NDC can be seen as successful in many ways, notably in relation to improved resident satisfaction levels, although there are also issues around whether or not it has resulted in change in other aspects, for example improvements in jobs. The evaluation and analysis of the NDC programme is incomplete, but it is nevertheless possible to detect a disjunction between the generally positive national survey findings and more critical case study research (Wallace, 2007) including several studies examining NDC areas in London (Perrons and Skyers, 2003; Bennington *et al.*, 2004; Dinham, 2005; 2007). In relation to the Salford NDC, Wallace (2007: 10) emphasises that he is not intending to dismiss some of the 'real achievements' of the NDC, but nevertheless his analysis emphasises the importance of context and how 'the challenge seems to be to shift the emphasis away from centrally defined outputs and models towards understanding and addressing the realities of local communities and those who work with them' (2007: 11).

I will now address some of the local realities Wallace mentions with reference mainly to a discussion of the findings contained in a CRESR (Centre for Regional Economic and Social Research) report by Bennington *et al.* (2004) on the ten London-based NDCs. Although housing is only one element in the five-fold thematic focus of NDCs, it played a central role in the London NDCs, accounting for a larger proportion of funding compared to the rest of England. This housing emphasis 'reflects the priorities of local residents, concerned not only about the condition of the housing stock but also the consequence of poor housing for their health, well-being and safety' (Bennington *et al.*, 2004). Many of the housing programmes involved major redevelopment schemes, for example at South Kilburn where £21 million was allocated to housing (see Stewart and Rhoden, 2003), but others were more small-scale (Bennington *et al.*, 2004: 13–14, table 4.1).

Bennington and colleagues highlight the way the London NDCs operate within a particular and even unique housing market context that impacts greatly upon their programmes. We have discussed this context above, but the following are worthy of further commentary. First, whilst house prices in London are extremely high, the London NDC residents have similarly deprived profiles to their peers in the rest of England. The result is that both residents and NDC officers considered home ownership an unrealistic goal, and this even applied to shared ownership. The result was that 'affordable housing was understood to mean social rented housing and more was thought to be needed to address problems of overcrowding, homelessness and the difficulties encountered by young people wanting to leave home but remain in their local area' (Bennington *et al.*, 2004: 12). Second, social renting has an even greater presence in the London NDC areas than elsewhere. Table 12.5 shows the tenure profile of the ten London NDC areas in comparison to London and England. Whereas social renting accommodates one-fifth of households in England and just over one-quarter in London, it accounts for over half in most of the London NDC areas. Furthermore, the social housing tenure composition is heavily weighted towards local authority rather than housing association renting in all the London NDC areas.

The main priorities for NDC action in relation to housing included addressing the poor housing conditions, notably the deterioration of the existing stock and overcrowding, and increasing the supply of affordable housing especially social renting. In achieving these goals, Bennington *et al.* (2004) identified several challenges and opportunities that they regarded as particular to NDCs in London arising from the special nature of the housing market. One opportunity facing the London NDCs was that a good deal of confidence regarding the long-term sustainability of the NDC neighbourhoods was expressed. However, the extremely high land prices in London rendered redevelopment of the social housing stock more expensive than elsewhere in England. Therefore a major challenge was that the large costs of redevelopment in London meant that funding gaps appeared. In those NDCs with large redevelopment programmes, 'the sums were reported to "just not add up"' (Bennington *et al.*, 2004: 13). Senior NDC

Table 12.5 Tenure profile of NDC areas in London, 2001 (household %)

NDC	London borough location of NDC	Tenure of NDC			
		LA rented	HA rented	Private rented[1]	Owner occupied[2]
Aylesbury Estate	Southwark	84.0	3.6	5.2	7.2
Clapham Park	Lambeth	44.8	5.1	17.8	32.3
Finsbury (EC1)	Islington	54.9	14.4	12.7	18.0
New Cross Gate	Lewisham	48.7	8.0	13.8	29.5
North Fulham	Hammersmith & Fulham	32.3	14.8	22.3	30.6
Ocean Estate	Tower Hamlets	50.3	11.9	14.9	22.9
Seven Sisters	Haringey	36.7	10.9	19.3	33.1
Shoreditch – Our Way	Hackney	53.0	12.4	11.9	22.7
South Kilburn	Brent	56.7	12.4	13.2	17.7
West Ham & Plaistow	Newham	39.7	14.1	15.1	31.1
London		17.1	9.1	17.3	56.5
England		13.2	6.1	12.0	68.7

Notes:
1. Private rented includes rented from private landlords, lettings agencies, employer, family, friends or living rent free.
2. Owner occupied includes shared ownership.
Source: Neighbourhood Statistics website, 2001 Census

officers thought that the programme had underestimated the extent of housing problems in some NDC areas and also failed to predict how important housing issues were to residents. Bridging the funding gap meant having to lever in large sums from the private sector that in turn brought compromises since it reduced the available land for affordable housing units and did little to meet the housing needs of existing residents. Finding partners brought delays and as a result 'faltering commitment to the NDC among local residents' (Bennington et al., 2004: 16). One option was stock transfer. The CRESR report provides a case study of an anonymous failed stock transfer NDC for which there was no obvious government funding mechanism that would provide the necessary capital given New Labour's insistence on either transfer, PFI or an ALMO. Bennington and colleagues also revealed challenges in relation to resident engagement. These stemmed from the ethnic diversity of the areas' population that was manifest partly in the plethora of local community organisations, but also in the tensions between the different groups involved in the NDC process.

Another challenge arose from the fact that a significant proportion of properties bought under the RTB by ex-tenants in London, especially inner London, are flats rather than houses as in the rest of England. This meant that there were large numbers of 'long-leaseholders' in many London NDC estates. According to Bennington et al. (2004), disputes arose between these lease-holders and councils over payment for costs of housing improvements, and in addition the NDC had to pay for compensation to leaseholders living in blocks earmarked for demolition, another funding drain on the NDC and additional potential source of conflict. Tensions also arose between leaseholders and tenants over improvements and payment responsibilities, as well as over stock transfers. In one NDC, the various conflicts of interest meant that the regeneration process was creating anything but 'a sustainable community':[3]

> The complex dynamic between the NDC, the local authority, lease-holders and tenants was reported to be fermenting tension within the local community, undercutting effective partnership working between the NDC and the local authority and delaying delivery of the NDC housing programme
>
> (Bennington et al., 2004: 22)

In relation to population changes, 'NDC officers and local authority staff tended to regard greater social mix as both an important objective and inevitable consequence of the NDCs housing programme' (Bennington et al., 2004: 29). This change would primarily result from the increasing number of new homes for sale rather than the displacement of existing residents, although it was thought that the latter would also occur. This 'social mixing' was regarded as an opportunity in that it was expected that the incoming higher income residents would raise the economic base of the area. However, existing residents, as well as NDC and LA officers, thought that the anticipated influx of new affluent people (a.k.a. gentrifiers) also represented a challenge that could result in tensions:

> I think there is a certain amount of, I suppose it's natural animosity about, it's like a social engineering thing, a sort of gentrification process and people are asking 'why are they bringing the rich in?'
>
> (NDC resident; Bennington *et al.*, 2004: 25)

The politically charged issue of working-class displacement in relation to urban regeneration and gentrification that Bennington and colleagues touch upon is one that is decidedly under-researched, as Slater (2006) and Watt (2008b) argue.

The CRESR report provides several policy lessons for the NDC programme in London, but 'underpinning virtually all these points is one issue; funding' (Bennington *et al.*, 2004; 30). Two of the policy implications in ensuring a 'successful' NDC are 'managing community expectations' and 'facing up to pragmatic realities' (Bennington *et al.*, 2004: 30-1). Given the scale of funding required for major housing redevelopment, such implications mean that NDCs have to emphasise to residents the practical realities about stock transfer, higher densities and gentrification, irrespective of whether or not they, the council or the residents themselves actually want these things to occur (ibid.). Despite the important data contained in the CRESR report and its many valuable lessons for social housing and regeneration, the authors tend to gloss over the way that their recommendations regarding 'pragmatic realities' and 'managing' community expectations sit uneasily with the other element of the NDC philosophy, i.e. community participation: 'by forging strong local alliances and ploughing back the knowledge and experience gained, NDC aims to enable local people to take charge of their own future' (ODPM, 2003c: 2). I examine these issues further in the east London context.

The New Deal for Communities and community participation in East London[4]

The Ocean Estate NDC is located in central Stepney in the east London Borough of Tower Hamlets (see figures 12.3 and 12.4). According to the Ocean NDC website, the core NDC area, centered on the large council-built Ocean estate, has approximately 6,500 residents living in 2,000 households. A large percentage of the properties on the Ocean NDC are social rented, mainly LA, whilst a significant minority of households are long-leaseholders under the RTB (see table 12.5). The residents are ethnically mixed but include a large Bangladeshi population. The Ocean NDC area suffers from multiple deprivation including poverty, overcrowding, ill health and worklessness (Anttila and Wright, 2004: 35-6; Beatty *et al.*, 2005). Overcrowding in the Ocean NDC area was over eleven times the national rate in 2001 and was also the highest level within the thirty-nine NDC areas (Beatty *et al.*, 2005: 7). A planning report indicated that 96 per cent of rented dwellings on the Ocean estate failed the Decent Homes Standard on one or more of four criteria (Mayor of London, 2005b). Despite the Ocean's manifold travails, it must be noted that poverty and deprivation are recurrent features across many parts of Tower Hamlets, one of the most deprived local authority areas in England (Watt and Finn, 2000; Ambrose, 2002; Hamnett, 2003; Anttila and Wright, 2004: 35–6; Shelter, 2004).

Because of the extent and depth of housing-related deprivation and needs in the Ocean estate, the NDC placed a large emphasis upon redevelopment of the housing stock; £21 million of the £56.6 million total grant was earmarked for the housing programme. However, the NDC Housing Masterplan estimated that the refurbishment and rebuilding bill could be over £340 million (Ocean NDC, 2002: 2). In order to meet the funding gap, the NDC and Tower Hamlets LA selected Sanctuary Housing Association (HA) as the partner to redevelop the properties following a mooted stock transfer to Sanctuary. Significant delays occurred to the housing programme however ('Ocean estate: new deal or old problems?', *BBC News 24*, 17 February 2004), whilst the stock transfer and anti-transfer campaigns on the Ocean estate took place in a politically charged atmosphere ('Tower Hamlets: the transfer battleground', *Inside Housing*, 2 March 2007). The pro-transfer view was that transferring to Sanctuary HA would inject large sums of otherwise unavailable finance into housing regeneration, whereas the local DCH campaign stressed 'privatisation' and what they thought would be a resulting under-supply of affordable properties for rent but increase in 'luxury' flats for sale. Eventually, in September 2006, the Ocean tenants decisively turned down the stock transfer option with a 63 per cent 'no vote' on a 67.8 per cent turnout (DCLG, 2007d). Consequently the housing programme part of the NDC came to an abrupt halt, as bluntly stated on the Ocean NDC website: 'The results of the housing stock transfer ballot on the Ocean returned a 'no' vote, meaning the majority of tenants who voted wish to remain with the council as their landlord. The Ocean NDC housing programme is therefore suspended.' (www.oceanndc.co.uk/index.php?projectdirectory, accessed 5 August 2007).

According to its newsletter, the Ocean NDC has brought improvements in many issues which affect Ocean estate residents, for example educational attainment and neighbourhood facilities (Ocean NDC, 2004). However, despite such achievements, the Ocean NDC's transformation of the estate into a 'place to be proud of' (see figure 12.3) is decidedly incomplete in relation to its ambitious and much-needed housing programme. Parts of the estate continued to have a run-down appearance in 2007 (see figure 12.4). Given Tower Hamlets council's own capacity to fund only minor repairs, it was announced during summer 2007 that the Ocean NDC Company was being wound up and that a new 'Regeneration Trust' would take on the delivery of the remaining NDC programme, including attracting new funding for housing regeneration, although tenants would remain with the council ('Ocean Estate improvements', *Tower Hamlets News Pages*, www.towerhamlets.gov.uk, 27 June 2007). It is too early, however, to tell what this might mean for the Ocean residents.

12.3
**Ocean NDC 'Welcomes
You'.**
Source: Paul Watt, 2007

What does the above tell us about community participation in regeneration, one of the key NDC programme aims? One can infer from the size of the 'no vote' in the stock transfer ballot that what most engaged Ocean tenants wanted, i.e. to remain with Tower Hamlets council as their landlord but also to have the major stock improvements that everyone agrees they need, did not occur. This 'choice', i.e. effectively the fourth option for council housing as advocated by DCH and discussed above, was denied to them, even though they voted for it in large numbers. Their 'choice' was ultimately hemmed in by the neo-liberal ideological and financial parameters of New Labour national housing policy, that if council tenants want major stock improvements they can only have them if they switch landlords (Ginsburg, 2005). Weaver (2001, cited in Imrie and Raco, 2003: 28) has identified a similar

12.4

Ocean Park: a rundown appearance?

Source: Paul Watt, 2007

'forced choice' scenario in the case of the Shoreditch NDC in the London Borough of Hackney.

Conclusion: future prospects

Considerable uncertainty exists regarding the direction of social housing policy (Cole, 2007). Early expectations of a positive shift in New Labour policy towards council housing as a result of Gordon Brown's accession to Prime Ministership ('Labour U-turn on council house building', *The Guardian* 14 July 2007) seems unlikely to be realised. The Housing Green Paper, published in July 2007, mentioned '45,000 new social homes a year by 2010-11' (DCLG, 2007f: 72), although its comments regarding local authorities' role are vague and fall well short of any 'Labour U-turn'.

The future for London's social housing is also uncertain because the Mayor of London's policy framework will not be fully in place until 2008. Amendments to the *London Plan* increased the overall housing target to 30,500 additional homes per annum (Mayor of London, 2006b: 16). The *London Plan* advocated that half the additional dwellings should be 'affordable', 70 per cent social and 30 per cent intermediate housing (GLA, 2004a: 63). Research commissioned by the

Greater London Authority suggests that the numbers of additional social housing units which will be needed over the next decade exceed those set out in the *London Plan* by a considerable margin (ORS, 2004). Although 'building more homes' is one of the policy areas recommended in the *Consultation Paper* (Mayor of London, 2006b: 8), commitments to social housing provision and pubic sector delivery in this paper are both sketchy. It is difficult to judge how far Ken Livingstone's targets will be realised, although existing trends are not fortuitous (see figure 12.2). For example, research on the Thames Gateway suggests there will be substantial shortfalls in affordable housing provision below the *London Plan* targets (LERI, 2006).

Existing policy and trends on housing provision in London therefore suggest that social housing is unlikely to be produced at the requisite level to meet the needs of the many thousands of ill-housed ordinary Londoners. If this remains the case, then any ABIs which attempt to foster sustainable communities in council-built estates will face an uphill struggle, as the discussion of London NDCs above suggests. NDCs face massive challenges in London, not least around funding for major housing renewal and the New Labour shibboleth of stock transfer. These can exacerbate local community tensions rather than foster cohesion as estate residents vie with each other over how programmes should be run. Such tensions overlay existing fault-lines of ethnicity and faith as Dinham's (2005, 2007) research indicates, but also tenure divisions between tenants and leaseholders as Bennington *et al.* (2004) show. Entirely new potential sources of social tension may even be generated, for example between those tenants who advocate transfer and those opposed to it.

Furthermore, social mixing, which is a corollary of large-scale redevelopment in London NDC areas, seems to mean bringing in the home-owning middle-classes to council-built estates (Bennington *et al.*, 2004). This is not something which existing deprived populations are necessarily going to gladly accept, as evidence from other London ABIs indicates (Lupton, 2003: 194–6). Poor urban working-class residents' anxieties (including concerns over displacement) over what can be conceptualised as 'state-led gentrification' are far from irrational even though they are currently under-explored by the academy (Slater, 2006; Watt, 2008b).

New Labour's efforts to 'tackle social exclusion' were symbolised by two of Tony Blair's visits, firstly to the Aylesbury estate in July 1997, and secondly to the Ocean estate in January 2001. Both estates were included in the NDC programme and both subsequently rejected stock transfer by large margins in ballots with substantial turnouts. As a consequence the housing renewal elements in each NDC stalled. After several years' involvement in New Labour's flagship regeneration scheme, neither neighbourhood has got what it deserved in terms of housing redevelopment, whatever other improvements the NDC might have brought. By RED social exclusion criteria of housing improvements and expansion of affordable housing for deprived populations, some London NDCs have struggled to deliver. The Ocean NDC housing programme was suspended whilst the Aylesbury estate is to be demolished. The latter decision has been dubbed 'social cleansing' by some local tenants' groups ('The big squeeze', *SocietyGuardian.co.uk*, 22 September 2005). Council tenants in these and other London NDC areas (Imrie and Raco, 2003: 28) were effectively penalised for not accepting the terms on which regeneration was being offered to them, terms in which the notion of 'community participation' is ambivalent at best and compromised at worst.

Acknowledgements

Thanks to the editors, Stuart Wilks-Heeg, Norman Ginsburg, Paul Burnham and Gareth Millington for their helpful comments on earlier versions of this chapter.

Notes

1   This oft-used definition begs the question 'how far below market levels?' Housing 'affordability' is really only meaningful in relation to other household costs and incomes, as Ambrose (2006) emphasises.

2   There is also a large and vigorous housing co-operative sector in London (Clapham and Kintrea, 1992; Holmes, 2006).

3   Perrons and Skyers (2003) make a similar point in relation to the Shoreditch – Our Way NDC.

4   This section draws upon documents, official data and websites related to the Ocean Estate NDC, an estate visit in August 2007 by the author, as well as existing research on the Ocean and Tower Hamlets. It is not being claimed that this discussion represents a comprehensive account of the Ocean NDC, not least given that this is in a transition phase; further research is clearly necessary.

Part IV

Community governance and urban change

Chapter 13

Regenerating the South Bank: reworking community and the emergence of post-political regeneration

Guy Baeten

The South Bank: the adversarial community, community incorporated and death by community

Regeneration efforts on the South Bank are an example of some of the basic contradictions London's development has gone through during the twentieth century. Plans for the South Bank have always sought an impossible balance between the local interests of inhabitants and the global interests of London's international flows of capital, investment, tourism and culture. The South Bank is one of London's prime battlegrounds where London's crisis is fought and its future re-invented. Over the past decades, the clashes of interest have resulted in unique victories and major defeats, for both corporate headquarters seeking development profits, and citizens seeking affordable housing. The South Bank is the borderland where the two Londons north and south of the river meet, and engage in conflict over who owns, controls and decides over local land use – and, by implication, the 'right' to inner London.

This chapter will argue that the South Bank is a key site in London to observe and analyse the emergence of 'post-political regeneration'. Following the work of Rancière, Mouffe, Badiou and Swyngedouw, amongst others, it will be argued that 'politics' have been evacuated from urban renewal efforts and that regeneration policies on the South Bank have been depoliticised through a range of 'post-political regeneration tactics'. The argument will unfold in three steps. First, I will briefly reconstruct the history of the Coin Street campaign of the

1970s and 1980s which saw the emergence of an 'adversarial community' on the South Bank and a (rare) moment of 'regeneration politics proper' in London. Second, I will briefly describe how the incorporation of the community into mighty business-friendly partnerships during the 1980s heralded the end of community-powered regeneration.

Third, current developments on the South Bank have effectively annihilated debate about alternative development visions for the neighbourhood. Contemporary power relations are such that dispute, conflict and contradiction between local and global interests have been largely suspended through the successful encapsulation of advocates of non-business interests into corporate-friendly organisations and partnerships that have installed a non-oppositional, post-political, non-democratic regime of regeneration. This chapter's contribution will focus on a range of post-political regeneration tactics through which the end of regeneration disputes is effectively achieved: neutralising dissent, particularising universal demand and localising the local, moralising regeneration, regeneration populism and regeneration-beyond-the-state.

Grand aspirations for the South Bank

The idea that the South Bank's nineteenth-century industrial infrastructure and working-class estates should be regenerated and integrated into the London of finance, commerce, culture and political power has dominated South Bank planning throughout the twentieth century. Planners tried for the first time to revive the area in 1915 through locating the London County Hall, the venue of the then London-wide government, on the South Bank (see figure 13.1). It was hoped that this prestigious landmark building would attract substantial investment towards the South Bank. This first regeneration effort failed and made the London planner Abercrombie conclude in his 1944 London County Plan that:

> it is one the great anomalies of the Capital that while the river, from Westminster eastwards, is lined on the north side with magnificent buildings and possesses a spacious and attractive embankment road, the corresponding south bank, except St Thomas's Hospital and County Hall, should present a depressing ... appearance lacking any sense of dignity and order appropriate to its location at the centre of London and fronting onto the great waterway.
>
> (Abercrombie, 1944: 112)

In the long term, the South Bank, according to Abercrombie, needed a 'Great Cultural Centre embracing amongst other features a modern theatre, a large concert hall and the headquarters of various organisations'.

Abercrombie's visionary ideas have strongly influenced post-war planning on the South Bank. The Royal Festival Hall, one of the major venues for the 1951 Festival of Britain, became Abercrombie's Great Cultural Centre and, in line

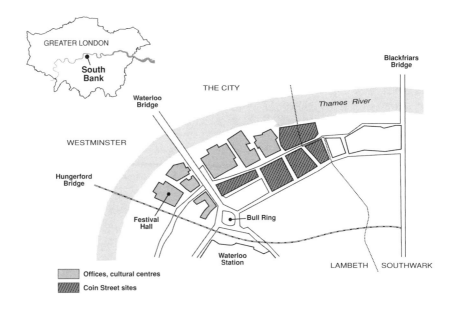

with his ideas, the National Theatre, the Hayward Gallery and the Queen Elizabeth Hall were added in the 1960s. The South Bank's cultural centres soon became synonymous with 'high brow arts' and remained isolated attraction poles for the middle classes in the midst of the South Bank's pockets of socio-economic deprivation and working-class estates. The efforts to regenerate the South Bank continued. As a Comprehensive Development Area in 1955, the South Bank was zoned for 'central uses', and both the 1962 Initial Development Plan for London and the 1969 Greater London Development Plan once again earmarked the South Bank as a preferred location for central area uses and office development. However, given the South Bank's marginal position on the London office market (some office blocks were constructed as a result of temporary boosts in office demand in Westminster and the City), none of these post-war master plans significantly altered the area. Meanwhile, industrial employment was disappearing, the population fell spectacularly from fifty thousand just after the war to a mere five thousand in the early 1970s, and most shops and schools had closed down. Great plans and planners, in their efforts to detach this southern border area from the south and integrate it in the political, economic and cultural grandeur of the north bank, had painfully failed to address the South Bank's local problems and needs.

The Coin Street campaign: the adversarial community

Community resistance on the South Bank started formally when the Waterloo Community Development Group (WCDG) was set up in 1972 to halt the extension of the Imperial War Museum into the adjacent public park. Through organising meetings with Lambeth planners and politicians, inspired by the 1971 Town and Country Planning Act which introduced public consultation in the planning process, WCDG managed to influence the contents of the 1977 Waterloo District Plan (WDP), which shifted its initial support for office development to housing (Self, 1979). The then Labour-controlled Greater London Council approved the WDP, but it also made it clear that planning permission for offices was not excluded. The authorities thus gave an ambivalent indication of what the planning priorities should be on the South Bank. When the GLC fell into Conservative hands in May 1977, it firmly favoured office development on the South Bank, in contrast with the WDP priorities.

The community battle for housing and against offices began in earnest in the late 1970s, when planning applications came in from Heron Corporation and the Vestey Company to erect a 140 m skyscraper hotel – possibly then the tallest hotel in Europe – and over 130,000 m² of offices on the Coin Street site. Half of the site was owned by the Vestey Company, the other half by the GLC itself (Tuckett, 1992). In an effort to counter the GLC, the borough of Lambeth applied for 251 mainly low-rise dwellings and also applied for a compulsory purchase order to acquire the sites from the GLC. And the Coin Street campaigners, who feared that 'their' plan, the housing-minded WDP, would soon be overrun by one of these developments, decided to develop their own plan for 360 low-rise dwellings, a riverside walk and park, shops and other facilities.

The then Environment Secretary Michael Heseltine called in all proposals for consideration at the inquiry that opened in May 1979. It would become 'one of the longest, costliest, most important and most confused planning enquiries ever held in Britain' (Tuckett, 1992). The fight between the local residents and the property developers was one between David and Goliath: the private developers had each appointed Queen's Counsels and the Conservative GLC had put most of its planning and legal staff at the disposal of the private developers. The local community did not have access to these powerful instruments to influence the course of the enquiry, but they successfully campaigned both on the streets and in the enquiry rooms, and kept the press aware (Cowan, 1979).

Michael Heseltine decided that none of the proposals would be approved. The office schemes were 'massive and over-dominant' while the housing schemes failed to 'exploit the employment potential of the site'. This conclusion was in fact an invitation to develop a compromise proposal that would scale down office development and would bring in more facilities for residents. The GLC and both the boroughs of Lambeth and Southwark put pressure on the community campaigners to accept this compromise, but they developed a new scheme that included even more houses than the previous scheme. Meanwhile, Greycoats and Commercial Properties had joined forces and formed Greycoat Commercial Estates Limited. Their revised development plan, designed by Richard Rogers and applauded by the architectural press, consisted of a rim of office towers along the river. There was no sense of compromise between the local community plans and the developers' plans. A second inquiry seemed inevitable.

The GLC, again Labour-controlled after the 1981 elections, thoroughly influenced the course of the second enquiry. The Coin Street campaigners received not only financial and technical help from the GLC but also political support. The GLC stated its commitment to housing development on the South Bank in its 1981 report *The Future of the South Bank Wider Area*, and it started to implement its Community Area Policy in sixteen neighbourhoods, including the South Bank, that had to be protected from gentrification and commercial development originating from the City and Westminster.

The second inquiry, which ran until March 1982, ended in a peculiar decision by the then Secretary of State Michael Heseltine. In contrast with the first inquiry, when none of the proposals were granted planning permission, this time both proposals for housing and offices were approved. This decision, again, seemed to be in favour of Greycoats: having already an option on the GLC-owned land, while owning the other half themselves, they now only had to obtain the necessary permits. But the campaign machinery was set to work again. In a remarkable alliance with all the planning authorities (the GLC and the boroughs of Lambeth and Southwark), Coin Street managed to systematically postpone the necessary permits for years. On top of that, the early 1980s witnessed a slackening demand for offices.

Greycoats decided in 1984 not to take the battle further and sold its holdings to the GLC. The GLC, in turn, sold the 13 acres of land to the newly set-up Coin Street Community Builders (CSCB), the organisation that on behalf of the campaigners would implement the housing plan. This event is still catalogued as a major 'community victory' in London. It is argued by some that the Coin Street success story could not have taken place without the GLC's exceptional generosity, or GLC's 'looniness' (Jeffery, 1997) (the land was sold to CSCB for a fraction of its 'real' value). But the then Chair of the GLC Planning Committee George Nicholson argues in an interview that the GLC acted neither illegally nor inappropriately. On the contrary, as a planning authority, it had the power to change land uses and as a strategic authority, it had to intervene in the land market, preferably when there was a bust in the land market.

Competitive partnership planning on the South Bank: community incorporated

Meanwhile, the urban regeneration climate in the UK was changing under Conservative rule. The Thatcher administration abolished the GLC in 1986, which implied the end of Community Area Policy, and hence the end of community-based development as a governmental policy. It also meant that the South Bank, which had been the Community Area Policy's showcase (receiving the bulk of CAP funding), saw its public financial support cut off. The Coin Street Community Builders now became fully dependent on private bank loans to implement the community's housing scheme – a new financial reality that significantly altered the development course of the South Bank. The Community Builders were now 'cast adrift in the shark-infested waters of the London property market in a small rowing boat' (Brindley, 2000:376).

The John Major administration subsequently introduced a shift from centrally controlled allocation of regeneration budgets to competition for regeneration budgets. Partnerships, consisting of local business elites, local authorities, the voluntary sector and the local community, now had to submit bid documents that would compete for scarce, centrally run regeneration budgets. The new approach to urban regeneration was underpinned by a range of new planning instruments that would marshal an evolution from planning as governmental regulation to planning as 'partnership' (Blackman, 1997). Partnership-based planning not only changed the nature of spending but also demanded a reworking of existing local power relations through the formation of partnerships between actors from the private sector, the community, the voluntary sector, local authorities and others. Although the local authorities were supposed to play the most decisive role in coordination, leadership and contact with central government, and although the 'local community' was supposed to play an important role in those partnerships, the epicentre of power shifted to non-accountable partnership boards with no statutory status (Cullingworth and Nadin, 1997).

Initially however, the new neo-liberal regeneration climate hardly affected the South Bank and its development: it remained relatively detached from, and untouched by, London's economic, cultural and political centres north of the river. The river continued to act as both a physical and a socio-cultural barrier between north and south. Throughout the 1980s and 1990s, the run-down areas on the South Bank remained largely perceived as unattractive places. Various spots on the South Bank, in particular the Bull Ring, would soon be hosting more than a hundred rough sleepers while the loss of population, shops and schools continued. This is how a local journalist described the South Bank:

> The South Bank should be a kind of place Londoners and visitors arriving at the new Waterloo International terminal inevitably make for . . . The South Bank dream is great, the reality is a nightmare . . . [The] first indication of the cardboard city is the strong stench of urine. It smells like a geriatric ward because the few older homeless inhabitants are often sick and incontinent. But the majority of the population is young and aggressive . . . The South Bank Centre . . . has recorded a fall of 21 per cent in average attendances at the Festival Hall over the past 21 years . . . Office-workers hurry through it at rush-hours . . . Beyond that, under the railway arch, there is a suburb of cardboard city which disturbs the police, the fire-brigade and massive employers like Shell, never mind the casual *visitor*.
>
> (Fay, 1993)

Images of, and realities on, the South Bank swiftly started to change after the community campaigners changed gear and found new allies in the corporate headquarters on the South Bank who showed an interest in making their immediate environment safer and more pleasant for their employees and visiting business relations. Key players in regeneration policies on the South Bank gradually moved away from the principles of community planning and adapted to the new partnership planning environment under Conservative rule. Coin Street Community Builders set up partnerships with other groups, such as the South Bank Employers Group (SBEG), local authorities and the Cross River Partnership. The 1990s have witnessed a continuous flow of public and private investments into the South Bank. Most of the derelict land has now been cleared and turned into housing, shops and restaurants, parks, public squares and riverside walks.

Oxo Tower Wharf and its landmark art deco tower, which would have been demolished under the office development scheme of the 1970s, now hosts seventy-eight housing units and symbolises the community victory ('houses instead of offices') on the South Bank (see figure 13.2). Homeless settlements have been removed and some major new tourist attraction poles (the giant IMAX cinema and the London Eye Ferris wheel) have been in operation for quite a while. Other major regeneration projects, including those on the nearby Bankside such as the new Tate Gallery and the Shakespeare Globe, make it far more acceptable for Londoners and tourists to 'cross the river' for other purposes than heading to the Royal Festival Hall, the National Theatre or Waterloo Station. It seems to be the case that the South Bank, after almost a century of good planning intentions and several failed efforts to cash in on its unique location in the heart of London, is finally linking up with the bustling centres on the North Bank. In total, more than thirty individual projects are implemented or planned on the South Bank and Bankside, the so-called 'Millennium Mile'.

13.2
The Oxo Tower: flagship of community-led regeneration on the South Bank.
Source: Guy Baeten

Some residents and representatives of local organisations consider the current successful regeneration projects on the South Bank to be a mere drop in an ocean of acute housing shortage, skyrocketing house prices and homelessness. The direct social impact of the regeneration schemes on the South Bank may indeed be limited, but its long-term contribution to 're-imagineering' the South Bank from an unsafe, deprived working-class neighbourhood to a safe, thriving middle-class area might be much larger. A marketing study by Bond Clarkson Russell (1995) states that the South Bank has no area identity, it is 'off the map', it is a bleak, hostile environment and the cultural centres are a mere place for 'highbrow arts'. The South Bank was perceived as a hostile, dangerous and unsafe place, home to the lower classes and the underclass, not part of the 'real London' north of the river. It is a place where the (affluent) middle classes would not go to and stay.

Some believe it is ironic that the South Bank redevelopment, which is invoked in the urban regeneration literature as a prime example of 'community planning' (Brindley *et al.* 1992), has actually completely moved away from 'community planning'. Other grass-roots movements in the area, such as the Waterloo Community Development Group, which initially stayed more faithful to the original objectives of the Coin Street campaign, overtly accused the Coin Street Community Builders and its allies of 'stealing' the land it acquired through community action from the residents' community and handing it over to power brokers whose regeneration objectives and ideology are no longer compatible with the initial cause (Baeten, 2000). In 2006 the CSCB even proposed a 54-metre high tower with mixed use on 'community land'.

Furthermore, in order to demonstrate the 'potential' and 'opportunities' for regeneration, bid documents tend to leave out the worst problems in the area and concentrate on commercial development. This entails a shift away from social concerns towards the priorities of promoting economic efficiency and industrial competitiveness (Oatley 1995). The attempt to develop a 'cultural quarter' on the South Bank is, according to Newman and Smith (2000: 9), 'an opportunist and image-based response to dominant property speculation'. Existing communities tend to be excluded and homeless residents moved out. Partnerships thrive on easy assumptions about the possibility of an inclusive society. According to Geddes (2000: 797), 'the dominant practice of local partnership – as opposed to some of its rhetoric – enshrines elitist, neocorporatist or neopluralist principles, and excludes or marginalises more radical egalitarian and solidaristic possibilities'. The idea of 'partnership' may intuitively be associated with local democracy and inclusion, but it remains in fact an overused and ambiguous term (see Hastings, 1996).

Coin Street Community Builders, accused of 'betraying' the community cause, saw several of its founding members leave, who continued their – marginalised – fight against unwanted regeneration projects within the philosophy of radical and local basic democracy. The 'local community', once united in its fight against its external enemy of office developers, was torn apart between *realos* (pragmatists) and *fundis* (idealists) as soon as the external enemy had gone and the local community, through CSCB, had to take up an entirely new 'big business' role as owner and property developer of one of the most wanted inner London sites. Like other partnership-based regeneration efforts, it has reduced the South Bank regeneration to an endless series of partnership initiatives and local experiments, and the fragmentation and disorganisation of local politics and policy (see Bassett, 1996).

Post-political regeneration: death by community

Politics proper and the absence of it

The general understanding of politics – a set of procedures that organises collectivities and powers, distributes places and roles for people, and legitimises that order, should, according to Rancière (1998), not be understood as 'politics' proper but rather as what he labels 'the police'. The police order is, essentially, 'the law', which defines whom has access to what and who has not. It is primarily

> an order of bodies that defines the allocation of ways of doing, ways of being, and ways of saying and sees that those bodies are assigned [. . .] to a particular place and task; it is an order of the visible and the sayable that sees that a particular activity is visible and another is not, that this speech is understood as discourse and another as noise.
>
> (Rancière, 1998: 29)

The police order ultimately determines the distinction between those who have a name and those who have not, those who can speak and will be listened to and those who will not be, in short those who have a part and those who have not.

Politics, then, is not about managing and sustaining this order through negotiation and consensus (Dikeç, 2002). Politics is the opposite of 'the police'. Politics arise when the police order is broken, when bodies are shifted away from the places assigned to them. Politics make visible what was not to be seen, it turns into discourse what was previously qualified as noise. Spectacularly or subtly, politics always undoes the perceptible divisions of the police order by implementing a heterogeneous assumption, 'that of a part of those who have no part'. The heterogeneous assumption will demonstrate 'the sheer contingency of the order' as it will expose the 'equality of any speaking being with any other speaking being' (Rancière, 1998: 30). Politics can arise when the logic of equality confronts the logic of 'the police'. Politics emerge when bodies step out of their assigned roles in the hierarchical order and occupy new roles and spaces. An important implication of this is that politics do not automatically occur simply because power relationships are at work. Power relationships may exist between groups and result in conflict but not necessarily in politics as the police order may be left untouched. 'For a thing to be political, it must give rise to a meeting of police logic and egalitarian logic that is never set up in advance' (Rancière, 1998: 32).

Post-political regeneration

Seen through this lens, urban regeneration politics are not necessarily political simply because power relationships between different stakeholders with conflicting interests exist and are dealt with at the negotiation table. Regeneration politics only start when one party steps out of its assigned negotiation role and puts forward a claim that threatens the existing police order, existing plans or existing negotiation procedures that underlie and reproduce existing inequalities in urban neighbourhoods. The incorporation of a pressure group in a regeneration partnership, however heated the debates this may trigger, is not political as it does not undermine the hierarchical assignment of bodies in places – perhaps quite the opposite. 'Nothing is political in itself for the political only happens by means of a principle that does not belong to it: equality' (Rancière, 1998: 33). The shift towards partnership planning and the annihilation of 'disorganised', non-institutionalised voice raising in regeneration efforts has precisely installed a regeneration order that is non-political. Regeneration efforts, exclusively conducted through the institutionalised channels of partnerships and governmental grants, create a *singular* discourse about what regeneration should be about, and reduce *any* alternative regeneration view, expressed by whomever whenever, to sheer background noise.

Parties expressing alternatives will be either labelled 'traditionalists' living in a romanticised past when urban politics were still possible, or 'fundamentalists' who do not understand contemporary requirements and conditions for successful regeneration. In today's harsh climate of global competition, urban planning and regeneration should not be left in lay hands but should be firmly steered by authoritarian technocratic conglomerates of professionals and politicians who pursue regeneration-beyond-the-state. Partnership planning makes equal partners – inhabitants and other unprofessional interest groups whose interests fall outside the economic logics of maximising land rent – invisible either through exclusion from the regeneration process or through incorporation and marginalisation within partnership organisations.

With the South Bank Employers Group currently deciding over all the important aspects of regeneration, the instalment of a regeneration police order, which assigns clear roles and places to individuals and groups and thus defines who is included in the regeneration process and who is not, is now complete on the South Bank. Uniquely steered by business-friendly agendas, regeneration *politics* are dead and can only be resurrected when the existing regeneration *police* are confronted with their antagonistic principle: equality. The idea that equal parties have equal voices in a regeneration process sounds odd in neo-liberal, post-political times as it could endanger and potentially undermine the hegemonic discourse and practice of pro-growth regeneration efforts.

Post-political regeneration tactics

Given the vast amount of scepticism and criticism partnership planning was receiving, some commentators concluded already after the first round of the SRB (late 1990s) that 'partnership' was a largely discredited notion in planning (see for example Colenutt, 1999). The New Labour government, however, was to take partnership planning to a new level the Conservatives could not have imagined. It is in this late stage of partnership planning, with its obsessive focus on dialogical, harmonious, communitarian cooperation between different interest groups, that 'post-political' regeneration effectively emerged. The elimination of dissensus, and therefore the end of politics proper (Rancière, 2003), takes place through an armature of post-political tactics that will be explored below.

Neutralising dissent

In the early years of the twenty-first century, a complex web of organisations (partners) involved in local planning has emerged on the South Bank – a network that is ultimately dominated by the local corporations through the South Bank Employers Group and its subsidiaries which control the SRB budget and decision procedures to allocate monies to projects. Non-business organisations are involved in partnerships but not in charge of budgets or procedures. The Coin Street Community Builders, once fighting office development as a symbol of corporate power in inner London, are now reduced to one of many partners in a web of non-accountable organisations, dominated by local corporate headquarters that steer local planning. Even the Waterloo Community Development Group, initially dismissed as Old Labour with old opposing tactics, eventually surrendered through adopting more 'constructive' tactics and seeking cooperation with SBEG and other organisations that are part of the regeneration mainstream. 'Communities' are no longer consisting of sub-entities with conflicting interests, but are now seen as 'beyond politics', as 'apolitical entities' (Rose, 2000).

'Community partnerships' is the vehicle through which post-political regeneration is introduced in the South Bank. Uniting all groups in one partnership effectively forecloses meaningful disagreement and dispute, and therefore democracy. Voices can be raised as far as they fit the overall regeneration aims laid down by the government and the existing partnership (financed largely by the government through the SRB). Other concerns are no longer able to come to the surface since no channels, organisations or resources are available under a regime of post-political regeneration; it is precisely the foreclosure of politics proper through the annihilation of the possibility of dissent that constitutes the essence of post-politics according to Žižek (1999). The us/them antagonism, or the fundamental opposition of interest which forms the essential starting point for politics, has been neutralised in Third Way politics (Mouffe, 1999, 2005).

In an age of post-democracy (Rancière, 1998), communities are now supposed to unite and fight for scarce regeneration resources, leave 'old' antagonisms behind and become reasonable, rational, sensible, communicative, responsible agents with smooth relations with central government and its funding bodies (see figure 13.3). In the process, however, a new friend/enemy relation is created, with, on one side, those who oppose the end of the adversarial model and do not

13.3

The idyll of depoliticised regeneration.
Source: South Bank Employers Group, South
Bank News, issue Feb–May 2006

comply with the idea of 'dialogue' between conflicting interest groups (Mouffe, 2005). Adversarial agents, then, are dismissed as irresponsible, unreasonable, 'politically motivated', irrational, fundamentalist, extremist, 'Old Labour'. In this way, antagonism between us and the mindless 'them' who do not understand how regeneration 'works today', can be safely ignored – the end of politics, death by partnership.

As a consequence, legitimate demands that fall outside the mainstream agenda and alternative development models (such as the famous Coin Street campaign) no longer exist. Nothing but consensus is acceptable (Rancière, 2007). In the process, communities are redefined and acknowledged by the government through the twin mechanism of inclusion and exclusion:

> If communities are seen to be positive in their attitudes towards development projects, then they are included and described as responsible bodies, representing community perspectives and needs in a positive and constructive manner. If, however, various community voices challenge the legitimacy of programmes or are overtly critical, then their views are dismissed as unrepresentative and motivated by other political agendas . . . This is exemplified by New Labour's unwillingness to include community groups that it sees as 'politically motivated' and critical of wider agendas.
>
> (Raco, 2003: 241)

Particularising universal demand, and localising the local

In post-political regeneration, particular demands (for example the demand for more schools) are kept particular (the demand for more schools) in an attempt to avoid them acquiring a wider, universal status (demand for universal state provision of high-quality public services) that could make them enter the sphere of the political. By centering regeneration policies on the 'local community', regeneration policies are depoliticised: community wish-lists are by definition local, particular (safe streets, schools, swimming pool) and do not transcend the local. 'What post-politics tends to prevent is [the] metaphoric universalization of particular demands: post-politics mobilizes the vast apparatus of experts, social workers, and so on, to reduce the overall demand (complaint) of a particular group to just this demand with its particular' (Žižek, 1999: 204).

The very localisation of regeneration policies reinforces the post-politicisation of regeneration: by locking particular political demands up in the sphere of the local, demands can be rendered post-political, disconnected from universal demands for welfare, or justice, or state involvement. Space thus plays a significant role in this process of post-politicisation (see Dikeç, 2005, for a discussion). Local inhabitants are asked, or summoned, to participate/engage in the 'community', since it is through communitarian action that regeneration funds will be triggered. But through this very engagement, people's demands are neutralised, 'post-politicised', since their demands are for the 'local' community only; they can have no relevance beyond the 'local', or the immediate 'community' to which they belong (residents, commuters, etc). Local concerns can no longer be the starting point for a more general critique of how urban society operates and the way it is governed.

In an attempt to depoliticise politics, SRB-style regeneration has initiated what, after Žižek (1999), could be labelled 'para-politics': political conflict is accepted but reformulated into a competition between acknowledged partners and agents; it is an attempt to de-antagonise politics by formulating clear rules to be obeyed so that the agonistic procedure of litigation does not explode into politics proper. Instead of uniting and rallying around universal demands for housing, employment and safe public spaces, deprived communities throughout London are now forced to compete with each other for limited regeneration funds. Through securing a substantial slice of the SRB fund, the South Bank has proved to play by the rules set by the government and effectively became a 'deserving community' as opposed to other communities with similar needs but wrong tactics.

Moralising regeneration

The effective removal of antagonist encounters between opposing regeneration ideas, or the removal of the friend/enemy relation as a basis for political conflict and negotiation, does not lead to the complete disappearance of antagonism. In the wake of the removal of the antagonism between a political 'right' and 'wrong', antagonism is reborn along moral divides. Those who oppose the end of the adversarial model and do not comply with the idea of 'dialogue', 'collaboration', 'communication' and 'partnership' are fundamentalists, traditionalists, or 'Old Labour' for that matter. Antagonism, in this way, can be safely ignored by 'dialogical' democrats who decide consensually what is best for the neighbourhood. The debate no longer revolves around what is right or wrong with regeneration policies but what is 'good' (partnerships) and 'evil' (opposition, conflict, disagreement). With the 'evil them' no agonistic debate is possible; they must be ignored if not eradicated. Condemnation, then, replaces proper political analysis. We can condemn the traditionalists and fundamentalists who do not fit into sensible reasonable liberal-democratic regeneration policies. Or, as the president of the SBEG put it in an interview: 'The defective people have been sidelined' (interview, 14 March 2007).

And the current head of the WCDG describes this turnaround as follows:

> The elected councillors in 1997 were a new breed, New Labourites, young, had not spent much time in the Party or the Union, management types. Labour changed, Lambeth changed, WCDG did not, we were old Labour, we were fighting old Labour style. Lambeth said why are we funding this group? We became isolated. When I came in in 2002 they wanted me to turn around the relation with Lambeth. I was a critical friend of Lambeth. I was on the inside, I was not on the outside screaming. They wanted me to establish a partnership – that was partly SRB-driven. And they wanted me to change the way we operated – more balanced, more inclusive, more consultative, so that we had a broader representation of views, so that our message would not be so hard-hitting, tell more than one story, a range of things. We have become that organisation. We now work in partnership in CSCB, SBEG, Lambeth, GLA, CRP. Lambeth now see us as a positive thing. We got more funding through this.
>
> (Interview, 14 March 2007)

The moralisation of antagonism along the good/evil divide justifies the way communities are disciplined into SRB-bidding:

> By focusing on area-based excluded communities, urban policy is characterised by its tendency to pathologise certain identifiable groups . . . it rewards those who demonstrate that they have the will and motivation to help themselves thereby relieving the state and civil society more broadly of their 'burden' . . . Responsibility for the problems faced by communities has been moved away from government policies of the past and placed firmly with 'degenerate', targeted communities themselves which are portrayed as somehow outside of (or excluded from) the normal values of civil society . . . Those who help themselves (and are, therefore, 'deserving', according to the government's criteria) require assistance to enhance their capacities and play a more active role in local politics.
>
> (Raco, 2003: 238)

Communities, then, are portrayed as a pathological underclass, entities that inculcate individuals with immoral values, but they are at the same time a source of moral good that is being corroded – something that needs to be rectified through regeneration (Imrie and Raco, 2003).

Regeneration populism

In post-political times, adversarial politics are considered hopelessly out of date. Disagreements are still possible but ultimately have to be dealt with within an overall model of consensus and compromise. In the process, depoliticised urban populism has come to replace politics proper and is now a key symptom of the post-democratic consensus. Following Swyngedouw (2007), populism, first, invokes *the* city and *the* people as a whole, or in the case of neighbourhood renewal, *the* neighbourhood and *the* community. In contemporary regeneration discourse, the neighbourhood and the community are often under threat from a common enemy. These fundamental threats, always present within the community, force the community into an eternal united fight, thereby silencing and neglecting basic conflicts *within* the community. Regeneration populism, second, is based on a politics of 'the community knows best', supported by a 'neutral' scientific technocracy, and it advocates a direct relationship between community and political participation (Swyngedouw, 2007: 67). Third, it invokes apocalyptic futures for the neighbourhood. Unless consensual technocratic post-democratic renewal policies are accepted, embraced even, the neighbourhood will face deprivation and downfall (Baeten, 2007). The apocalyptic threat ultimately promises absolutely nothing: it urges people to comply with existing policies in the hope to stave off disaster; it forces people to accept 'the way things are' in an attempt to steer the neighbourhood away from the abyss.

Fourth, populist regeneration does not identify a privileged subject of change (like the proletariat for Marx, women for feminists, or the creative class for neo-liberal capitalism), but a common condition or predicament (Swyngedouw, 2007). The neighbourhood is not challenged by a nameable threat but rather by intangible sociological categories (deviance, disorder, decline) that are everywhere and nowhere, and are ineradicable due to their relative nature. The neighbourhood is under threat from an intruder (globalisation, crime) who has corrupted the system. It is not flaws in the regeneration system itself but external foes that are undermining an otherwise benign regeneration machine. Fifth, regeneration populism is addressed at the elites: it is the professionals, the partnership boards and the regeneration fund boards that initiate and oversee regeneration projects. Regeneration populism does not seek to overthrow the elites but, contrarily, bestow them with responsibility and the right to act and speak on behalf of 'the' community.

Regeneration-beyond-the-state

In the absence of a state setting local planning agendas and drawing up meaningful local spatial plans, non-state actors, engaged in partnerships, now determine in almost full detail the outlook and future of the South Bank. In the process, 'community became a metaphor for the absence or withdrawal of services by the state' (Hoggett, 1997: 10). Regeneration on the South Bank is now characterised by a peculiar mix of post-political, neo-liberal, communitarian policies, resulting in effective forms of governance-beyond-the-state (Swyngedouw, 2005). The South Bank is a 'deserving' community that has been given assistance by the government to help itself. SRB-style regeneration has effectively led to the withdrawal of guaranteed universal public services. Only when the community shows the courage and will to unite and fight for its rights that it is entitled to as citizens and tax-payers, its rights will be (partly) met by the government through allocating a certain sum of money. What in many other European societies is almost a matter of bureaucracy (building schools when there is a shortage of places available) becomes a matter of charity in the regeneration of London. Only when the community is defined as deserving will money be freed to provide basic services. The delivery of 'normal' public services, then, becomes a matter of 'regeneration'. 'Regeneration', then, is no longer aimed at improving the area but at the fragmented and piecemeal delivery of ordinary urban public services to deprived London.

By casting the delivery of ordinary public services under 'regeneration' for which the community has to prepare a bid, the overhead costs are huge compared to an ordinary, bureaucratic, universal way of allocating budgets to, say, street cleaning. The withdrawal of universal state provision makes collective services hopelessly inefficient and therefore reaches exactly the opposite of what it was aiming at. London neighbourhoods are now living in a surreal world where no public service can be taken for granted. Neighbourhoods do not know what they are exactly entitled to or what to expect from government. It is the accidental success of 'the bid' that will decide. The government's interest in the well-being of neighbourhoods is fragmented, temporary, elusive, while it expects citizens to behave like citizens and organise themselves through consistent, coherent and consequent community initiatives. Instead of the birth of a 'communitarian' generation of citizens concerned about their neighbourhood, post-political regeneration may create a generation that feels alienated from politics since there is no outlet for dissident voices (other than the street). This could result in a crisis of legitimacy of regeneration policies.

Conclusion

In sum, after almost a century of regeneration efforts, the hope to make the South Bank part of the thriving London north of the river is finally becoming true. What successive paradigms of regeneration failed to achieve is finally realised under 'Third Way regeneration' or 'post-political regeneration': the appropriation of the South Bank by grand capital. The Coin Street campaign was adversarial, antagonistic and therefore political. A new type of regeneration effort, centred on 'community plans', adopted by the then GLC, emerged from it. In an ironical twist, 'community', then the driving force behind the politicisation of the needs of deprived neighbourhoods, has now been appropriated by the New Labour administration, catapulted into the core of regeneration policies and effectively rendered politically impotent through the twin process of inclusion and exclusion from 'community'.

South Bank's past, that of the promise of office towers eliminating a once vibrant residential and industrial community at the heart of London, is haunting the South Bank's immediate future. Towers are emerging again in architects' drawings for the South Bank, ironically commissioned by the Coin Street Community Builders who were once fighting tower development. And the head of the SBEG has a blunt vision for the neighbourhood that would ban the achievements of the Coin Street campaign to planning history books:

> The total opportunity here is on the scale of the Canary Wharf in the first phase. People have not really grasped that. If you look at the actual developments and the potential developments in the draft Waterloo Development Framework then there is huge potential.
>
> (Interview, 14 March 2007)

The South Bank has come full circle: what was impossible in a time of politics – the development of a business and leisure district – will be realised in post-political times.

Chapter 14

The disputed place of ethnic diversity: an ethnography of the redevelopment of a street market in East London

Nick Dines

Introduction

Considerations on the position of markets in contemporary London

It is a blustery but sunny Saturday afternoon in early December. Queens Market is packed with people going about their weekend shopping trips. The smells of fish, meat and coriander waft through the air as the solitary cries of traders are drowned out by the multilingual chatter. Four Black Caribbean men in their sixties hanging outside a kiosk taunt a fruit and veg trader about West Ham United's latest plight in the Championship. Groups of Asian and African women chat as they rummage through rolls of material on a stall tended by two young white men. In front of the canopy a few people are collecting signatures to 'save Queens Market'. One of them, a middle-aged Asian man, is relaying information in Hindi through a megaphone. Discarded empty boxes are littered around stalls and a number of plastic bags eddy in the aisles. In a quiet square adjoining the market, a few people are milling around a caravan belonging to a property development company. An exhibit has been erected displaying designs for a new complex featuring a superstore, a new market, shops and apartments. Leaflets are being handed out to the few passers-by, asking for their thoughts on the plans. Printed on the front of them are the words: 'The New Queens Market. Towards a Safe, Clean, Vibrant and Lively Shopping and Living Environment'.

(Field notes, December 2004)

Queens Market has operated next to Upton Park tube station in Newham, east London, for just over a century (see figure 14.1). Since 1968 the market has been located underneath a purpose-built, open-ended steel and concrete structure which currently houses eighty stalls trading four days a week as well as a series of independently run shops and kiosks (see figure 14.2). Besides providing residents with cheap food and household goods, Queens Market has long been a focal point for minority groups, from East European Jews and Germans at the beginning of the twentieth century to the Caribbean and South Asian groups who started to arrive after the Second World War to more recent migrants such as West Africans and East Europeans.

The London borough of Newham (LBN) has the highest non-white population of any local authority area in the United Kingdom. According to the 2001 census, 60.6 per cent of its 237,900 residents were from Black and Minority Ethnic groups, compared to 7.9 per cent nationally and 28.8 per cent in London. In contrast to the neighbouring borough of Tower Hamlets with its large Bangladeshi population, the ethnic minority composition is extremely diverse. The principal ethnic groups are: Black African (13.1 per cent); Indian (12.1 per cent); Bangladeshi (8.8 per cent); Pakistani (8.4 per cent) and Black Caribbean (7.3 per cent). The borough's dense web of social networks and relatively cheap housing has meant that it remains a first point of arrival for refugees and migrants. Newham's 'super-diversity' (Vertovec, 2006) is most vividly captured in Queens

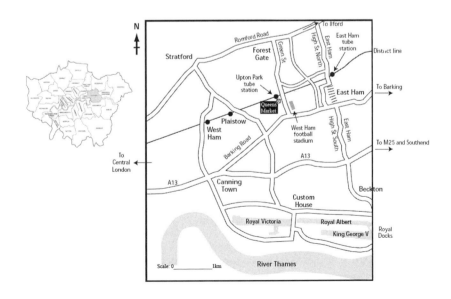

14.1

Map of Newham.
Source: Nick Dines,
2008

14.2
Queens Market, Newham.
Source: Dan Sayer, 2004

Market. Indeed, the market is often locally considered to be the 'multicultural' hub of Newham on account of its particular history, the variety of ethnic products on sale, the mix of people who trade and shop there, and the fact that it lies at the geographical centre of the borough.

In September 2004 the Labour-run local authority announced plans to demolish Queens Market and rearrange it within a new shopping precinct. Promoters of the scheme argue that the current market is unsafe and dirty as well as a drain on the council's limited resources. Redevelopment of the site, to be financed and carried out by a private developer, would instead provide Newham residents with improved housing and retail facilities and at the same time attract new people and businesses to the borough. During the same period, an umbrella group called 'Friends of Queens Market' (FoQM), consisting of shoppers, traders, community organisations, opposition councillors and local political parties, has coordinated opposition to the scheme and has instead called for refurbishment to the existing structure. As well as emphasising its continuing popularity, campaigners have made a point of celebrating the particular cultural diversity of the current market. This, they feel, would be irrevocably lost in the event of redevelopment.

The market offers a particular lens through which to explore struggles over the meaning and shape of public space in contemporary London. Until recently, scarce attention has been paid to street markets in the literature on regeneration in the UK. Yet markets have historically played a key role in British urban life as sites of commerce, consumption and social interaction (Watson and Studdert, 2006). As distinct public spaces and crucial nodes in people's social and economic networks, they have also been closely bound up with notions of place identity, particularly so in London (Sinclair, 2006). However, as Stallybrass and White (1986) remind us, the market has held a somewhat equivocal position in the modern city:

> A marketplace is the epitome of local identity (often indeed it is what defined a place as more significant than surrounding communities) and the unsettling of that identity by the trade and traffic of goods from elsewhere. At the market centre of the polis we discover a co-mingling of categories usually

kept separate and opposed: centre and periphery, inside and outside, stranger and local, commerce and festivity, high and low.

(Stallybrass and White, 1986: 27)

This inherent promiscuity of the market can create feelings of anxiety by disturbing a sense of order (Sibley, 1995), but may also be a source of attraction by providing a less regulated social realm than other spaces of the city. In addition, the market has traditionally been a politically ambivalent space; on the one hand functioning as an inclusive everyday public sphere, while on the other representing a place of petty bourgeois reaction and nostalgia (Watson and Wells, 2005). The key question that needs to be asked is, if the market has constituted a particular experience at the city's core, one that is both mundane and exceptional, what might its 'regeneration' entail?

During the last two decades there has been a narrative about the decline of markets. Traditional markets have found themselves closed down, under threat or relocated outside urban centres, largely as a result of growing competition from superstores and out-of-town shopping malls and a lack of investment from local authorities which have redirected finances towards higher priorities such as housing and education (Watson and Studdert, 2006). However, the idea of 'decline' is at the same time problematic. Conceived simply as a drop in customer footfall, it overlooks the ongoing, less tangible social role of markets. The term can also be used to simply express a negative evaluation that positions a market in relation to transformations that have occurred in a surrounding area. For example, Jane Jacobs discusses how the allure of the fruit and vegetable market in Spitalfields, East London, swiftly diminished for new middle-class residents as its noise and clutter began to disturb their gentrified vision of turning the district into 'a restored monument to early Georgian London' (Jacobs, 1996: 85). As such, the notion of 'decline' is employed to legitimate that other powerful metaphor 'regeneration' (Furbey, 1999).

More recently there has been an equally insistent narrative of 'revival'. The demise of street markets has been checked in the last decade by a growth in popularity of specialist and farmers' markets, although these have tended to attract a more affluent public and have been unsuccessful in ethnically diverse parts of London (Watson and Studdert, 2006).[1] In order to revitalise trade, existing markets, such as Queens Crescent market in Gospel Oak and Broadway Market in Hackney, have begun introducing new stalls selling international gourmet foods and handicrafts in order to attract higher-income residents who have moved into the local area. This has sometimes given rise to tensions between 'indigenous' market users and newcomers around questions of cost and taste and, where increased popularity has attracted major property investors, has led to outright conflict, as in the case of the protracted 'Battle of Broadway Market' between 2005 and 2006 when residents and activists physically resisted the eviction of a local café owner (Kunzru, 2005; Iles and Seymour, 2006).

During this period of 'decline' and 'revival', urban policy has paid scant attention to street markets. Despite growing cross-departmental interest in the public realm under a New Labour government and the inclusion of markets in its planning agenda for town centres (ODPM, 2005), there has been little emphasis on understanding how markets function as social spaces. In response to this policy gap, a number of recent studies have sought to highlight the benefits of markets; underlining, for instance, the opportunities they offer for social interaction and inclusion (Taylor et al., 2005; Dines et al., 2006; Watson and Studdert, 2006). In a global metropolis like London, markets are seen to serve a diverse public and to act as entry points for new arrivals. As the authors of a report produced for the London Development Authority remarked, 'markets create a sense of neighbourhood and social capital that can be difficult to find in London' (Taylor et al., 2005, p.44). The reports have all called on local authorities to strengthen their support for markets by incorporating them within sustainable community, social inclusion and regeneration initiatives. However, it remains to be seen how and to what extent their 'virtuous' attributes might be incorporated within the wider picture of urban change.

By the time these noble policy recommendations were published, the proposed redevelopment of Queens Market had already become a local and national cause célèbre (see, for instance, Muir 2005a). The market has encapsulated a series of interconnected conflicts surrounding urban regeneration: from questions of consumer identity and architectural design to class composition, the privatisation of public space and local democracy. This chapter explores the meanings assigned to Queens Market by local people, the local council, private developers and the campaign group in order to analyse in depth the complex relationship between markets and regeneration. Many of the issues raised by the redevelopment, such as the role of private developers vis-à-vis public space, connect with general questions about markets and regeneration projects in the rest of London. At the same time, the case demands a degree of sensitivity to context. Newham does not neatly fit the concept of the 'inner city' with its particular built environment and class fault lines that is commonly identified and imagined in the regeneration literature. The borough does not possess the desirable Victoriana enclaves of neighbouring Tower Hamlets and Hackney and until recently there has been very little gentrification of its existing housing stock,[2] while Queens Market has yet to attract the middle-class visitors of other east London markets closer to the city centre such as Brick Lane and Broadway Market. As one of Queens Market's defining characteristics, particular attention will be paid here to the issue of ethnic diversity.

The multiethnic composition of Queens Market has, itself, not been a matter of controversy. Rather, discordance has arisen between, on the one hand, grounded experiences of a diversity that both constitutes and is constituted by the space of the current market and, on the other, a top-down, decontextualised vision of diversity contemplated by regeneration. As Lees has pointed out, 'diversity' is a composite concept comprising a series of social, ethnic, cultural and economic elements that has been embraced in contemporary planning processes but which is marked by inherent contradictions between the celebration of pluralism and the concurrent pursuit for consensus and between 'the promotion of diversity as an end in itself and as a means of attaining the higher goal of economic development' (Lees, 2003b: 623). How, therefore, might the redevelopment scheme's objective of fostering a greater social mix relate to the ethnic diversity of Queens Market?

The chapter takes the form of an ethnography that critically considers regeneration in the light of the disparate voices, discourses, visual representations and political actions that have surrounded the market. It partly draws on qualitative research conducted between June 2004 and December 2005 for a Joseph Rowntree-funded study that examined the social and therapeutic role of public spaces in east London (Dines *et al.*, 2006). A few months after the research commenced, the redevelopment scheme for Queens Market was announced. This enabled me to examine how the proposed plans influenced people's narratives about the market. Local and national media coverage about the market was closely followed while public meetings and exhibitions about the redevelopment were attended between June 2004 and July 2007, initially as an interested researcher and, from late 2004 onwards, also as a committee member of Friends of Queens Market. The views expressed here are, however, entirely my own and do not necessarily reflect the views of FoQM.

The chapter starts by discussing regeneration in Newham in relation to the urban agenda and politics of race of New Labour, before outlining the evolution of the redevelopment proposals for Queens Market. It proceeds to explore local people's discussions of the current market and how a perceived threat to its existence led to organised opposition to redevelopment. It then analyses the divergent public representations of the market and how these have been cut across by particular understandings of diversity. By doing so, the chapter attempts to unpack the contested significance of ethnic diversity in the context of regeneration, from the everyday experience of interaction and a resource that is mobilised by campaigners to the gentrifying trajectory that is inherent in the redevelopment scheme.

Urban regeneration in the London Borough of Newham (LBN)

> By 2010 Newham will be a place where people choose to live and work.
> (London Borough of Newham Regeneration Vision,
> www.newham.gov.uk/topics/RegeneratingNewham/)

During the last decade, Newham has been at the centre of one of the most extensive regeneration programmes in Britain. This has included both large-scale capital projects on brownfield sites along the borough's western and southern perimeters such as the new commercial and residential Stratford City district and neighbourhood-based initiatives like the West Ham and Plaistow New Deal for Communities (NDC). As one of London's most disadvantaged boroughs and strategically situated within two designated growth areas (the Thames Gateway and the London–Stansted–Cambridge corridor), Newham has qualified for most of the government's regeneration schemes, receiving over £300 million between 1996 and 2004 (North and Syrett, 2006). Regeneration has been overseen and actively promoted by the Labour-controlled local authority (at the time of writing, fifty-four out of sixty councillors were Labour party members) that since 2002 has been run on a mayoral and cabinet system. The full executive power of the mayor was seen to provide local communities with 'strong, identifiable, visionary local leadership', especially to meet the challenge of urban renewal (LBN website).

A central goal of regeneration has been to exploit Newham's strategic position in London in order to attract new investment and jobs to the area and to integrate traditionally 'excluded' sections of the population into the labour market. Despite persistent structural inequalities in the borough (North and Syrett, 2006) and the fact that the most visible change, as the local authority itself admits, has been to land and property, regeneration is seen to have long-term social benefits such as raising educational standards, improving the public realm and reducing crime (LBN, 2004a). In line with the communitarian approach to governance at the heart of the New Labour project, LBN has placed much emphasis upon public-private partnerships, local capacity building and the direct participation of citizens in neighbourhood renewal. An example of the latter was the recent local involvement in the refurbishment of a park in the NDC area that aimed to provide high-quality public facilities and measures to curb social disorder. While these practices have introduced a degree of participatory democracy, many researchers have demonstrated that the mechanisms for involvement, the economic and social objectives of schemes, as well as the very definition of community, are usually stipulated by those in positions of power, in particular local authorities and funding bodies (Edwards, 2001; North, 2003). In Newham, the power to control the direction of regeneration strategy and allocation of resources is seen to be increasingly concentrated in the figure of the mayor which has led to widespread disillusionment amongst those, especially in the voluntary sector, involved in neighbourhood renewal (North and Syrett, 2006).

At the same time as seeking improvements for (and through) the local community, the borough has also been keen to attract more affluent residents to new-build developments and to increase the social mix of traditionally undesirable areas such as Canning Town through new housing and the refurbishment of existing local authority stock (LBN, 2004b). The high concentrations of poverty, low aspirations and welfare dependency in certain areas are seen to be the products of 'unregenerated' (Furbey, 1999) social and physical environments. As numerous commentators have argued, the axiomatic rhetoric that social and tenure mix provides a panacea to such pathologies has in reality acted as a thin veil over the gentrifying tendencies inherent within urban policy (Davidson and Lees, 2005; Lees et al., 2008). For example, Stephen Jacobs, chief executive of the Stratford Development Partnership, imagines an 'ordinary' future for Canning Town post-neighbourhood renewal where, among other things, 'Marks & Spencer will have opened several new Metro stores to cash in on the increased amount of disposable income among Canning Town residents' and its 'Thames-side location [. . .] will have been exploited by a huge number of riverside residential and commercial developments, providing yet more jobs for the highly skilled local workforce' (Jacobs, 2000: 97–8). Here the benevolent vision of a competitive mixed neighbourhood with a thriving housing market does not envisage the classic rarefied traits of gentrification such as fashionable clothes outlets and coffee bars but rather a normalised residential and retail environment that will, commonsensibly, be advantageous to everyone. This particular notion of 'ordinariness' would resonate through the council's vision for Queens Market.

Ethnic diversity and regeneration

Newham's regeneration vision received a boost in July 2005 when East London (and Newham in particular) was chosen as the venue for the 2012 Olympic Games. Nationally, the Olympics were seen as providing an opportunity to regenerate 'one of the most deprived areas of Europe' (Gillan, 2005). At the same time East London's ethnic mix was seen as a key winning ingredient in the capital's bid. The cultural diversity of many of Britain's major cities within the context of regeneration policy has been both a challenge – to involve and benefit minority groups that have traditionally been excluded from urban processes – and a resource; for instance, in reimaging urban areas as 'cosmopolitan' and therefore attractive to new residents (Young *et al.*, 2006). This celebration of diversity has sat, often uncomfortably, alongside the government's discourse of 'community cohesion' (Worley, 2005); the lack of which was seen to have been a major motivating factor in the social unrest between British Asian and White groups in northern English cities in 2001 (Home Office, 2001). It has been argued that the New Labour project has had an ambiguous relation to race and diversity (Back *et al.*, 2002). On the one hand the government has embraced cultural diversity and placed institutional racism on the agenda, on the other it has adopted an increasingly assimilationist rhetoric, especially after 2001, that has censured the apparent lack of integration of some minority groups and signalled a shift to the right in asylum and immigration policy. According to Back *et al.*, the Janus-faced nature of New Labour's politics of race reflects 'the contradictions that surface in both liberal models of social inclusion and the attempt to define a social democratic model of national economic growth in a globalised economy' (2002: 447).

The Cantle Report, published in response to the disturbances of 2001, called upon local authorities to draw up a 'local community cohesion plan' which would include 'the promotion of cross cultural contact between different communities at all levels, foster understanding and respect, and break down barriers' (quoted in Worley, 2005: 487). The localisation of the management of diversity has produced its own set of problems however. In particular, neighbourhood renewal schemes based on consensus building have tended to assume simplified notions of community that overlook the multiple identities between and within ethnic groups. Moreover, the goal of community cohesion presupposes that this does not already exist and neglects the fact that it might instead be dependent upon circuits and spaces inconsistent with certain regeneration visions (Amin, 2002; Phillips *et al.*, 2007). The example of Queens Market indicates that place attachments do not exist only on the basis of *ethnicity* (Amin, 2002) but also, crucially, upon particular understandings of *diversity*.

As noted, Newham is one of the most diverse local authority areas in Britain. Although it has had some of the highest levels of reported racial harassment in the country (Prasad, 2000), it also possesses a strong anti-racist tradition (for example the Newham Monitoring Group, set up in 1980 to counter, among other things, racism within the police force, was the first organisation of its kind in the country), while the British Nationalist Party is now more or less non-existent, in stark contrast to the neighbouring borough of Barking and Dagenham where it possesses a number of councillors. While there have been conflicts over the political representation of minorities in Newham,[3] LBN has generally appeared comfortable in celebrating the borough's cultural diversity. As well as drawing up a community strategy in 2004 that emphasised building 'an active and inclusive community' (LBN, 2004b), it has promoted its multiethnic heritage; for instance by marketing Green Street (adjacent to Queens Market) as a major multiethnic retail centre and tourist attraction (Carey and Ahmed, 2006). This was one of the outcomes of an £8.5 million SRB-funded regeneration programme between 1994 and 2001 that carried out environmental improvements in the area. Reluctant to follow the example of 'Banglatown' in Brick Lane with its focus on a single community and deliberate use of orientalist imagery, the programme emphasised the diversity of Green Street, even funding at its southern end a statue to the West Ham footballer Bobby Moore (Shaw *et al.*, 2004). This low-key approach to creating and sustaining an 'ethnoscape' (Shaw *et al.*, 2004) has been overshadowed by the active promotion of socially mixed communities that makes no direct reference to ethnicity. This was indeed the case, at least initially, with the Queens Market scheme.

The redevelopment plans for Queens Market

In the late 1990s, minor renovation was carried out on Queens Market as part of the regeneration of Green Street. This included the instalment of CCTV and canopies at the front of the market. The market was even featured in the council's 'This is Green Street' promotional campaign. Shoppers and traders still grumble about the removal of the original public toilets and the leaky roof that was not properly fixed, but overall the interventions did little to disturb the day-to-day functioning of the market.

During the course of 2004 there were a number of reports in the local press as well as increasingly persistent rumours in the community about the imminent demolition of Queens Market and the arrival of a major supermarket. After initially declaring that nothing had been decided, LBN suddenly announced in September 2004 that it had appointed St Modwen, a property developer and self-proclaimed 'leading regeneration specialist', to redevelop the site. St Modwen's architects had even produced a proposed scheme. The designs, presented to the local

Green Street Community Forum on 14 September 2004, envisaged the replacement of the existing structure with a new shopping and residential complex fronted by a small square. At the centre of the complex was a large supermarket. This was flanked by retail units, a new residential block consisting of mainly one and two-bedroom flats and a small gated market relocated to an adjoining space. During the presentation, the Deputy Mayor of Newham emphasised that the retention of Queens Market was central to the council's plans for the site and that the major investment and subsequent management (on a 150-year lease) by their private partner would insure the market's long-term future. Regeneration, it was argued, would improve the quality of retail facilities, enabling the area to compete with the new shopping centres elsewhere in the borough. The mixed-tenure housing units in front of Upton Park tube station would increase the social mix in the immediate area by offering affordable homes to local people and attracting buyers who would not normally consider living in central Newham. In order to placate the dismay among Community Forum attendees that such a full-fledged project already existed, the Deputy Mayor insisted that the architects' sketches would evolve to reflect the views of local people.

The first design had an unequivocally corporate identity. Shopping parks such as Gallions Reach in nearby Beckton were seen in unproblematic terms as models for retail regeneration (Rubin *et al.*, 2006). Indeed, for many people locally, the project became synonymous with the supermarket chain. Following consultation commissioned by LBN at the end of 2004 and a series of meetings with market traders and shopkeepers, St Modwen produced a revised proposal in autumn 2005 which saw the supermarket reduced in size and its food section moved to the first floor, an increase in the number of independent shops and a larger open-sided market hall that retained all the existing stalls. The new design also included the relocation of Green Street Library and a service centre into an 'iconic building' that would be built over the market. The corporate excesses of the 'standard modern shopping centre' (LBN, 2005) of the first proposal were tempered through the incorporation of functions and design features 'promoting community cohesion' (LBN, 2005). Both the developers and the council increasingly drew on the terminology of 'urban renaissance' (DETR, 1999; Lees, 2003a), emphasising words such as 'plaza' and 'iconic building', to intimate the creation of a high-quality public space.

Further alterations were made to the scheme after the superstore pulled out of the project in June 2006, largely as a result of local hostility and adverse publicity surrounding its inclusion in the scheme (Balakrishnan, 2006).[4] A third project was revealed in October 2006 in which the market was expanded in size to take up the entire ground floor of the development. Besides the retention of community facilities, the design for the enlarged market sought to reflect the cultural diversity of the local area by proposing, inter alia, murals coordinated by a 'respected and experienced arts consultant' to 'reflect the area's heritage and international feel' and to 'enhance [the market's] appearance' for both its current and future users (St Modwen-LBN, 2006). At the time of writing, this final version awaits planning permission.[5]

The redevelopment scheme therefore passed through three stages: the first represented the private developer's blueprint based on the council's brief, the second accommodated the public consultation exercise, while the third appeared a riposte to the unexpected withdrawal of the commercial anchor and widespread public opposition. By the final project, the shopping centre and residential complex of the first proposal had been dressed in the language of 'community' and 'diversity'. But while the third project assumed a seemingly more benevolent, democratic guise, key decisions such as the demolition of the present market and the private management of the new complex were never negotiable.[6] By the time it came to canvass the views of the public, LBN seemed already adamant that the present market was not good enough for Newham and that its redevelopment through a public-private partnership was the only viable option (LBN, 2005).

From place attachments to opposition to the redevelopment scheme

Before examining how the council and developers represented the market as a public space, it is necessary to consider the various meanings that Queens Market held for local people, also in order to understand why there was such rooted opposition to redevelopment. The interviews conducted between June 2004 and December 2005 in Newham focused on people's social relations, perceptions of community, daily routines and encounters with ethnic difference in order to evaluate the relative importance of public spaces in everyday lives. This led to discussions about a wide range of places, from parks, high streets and markets to 'nondescript' neighbourhood spaces such as forecourts and street corners. Queens Market captured, more than any other place discussed, a series of aspects that were collectively valued about public space. Many informants spoke at length about how the existing site encapsulated the overlapping 'East End', 'working class' and 'multicultural' identities of Newham. The fact that the market was also described as 'scruffy' and 'dirty' (complaints often directed at 'the Council') did not detract from it being perceived as an important place in people's everyday lives and a source of their attachment to the local area. At the same time as providing cheap fresh food and ethnic produce, it was the setting for routine and unexpected encounters between people. The spatial configuration – the wide aisles between stalls and the fact that it was set back from the busy pavements of Green Street – turned the market into a sort of surrogate town square. This was a place where older people in particular felt comfortable to linger. A group of Asian elders, for example, described it as a place where they could 'hang out' without necessarily having to buy anything. The social vibrancy of the market was also seen by some informants to contribute to a sense of well-being. As well as being variously described as 'fun' and 'uplifting', it provided respite to those people who felt uneasy in other neighbourhood spaces. A thirteen-year-old Afghan boy who had been bullied by white teenagers in his local park saw the market as a safe haven where the same individuals (who sometimes worked on the stalls) no longer posed a threat.

People's sense of comfort in the market was often tied to their appreciation of it as a 'multicultural' space. Crucially, this epithet was used not simply to reflect the mix of traders and shoppers or the range of products on sale, but also because the market was seen to enable casual encounters between different ethnic groups who would otherwise not come into contact. According to a white British woman and member of Friends of Queens Market, this applied both to shoppers and traders:

> Next to the Bengalis selling biscuits is a Jewish guy selling curtains. They would never have met a Jewish bloke [. . .] It's most unlikely that they'd find themselves in a colleague situation where they can ask questions, they can joke with him. [. . .] And he could ask them about their religion. I can't see another space where that could possibly happen. You could set up a society to bring Jews and Muslims together: he wouldn't turn up and they wouldn't turn up, because these sorts of outfits attract special people.

For a Pakistani woman, the market represented a rare environment where she would find herself speaking to strangers:

> We meet different cultures. I might be buying vegetables that I don't know how to cook, and the lady from another part of India will tell me how to cook it. Normally I would never talk, I would never know such things. And you could hear the same story for many market users who go regularly.

The mundane, unorganised nature of these encounters – resonant with the 'liberating ordinariness of race' contemplated by Paul Gilroy (1987) – elicited a greater deliberation upon the significance of the market as a public space. But although diversity was generally seen to be integral to the market's identity, this was sometimes acknowledged with a degree of ambivalence. An elderly white British woman, living on the same estate as the Pakistani woman, complained that 'they' (referring to ethnic minorities, and principally Asians) 'are always pushing past us' and that 'they do not know how to queue like the English'. However, she went on to note that there were 'other ways of doing things' and that people held different relationships with the market: 'it's a case of us understanding them but they need to understand us as well'. Recent research on a market in South London has suggested that indigenous white residents and traders possessed nostalgic views about an ethnically 'authentic' market that had been lost through waves of immigration (Watson and Wells, 2005).

However, people's views of Queens Market indicate a more complex situation. First, the market was commonly understood to have never been an exclusively 'white-English' space. During the first half of the twentieth century, many of the traders and customers were East European Jewish, Irish and German immigrants. Indeed, some older white people's narratives about Queens Market and Green Street were nostalgic about a different 'cosmopolitan' mix rather than an ethnically homogenous past. Second, the market, with less rigid symbolic boundaries than elsewhere, remained a key site where people encountered, negotiated and reflected upon the demographic changes in the area. In contrast to certain descriptions of residential streets, people were less likely to perceive the market as being 'defiled' by a changing public (Sibley, 1995). Despite her complaints, the same British woman's strong support for the market as an important community facility was undiminished.

Not everybody was fond of Queens Market. A few disliked it because they were generally not keen on busy places. Many younger people and children were amongst its most vociferous critics, variously describing the market as 'rubbish' and 'too noisy'. At the same time, younger people were far less interested in Queens Market as a social space. Their meeting points were often independently established in quieter or underused places. Many of those who disliked the current market nevertheless criticised the redevelopment proposals, largely because they appreciated the market's advantages as a social resource for other people. A 22-year old British Pakistani man for instance exclaimed:

> I don't like the place, but I do understand why people are upset, that it's not going to be there in a couple of years time. If it's going to disappear, where else are they going to go?'

The attention surrounding redevelopment heightened people's reflections upon the significance of the present market. Most thought that the general conditions in the market needed to be improved but were critical about the preliminary plans to redevelop the market around a superstore. Significantly, nobody imagined how the future site would function as a public space if the scheme went ahead. At most, a large supermarket nearby could be convenient. Many instead believed that regeneration would remove part of the local area's history and destroy a fundamental social space. A black British man who had continually visited the market since he was a child commented:

> I don't think they should get rid of it because it is tradition, it's been there for so long. As I say, people gather there, it's like a communities place; like you'd say 'I'll meet you at the Market'. It's like a landmark [. . .] and to take that away, I think you're taking a bit of history away.[7]

Organised opposition to the proposed redevelopment grew out of the practical concerns of traders and shoppers but also deep-seated attachments to the current market. Friends of Queens Market (FoQM) already existed as a small group before redevelopment was confirmed and its membership swiftly grew after St Modwen's first design was released. Campaign members have emphasised the common-held view that Queens Market in its present form is one of the most popular general street markets in London, and hence it did not have to compete with other retail developments. FoQM firmly believed that regeneration would actually destroy the market's unique appeal as well as jeopardise the livelihoods of traders and shopkeepers and the low prices of produce on offer. The many traders who were members of supporters of FoQM were sceptical about reassurances from St Modwen that all stalls would be retained and rents would remain frozen for five years because unlike the council, the developer was a private company whose priority was to maximise financial returns for its shareholders (and, as such, the housing and new shops were far more commercially important than the market to the overall scheme). Although the superstore was removed from the third project, it was pointed out that Queens Market would still change in definition from a 'public highway' to a privately run 'market-in-a-mall'.

Since 2004 FoQM has had a regular presence in the market; collecting signatures for a petition to save the market[8] as well as distributing its own newsletters about the redevelopment and the campaign. It has also criticised the political process surrounding the scheme at public meetings and through frequent letters to the local press. The perception that the council had closed the door on negotiation led FoQM to exert pressure through a range of local and regional media (press, radio and television) and through building alliances with national organisations such as Friends of the Earth and the New Economics Foundation, which subsequently produced a report on the market (Rubin *et al.*, 2006). The dual strategy of high-profile publicity and local campaigning enabled FoQM to maintain momentum following the supermarket's withdrawal in 2006. The supermarket had provided the public with a clear-cut enemy but its 'defeat' risked turning into a pyrrhic victory. However, FoQM had formulated its position around specific conceptions of the market as a public space and not simply in reaction to the corporate character of the scheme. At the end of 2005, FoQM publicly presented its own alternative plan for a 'sensitive' refurbishment of the market (FoQM, 2005). This included substantial renovation of the existing environment, an improved cleaning regime as well as promotional advertising. It also envisaged setting up a trust comprising traders, shoppers and the council to develop and manage the market.

Contested notions of public space and ethnic diversity

Initially, LBN Council and St Modwen showed little interest in comprehending the variety of affective ties between local people and Queens Market. Its present incarnation was, for the most part, negatively portrayed. In its preliminary consultation leaflet, St Modwen stated:

> Queens Market is largely a covered, architecturally undistinguished box with open ends and lacking in modern facilities. It has acknowledged problems relating to crime, hygiene and waste disposal. It

> suffers from a proliferation of certain uses such as meat sales and fruit and vegetables. [. . .] The new market will accommodate permanent stalls and market shops in a design that gives a more coordinated appearance to the market.
>
> (St Modwen-LBN, 2004)

The council acknowledged more readily the market's popularity but this did not subdue its conviction that it needed to be redeveloped:

> We have a good market, but we have bad use of space. That space is just poorly designed, poorly structured, poorly maintained and we need to relocate the market.
>
> (Deputy Mayor, Green Street Community Forum meeting 14/09/04)

According to promoters of the redevelopment, the market had no aesthetic value but was rather an 'undistinguished' and 'poorly designed' space. Its demolition was not perceived in any way to be a loss because, as a purely commercial amenity, it was seen to be eminently replaceable and improvable. When the market's social aspects were considered these were invariably pernicious: it was typically an unsafe and dirty place where prostitution and petty crime took place unabated. As public consultation was carried out, official descriptions of the market as a site of anti-social behaviour became less dominant as the focus switched to the vision of a cleaner, safer and more organised environment.

Significantly, it was only after the present market had been sufficiently discredited that the ethnic diversity of Queens Market began to be acknowledged. LBN's first public newsletter about the redevelopment in November 2004 had juxtaposed St Modwen's plans with two photographs of the present market: one displaying an empty aisle during a non-trading day and the other showing rubbish behind a staircase. By its fourth and last newsletter in August 2005, the visual focus had shifted to close-ups of smiling shoppers and traders. These facial portraits convey a multiethnic milieu that is at the same time disconnected from the spatial dimension of the current market; thus rendering diversity readily transposable into a future, regenerated setting. In the redevelopment plans themselves, the question of diversity was initially absent. In fact, St Modwen had to hastily alter its preliminary drawings after it was noted during the public presentation that all the human figures were conspicuously white (in the revised version some were redressed in headscarves and shalwar qamizes).

By its third project, St Modwen had started to play up the 'international feel' of a market that 'provid[ed] an opportunity for people of different cultures and backgrounds to meet and communicate' (St Modwen-LBN, 2006), and even confidently included photographs of Green Street and Queens Market alongside its designs. The computer-generated drawings also communicated a clear discursive turn: the pencil-outlined figures of the first design had been replaced by actual photographs of people (again, ethnically distinguishable by their garments) and had been brought off the street into the bright and uncluttered environment of a new market. The achromic, multiethnic crowd that had previously provided contrast to the colour and scale of the project was now transformed into an orderly assembly of participating consumers. This message was reiterated in the council's 2006 Equality Impact Assessment of the proposed plans where diversity was conceived in terms of access to ethnic products. Any adverse affect from redevelopment would instead be offset by its 'high quality and inclusive design' (LBN, 2006).

Friends of Queens Market gathered a broad range of people from different social and ethnic backgrounds and consequently there were many different relationships with the market. Some had specific interests in resisting development: traders were concerned about their livelihood; shoppers about prices and supply. There was, nevertheless, general consensus on a number of key issues. Queens Market was more than just a retail site: it was a unique and important amenity for the local community both as a shopping centre *and* as a social place. Campaigners were particularly angry about what they saw as a wilful misrepresentation on the part of the council and the developers of what was an extremely popular market. While many recognised that the building was, in the words of one trader, 'not the prettiest place in London' (deputation to LBN council, 20/09/04), this did not diminish its success and vitality as a public space. In contrast, the redevelopment scheme would 'sanitise' the market and transform the area into a 'clone town' consisting prevalently of chain shops which, it was argued, was already the case of nearly every other shopping area in the borough (deputation to LBN council, 20/09/04).

While there were moments of tension within the campaigning group regarding political positions, individual commitments and the direction of strategy, there was never any dispute over the question of diversity. From the outset, the multiethnic composition of the market was seen as a key resource in mobilising support for the campaign. FoQM capitalised on St Modwen's lack of knowledge and insensitivity to local context (exemplified by the faux pas in its first drawings) and in doing so questioned the reasoning behind the council's decision to appoint them as partners. During the deputation to LBN council, a white British trader described the market as a continually evolving place that presented a window on the sociodemographic transformation of London. This risked disappearing if the market were redeveloped:

> When I first began working there fifteen years ago it was almost purely Asian with some Caribbean people and then we saw more African people come in and now, more recently, we've seen many more Eastern European people. [. . .] Places like Queens Market are a first base for people. People travel from all over London to come to Queens Market. They won't travel to come to ASDA or Waitrose or Sainsbury's. They've got one locally. We're not short of supermarkets and as much as they may give you the highest revenue, and they may provide you with the cleanest, sanitised environment with which to present

Newham, it doesn't mean it will offer the best for the people of Newham.

(Interview, 20/09/04)

In its 2005 refurbishment plan, FoQM made a point of articulating the particular diversity of the market, for instance remarking, 'like a coral reef this multi-layered and multi-faceted community is a fragile form, easily destroyed, yet near impossible to replicate' (FoQM, 2005: 24). Hence, it was not diversity per se that was threatened by redevelopment but a diversity contingent to time and space. Moreover, campaigners were plainly aware that class and other factors cut across ethnic difference, and that this distinguished their outlook from that of the council.

Conclusions: (dis)placing diversity

Queens Market has provided a particular site through which to examine conflicting interpretations of the significance of public space when this is designated for regeneration. It has also demonstrated how the notion of ethnic diversity, just like the concept of community, is not simply an 'arbiter of moral worth' but rather 'becomes a battleground of competing ethics' (Back et al., 2002, p.448). For the campaigners, diversity is an integral element of an irreplaceable social environment; for the redevelopers, it is an appendage to a new retail and residential complex. The major fault line runs not between inclusion and exclusion, or tolerance and discrimination, but in between the embodied, everyday experience of ethnic diversity on the one hand, and a disembodied, supra-quotidian vision on the other.

Many of the local informants interpreted Queens Market as a flexible, multi-layered space that accommodated a range of attachments. Regardless of the market's actual physical state and aesthetic qualities, no other local space was seen to play such an important role for so many people. The uncompromising late-1960s Brutalist architecture was but a shell, as one FoQM campaigner put it, 'to the heart that is throbbing beneath'. In contrast, promoters of the redevelopment assigned unambiguous, peremptory definitions to Queens Market: it was dirty, badly designed, a site of anti-social behaviour and, ultimately, a redundant space that evoked the welfare-dependent and unaspirational Newham of yesteryear. Instead, a regeneration agenda that spoke of urban renaissance and social mix assumed precedence over any attempt to appreciate its significance for local people. The desire to attract new residents was spelt out by Stephen Jacobs, the former head of the Stratford Development Partnership, during a meeting with FoQM:

It's not just a market development: we're very keen to build a newer community there . . . [The council] wants areas to become – if I can be blunt about this – like any other area where you want to buy, rent, come in and come out. We've got areas which are just all rented or all . . . you know, it's just not good.

(Meeting at Newham Housing Services, Stratford, 26/10/04)

Leaving aside the fact that the area around Queens Market was already characterised by a mixture of housing tenures, Jacobs' words underline the ambivalence inherent within the council's vision that 'by 2010 Newham will be a place where people choose to live and work'. Queens Market, presumably used at the moment more through constraint than out of choice, should become 'like any other area'. Indeed, during consultation the public was alerted that redevelopment might transform the market's cultural mix (LBN-Mori, 2005: 100). This is instead recuperated in the developers' third project through public art murals and new surroundings that provide 'opportunities to meet and communicate' (St Modwen-LBN, 2006). Like Jacobs' vision of an 'ordinary' Canning Town, the exceptionally mundane diversity of Queens Market is normalised and rendered manageable. Diversity itself has undergone a process of gentrification: having been dislodged from the temporal and spatial context of the old market, it is now also amenable to a different type of higher-income user. It is perhaps indicative of the underlying trajectory of New Labour's 'neo-liberal communitarian' (DeFilippis *et al.*, 2006) urban agenda and its enclosure of discourses about 'community cohesion' and 'social mix', that a place like Queens Market, considered crucial to local understandings and experiences of multiethnicity, cannot be valued in the here and now. As long as regeneration programmes remain insensitive to the constitutive role of (unregenerate) places in sociocultural interactions, posterior winks to multiculturalism will be but hollow rhetoric.

Across London there has been growing resistance to the redevelopment of social and economic spaces in the name of the telos of regeneration, from the occupations in Broadway Market to the recent protests at the demolition of the East Asian shopping centre Oriental City in North London (Brannigan, 2006). The campaign to save Queens Market has frustrated the council and developers by challenging all aspects of the redevelopment while continually questioning its raison-d'être. It has also effectively maintained local and national media attention on the market, which was instrumental in forcing the withdrawal of the superstore from the project in 2006. The promoters of redevelopment have tended to deride the opposition or consider it simply irrelevant. Campaigners were accused of 'refusing change'. Like the market, they too were seen to be part of a bygone era.

And yet the 'old' Queens Market is important exactly because it provides an arena in which social and cultural change is experienced and negotiated. Moreover, the campaign itself has played its own part in 'community cohesion' by forging and consolidating ties between different groups of people. Whatever the final outcome of the redevelopment scheme, both Queens Market and the politics of diversity have already been reconfigured by grass-roots struggle.

Acknowledgements

I would like to thank my former colleagues at Queen Mary University of London, Vicky Cattell, Wil Gesler and Sarah Curtis, with whom I worked on the JRF-funded project 'Public Spaces, Social Relations and Well-being in East London'. While some of the fieldwork conducted for the project forms the basis of this chapter, the arguments contained here within are entirely my own. A version of this chapter was presented at the Third EURODIV Conference 'Diversity in Cities: Visible and Invisible Walls' at University College London, 12 September 2007. Many thanks also to the editors, Rob Imrie, Loretta Lees and Mike Raco, for their helpful comments on an earlier draft of this chapter.

Notes

1   First established in 1997, by definition a farmers market in London is where producers from within 100 miles of the M25 motorway sell their produce direct to the public. Watson and Studdert note that part of the reason why attempts to introduce a farmer's market in Tower Hamlets were unsuccessful was because the local Bengali population wanted to buy products from Bangladesh. (2006: 32).

2   On the new-build residential developments, a different case in point, located mainly in the south of the borough, see Butler and Robson (2003).

3   Despite having the largest non-white population in the UK, Newham has never had an ethnic minority MP. In 2005 a row erupted over the selection of the new Labour candidate for the West Ham constituency after the Labour NEC decided upon an all-woman rather than an all-black short list and local party members selected a white LBN councillor (Muir 2005b).

4   The redevelopment of Queens Market also featured in the US documentary *Wal-Mart: The High Cost of Low Price*, premiered in the UK in April 2006, which increased national attention around the scheme.

5   In May 2008, after this chapter was completed, St Modwen officially submitted a revised fourth plan to LBN for planning permission (for images, see www.newqueensmarket.co.uk). The key elements remain the same as those of the third project: an enlarged market (but now 'laid out almost exactly as it is at present'), a community building including a library and new housing units, mostly in high-rise blocks located around the market.

6   After the presentation of the first scheme in September 2004, it emerged that the premise for redevelopment was based on a feasibility plan commissioned in 2000, but not released until early 2005 which actually showed that there was no overwhelming support for redevelopment among traders or members of the public (Weatherall 2000).

7   There is a rich and long-standing literature that explores the negative impact of neighbourhood renewal schemes upon the social networks and mental well-being of residents, either as a result of their displacement or through the elimination of their spaces of socialisation. See, for example, Young and Willmott (1957); Fried (1963); Fullilove (2001).

8   This petition, the largest in the history of Newham, was delivered to the Mayor of London at City Hall in September 2005.

Chapter 15

From a 'society of fear' to a 'society of respect': the transformation of Hackney's Holly Street Estate

Tony Manzi and Keith Jacobs

Here, now, today, people have had enough of this part of the 1960s consensus. People do not want a return to old prejudices and ugly discrimination. But they do want rules, order and proper behaviour. They know there is such a thing as society. They want a society of respect. They want a society of responsibility. They want a community where the decent law-abiding majority are in charge; where those that play by the rules do well; and those that don't, get punished.

For me this has always been something of a personal crusade. I got used to the society of fear on the Holly Street estate in Hackney in the 1980s when people were too scared to open the door and the letterboxes had burn marks round them where lighted rags had been shoved through them.

Tony Blair's speech on the launch of the five-year strategy on crime
('Labour unveils crime 'crusade'', 19 July 2004)

Introduction

In 1992 the London borough of Hackney embarked on a £300 million regeneration scheme on five system-built public housing estates (see figure 15.1). Known as the Comprehensive Estates Initiative (CEI), the initiative offered an early example of: the ability to combine public and private funding sources; partnership working between statutory and voluntary sector organisations; and an ambitious community participation strategy with local residents. Heralded by politicians and presented in the media as a major success, the CEI offered a prototype for future local authority regeneration projects. Fifteen years from its inception, it is now possible to consider the impact of the CEI and assess its significance in terms of the wider politics of regeneration in London.

This chapter uses the Holly Street estate as a case study to discuss the efficacy of regeneration activity, highlighting the substantial progress made as well as some of the lessons that can be learned from a large-scale project. We argue that Holly Street's significance is that it encapsulates many of the wider debates about regeneration policy that have been a feature of the London context since the 1990s; for these reasons it can be viewed as emblematic of the direction of urban policy in inner-city London in the early twenty-first century. Our approach has been informed by a set of theoretical assumptions: first: that the capacity of regeneration agencies to affect change is limited by resources, competing demands, local economic contexts and neo-liberal ideologies that have infused regeneration practices with a heavy dose of 'communitarianism', an approach which lays strong emphasis on emphasising both rights and responsibilities (Etzioni, 2004). Whilst political communitarianism has been shown to be a core component of New Labour philosophy (DeFilippis and North, 2004), there has been less attention to the potentially repressive and intolerant character of communities (Lees, 2003b).

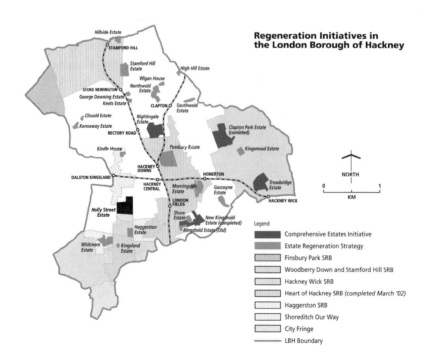

15.1

The Holly Street Estate, Hackney.

Source: Adapted from LB Hackney, 2007

Second, the willingness by policy-makers to embrace regeneration in the 1990s and its continuation through to the present can be viewed as part of the 'territorialising' component of local state governmentality (Hillier, 2007). We use the term 'territorialising' to denote the ways in which local state housing policy extended from economic and material issues to matters of individual responsibility. Hence the major change in local housing policy from the 1980s onwards was the emphasis placed on community empowerment and participation. This shift can be viewed as a reaction to the ideological attacks on the local state throughout the 1980s.

In short, local authorities like Hackney embraced community empowerment as a way of legitimising their activities in the face of this onslaught (Pierson and Worley, 2005). Third, while community empowerment and private sector engagement are used as legitimation strategies for regeneration schemes, approaches that simply provide symbolic reassurance to community involvement are likely to raise expectations but fall short in terms of delivery. Hence, the emphasis placed upon community participation is promoted by governments as a way of overcoming social and political fragmentation. The Foucauldian-inspired work of Dean (1999), Flint (2002), Rose and Miller (1992), Rose (1996) and Raco and Imrie (2000) are relevant in this respect. For example, Rose (1996: 337) argued that governments have utilised the language of community politics and the active citizen to refigure the practices of government away from the 'social' in favour of the 'community'. In making this point he is suggesting that traditional patterns of intervention in which the state took an active and organising role are being replaced with an emphasis on the individual and the community as an active agency. State housing policy entails a complex mix of competing ideologies such as with policies that seek to control and manage the individual behaviour of tenants through rules of regulation alongside an increasing emphasis on community participation (Haworth and Manzi, 1999; Flint, 2006). As we suggest, it is the combination of individualism with the collectivist rhetoric of participation that has created particular tensions within regeneration schemes such as Holly Street.

Background to the CEI: Holly Street pre-regeneration

The Holly Street estate was initially developed in 1971 and, as depicted in figure 15.2, consisted of nineteen five-storey 'snake' blocks and four nineteen-storey tower blocks (a total of 1145 units). By early 1992, the local authority had described it as having 'some of the most extraordinary design flaws in post-war British public housing'. As figure 15.3 indicates, faults included leaking roofs, condensation, cockroach infestation and poor insulation. The estate was used as a model of design failure by the Commission for Architecture and the Built Environment (CABE). In a publication entitled *The Cost of Bad Design*, Holly Street was cited as a design that was 'completely alien to Hackney's principal residential urban form of grids of terrace streets alongside parks and squares' (Simmons, 2006: 21); one that had to be demolished twenty years into an intended sixty-year

15.2
The Holly Street 'snake blocks'.
Source: Levitt Bernstein Associates, 2008

design life. The design of the estate almost certainly accentuated opportunities for crime. Indicators of deprivation in the early 1990s revealed that the neighbourhood was suffering from a multitude of problems.

Over 31 per cent of all those potentially economically active were unemployed compared with 19 per cent for the borough as a whole. Over 21 per cent of all households were headed by a single parent compared with 8 per cent for the borough as a whole; the highest for any London borough. Approximately 63 per cent of the tenants were in receipt of housing benefit. A significant number of residents suffered from mental health problems (Ambrose and Randles, 1999; Woodin Consultancies, 1996). About 80 per cent of tenants had registered to be transferred away from the estate, over one-third of the dwellings were officially classified as difficult to let and the level of rent arrears was over twice the borough's average (Higgins Construction, 2003: 1).

The renewal of Holly Street and the modernisation of local government

The CEI entailed a large reconstruction of existing system-built housing estates including Holly Street, Clapton Park, Trowbridge, Nightingale and New Kingshold, with a projected expenditure of £180 million over a five-year period (although the figure eventually turned out to be nearer £300 million). The significance of the regeneration scheme in the early 1990s was that it coincided with a period, following the Housing Act 1988, when central government was highly sceptical about the ability of local authorities to improve and manage their existing stock. The strategy of 'demunicipalisation' and reductions in government funding in the Local Government and Housing Act 1989 meant that local authorities were

15.3
The 'old' Holly Street.
Source: Levitt Bernstein
Associates, 2008

compelled to find alternative sources of funding and to rely on private sector partners to carry out major regeneration projects (Kemp, 1989).

Holly Street itself received £97 million in funding (LBH, 1999a) using an early public-private partnership financial arrangement and the regeneration was managed by a consortium of housing associations (The Holly Street Partnership). Alongside the physical renewal, the CEI also committed funds to job creation projects with the development of the Queensbridge Community Trust in Holly Street established as an agency intended to channel community funds and economic development through joint management between residents and housing associations.

The council firmly believed that the regeneration of the Holly Street estate provided concrete evidence of success in housing management and regeneration and was determined to use the estate to showcase its achievements. For example, it produced a glossy booklet entitled *Holly Street Estate, Blueprint for Success* (1999b) which claimed that post-regeneration 93 per cent of the residents wanted to remain on the estate long-term (LBH, 1999b: 3), that only 5 per cent had concerns over community safety (pre-regeneration this figure was 60 per cent) and that it was 'one of the most popular choices for tenants on the waiting list' (LBH, 1999b: 21). By 2003 measurable indicators of success included:

> A newly created neighbourhood of small streets, with 374 low-rise homes (small blocks of flats and brick-built houses), with pitched roofs and gardens; a sport and community centre, an elderly persons day centre and health centre based in the estate; a figure of 93 per cent of tenants who stated that they were happy to stay on the estate with 'a thriving tenant's association'. Fear of crime is only 5 per cent, the physical environment is practically graffiti and litter free. The local beat officer commented recently that there were only four minor incidents reported over a three-month period, when the typical amount of reported crime was over four incidents per day. Improving the mental and physical health of residents reduced the call on health services by over a third.
>
> (Higgins Construction, 2003: 1)

The election of a New Labour government in 1997 heralded a commitment to tackling social exclusion, but the focus on 'joined-up government' marked a continuation of the strategy of excluding municipal solutions to existing urban problems (SEU, 1998). At the same time, the discourse of community was a 'prerequisite for the economic revival of cities' (Imrie and Raco, 2003: 5) and Holly Street was viewed as an archetypical site wherein these concepts had been successfully applied. The innovative combination of public and private finance and the effective use of multi-agency partnership models were enthusiastically embraced by the incoming Labour government as a model for the wider modernisation of local government. For example Tony Blair unveiled his flagship New Deal for Communities scheme in September 1998 and had this to say about the estate:

> The change I have seen here is a remarkable tribute to the partnership and all the people who live here who have decided to take their lives into their own hands. What an incredible transformation. This is the type of initiative we need to see replicated across the country. Holly Street is a symbol of what a neighbourhood can do and how it can rebuild itself. . . . Holly Street shows it can be done.
>
> (Quoted in LBH, 1998)

The Holly Street estate in the early 1990s represented the clearest possible example of, in Tony Blair's words, 'everything we needed to change in inner city life'. As noted above, on almost every socio-economic indicator – design faults, levels of resident dissatisfaction, lack of safety and security – the estate could be seen as failing. As the local MP recalled: 'It wasn't an area you would walk through. It was hideous' (Interview with Meg Hillier MP, 1 March 2007). In contrast, the regeneration of the Holly Street estate encapsulated core themes of new governance, community leadership and sustainability; themes that would constitute central aspects of New Labour's 'urban renaissance' in the late 1990s (Imrie and Raco, 2003) and government ministers were able to use the supposed successes of the Holly Street regeneration programme as vindication of a new discourse in urban policy (see figure 15.4 for evidence of the scale of visual change).

The emblematic status of Holly Street is evident in the way it is considered a benchmark for development, 'known to have inspired many similar schemes around the world' and 'recognised as a flagship demonstration of just how much can be achieved by investing in good quality social housing' (community development manager, quoted in *Inside Housing* magazine, 1 December 2004). In particular the Comprehensive Estates Initiative provided an early blueprint for governance mechanisms which excluded local authority institutional structures; community-based approaches to urban renewal, based around concepts of resident involvement; and management structures designed to achieve 'sustainable' outcomes. These concepts would be used as central features of later New Labour regeneration initiatives, such as the New Deal for Communities and the National Strategy for Neighbourhood Renewal (Imrie and Raco, 2003). Fifteen years on from the regeneration programme, it is pertinent to interrogate the key aspects of the success of

15.4

The regenerated Holly Street.

Source: Levitt Bernstein Associates, 2008

the scheme. How significant are the changes? What were the core features? To what extent might these improvements have an impact on the wider governance of London? Before exploring these issues, we outline our approach and data collection methods.

Methods

In this chapter we have adopted an historical approach by tracing the regeneration project from its inception in the early 1990s to the present day. This approach enabled us to make explicit the continuity and changes over time that have impacted on regeneration policy; an approach which is not generally accessible for researchers engaging in contemporaneous analysis (Jacobs, 2001). Undertaking such a task required us to make assessments about the progress that has been achieved and the problematic aspects of the regeneration. Our approach was to draw on both early and existing policy documents, media articles and interviews with key actors, some of whom were involved in the early stages of the project, as well as those who are now responsible for managing Holly Street. Eight in-depth interviews were conducted, incorporating important stakeholders in the project, for example the local ward councillor, the local MP, professional staff with responsibility for the neighbourhood, the Chair of Housing, the lead architect in the scheme, as well as a long-standing tenant representative.

All of the interviewees have served either in a representative capacity or have been professionally involved in the regeneration initiative. The challenge for us was to encourage a critical perspective and steer interviewees away from a simplistic narrative of success. We asked our interviewees to use hindsight to dwell upon the changes that have taken place over the last fifteen years and consider what lessons can be learnt for future regeneration practices. The challenge of interviewing elite actors was to encourage open and frank discussion of both success and failure; to allow reflection on their experience over a significant period of time (over ten years in this case) and to consider what improvements might have been made, given the benefit of hindsight.

The data we collected was categorised thematically to enable us to consider the appropriateness of *governance structures*, the levels of *sustainability* and commitment to *community involvement*. In respect of secondary data we felt it important that we differentiated between, on the one hand, the promotional and rhetorical component of regeneration practice and, on the other hand, those policies that were supported with financial resources and therefore likely to have a more significant material effect. The legacy of the Holly Street regeneration is therefore researched and evaluated through qualitative themes that both challenge official narratives and enable a more nuanced reading of policy to be developed.

Holly Street and the legacy of regeneration

The next sections of the chapter consider the regeneration of Holly Street by reference to in-depth interviews, classified under the themes set out above.

Governance structures

A core feature of the Holly Street regeneration scheme was an emphasis on new approaches to urban governance. In particular a central focus was to move away from what were seen as discredited municipal approaches to service provision and to encourage partnership working in the neighbourhood. Consequently a consortium was established – the Holly Street Partnership – comprising the four main housing associations or Registered Social Landlords (RSLs) then working in the neighbourhood. A commitment to partnership working was central to how the estate was to be managed; this raised particular problems for a housing association sector that was keen to emphasise organisational autonomy:

> RSLs are very precious about their identity . . . we are a brand, we have to sell ourselves . . . We develop, we are a business . . . And the idea of actually sacrificing your identity in order to have a joint identity through the Holly Street Partnership was quite different.
> (Interview, housing association manager, 9 February 2007)

One of the most difficult features of the partnership arrangement was the need for joint management arrangements which one manager described as a 'bloody disaster' (Interview, housing association manager, 9 February 2007). Significantly, this principle of joint management did not endure. One organisation refused to join the partnership initially, one chose to sell their properties and another subsequently left, claiming they were unhappy with the services provided. One manager commented that the largest organisation viewed day-to-day management as 'a bit beneath his attention', whilst smaller ones experienced significant resource difficulties (Interview, housing association manager, 9 February 2007). The local MP also mentioned the problem of divided lines of responsibility: 'having different people managing it is not helpful' (interview with Meg Hillier MP, 1 March 2007).

One of the difficulties was that the role of the RSLs was never clearly defined. As a ward councillor commented:

> they are not simply providing houses; like with councils and council-lors, they also have a community leadership role. In that way they are no different from local authorities. I think they are now having a more pro-active role but it's taken them a number of years to achieve that.
>
> (Interview, 10 April 2007)

These tensions suggested that while there was initial commitment to the prin-ciple of partnership from some (although not all) of the RSL partners, there was also reluctance to commit resources and to devolve management responsibili-ties. Without a clear lead agency, these kinds of schemes have been shown to be highly problematic (Manzi and Smith-Bowers, 2004). In particular, one of the central criticisms levelled was the lack of involvement from the local council:

> There weren't any drivers; I think Hackney disengaged from Holly Street quite a while ago. I think almost inadvertently; I'm not sure it was done with any strategic purpose. But when you are trying to deal with an estate which has been demolished and rebuilt; which has been substantially transformed with old communities moving out and new communities moving in, there is some missing link there.
>
> (Interview, housing association manager, 30 March 2007)

This comment illustrated the difficulty surrounding forms of urban governance that bypass local authority institutional structures. The neo-liberal rationale is that local authority control should be reined back to embed community activity even if gaps in service provision become apparent. The emphasis on new forms of governance has been a feature of regeneration policy since the 1980s and can be viewed as an attempt by the state both to legitimise its own interventions in the light of previous policy fail-ures but also as a mode of communitarian practice intended to facilitate engagement with socially excluded groups residing in public housing (see DeFilippis and North, 2004 for a discussion of similar issues in the Elephant and Castle area in South London).

Sustainability: 'tokenism on a very grand scale'

As mentioned above, there were significant measurable successes evident on Holly Street. These successes were largely attributed to the high level of resources allocated to the initiative. Hence:

> Holly Street is the last project you will probably ever see looking anything like it does; it was incredibly expensive . . . that level of money . . . just isn't around any more . . . The streets are wide; it is designed on such a spacious, airy basis.
>
> (Interview, housing association manager, 9 February 2007)

At the same time managers felt that one of the central lessons learned from the regeneration process was the need to consider both long- and short-term objectives. This was a point stressed by the main architect responsible for the masterplan:

> What effectively happened is that projects like this have an enormous amount of momentum and energy and (in an institutional sense) charisma for a certain period of their life. And then when they get into the exit strategy suddenly they are not that important any more and the 'place to be' moves somewhere else.
>
> (Interview, architect, 20 April 2007)

This comment illustrated the importance of maintaining interest, in particular in the shift from capital to revenue funding. It is this issue of institutional momentum that is crucial to ensuring whether or not projects can be 'sustainable' over the longer term. This was described as a need to acknowledge that key, dynamic individuals would leave schemes to move to other projects (Interview, architect, 20 April 2007). Simultaneously, whilst it became clear that there had been substantial physical improvements, it was the intangible features that were seen to be most problematic: 'It's a brilliant model, but the community development let it down' (Interview, housing association manager, 30 March 2007).

Holly Street's regeneration programme entailed an elaborate structure of consultative bodies. This included a Joint Management Board (JMB), an Estate Development Committee (EDC), and a Community Development Trust – the Queensbridge Trust. Throughout the 1990s socio-economic regeneration was viewed as a necessary condition for regeneration programmes to achieve sustainable outcomes and the Queensbridge Community Trust was created specifically to provide wider economic benefits to the community. It was always acknowledged that to accompany the problems originally at Holly Street – high levels of crime, vandalism, deprivation and despair – efforts should be made to have a commitment to wider regeneration objectives:

> The Borough insisted that this body ought to be overseen by local residents who would look after this organisation and provide all forms of services and benefits locally; it would provide training; it would do the cleaning on the estate; it would also do the gardening.
>
> (Interview, housing association manager, 9 February 2007)

However, respondents were highly critical of this vehicle and it was described by one manager as 'a catalogue of disasters' (Interview, housing association manager, 9 February 2007). Managers were particularly frustrated that they were compelled to put significant resources into the programme, placing some of the smaller organisations in significant financial difficulties. This attempt to promote wider regeneration was described as 'tokenism on a very grand scale'.

A particular difficulty with the regeneration programme was the development of a leisure centre within the neighbourhood; although this was seen as a valuable resource, there were significant costs:

> There is this wonderful building there where you can do sports and have all sorts of meetings but running a building like that is chronically expensive. In order to raise money you have to charge people for its use and in order to start charging for its use you start to exclude some of the people you want to use it.
>
> (Interview, housing association manager, 9 February 2007)

Seen as 'the fatal flaw in the regeneration of the area' (Interview, housing association manager, 30 March 2007) this facility was described as 'slightly patronising . . . let's build them a building' (Interview, housing association manager, 9 February 2007). As a local authority officer commented: 'I don't think we looked at it as a financial asset; we looked at it as an asset to keep young people off the street' (Interview, 2 March 2007). The central difficulty was that there existed 'broader, deeper, serious, underlying issues which you can't really see unless you are in touch with the subcultures in the neighbourhood' (Interview, housing association manager, 30 March 2007). The major problem was expressed as one of 'gangs and guns and drugs and really frightening tensions and conflicts within these subcultures' (Interview, housing association manager, 30 March 2007). These difficulties are ones noted in other regeneration programmes; for example Morrison's (2003) case study of the Blackbird Leys estate in Oxford illustrated how the issue of social justice addressed the economic rather than cultural considerations that contribute to social exclusion.

Hence, wider regeneration activity was needed and the Queensbridge Trust was replaced by the Holly Street Youth Partnership (established in 2007). This latter body was intended to address the wider issues of social exclusion amongst young people and in particular to offer support for drug abuse; in other words to fill the gaps left in the previous attempt at regeneration, with the local authority this time playing a leading role in the partnership.

Community involvement

Our third theme focused on tenant participation and community leadership. The major strand of political communitarianism was evident in the strong emphasis on resident involvement in the scheme. In the broad field that constitutes regeneration practice, tenant participation is seen as a prerequisite; the emphasis placed on participation stems from the perceived failures of post-war slum clearance programmes when in many of Britain's cities, Victorian housing was demolished to make way for system-built municipal housing. The criticisms of slum clearance continue to reverberate and help explain the lengths to which local government agencies engage in consultation. Within Holly Street it was evident that there was an initial optimism about what could be achieved for the area:

> A lot of residents had lived there for some time and there was a real sense of ownership, a real desire for change, talking about the errors

of the past and how Holly Street was gong to be new and different and how we are going to make things better.

(Interview, housing association manager, 9 February 2007)

Furthermore, there was a strong consensus that the residents had acted as a force for good in the neighbourhood and had overseen real physical and neighbourhood improvements, such as depicted in figure 15.5. They had done so by avoiding the tensions between residents and local authorities that have occurred on other regeneration projects such as the Elephant Links Regeneration Programme (Defilippis and North, 2004; Maginn, 2004). As the local MP commented: 'the unifying factor is the residents association' (Interview with Meg Hillier MP, 1 March 2007). A resident who had been active in the consultation stage of the CEI recalled how tenants groups negotiated with local government and professional staff at the start of the CEI process:

> When we were first set up the council and the CEI people dominated the meeting until we said 'we will invite who we want to come along to our meetings to discuss different aspects of the development' . . . That worked because the local council, builders, architects, suddenly realised that we weren't stupid people. We did care what we were doing and basically I suppose we learned to speak their language.
>
> (Interview resident representative, 2 March 2007)

This comment was revealing in that the locus of power remained with the professional groups, with community 'empowerment' restricted to those able to participate

15.5
A new children's playground.
Source: Levitt Bernstein Associates, 2008

in a specialised discourse, a process found in similar studies (such as Morrison, 2003). This process, like all negotiations, entailed conflict but nothing that resulted in major schisms or tensions that delayed the project. One resident suggested that 'it was a case of compromising with each other' (Interview, resident representative, 2 March 2007). A notable success identified by respondents interviewed was the decision to demolish three out of the four tower blocks, and the refurbishment of the remaining one for over-fifties households without children; a decision that was taken by residents themselves. This tower block was seen as a substantial improvement, it included a twenty-four-hour concierge service managed by a resident body (the Tower Management Organisation) (see figure 15.6). Residents were responsible for ordering and commissioning minor repairs and the local authority was responsible for major repairs. Any surpluses that the residents were able to generate could be used to improve the block, for example painting and internal improvements.

At the same time there was also an underlying concern about the bureaucracy that was assembled to orchestrate tenant involvement and uneasiness about overlapping responsibilities with the same residents acting as representatives on different bodies with possible conflicts of interest, with some complaints about 'resident involvement overload' (Interview, housing association

15.6
The Holly Street tower block.
Source: Tony Manzi

manager, 9 February 2007). This manager felt that Hackney Council was at times over-indulgent to the needs and demands of residents: 'Part of involvement is doing things for yourselves, whereas Hackney were so keen to be responding to tenants that they would do everything for them' (Interview, housing association manager, 9 February 2007). Yet, consultation often brings to the fore tensions that exist within housing estates along the lines of gender, identity and ethnicity (Maginn, 2004). At the same time, managers were keen to stress that problems arose due to a lack of support from the statutory bodies rather than through any fault on the part of the residents: 'The residents in charge were actually blame-less, but they were not supported. They were told "you've got to take control of your own lives" and one of the ways is to be on the Board of this organisation' (Interview, housing association manager, 9 February 2007).

Proposals ostensibly designed to empower residents were seen as poorly conceived. In particular, a communitarian emphasis on rights and responsi-bilities enabled governing bodies to lose interest and subsequently to blame resi-dents for policy failures. Others were critical in their view of what was achieved. As one ward councillor commented: 'There was a sense of idealism ten years ago, but if you speak to the residents there is a fair degree of cynicism, the communities have not been engaged' (Interview, 10 April 2007). As this councillor explained:

> the key challenge which has not been realised is about the community being at the heart of decision making and local activism. Basically it was because the council were going through a crisis at the time,[1] they probably took their eye off the ball; they were going through financial meltdown.
>
> (Interview, 10 April 2007)

The key difficulty was that 'people were left to fend for themselves'. This problem was most evident in the arrangements for the joint management board: 'It was really just a residents association; to call it a joint management board gives the impression that residents had access to budgets, or could make decisions on budgets, but that was not the case. Actually it was quite misleading' (Interview, 10 April 2007). In addition, there was a strong sense that the participation arrange-ments had not provided sufficient institutional support. For example:

> I think there is a desire to participate; a lot of people attended meet-ings with the police about crime and anti-social behaviour. A lot of people are angry and want to be involved. There are people out there who have got ideas, but they are not being given the permission, the opportunity or the resources to participate. It's about creating a space and a platform to say 'yes you can help and we will help you to do it'.
>
> (Interview, ward councillor, 10 April 2007)

This experience is one that has been noted in other regeneration case studies, for example North's analysis of 'Project Vauxhall' in South London that 'followed an agenda that was developed by the council, but which left so much in the hands of local residents that it was accused of a failure of leadership' (2003: 135). Whilst participation on the Holly Street Estate had not broken down in the way that other similar schemes in London had, for example in the Elephant Links programme in South London (DeFilippis and North, 2004), the example of the Queensbridge Trust illustrated that the shift to community leadership carried inherent difficulties if residents were not offered substantial institutional and financial support.

Conclusion: the legacy of the Comprehensive Estates Initiative and the wider governance of London

In 2006 a popular television property show evaluated the best and worst places to live in Britain; the London borough of Hackney was deemed to be amongst the worst, 'home to endemic crime and urban deprivation', with 'all of its 19 wards among the most deprived in England'.[2] Whilst this view of Hackney reveals a common set of prejudices, the example of Holly Street illustrates the way in which regeneration schemes can be used to counteract stigma and offset images of social and economic deprivation. In the context of east London, Holly Street is more likely to be viewed as a desirable place to live, property prices are high relative to the area and the design is widely regarded as good quality. However, the important fact about Holly Street is that it required very high levels of investment at the same time as being constructed at low levels of density. These are features that in today's environment would be unlikely to be replicated.

Holly Street's regeneration serves as an example of what can be achieved when agencies actually commit material resources to address poverty. In our view, it was not so much that the CEI entailed a partnership or engaged in community programmes, rather that its impact was the result of budgets being set aside for renewal. Nevertheless, the policy changes of the 1980s and 1990s involved an emasculation of the local state in favour of an emphasis on community involvement; one which left a vacuum at the heart of urban policy, with residents 'left to fend for themselves', unsupported, and local authorities vulnerable to the accusation of 'taking their eye off the ball'. The consequence was widespread cynicism and the perception that attempts to develop social capital and capacity building were largely symbolic and rhetorical. The key lesson that can be learned was that sustainable regeneration programmes require institutional as well as financial support; it is the local authority that is best placed to offer this institutional assistance. This means that partnership and participation is a necessary but not a sufficient condition for successful regeneration.

For London as a whole, the legacy of the CEI in Hackney was threefold: it showed how new institutional structures could be applied to entrenched social problems, in particular through multi-agency partnership working. Second, it demonstrated how sustainable improvements needed to incorporate socioeconomic factors, and third, that community leadership was central to success. However, the Holly Street case study also indicated the limitations of these models. Partnership working was problematic if it merely involved an absence of local authority oversight, socio-economic regeneration had a tendency to become token-istic if support mechanisms were not provided and community leadership needed to be adequately resourced (both in financial and institutional terms). Within Holly Street the initial concept of partnership based on a number of organisations with different responsibilities was subsequently abandoned, but the fact that the central features of the initiative have been widely copied elsewhere illustrates how Holly Street came to reflect an image of both the failure of council housing and the success of subsequent regeneration strategies. This is why Holly Street became such a potent symbol of both the past and future of social housing.

Holly Street provided a model for the way in which the governance of regeneration programmes would develop in the future: through a communitarian emphasis on individual responsibility; through stock transfer to alternative land-lords; through partnership arrangements between statutory, private and volun-tary sectors; and through innovative private finance schemes. In particular, the CEI initiative illustrated the offer of substantial resources in exchange for a willing-ness to engage with private sector partners alongside a commitment to commu-nity participation and an emphasis on social sustainability.

Holly Street's regeneration can therefore be viewed as an example of how the local state has engaged with territorialising components of neo-liberal policy making. While the initiative can be critiqued for establishing complex bureaucratic structures and sometimes misplaced faith in the capacity of commu-nity involvement to secure benefits, it does, nonetheless, represent an example of what can be achieved when funds are made available. Despite mistakes, Holly Street provided a schematic example of how regeneration policy would develop into a wider governmental remit for London.

At the same time the programme illustrated some of the contradic-tions at the heart of the government's strategy. Programmes were aimed at collective goals (such as community empowerment) but were also dependent on individualistic mechanisms (such as private finance and voluntary sector involve-ment) and this created inevitable tensions within regeneration schemes such as Holly Street; its legacy shows that community involvement strategies, active resi-dent participation, institutional partnerships and attempts to engender wider socio-economic regeneration are only meaningful if underpinned by substantial financial investment and by an enduring institutional momentum.

Acknowledgement

The Authors would like to thank Patrick Hammill from Levitt Bernstein Associates for providing pictures of Holly Street.

Notes

1 Labour lost its majority on Hackney Council in May 1998 after seventeen Labour councillors resigned from the party and formed an independent grouping (Jacobs, 1999).

2 (http://www.channel4.com/4homes/ontv/best&worst/2006/hackney.html, retrieved 23 March 2007.)

Chapter 16

Young people and the regeneration of the King's Cross Ten Estates

Nina Brown and Loretta Lees

> The relationship between sustainable development and children's lives
> is not about adult roles as stewards and their capacity to act on behalf
> of the child – it is also about recognising the capacity for children and
> youth to be authentic participants in planning, development and imple-
> mentation processes. Democratic behaviour is learnt through experi-
> ence, so children must be given a voice in their communities so they
> will be able to, now and in the future, participate in civil society.
>
> (Malone, 2001: 8)

Introduction

This chapter explores the regeneration of the 'Ten Estates' in King's Cross London
after they were stock transferred from Islington Borough Council to the Peabody
Trust in 1999. A number of London's large and decaying council estates have
been stock transferred to housing associations and other social landlords by local
councils unable to afford to regenerate their housing stock (see chapter 12 in this
volume). The Peabody Trust is one of the largest social landlords in London and it
sought to improve the fabric and community of these ten decaying and disparate
ex-council estates in King's Cross. The initial £15.2 million five-year regeneration
programme that ensued was, at the time, the Trust's largest stock transfer and
represented a plethora of specific social and physical regeneration challenges. At
the core of the regeneration programme the Trust sought to improve the quality
of the estate and in turn the quality of life for residents, including young people.
Since the 1990s urban policy in Britain has been premised on the importance of
public participation in local regeneration and governance, with a view to empowerment and developing citizenship. However, one group frequently overlooked by

the participation process is young people, precisely the group whose perceived lack of citizenship causes such concern to many (Speak, 2000). Although young people's needs were part of the regeneration programme on the Ten Estates and local residents were involved in the decision-making process, young people's participation in the regeneration programme was minimal – tokenistic. In this chapter, we demonstrate the failures that arose as a result of the exclusion of young people from the decision-making process, as well as some of the successes of the regeneration programme for young people.

This chapter draws on research into the spatial needs of young people living on the Ten Estates and how the regeneration programme undertaken by the Peabody Trust dealt with these. Such a study is of particular importance in light of recent concerns about young people spending an increasing amount of time indoors and under adult supervision (Aitken, 1994; Valentine, 1996; Fitzpatrick et al, 1998). In 2000 the Office of the Children's Rights Commissioner for London conducted a survey into children's experiences of London and found that they 'were more and more restricted as their place to play gets smaller', which is problematic as social and play opportunities are important to young people's quality of life and social development (Barnardos, 1994; Valentine 1997). The study is also important in light of recent concerns about the anti-social behaviour of London's young people, especially on council estates:

> From the murderers of the 10-year-old Damilola Taylor in 2000 to the uncontrollable 'children from hell' on inner-city estates to the 13-, 12-, 11-year-olds increasingly suspected of a whole gamut of crimes from rape to robbery with violence, London seems to be spawning ominous and sinister children, perhaps as never before.
>
> (Bavidge and Gibson, 2003: 44)

Indeed young people in London have long been demonised and current debates follow established patterns:

> They particularly resemble nineteenth-century arguments about the presence of women in public spaces, and are similarly fraught with anxieties about moral geographies, the dangers supposedly inherent in movement around the city . . . The question of the particular places in the city that children should and should not occupy has become an intensely moral one . . . However inadequate as a substitute, institu-tionalized, tightly regulated (and commercialized) 'spaces of play' appear to be the only option.
>
> (Bavidge and Gibson, 2003:43)

By focusing on the geographies of young people on the Ten Estates, this study highlights the socio-spatial exclusion that they experience within the regenerated communal and play spaces of the Ten Estates, which, as this chapter will high-light, leads to a socio-spatial exclusion that impacts their quality of life in different ways. There has been little work within the regeneration literature in the UK that has specifically focused on young people's experiences. The research that has been undertaken (e.g. Fitzpatrick *et al.*, 1998, 2000; Matthews, 2001; O'Brien, 2003) has tended to focus on children at the expense of older young people and has not looked at young people's geographies, but as this study shows, children and teenagers have quite different needs from the regeneration of their estates. Overall there are two main concerns that frame the study: i) the marginalisation, if not outright exclusion, of young people from the decision-making about the urban regeneration of their estates, and ii) the way that a design-led regeneration has further excluded young people from the public spaces around their homes.

The study

The research was funded through an ESRC-CASE studentship, the CASE or collaborative partner being the Peabody Trust. One of the key aims of the research was to develop it as a piece of participatory action research, designed to encourage the participation of both the Peabody Trust and the young people on the Ten Estates. The study focused on the complex tensions and conflicts that young people on the Ten Estates experienced on a day-to-day basis in the use of their local built environment.

A multi-method approach was used that combined qualitative methods like interviews and surveys with visual methods such as photography and video. As Christensen and O'Brien (2003:3) argue, 'there is much scope for using a mixed-method approach, which can draw on the strength of each perspective and at the same time can combine these with more in-depth and sensitive analysis of what life in the city means to children'. The sixty-seven young people, aged eight to nineteen, who participated over a period of three years, were given a choice over the way they wanted to communicate their lived experiences on the Ten Estates – oral/verbal (interview), written (survey or diary) or visual (photos, video). They could choose to participate for fifteen minutes, a whole day or for some for over several years. This captured the voices of young people in an enjoyable, engaging and participatory way. It also tackled the particular challenges associated with working with 'disadvantaged' young people. The young people could keep their maps, photos, photo notebooks and videos, and as such all the participants shared ownership of the data (Young and Barrett, 2001). Gaining access to, and the trust of, the young people was difficult and time consuming. Some young people were contacted through youth clubs and summer play programmes, but more were contacted by hanging out in the public spaces around the estates, so as to make sure the sample was as representative as possible.

Participatory approaches to community research with young people such as this have demonstrated the multiple benefits of engaging with young people: challenging their social exclusion, redistributing power within the research process, and allowing and enabling them to analyse and potentially transform their own lives through the skills they might learn. In addition it gave the Peabody

Trust the opportunity to evaluate their regeneration programme openly – considering both the successes and failures for the Ten Estates in general and specifically with regards to the young people concerned. Although this research supported an impetus already in place at the Trust's youth service – to be more inclusive towards young people – this project aided cross-departmental awareness and discussion about young people's socio-spatial needs, which was especially insightful for departments outside the youth service at the Peabody Trust.

The Ten Estates

The location of the Ten Estates near to King's Cross in central London, an area infamous for prostitution and more recently drugs, which is itself undergoing regeneration, is important (see figure 16.1) (see chapter 6 in this volume). All of the estates had experienced drug and prostitution related activities for many years, and in discussions with residents and Peabody staff it was made clear that those estates closest to King's Cross suffered the most. The number and size of the Ten Estates also marks out this study. The ten estates that now make up the Ten Estates differ not just in terms of location but also in terms of architectural style, age and size. The estates built before the war tend to be low-rise brick buildings with small one- and two-bed flats with a courtyard internal to the estate; those built after the 1970s are higher rise concrete buildings with a combination of flat sizes from bedsit to three-bed and with larger communal spaces and parking facilities. Many of the estates had been experiencing problems for years, Pollard House, for example, had attracted drugs and prostitution for a number of years:

> I spoke to a guy . . . he is in his seventies and he remembers Pollard House . . . as being a massive brothel and ministers jumping out of the windows when there were police raids, to get away. I mean he remembers that from years ago – so it must have been going on for many years.
> (Interview, Ten Estates Community Regeneration Officer, 2002)

And on the largest estate – Priory Green, designed by Berthold Lubetkin – there were numerous anti-social behaviours evident: 'there are needles on the stairs, and I am scared they are going to stick in me . . . they just wee and pooh in the lift, it is disgusting' (Interview, female, age eleven).

The Priors Estate, the second largest of the Ten Estates, had a large concrete communal area between the buildings, underneath which were the residents' garages. Drug users, prostitutes and other itinerant people frequented the underground area and the estate had no social or play areas at all. Most of the regeneration of the Ten Estates had begun when the research began; indeed some of the estates had already been regenerated.

In many ways it is the specifics associated with social housing in central London that come to the fore of this study, issues such as overcrowding, significant ethnic diversity, poverty, crime and markedly a sense of class-based marginalisation and social exclusion. The latter was especially evident when the young people left the Ten Estates to go to the nearby commercial and recreational facilities on offer in Angel (see Butler and Lees, 2006, on this part of gentrified inner London) where they were placed under surveillance in these spaces due to their embodiment as young and poor (see the section on successes and failure at the end of this chapter).

The stock transfer and the state of the estates at transfer

Towards the end of the twentieth century significant reinvestment was needed in order to improve and modernise a social housing stock that had fallen into disrepair. Local governments began to look towards alternative routes to inject funds into improvements and maintenance. The first stock transfers of social housing from local councils to registered social landlords began under the Conservatives, but it became more extensive under New Labour. Towards the end of the 1990s, without the money to improve all of their social housing stock, Islington Borough Council sought to transfer some of their worst stock to other social landlords in a bidding process. The King's Cross Ten Estates, not originally called the Ten Estates and not previously sharing any association beyond locality and ownership, formed part of this stock transfer. The Peabody Trust put in a bid for the stock transfer and to regenerate these estates. In 1999 they won the tenants' vote with a strong majority and the King's Cross Ten Estates, as they were then named, were transferred to the Peabody Trust. The Peabody Trust had a good reputation and persua-

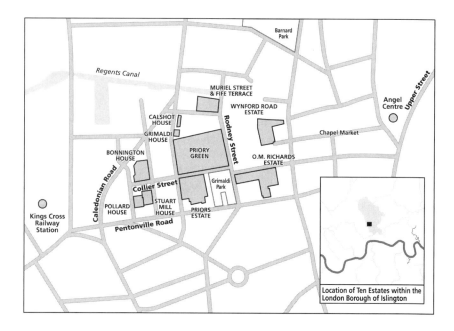

16.1
Location of King's Cross Ten Estates.
Source: Nina Brown and Loretta Lees, 2008

sive improvement plans, as the economic and community development manager at the Peabody Trust explained: 'I think they were obviously quite interested in the Peabody because we do a lot of regeneration, but more because we had a good reputation as a social landlord and I think that that probably swung it' (interview, 2002). The community development manager added that the residents had little choice but to transfer:

> local authorities are transferring estates that have had no investment for an awfully long time and . . . they are transferring them because their stock is crumbling, it's falling down around their ears. There's no value unless the amounts of money are spent on it and tenants are dissatisfied with everything and that's the only thing that swings the vote.
>
> (Interview, 2002)

As a historically philanthropic organisation dedicated to improving housing for London's poor, the Peabody Trust at the time were keen to extend their stock, which is exclusively and unusually London based. They sought to extend their stock through new developments on brownfield sites and stock transfers, of which at the time the King's Cross Ten Estates was the Trust's second, largest and most challenging stock transfer. The Ten Estates were architecturally and socially different to the traditional Peabody estates, but as the community development manager explained, the Ten Estates 'presented the opportunity for us to build other partnerships and lever in additional funds to be able to work on the Ten Estates' (interview, 2002).

At their transfer the estates were suffering from a plethora of social and physical problems, which led one community development worker to describe the Ten Estates as having 'the mad, the bad, and the sad . . . living there' (Brown, meeting notes, 2002). Surveys undertaken by the Peabody Trust revealed the extent of the underinvestment and lack of maintenance that had happened over a number of years, resulting in poor lighting, overgrown green spaces and broken doors, entrances and gates, which left the estates insecure and with an impression of neglect. Their lack of maintenance and security attracted prostitutes, drug dealers and drug users. There was escalating youth-related anti-social behaviour and alcohol/drug abuse among residents with some properties being used as 'crack dens'. This had a significant impact on the residents of the Ten Estates, with some elderly residents having to take action themselves, for example one elderly male resident:

> ended having to chase them with a spade. I was so fed up. They were always there in the corridors, lifts . . . my grand-kids were round and I saw then by the cars. I just got a spade and chased them out.
>
> (Interview, 2003)

A Peabody Community Regeneration document reported that the lack of 'safe play spaces' on the Ten Estates posed a serious threat to the young people, who had restricted opportunities to use their leisure time 'positively' (CR Doc 3, p.4). As the Islington Play and Youth Service report reiterated, 76.2 per cent of children in Islington lived in rented accommodation, few of them had private gardens (the Ten Estates had a total of only fifteen private gardens attached to some of the ground-floor properties on two of its estates) and as such they were dependent on local public spaces for play. However, with only 5.6 per cent of Islington's total area as public open space (IPYS Doc) and limited space within the estates, there was a shortage of both public and safe spaces for young people. High levels of crime and poverty in King's Cross compounded this shortage of public open space. As the Islington Play Association reported:

> poverty in Islington is increasingly found in families with children. For these children, there is too little opportunity for the essential self-development that only free, safe and nurtured play can bring. Instead they face a dangerous traffic ridden urban landscape desperately deficient in developmental stimuli where they are more likely to be the victims of crime than the perpetrators.
>
> (IPA Doc 1: 2)

A local Sure Start report also stated that it was difficult for families living in the area to move into accommodation that was more suitable for young children, that young people's living conditions were exacerbated by parental drug use, and that the high crime rate in the local area made it unsafe to go out (Sure Start Copenhagen Report, 2000 – SS Doc 2). This was reiterated by a community police officer in interview: 'a lot of these children come from beaten, very appalling backgrounds, a lot of abuse' (interview, 2003).

With no way to escape such problems in all realms (public and private), the quality of life for young people on the Ten Estates was seriously affected. Here is a sample of the stark comments from young people on some of the estates prior to their regeneration:

> There are drug needles outside my house . . . makes me feel sick . . . cause people, I don't want them druggies in my flat.
>
> (Interview, male, age twelve, 2002; see figure 16.2)

> It's like everywhere you go, poop and graffiti.
>
> (Interview, male, age twelve, 2002)

> My sister had a baby and she always used to come around, but people used to piss and that, it smells and the baby is there. It's unhygienic and that . . .
>
> (Interview, female, age thirteen, 2002)

> yeah, but people who don't live here, they come and do [embarrassed to say] and put it in there, and you know walk away. They don't care.
>
> (Interview, male, age seven, 2002)

16.2
Drug needle outside young person's home.
Source: Nina Brown, 2008

The young people explained they rarely used the recreational areas on their estates because they were broken, overgrown and dirty, and some had been taken over by drug addicts and prostitutes; they were especially afraid of used needles lurking in the bushes and undergrowth. They resorted to other measures:

> We used to have these pop-up tents, me and my friends used to take them down there [at the base of their building] and we used to put them up and we would get covers and food and that, and we used to sit in the tent all afternoon on a Saturday, so at least we could get out of the house.
> (Interview, female, age twelve, 2002)

The poor state of the Ten Estates was obviously affecting their quality of life and self-perception:

> where we live is crap!
> (Interview, female, age twelve, 2002)

> horrible . . . everything. The area, the playing, the flats are all manky . . . a bit too squashy . . . it's unpleasant. The lifts are disgusting and stinky.
> (Interview, female, age twelve, 2002)

Needless to say when the Peabody Trust took over the Ten Estates and began a programme of regeneration, adult residents and young people were excited and optimistic about the future of the Ten Estates.

The programme of regeneration

The Ten Estates were to undergo a £15.2 million regeneration programme over a period of five years. The Peabody Trust's ECRF bid focused on four areas:

- *Resident Involvement* – featured throughout the bid document and indicated strongly that residents were key and central to the entire modernisation programme. By involving residents formally (through resident groups) and informally (knocking on doors, etc.), supporting residents practically and financially, the Trust was attempting to tackle barriers to resident participation (interview, Community Development Manager, Peabody Trust, 2002). This reflected the Trust's general approach to residents and policy arguments that resident involvement was the core to successful and sustainable regeneration.

- *Development and Improvement Programme* – the programme of works would address physical and safety issues within the estates and would reflect the needs of the residents. It would involve them in decision-making on issues ranging from the appearance of the estates to more fundamental issues such as safety and security. The overall aim was to raise the standard of the housing and to improve the quality of life for the residents.
- *Housing Services* – the Peabody Trust believed that a central component of area regeneration was local estate-based management. They argued that through on-site management housing standards could be maintained by dealing with minor repairs, estate cleanliness, safety and security problems, and resident satisfaction more readily.
- *Community Development* – a joined-up approach that would tackle both physical and social problems was central to the Trust's bid. They committed to an ongoing programme of community development for all residents, young and old, beyond just including them in decision-making about the modernisation programme.

These four key areas of the bid reflect many of the ideas outlined in the government's Urban White Paper (DETR, 2000a), regeneration as an inclusive, joined-up, sensitive and sustainable approach. With funding from ECRF, the Heritage Lottery Fund and the Peabody Trust, the initial £15.2 million programme of regeneration would 'tackle more than bricks and mortar' (interview, Community Development Manager, Peabody Trust, 2002), for the Peabody Trust were committed to 'building sustainable communities on its estates' (PT Doc 14, p.15).

Following resident and other professional consultations the regeneration documents focused on five main aims:

- to create a safer environment for residents (focusing on security and access issues)
- to remedy the structural and other physical problems of the estate buildings
- to create a common landscape identity among the Ten Estates
- to meet the needs of the estate buildings and their residents, individually and collectively
- to tackle social and community regeneration and development.

Although the initial budget for the regeneration programme was £15.2 million, the final cost of redeveloping the Ten Estates exceeded £50 million.

Resident participation – space for young people?

The regeneration of the Ten Estates was a design-led regeneration strategy, in other words the Peabody Trust felt that if they improved the physical fabric of the estates this would have a positive impact on sense of community, well-being and anti-social behaviour (CR Doc 4). Resident participation in the decision-making process that was to design the regeneration programme was important to the Peabody Trust. The participation of residents would not only mean that the regeneration programme reflected their needs, it would also be a sustainable approach because it would empower residents and re-establish their connection to the built environment (interview, Peabody Trust Resident Involvement Officer, 2002). The latter was considered to be particularly important for the Ten Estates because the residents had limited private space to attach a personal identity to, and therefore it was important to try and create this attachment through communal areas. In doing so it was hoped that residents would identify these areas as their own, which would stimulate interest and attachment, and make these areas less prone to abuse by residents (FHA Doc 1). Finally, the Trust hoped that participation might empower the residents and provide skills training (interview, Peabody Trust Resident Involvement Officer, 2002).

Acknowledging that resident participation would need support, the Trust employed a number of different methods to support and sustain resident participation on the Ten Estates:

- it established formal groups, including an area steering group committee, a tenants association (TA), and tenant management organisations (TMO)
- it held community events, such as public meetings, exhibitions and open days
- it produced newsletters and undertook door knocking to inform residents of participation activities and regeneration plans, and questionnaire surveys were utilised to extend participation
- it offered financial and practical support to the TA and TMOs to assist their ability to participate in the decision-making
- it conducted external research, such as a community mapping consultation to inform and support community development.

Those involved in the resident participation were aware that resident participation on the Ten Estates was not representative and to attract underrepresented groups a different approach was needed. Ethnic minority residents were identified as one underrepresented group who needed a different involvement strategy. Young people, however, were not identified as an underrepresented group and were not formally identified in the participation and decision-making process. The Trust did create some opportunities for the young people to be involved. They asked young people to enter competitions to design play areas at community fun days – the winner would get some of their ideas realised, they tried to attract them and their carers[1] with children's activities, such as bouncy castles, they were welcome at the exhibitions, and in some cases were also able to choose the colours for the play area and discuss formal play equipment. But these did not engage the young people in discussions about what they wanted and needed, as these comments illustrate:

> they used to come and entertain people by food and talk downstairs and all the adults of the houses used to come downstairs and talk with the new people at Peabody.
>
> (Interview, female resident, age thirteen, 2003)

> it wasn't on a particularly deep level. I don't think it was more than a free fun day so they came along and we hoped that in doing that their parents may come along and we could talk to them as well.
>
> (Interview, Peabody Stock Transfer Team, 2002)

Even a senior Peabody youth worker was critical of the tokenistic efforts by the Trust to include young people in the decision-making; he was especially critical of the way that they got the hopes of young people up in terms of using their ideas and then not doing so, and of the disappointment that ensued:

> the kids believe that this is going to happen because at the time the staff had been really enthusiastic about their drawings, saying that they were really good, but in the end they didn't do anything about them.
>
> (Interview, senior Peabody youth worker, 2002)

Moreover, drawing pictures and choosing colours for play equipment did not attract older young people, and as such they were significantly underrepresented in the decision-making process. This was ironic given that they were often seen to be the root of certain problem behaviours and that these were the largest group of residents that were likely to want to use the communal and recreational spaces around the estates. Participating in this study was the first time that the young people, especially the older young people, on the Ten Estates had a real opportunity to talk about where they lived and the regeneration programme.

Young people are in an interesting position in terms of urban regeneration because of the ambivalence around their position (see Lees, 2003b): urban regeneration programmes often set out to both include but also exclude them, to integrate them into the process of provision for them, but at the same time to disperse their less desirable behaviours. As such young people as key users of public space remain awkwardly balanced between a rhetoric of 'provision and protection' and 'demonisation and legislation' (Valentine, 2004).

Successes and failures

The consultation process revealed that safety and security issues were the residents' main and constant priority; this was reiterated in discussions with the young people who thought that good security was also important to them: 'make high security, like guards at every doors and on every floor . . . to be safe. To keep people out' (interview, male, age twelve, 2002).

As a landscape architect who had worked on the redesign commented: 'They had been living in these conditions for so long that it [security] was all they could see' (interview, 2002). As stated earlier, the physical regeneration and redesign of the Ten Estates was linked in the minds of the Peabody Trust to the social regeneration of the estates. The regeneration strategy was one of design determinism. It was thought that physical and cosmetic changes to the estates would increase people's feelings of safety and ownership, therein improving morale and anti-social behaviour. But it was also recognised that increased security and good quality housing alone would ultimately not sustain community on the estates (interview, Peabody Trust community development manager, 2002).

The first step was to secure the estates from non-residents and to deal with the problematic behaviour of a minority of residents. Before the physical regeneration even began the Peabody Trust worked with the local police to get a number of crack houses shut down, demonstrating to both residents and non-residents that such criminal activities were no longer tolerated on the estates. The Peabody Trust's ability to do this was aided by their estate-based management strategy that highlighted that the estates were now under daily observation and by the serving of a number of anti-social behaviour orders (ASBOs). As one young person said: 'they [Islington Council] didn't do anything . . . the Peabody came and they were like, we are going to sort the place out' (interview, male age 14, 2002).

Controlling access to all the estate buildings was the next stage in securing the estate from non-residents. Boundary railings were installed around the periphery of each estate to both secure them and to signify the change of management/identity of the Ten Estates (see figure 16.3). They also changed the layout of certain spaces so as to enhance natural, resident surveillance (see figures 16.4 and 16.5). Instead of the numerous entry and exit points throughout the Ten Estates, central entry and exit points were developed into gateways (see figure

16.3
Photo of the newly bounded Priory Green Estate after regeneration. Source: Nina Brown, 2008

16.4

Poor natural surveillance over recreation area between Redington and Kendal House on the Priory Green Estate before regeneration.
Source: Nina Brown, 2008

16.5

Good natural surveillance over recreation area between Redington and Kendal House on the Priory Green Estate after regeneration.
Source: Nina Brown, 2008

16.6). By minimising the number of entry points it was easier to control, monitor and secure access into the estate buildings and communal areas (FHA Doc 1). Residents could only gain access to their estate using an electronic key, which could only be replaced/replicated by the Peabody Trust. After they had secured access they began to monitor the estates using surveillance technology. CCTV systems were installed throughout the Ten Estates in entrances, corridors, lifts and recreation areas, and some of the estates were linked up to a twenty-four-hour concierge system in Hugh Cubbit House on Priory Green in the centre of the Ten Estates. Other strategies included improving signage and lighting on the estates.

This defensible approach to regeneration reflected some of the principles of Alice Coleman's[2] Design Improvement Controlled Experiment (DICE) in the late 1980s/early 1990s for 'securing significant and long-lasting improvements in the physical and social conditions on housing estates through rectifying poor design characteristics' (ODPM, 2006b). This approach increased residents', including young

16.6

New entrance for Redington and Kendal House on the Priory Green Estate.
Source: Nina Brown, 2008

people's, feelings of safety on the estates almost immediately: 'now it's definitely got better, better than it was. It's a smaller amount of people [causing trouble] cos most of them have just gone away now' (interview, female age fourteen).

It is clear from this research that making regeneration visible to residents and non-residents is crucial (see also Dean and Hastings, 2000).

However, although the problems with non-residents declined, the security measures still failed or broke down (see also chapter 9 in this volume). This made young people's new sense of safety fragile:

> Security guards not great. They are not doing much. Some of them are rude . . . the doors keep breaking . . . I don't trust the security guards. One of them got fired cos drunk-druggie.
>
> (Interview, male, age twelve, 2002)

> the door in the back can be pulled open. There is a hole in the park that you can climb in as well.
>
> (Interview, male, age twelve, 2002)

On a couple of occasions an almost frenzied atmosphere was observed when young people didn't recognise someone on the estate. Nevertheless the improved security features did create a greater attachment of young people to their estate; indeed they became part of the natural surveillance and gained a sense of control, as they were able to report misuse and access by non-residents. They developed a sense of pride:

> I feel better about the area. [Regeneration] has given the area a good name and reputations. Like when family come over because I am proud. I wouldn't invite them round before, cos looked really bad. Now invite all my cousins and they are really impressed.
>
> (Interview, male, age eighteen, 2004)

> there's more stuff and I like the way it looks, it's fancy. I am real proud of it cause it's a good place, innit, and they [his family in the buildings] can see you.
>
> (Interview, male, age ten, 2003)

The second step was improvements to the physical, structural and safety elements of all the buildings and the modernisation of the residents' flats (new windows, doors, bathrooms, kitchens, redecorating, etc). The modernisation of the buildings was extensive and reflected the poor physical state they were in on transfer. Although few young people were involved in the decision-making about the modernisation of their flats, almost all of them were pleased with the improvements to their homes. But given that the private spaces of the young people's homes were to remain much the same, just cosmetically improved, it was the regeneration work to the public spaces around their buildings that was most pertinent to them. The Peabody Trust began by reducing the number of car parking spaces and increasing the communal space on the estates. The recreational spaces were redeveloped with safer, more durable play equipment and adjacent seating to enable supervision and surveillance. There was new planting and vegetation, bushes and shrubs that had previously hidden attackers or intruders were removed and replaced with spikey plants that discouraged access, and other plants were used to screen areas, channel pedestrian movement and create privacy etc. The majority of the young people said that this regeneration had improved their feelings of safety and access to these areas, some stating that their parents now let them out on their own:

> my mum let me out today . . . I am not usually let out since my dad died, as my mum doesn't think it is safe for me, but she thinks its better now cause she can see me.
>
> (Interview, male age nine, 2003)

> it's better . . . bigger with better facilities. I can hang out with friends more now. Kids came out less before cos the park wasn't good, innit. Now it's good, so we can get together here. Met loads more people since they changed it.
>
> (Interview, male age twelve, 2003)

Although young people were not formally involved in the decision-making process, their needs were taken into consideration in the regeneration programme on the Ten Estates. The programme took into account that young people had limited access to safe places and developed play spaces that were more secure, functional and visually appealing. This took account of the Islington Play Association who argued that 'the key component of social exclusion is quality play provision' (IPA Doc 1, p.2). The Peabody Trust identified the fact of play equipment that was 'outdated, unimaginative and offered limited play value with little variety for different age groups' (FHA Doc 1). A sift through the various community development documents at the time also shows that the Peabody Trust saw that opportunities for young people to use their leisure time positively needed to be created in order to avoid the problems of offending behaviour. The regeneration of the recreational areas on the estates significantly increased the young people's access to and use of these spaces, because the spaces were now better equipped and were safer. However, it was these communal recreational and play spaces that bore the brunt of the criticism of the regeneration programme from the young people, especially the older young people. They argued that the spaces had been developed for younger users not for older young people and that they did not reflect the way that they used these spaces (see figure 16.7):

> [Peabody] bought all stuff for children, for younger children, and I think they should have built more stuff for bigger children and adults. There isn't much stuff we can go on.
>
> (Interview, female, age twelve, 2003)

16.7
**Extract from photo
notebook, female age 13.
Source: Nina Brown,
2008**

I would give this picture a 🙂
This is the playground.
This is the playground I was talking about on the
writing opposite. When peabody made this playground
they were only thinking about the little kids and
not the big kids.
I think they could not even put a round about or even
a few swings and then that would be ok, but they
did not even do that. So while the little kids are
playing on the climbing fame the big ones have to
stay indoors out because there was nothing for them
to do.

the hills are a waste of time. We need basketball and football, then everyone would come out and if got coaches teach you it would be even better.

(Interview, male age sixteen, 2003)

I think they should make a place for little kids, big kids and that, and grown ups like to sit down in the corner.

(Interview, male, age twelve, 2003)

The result was that older young people often creatively appropriated these spaces for their own needs (see figure 16.8), using equipment to socialise on, making

16.8
**Photo of young people playing
football after tying up swings to make
a goal.
Source: Nina Brown, 2008**

bike ramps, and so on (compare Matthews *et al.*, 1999). This often led to conflict with the carers of the younger children.

In reality the regeneration of the recreational spaces on the estates was a narrow view of young people's access to, and use of, the built environment. It reduced the needs of young people to formal (and quite childish) play spaces and play equipment. When discussing this with a professional involved in the decision-making about the recreation areas, he explained that the residents had requested play equipment for small children for two reasons. First, they wanted somewhere for their grand-children to play, and second, they didn't want to attract older young people to 'hang out' in these areas, as they would bring trouble and noise. This was reiterated by the Peabody Youth Service who explained: 'although residents want the kids to be doing something, they don't want it done on their doorstep because it attracts congregations of kids' (interview, senior Peabody youth worker, 2003). It seems then that the regeneration of the play areas was deliberately designed to exclude people of a particular age (those over ten years old). In interview the community development manager argued:

> one of the big problems at King's Cross is that tenant representation is largely elderly, white and male. They are no longer in employment. They no longer have young kids . . . their interests aren't towards the more positive sides of community regeneration . . . it's about wanting a nice place without drug dealers and crack houses, gates to keep kids out [and that has] an impact on the work that you can do . . . you won't solve those problems by talking to five year old guys at King's Cross, frankly because their reality is not the same reality as the majority of the people living there.

Unlike the children, the older young people, those over approximately twelve years old, sought areas to socialise in that would provide them with a degree of privacy. Grimaldi Park (see figures 16.1 and 16.9), the largest public space adjacent to the Ten Estates, was the main space that older young people sought to socialise in.

16.9
Grimaldi Park.
Source: Nina Brown, 2008

Although the Peabody Trust saw it to be a significant potential amenity for the residents, tightening purse strings meant that Grimaldi Park was not significantly regenerated. It was not formally controlled (in comparison to all the other communal and public spaces around the Ten Estates) and as a result it became attractive to teenagers. It did have an area of play equipment designed for children but it was also one of the few spaces that had things suitable for older young people, such as a caged playing area for team sports like football and basketball (see figure 16.10).

The park was divided into four sections, two of these at the back along Pentonville Road offered the most privacy because people rarely passed through them, they were away from the play spaces in the park and furthest from the estates. A low brick wall allowed a vantage point from which teenagers could view the park largely hidden (see figure 16.11). Teenagers often used this part of the park for what they described as 'private stuff' – activities they didn't want adults (parents/carers, residents, the police or the Peabody Trust) or other young people to witness. They used this space for intimate encounters, to smoke cigarettes or drugs, and have a private conversation.

This behaviour demonstrated the needs of teenagers living on large, communal estates such as these for a degree of privacy away from parents/carers and other residents. There was nowhere else for them to go. Their flats were often small and overcrowded:

> very, very small. Our kitchen is so small yeah, only two or three people can get in it.
>
> (Interview, male, age twelve, 2002)

and they couldn't always afford the more commercial places or public leisure facilities where youth tend to hang out, such as shops, cinemas, swimming pools, clubs, etc. They were also often under surveillance in these spaces, due to their embodiment as young and poor, producing exclusion:

16.10
Caged play area Grimaldi Park.
Source: Nina Brown, 2008

16.11
Private area Grimaldi Park.
Source: Nina Brown, 2008

> the Warner Cinema, that costs X for a family, who can afford that?
>
> the security guard follows you round, checking you don't nick anything
>
> you know the shops, they are alright but some of them are rude . . . like if you're in with your friend they are saying like, 'two at a time', Then if you all go in they start shouting at you 'Get out of my shop'
>
> (Interview, female, age twelve, 2003)

Significantly, they also wanted to be away from younger children. As the young people grew older they sought social and physical separation from the younger children. They argued that this was of benefit to both themselves and to the children, as their conversations and activities were unsuitable or a bad influence on younger children:

> do my own things [in Grimaldi Park]. No one hassles you. You get to go there with the older kids and get away from all the younger kids who grass you up.
>
> (Interview, male, age seventeen, 2003)

> the little ones just copy everything we do, they hang about with us. That's not good, they shouldn't follow our world and that's why I go to Grimaldi.
>
> (Interview, male, age seventeen, 2003)

Despite a growing emphasis on the autonomy of young people and on their rights of participation (see Frank, 2006) they are increasingly finding themselves segregated from or marginalised from public urban spaces. Sustainable urban regeneration requires not just the participation of young people but also that the regeneration results in a quality, safe and liveable environment for *all* young people. This study shows that a balance needs to be struck between the provision of appropriate urban space for children and that for older young people. Overall the regeneration of the Ten Estates created an adult space with pockets of space suitable for children but little space suitable for older young people – the resident teenagers and young adults.

Conclusion

> Across Europe and internationally, there is a move to place children's needs and rights at the centre of planning our cities. This development understands that if your major cities are to become genuinely sustainable – places where families choose to bring up their children and where all young people feel valued and included, we must listen to their concerns – and act on them.
>
> (GLA, 2004b: foreword by Ken Livingstone).

Despite shifts in urban policy towards community participation, international shifts towards young people's rights, of which the right to participate in decisions that affect them is one, literature to support and emphasise the importance of including young people, and evidence of varying degrees of good practice across Britain (see Matthews, 2001), there is still a gap between this rhetoric of broadening participation and practice, with 'participation by young people . . . still the exception not the rule' (Matthews, 2001:155). Although young people were featured within the regeneration plans for the Ten Estates, they were not included in the decision-making beyond a few tokenistic efforts. The efforts that were made compartmentalised young people's needs, rather than allowing them to contribute to the overall strategic planning and development (Elsley, 2004; Matthews, 2001; Fitzpatrick et al., 1998). As Matthews et al. (1999:135) argue: 'for the most part, young people are provided with few opportunities to engage in discussions about their economic, social and environmental futures . . . [and] it would seem that participation is still conceived to be an adult activity' (see also Matthews, 2001, 1992).

The aim of including the local community (the residents of the Ten Estates) in the regeneration programme was to reflect the needs of the local community, to make the regeneration sustainable, and to (re)establish a connection between the communities and place. Although one community regeneration document recognised that 'young people in the area have many needs associated with life in an inner city, multicultural society' (CR Doc 3, p.4), in reality there was little acknowledgement of the young people's complex social and spatial needs. As Dodman (2004) argues, it is necessary to understand the heterogeneous ways young people perceive their environment if effective means are to be developed to foster inclusion in urban governance, deal with problems, and develop attachment. As Matthews (2003) discusses, participation offers a way out of the problematisation of young people, especially in the context of neighbourhood renewal. Whilst young people were only offered token involvement in this regeneration project, the empirical research with the young people on the Ten Estates has shown that they are capable of the same involvement as adults (see Speak, 2000). We leave this chapter with a comment from one of the young people on the Ten Estates:

> This was the first time someone has asked me what I think . . . it's been good . . . It was good to talk about it.
>
> (Interview, male age 13, 2003)

Documents used

CR Doc 3: Draft for Partnership Youth Strategy, Jim Kennedy (1999).
CR Doc 4: King's Cross 10 Estates Community Development Strategy, Peabody Trust.

FHA Doc 1: King's Cross Ten Estates Urban Design Masterplan: survey, analysis, and recommendations by Farrer Huxley Associates, September, 2000.

IPA Doc 1: Islington Play Council, annual report, 1999.

IPYS Doc: A Discussion Paper from Islington Play and Youth Service: developing play and youth work in the Copenhagen neighbourhood – draft document, Tom Murphy, Play and Youth Officer, London Borough of Islington, June 1999.

PT Doc 14: London Borough of Islington, King's Cross ERCF Bid, 10 Estates, Peabody Trust, Feb 1998.

SS Doc 2: Issues Identified by workers and organisation who provide services for families with young children in the Sure Start Copenhagen Area, Companion Document of the Sure Start Copenhagen Islington, London Delivery Plan, May 2000.

Notes

1   In discussion with the Peabody Trust it became apparent that these fun days were more a way of attracting young people with their parents/carers, so that the Trust could gain access to the adults with respect to their participation rather than as a method to specifically target young people as participants.

2   Alice Coleman was Professor of Geography at King's College London and Head of the Landscape Research Unit. Drawing on Oscar Newman's (1971) ideas on 'defensible space' she launched an attack on the design of post-war (especially high-rise) council estates in the UK (Coleman, 1985). As a result of this work, the Thatcher government gave her a significant sum of money to redesign, using defensible space principles, a number of council dwellings (see Warwick, 2008).

Part V

Conclusions

Chapter 17

London: regeneration or rebirth?

Allan Cochrane

Introduction

London's particular – not to say peculiar – position within national and international urban hierarchies raises some fundamental questions for the analysis of regeneration strategies within the city. London is not only a world city, but also the national capital. It is a diverse and multicultural city, a feature celebrated by local (and even national) politicians. It has a growing middle-class population and workforce but at the same time it is a deeply divided city, characterised by growing inequality. And it is the centre of a wider urban region that draws in millions more. It has a nationally significant economic role, to the extent that its continued success is frequently identified by government as a necessary condition for the maintenance of the UK's prosperity. This chapter reflects on these different understandings and the relationships between them as a means of revisiting and reflecting on some of the arguments arising from earlier chapters.

Living in a world city

A focus on London's role as world city highlights the importance of its connections into wider global networks of one sort or another. From this perspective, it is these connections that have come to define it, to the extent that its relationship to the rest of British economy and society is almost vestigial, and certainly secondary. London is understood to 'compete' with other global cities. It is sometimes even suggested that a new networked global politics is emerging that is based around those connections to supersede forms of international relations organised around national state structures (see for example Taylor, 2004). In some respects, of course, this is a persuasive story, and it places London as a node in a particular set of global networks (whether characterised as finance, advanced producer services or anything else).

But it leaves open the nature of the urban society experienced by those living and working in the node. Some residents of the city, such as those

Taylor (2004: 214) identifies as the 'network bourgeoisie', may be defined through their involvement in transnational networks but Castells suggests that the networked, interconnected world is one with significant 'holes' in it. He identifies 'multiple black holes of social exclusion throughout the planet' which are 'present in literally every country, and every city, in this new geography of social exclusion' (Castells, 1998: 164). In this context, it is perhaps not surprising that there is a strong tradition in academic writing on London, which suggests that it is a 'dual' or 'divided' city (Sassen, 2001; Fainstein et al., 1992). Most recently, emphasis has been placed on the sharp disjunction between the (connected) urban elites and the new migrants who have a rather different position in global networks and have the task of servicing the business operations of the elites as well as supporting their leisure and consumption activities (May et al., 2007).

This emphasis on division captures one aspect of contemporary London (and similar points are made by Poynter in chapter 8 where the danger of division based around the existence of an unskilled workforce in the east of the city, whose role is serving an 'entrepreneurial, global city', is explicitly identified). However, it is important to recognise that the nature of the divisions within London cannot be captured effectively by such straightforward binaries. So, for example, in chapter 12, Watt discusses some of the specificities of social housing in London in ways that highlight aspects of the complexity of social relations in the city. In inner London, he notes, social housing represents a much larger share of tenure than nationally (around one-third, compared to less than one-fifth nationally). More importantly in this context, he confirms that the process of residualisation is less extensive in London than across England as a whole. An apparently disproportionate share of national expenditure on housing benefit goes to tenants in London because rents (particularly private rents) are higher there (Hills, 2007: 114). But London council housing also continues to be attractive to those who are ineligible for housing benefit, not least because rents are substantially lower than they would be in private rented accommodation (Hills, 2007: 63–4, 80).

As Butler and Hamnett point out in chapter 3 (building on a longer programme of research), the process of social change and division in London cannot be captured in a vision of sharp polarisation (see particularly Hamnett, 2003). Instead they identify significant changes in London's occupational class structure. The growth of the professional and managerial middle classes means, they conclude, that a majority of London's population can now be characterised as non-manual middle class. However, this does not mean that inequality is no longer an issue. On the contrary there is strong evidence that inequality continues to grow, reflecting the development of an increasingly wealthy urban elite, alongside the existence of groups living in deep poverty (reinforced by the attraction of migrant labour whose position is not recorded in official data). In this context, the growing middle class faces pressures of its own – as it is left behind by the elite while having to survive in a city where housing and other costs take an increasingly big share of household income.

Beyond the world city

Focusing on London's role as world city – or what Massey calls a 'global centre of command' (2007: 39) – also encourages an emphasis on those areas of the city that are most closely associated with its 'global' activities, namely the City of London and its related social and economic impacts (whether in terms of housing, transport networks, cultural provision or the consumption patterns of its employees). However, 'London' must be understood to cover a much wider area of the south-east of England than can be captured even by the institutional borders of Greater London. As Gordon *et al.* argue, 'the effective London economy extends well beyond the borders of Greater London, encompassing most of South Eastern England and perhaps some areas beyond, in what is for many purposes a single labour market' (2004: 30). 'In this regionalized version of London,' says Gordon, 'outer areas now substantially contribute to its agglomeration economies, as well as continuing to benefit from those rooted in central London' (2004a: 41. See also Buck *et al.*, 2002; Dorling and Thomas, 2004: 183). Hall *et al.* (2006) identify it as a global 'polycentric metropolis' or 'polycentric mega-region' – a polycentric urban system.

In some versions of this extended region, around half of England's population find themselves incorporated within it (see discussion in Cochrane, 2006). In other words, London has a strong material impact that is helping to generate an urban experience that stretches far beyond any existing institutional boundaries. Given the nature of this connected economic activity space and the social relations associated with it, it is perhaps already clear that the placing or settling of London is important – it cannot just be defined through its position in global networks. But this is reinforced by the need to recognise both the diversity of London's economy (which is not reducible to finance or even the cultural industries) and the importance of its economic linkages to the rest of the United Kingdom. London's role as a world city (or with a particular position within world city networks) does not mean that its economy (and society) is effectively divorced from the rest of the UK. Drawing on Gordon (2004b), Massey (2007: 38) notes that 'London's main export market is in fact the "rest of the UK"', even for the financial services products which are generally assumed to be the most tradable and traded in global markets.

The recognition of London's role in the national economy is not the end of the story, however. On the contrary, there is a sharp tension between those who see London as driver of the national economy and those who see it as an active agent in generating wider regional inequality. So, for example, Gordon *et al.* (2003: 65–80) strongly argue that London is a net contributor to the rest of the country through its taxes and the public expenditure for which they pay (see, also, Hall's interview in chapter 2). In policy terms, this broad understanding can be seen as confirmation of the role which London and the South-East play in the context of a wider neo-liberal vision of the UK social economy – providing evidence of the success of the new economy and high-lighting the weaknesses of the old (industrial) economy, as well as, apparently, offering support to the argument that freedom from state interference is the key (Allen *et al.*, 1998).

From another perspective, however, the matter is understood quite differently. Amin *et al.* (2003: 17) argue that the centralisation of power in London means that a 'significant element of 'national policy making effectively functions as an unacknowledged regional policy for the South Eastern part of England'. As a result, they argue that national economic policy is overly influ-enced by the state of the regional economy in London and the South-East, with steps being taken to restrain the economy when the region is 'overheating', even when the rest of the country still has significant capacity for growth (see also Morgan, 2002: 800). The rise of a wider city region agenda (apparently focused on England's so-called 'core cities') might have been expected to disrupt this powerful narrative, but, as Morgan (2007: 1244) notes, it has 'certainly not devalued the hegemony of London and southern England in the corridors of political power'.

In this context, Massey suggests that the emphasis on London's global role is a political strategy (as much as an economic reality) because of the way in which it reinforces particular ways of thinking (which she identifies as neo-liberal). The 'geographical concentration' of the very wealthy in London and the South East, 'into a self-referential echo chamber reinforces their distance from the rest of us' (Massey, 2007: 66), and serves to reinforce a policy agenda which includes a commitment to deregulation, an emphasis on the 'untoucha-bility' of the financial sector, and a drive to privatisation of various sorts (including 'competitive individualism and personal self-reliance') (Massey, 2007: 38–40). The 'global' is mobilised precisely to reinforce the city's national dominance to the extent that the 'Reinvigoration of London . . . represents the rise of a new elite, and the culture in which it is embedded' (Massey, 2007: 49).

More prosaically it also feeds into the sustenance of what has been identified as an 'implicit' (and active) regional strategy which benefits the 'London super-region' (Marvin *et al.* 2006). One expression of this is to be found in initiatives like those associated with the 'sustainable communities plan' (ODPM, 2003b) which is justified in terms that stress the need to ensure that there is enough affordable housing in the urban region to ensure that London's economic strength is not undermined by labour shortages, increased labour costs or the lack of necessary social infrastructure (e.g. because public sector professionals cannot afford to live in the region) (see, for example, Allen and Cochrane, 2007; Raco, 2007a). Even before the arrival of the Olympics, the scale of the investment in 'sustainable development' promised for the Thames Gateway far outstripped anything promised for any of England's other urban areas (Raco, 2005).

Social division and inequality

As the chapters of this book demonstrate, however, London cannot solely be understood in terms that identify it as a privileged space, or a place whose residents all benefit from the arrangements that give it such a central position in national hierarchies of power and wealth. London is a fundamentally divided city in which poverty and wealth grow alongside each other. Although, as Massey (2007) notes, these different – and co-existing – aspects of London are often presented in terms of paradox, particularly because the growing wealth of the city and some of its residents exists alongside continuing poverty for many, this is not some paradoxical outcome but, rather, an inherent part of the development process.

She suggests that the process by which inequality in London is not only reproduced but actively produced and increased is a direct consequence of the way in which the city is re-imagined as a global city – that is, one in which the priorities of global financial markets are taken for granted and the need to keep and attract the financial institutions and the staff associated with them is assumed – and this has had a dramatic effect. But this also means, says Massey, that 'London's poor . . . and those without higher level skills, are caught in the crossfire of the city's reinvention' (Massey, 2007: 64). Most of the new jobs, she points out, are not ones for which those who are unskilled or with traditional skills are well suited and those which are created for the lower end of the labour market may be taken on by labour drawn in from around the globe (Massey, 2007: 64–5; see also the arguments developed by Poynter in chapter 8 of this volume).

These issues are reflected particularly strongly in the labour market in inner London because of the shift in forms of employment to higher end service roles, which attract high levels of in-commuting from the suburbs while local residents with different skill sets remain unable to access them (see Green and Owen, 2006, who confirm both that the London labour market is highly polarised and that levels of employment for local residents are substantially lower than might be expected). Even for London as a whole the data suggest that inequality has become more marked. In 1980 weekly earnings of the top 10 per cent of male full-time employees were just over twice as much as those of the bottom 10 per cent, while in 2000 the ratio had moved to over four times as much (GLA, 2004a: 32; cited in Massey, 2007: 89). Edwards identifies London as a 'wealth machine and poverty machine' (2002: 29; cited in Massey, 2007: 70) highlighting the ways in which the two processes are linked together and reinforce each other.

The challenges of regeneration

So, how does this relate to the possibilities of regeneration in London that have been the focus of the earlier chapters of the book? What opportunities can be created for the excluded or for the re-imagination of parts of the city? The chapters of this book draw on a particular understanding of London, highlighting some of the tensions associated with urban regeneration and renaissance. Most of them focus on divisions within London, rather than between London and the rest of the UK. And in practice, they are concerned with particular parts of London – not the suburbs, not the City, not the gentrified (or already rich) urban neighbourhoods. The focus is on areas that have been bypassed by world city growth or by social groups whose members have gained little benefit from it, but the chapters also point to some of the tensions and ambiguities that are inherent in the growth and development process itself.

London itself is substantially divided and, even as some areas reflect an influx of wealth and property, or exhibit forms of economic revitalisation, others seem stubbornly trapped in decline. There is a tension between those areas which offer opportunities for regeneration (that is rediscovery or reinvention as areas suitable for economic revival or gentrification) and those in which regeneration is likely to be hard fought – a consequence of active public policy engagement (possibly reflecting needs of local populations). In his interview with the editors, Hall points to a series of apparent paradoxes: regeneration against a background of booming growth, the emergence both of what he calls a super class and an underclass, the experience of immigration alongside localised unemployment.

The various 'geographical imaginaries' (Massey, 2007) of London come together uneasily in any discussion of public policy relating to the city. The very nature or definition of regeneration reflects the tensions inherent in the process. For Butler and Hamnett, in chapter 3, regeneration has a specific meaning – they use it to mean any process of re-growth within the city, any ways in which shifts in use bring change that brings areas of the city back into economic sustainability, in a sense a model that emphasises the way in which 'excluded' areas become incorporated once more into the mainstream economy. From this perspective, therefore, the development of new shopping and employment areas within London is a form of regeneration, as is the process of gentrification, while the process of re-growth in central London is better understood as development rather than regeneration (since the area has remained economically productive throughout).

It is this understanding that enables them to explain what they see as the paradox of regeneration in one of the most prosperous cities in the world – the survival of development opportunities because of historical patterns of growth and decline that have left economically unproductive space ready to be brought into profitable use as opportunities have arisen. In many respects this is a helpful way of framing the process, particularly in capturing the development process beyond the state. So, for example, Imrie's discussion of the King's Cross development, in chapter 6, highlights the active process by which developers draw on notions of community to find ways of achieving development that is sensitive to local context, even if it is still a hierarchical process in which the developer is able to mobilise resources inaccessible to the local community (see also Allen, 2003). Ultimately this remains regeneration as re-growth, opening up new investment opportunities for the developers, even if it also requires some engagement with local interests.

In other contexts, regeneration implies a more active process of state-led renewal. In some cases, however, this may have similar results and a similar focus as stress is placed on ways of remaking places in ways that help generate opportunity for profitable redevelopment. So, for example, in their discussion of the development of Paddington Basin in chapter 7, Raco and Henderson emphasise the role of local government in leading a process of flagship regeneration. They suggest that a focus on partnership may understate the significance of the active role taken by local government. But the planned outcome is precisely to achieve regeneration that produces a new economic centre for the city. The balance between community gain and developer gain is an uneasy one, as spaces are opened up for high-end shops and offices.

In chapter 13, Baeten's discussion of development on London's South Bank approaches the issue from a different angle, but his review of the process emphasises the extent to which regeneration has come to be understood as 'post-political', so that the more effective integration of the South Bank into the rest of central London no longer allows space for contestation and alternative models. As Davidson's case study in chapter 10 confirms, even when planners sponsor an inclusive vision of regeneration the reality provides limited evidence of social mixing, as the process of 'Riverside renaissance' delivers outcomes that seem closer to gentrification (see also GLA, 2004a: 193–218). Attempts to generate increased social mixing by bringing members of different social groups into proximity with each other, however well meaning, are in themselves (as Middleton in chapter 11 shows in her discussion of attempts to encourage walking through the city) unlikely to have the hoped for outcomes.

But in other contexts regeneration is given rather a different framing, a rather different emphasis, with a focus on it as a process through which the position of disadvantaged groups may be improved, and existing inequalities challenged. Brown and Lees in chapter 16 highlight the spatial needs of young people in the process by which council estates are being regenerated in King's Cross. They draw attention to some of the tensions faced by those who have the daily experience of decay even as they live in a wider 'sea of renewal' (regeneration that is apparently transforming the surroundings). At the same time regeneration creates new tensions, for example, reflected in conflicts over space between young people living on the estates.

The role of traditional high-rise housing is revisited by Baxter and Lees in chapter 9 who point to the possibilities that lie within it – emphasising that it is not appropriate simply to dismiss high-rise living as a possibility for a range of people. They emphasise that when considering the value of high-rise housing, it is necessary to consider a range of features, including its material condition and maintenance; its physical design and security; the extent of anti-social behaviour; and the neighbourhood and community context. In some places, these factors may come together to create housing that is unliveable, but in others the opposite will be the case. Here regeneration is about creating liveable conditions – enabling a form of rebirth – rather than necessarily looking to ways of redeveloping the built environment or replacing the existing population. In their chapter drawing on the experience of Holly Street in Hackney, Manzi and Jacobs confirm that it is possible to undertake regeneration along these lines, but emphasise that it is not an easy option – community involvement can only help deliver effective regeneration and improvements for those living in areas like Holly Street, if it is accompanied by significant direct spending by local government or other public agencies.

The challenge (as well as the opportunity) of urban regeneration in London lies in finding ways of balancing social regeneration of these sorts with the economic, market-driven regeneration discussed earlier.

Beyond regeneration?

In many respects debates about regeneration understandably tend to focus on relatively small areas of cities. The promise of regeneration relates to possibilities of upgrading those areas and sometimes of benefiting those living in them. But in important respects, as Michael Keith suggests in chapter 5, the notion of regeneration also offers us the prospect of what he calls 'future thinking' – of rooting visions of the future in the practice and experience of the present. 'Future thinking', he argues, also inhabits the cities of the present, in the sense that different visions of the future are always in contention (see also Cochrane, 2007: 145). He illustrates this and explores its usefulness as a way of thinking in his discussion of the Thames Gateway and plans for its regeneration. As well as being a project in its own right, the Gateway provides us with a frame through which wider issues can be explored.

Keith focuses particularly on the tension between the Barker Report on housing in the South East (Barker, 2004; see also Barker, 2006), which identifies the constraints of limited housing supply as crucial limits to the growth of the South-East, and Hills' work on social housing (Hills, 2007), which highlights the fundamental limits of the approach which has shifted attention away from the building of social housing towards the provision of subsidy to those on low incomes. In his interview, Hall similarly notes that the effective end of social housing has led to a decline in the total amount of housing available. For Barker, the solution is to free up the market, to remove restrictions on land use and to allow developers to build where previously they have been unable to do so, because of planning restrictions; for Hills the answer is for the state to move more actively into the development of social housing.

In a sense, therefore, both incorporate forms of 'future thinking', a different vision of what is possible – although each is also fundamentally concerned about the city as it currently is. Keith suggests that the plans for the Thames Gateway very clearly involve forms of 'future thinking' and take the form of a compromise between the paradigms developed by Barker and Hills – a 'compromise or stand off between state and market that the logics of partnership based urban regeneration imply'. In other words, he argues that the model of development needed to underpin successful regeneration, which will benefit existing residents as well as providing the base for further growth, will be based around hybrids of state and market, public and private initiative. In this context, he identifies registered social landlords as providing a potential base on which housing accessible to low and middle income residents can be delivered. He firmly locates the Gateway within the wider city region, noting that South-East growth is likely to be under threat if places such as the new business district of the Isle of Dogs and growth sites such as a post-Olympics Stratford cannot be made to work.

Although Keith focuses policy attention on a slice of post-industrial (mainly inner city) Greater London, which has been the target of many regeneration initiatives, he sets his agenda firmly within the wider urban context of the London 'super-region'. In his interview, Peter Hall takes this further to suggest ways in which London's regeneration or rebirth might be positioned within a wider national urban and regional strategy. Alongside a commitment to a strategy based around city regions centred on what have been (self-)identified as England's core cities (Birmingham, Bristol, Leeds, Liverpool, Manchester, Newcastle, Nottingham and Sheffield) (see www.corecities.com), he sees the apparently inexorable expansion of the South-East (which he identifies as a mega city region) as offering the possibility of drawing more of the country into the region's growth and prosperity. On this model, and as part of a deliberate planning process Birmingham and the West Midlands might become part of London and the South-East, with an emphasis on making it more multi-centred. This is another quite distinctive form of 'future thinking', around which regeneration might be organised, namely one in which London becomes solution to, as well as cause of, regional inequality in England. And, of course, it fits uneasily with the approach and thinking associated with Massey and others that was introduced earlier (Massey, 2007).

Conclusions and reflections

Twenty-five years ago, the prognosis for London (as well as for other large British cities) was almost overwhelmingly negative. Population loss was the defining characteristic. Everybody, it was said, was moving to small towns, market towns. So London's transformation into (and reimagination as) a dynamic 'world city' (see, for example, London Planning Advisory Committee, 1991) is a remarkable one. And it might be appropriate to label it a rebirth, since this is a London with a new role and new status only made possible because of the particular form taken by globalisation and the positioning of London within the world networks associated with it.

However, as we have seen, this form of rebirth tells us little about how people live in the urban spaces produced by it. Some forms of 'regeneration' may flow from it, as previously declining areas are reworked as spaces for retail, office development or even housing through gentrification. But this leaves others and some groups on the outside looking in, sometimes up against the 'new' even as the old survives or themselves part of the 'new' – for example, low paid workers drawn in from overseas – look for ways of surviving. In that context the challenge for regeneration as an active form of public policy is to take on a different set of meanings, as an active programme of social renewal, seeking to draw in those people and those areas that might otherwise be actively disadvantaged or marginalised.

There is some evidence that targeted schemes can have an impact here, can generate forms of regeneration that are not solely driven by development opportunities. And, in their different ways, with their different future visions, both Michael Keith and Peter Hall offer ways of imagining more inclusive forms of development – ways of re-imagining regeneration through the combination of state and market in what Keith calls 'hybrid' forms. Of course, the extent to which such politics can be translated from imagination to reality remains open, and in London the opportunities for development, framed by a world city rhetoric, often makes the balance difficult to maintain. It sometimes looks as if the prime role of state institutions is to underpin development opportunities. In other words, the political and public policy challenge is to find ways of ensuring that a commitment to the delivery of social and community regeneration is actively maintained and not lost in the drive for economic renewal.

Bibliography

Abercrombie, P. (1944), *Greater London Plan*, HMSO: London.

Ackroyd, P. (2000) *London: The Biography*, Chatto & Windus: London.

AIG (2006) *Legible London: A Wayfinding Study*, AIG Publications: London.

Aitken, S. (1994) *Putting Children in Their Place*, AAG Resource Publications: Washington.

Alexander, J. and Burdekin, O. (2002) 'Live, work, and play', *Locum Destination Review*, 7: 8–12.

Allen, J. (2000) 'On Georg Simmel: proximity, distance and movement', in M. Crang and N. Thrift (eds), *Thinking Space*, Routledge: London, pp.54–70.

Allen, J. (2003) *Lost Geographies of Power*, Blackwell: Oxford.

Allen, J. and Cochrane, A. (2007) 'Beyond the territorial fix: regional assemblages, politics and power', *Regional Studies*, 41: 1161–75.

Allen, J., Massey, D. and Cochrane, A. (1998) *Rethinking the Region*, Routledge: London.

Álvarez-Rivadulla, M. (2007) 'Golden ghettos: gated communities and class residential segregation in Montevideo, Uruguay', *Environment and Planning A*, 39: 47–63.

Ambrose, P. (1994) *Urban Processes and Power*, Routledge: London.

Ambrose, P. (2002) *Second Best Value: The Central Stepney SRB – How Non-joined-up Government Policies Undermine Cost-effectiveness in Regeneration*, Health and Social Policy Research Centre, University of Brighton: Brighton.

Ambrose, P. (2006) 'Declining affordability in a diverse society: trends, causes and consequences', in S. Darby, P. Flatau and I. Hafekost (eds), *Building For Diversity: National Housing Conference 2005*, Western Australia Dept. Of Housing and Works/AHURI: Perth, pp.34–48.

Ambrose, P. and Colenutt, B. (1975) *The Property Machine*, Penguin: London.

Ambrose, P. and Randles, J. (1999) *Looking for the Jobs: A qualitative study of interagency working in Holly Street and Hackney*, Centre for Urban and Regional Research, University of Sussex.

Amin, A. (2002) 'Ethnicity and the multicultural city: living with diversity', *Environment and Planning A*, 34: 959–80.

Amin, A. (2005) 'Local community on trial', *Economy and Society*, 34: 612–33.

Amin, A. and Thrift, N. (2002) *Cities: Re-imagining the Urban*, Polity Press: Cambridge.

Amin, A., Massey, D. and Thrift, N. (2000) *Cities for the Many Not the Few*, The Policy Press: Bristol.

Amin, A., Massey, D. and Thrift, N. (2003) *Decentering the Nation: A Radical Approach to Regional Inequality*, Catalyst: London.

Andranovich, G., Burban, M. and Heying, C. (2001) 'Olympic cities: lessons learned from mega-event politics', *Journal Of Urban Affairs*, 23: 113–31.

Anttila, C. and Wright, G. (2004) *Multiple Deprivation in New Deal for Communities Areas*, Social Disadvantage Research Centre, Department of Social Policy and Social Work, University of Oxford: Oxford.

Arup (2001) *Our Principles for a Human City*, Arup: London.

Arup (2002) *London Olympics 2012: Costs and Benefits*, Arup: London.

Arup (2004) *King's Cross Central: Regeneration Strategy*, Arup: London.

Atkinson, G., Mourato, S. and Szymanski, S. (2006) *Are We Willing to Pay Enough to Back the Bid?*, London School of Economics: London.

Audit Commission (1989) *Urban Regeneration and Economic Development*, HMSO: London.

Back, L., Keith, M., Khan, A., Shukra, K. and Solomos, J. (2002) 'New Labour's white heart: politics, multiculturalism and the return of assimilation', *The Political Quarterly*, 73: 445–54.

Bacon, R. and Eltis, W. (1976) *Britain's Economic Problem: Too Few Producers*, Macmillan: London.

Baeten, G. (2000) 'From community planning to partnership planning: urban regeneration and shifting power relations on the South Bank, London', *Geojournal*, 51: 293–300.

Baeten, G. (2007) 'The uses of deprivation in the neo-liberal city', in N. Bavo (ed.), *Urban Politics Now: Re-imagining Democracy in the Neo-liberal City*, Nai Publishers: Amsterdam, pp.44–57.

Balakrishnan, A. (2006) 'Asda Pulls Out', *The Guardian*, 17 June.

Ball, M. (2004) 'Co-operation with the community in property-led urban regeneration', *Journal of Property Research*, 21: 119–42.

Ball, M. and Maginn P. (2005) 'Urban change and conflict: evaluating the role of partnerships in urban regeneration in the UK', *Housing Studies* 20: 9–28.

Ball, M., Le Ny, L. and Maginn, P.J. (2003) 'Synergy in urban regeneration partnerships: property agents' perspectives', *Urban Studies* 40: 2239–53.

Barker, K. (2004) *Delivering Stability: Securing Our Future Housing Needs*, HMSO: London.

Barker, K. (2006) *Barker Report on Land Use Planning: Final Report – Recommendations*, HMSO: London.

Barnardo's (1994) *The Facts of Life: The Changing Face of Childhood*, Barnardo's: London.

Bassett, K. (1996) 'Partnerships, business elites and urban politics: new forms of governance in an English city?', *Urban Studies*, 33: 539–55.

Bavidge, J. and Gibson, A. (2003) 'The metropolitan playground: London's children', in J. Kerr and A. Gibson (eds), *London: From Punk to Blair*, Reaktion Books: London, pp.15–30.

Baxter, R. (2005) *The Residential High-rise In London: Towards An Urban Renaissance*, ESRC/ODPM Postgraduate Research Programme, Working Paper 18.

Beatty, C., Jones, C. and Lawless, P. (2005) *The NDC Programme: an Overview of the 2001 Census*, CRESR, Sheffield Hallam University: Sheffield.

Beck, U. (1996) *The Reinvention of Politics: Rethinking Modernity in the Global Social Order*, Polity Press, Cambridge.

Benjamin, W. (1983) 'Der Flaneur', in W. Benjamin, *Das Passagen-Werk*, 2 Bde, Suhrkamp: Frankfurt, pp.524–69.

Bennett, J. and Morris, J. (2006) *Thames Gateway People: The Aspirations and Attitudes of Prospective and Existing Residents of Thames Gateway*, Institute of Public Policy Research: London.

Bennington, J., Fordham, T. and Robinson, D. (2004) *Housing in London NDCs: Situations, Challenges and Opportunities* (Research Report 59), CRESR, Sheffield Hallam University: Sheffield.

Berry, B., Parsons, S. and Platt, R. (1968) *The Impact of Urban Renewal on Small Businesses: The Hyde Park-Kenwood Case*, University of Chicago Press: Chicago.

Blackman, T. (1997) 'Urban planning in the United Kingdom', in M. Pacione (ed.), *Britain's Cities: Geographies of Division in Urban Britain*, Routledge: London, pp.128–49.

Blears, H. (2008) *Putting Communities in Control*, found at: www.communities.gov.uk/news/corporate/ 712771

Bond Clarksson Russell (1995), *South Bank Marketing*, Bond Clarkson Russell: Guildford.

Borough of Tower Hamlets (2008) *Borough Profile*, accessed 13 March 2008 at: www.towerhamlets.gov.uk/ data/discover/data/borough-profile/data/borough-profile/creating-sharing.cfm

Brannigan, T. (2006) 'Campaigners battle to save "Real Chinatown"', *The Guardian*, 21 November.

Brenner, N. (2004) *New State Spaces: Urban Governance and the Re-scaling of Statehood*, Oxford University Press: Oxford.

Brindley, T. (2000) 'Community roles in urban regeneration: new partnerships on London's South Bank', *City*, 4: 364–77.

Brindley, T., Rydin, Y. and Stoker, G. (1992) *Remaking Planning: The Politics of Urban Change*, Routledge: London.

British Olympics Association (2007) *London 2012 Olympic Bid: An Eight Year, Journey*, www.boa.org.uk

Brown, P. (2003) 'Lofty solutions to housing crisis: Architects propose 200m towers', *The Guardian*, 11 February.

Brownill, S. (1990) *Developing London's Docklands: Another Great Planning Disaster?*, Paul Chapman Publishing: London.

Brownill, S. (1999) 'Turning the East End into the West End: the lessons and legacies of the London Dock-lands Development Corporation', in R. Imrie and H. Thomas (eds), *British Urban Policy and the Urban Development Corporations*, Sage: London, pp.43–63.

Brownill, S., K. Razzaque and Kochan, B. (1998) 'From exclusion to partnership: the LDDC and community consultation and participation', *Rising East*, 2: 42–72.

Buck, N., Gordon, I. and Young. K. (1986) *The London Employment Problem*, The Clarendon Press: Oxford.

Buck, N., Gordon, I., Hall, P., Harloe, M. and Kleinman, M. (2002) *Working Capital: Life and Labour in Contemporary London*, Routledge: London.

Budd, L. C. (2006) 'London: city-state or city region?', in M. Baker, I. Hardill, P. Benneworth and L. Budd (eds), *The Rise of the English Regions?*, Routledge: Oxon.

Butler, T. (2007) 'Re-urbanising Docklands: neither gentrification nor suburbanisation?', *International Journal of Urban and Regional Research*, 31: 759–81.

Butler, T. and Lees, L. (2006) 'Super-gentrification in Barnsbury, London: globalisation and gentrifying global elites at the neighbourhood level', *Transactions of the Institute of British Geographers*, 31: 467–87.

Butler, T. and Robson. G. (2003a) 'Plotting the middle classes: gentrification and circuits of education', *Housing Studies*, 18: 5–28.

Butler, T. and Robson, G. (2003b) *London Calling: The Middle Classes and the Re-making of Inner London*, Berg: Oxford.

Butler, T. and Watt, P. (2007) *Understanding Social Inequality*, Sage: London.

Butler, T., Hamnett, C. and Ramsden, M. (2008) 'Inward and upward? Marking out social class change in London 1981-2001', *Urban Studies*, 45: 67–88.

Cadman, D. and Austin-Crowe, L. (1983) *Property Development*, Spon: London.

Carey, S. and Ahmed, N. (2006) *Bridging the Gap. The London Olympics 2012 and South Asian-owned Businesses in Brick Lane and Green Street*, Young Foundation: London.

Castells M. (1980) *The Economic Crisis And American Society*, Blackwell: Oxford.

Castells, M. (1998) *End Of Millennium: The Information Age. Economy, Society and Culture*, Blackwell: Oxford.

Central London Partnership (2001) *A Walking Strategy for Central London*, Central London Partnership: London.

Centre for Regional Economic and Social Research (CRESR) (2005) *The 39 NDC Areas Brief Pen Portraits, New Deal for Communities: The National Evaluation*, Data Analysis Paper 41, Sheffield Hallam University: Sheffield.

Chalkley, B. and Essex, S. (1999) 'Urban development through hosting international events: a history of the Olympic Games', *Planning Perspectives*, 14: 369–94.

Champion, A. and Coombes, M. (2007) 'Using the 2001 Census to study human capital movements affecting Britain's larger cities: insights and issues', *Journal of the Royal Statistical Society*, 170: 447–67.

Charney, I. (2007) 'The politics of design: architecture, tall buildings and the skyline of Central London', *Area*, 39: 195–205.

Christensen, P., and O'Brien, M. (eds) (2003) *Children in the City: Home, Neighbourhood and Community*, Routledge Falmer: London.

Church, C. and Gale, T. (2000) *Streets in the Sky: Towards Improving the Quality of Life in Tower Blocks in the UK*, Birmingham National Sustainable Tower Blocks Initiative: Birmingham.

Clapham, D. and Kintrea, K. (1992) *Housing Co-operatives in Britain*, Longman: Harlow.

Clarke, J. and Newman, J. (1997) *The Managerial State*, Sage: London.

Cochrane, A. (2006) 'Looking for the south-east', in I. Hardill, P. Benneworth, M. Baker and L. Budd (eds), *The Rise of the English Regions*, Routledge: Oxon, pp.227–44.

Cochrane, A. (2007) *Understanding Urban Policy: A Critical Approach*, Blackwell: Oxford.

Cohen, P. and Rustin, M. (eds) (2007) *London's Turning: The Prospect of Thames Gateway*, Ashgate: Dover.

Cole, I. (2007) 'What future for social housing in England?', *People, Place & Policy Online*, 1: 3–13.

Coleman, A. (1985) *Utopia on Trial: Vision and Reality in Planned Housing*, Hilary Shipman: London.

Colenutt, B. (1999) 'New deal or no deal for people based regeneration?', in R. Imrie and H. Thomas (eds), *British Urban Policy: An Evaluation of the Urban Development Corporations*, Sage: London, pp.233–45.

Collins, M. (1999) 'Land-use planning since 1947', in J. Simmie (ed.), *Planning London*, UCL Press: London, pp.90–140.

Colomb, C. (2007) 'Unpacking New Labour's "Urban Renaissance" agenda: towards a socially sustainable re-urbanization of British cities', *Planning Practice and Research*, 22: 1–24.

Commission for Architecture and the Built Environment (CABE) (2003) *Building Sustainable Communities: Actions for Housing Market Renewal*, CABE: London.

Commission for Architecture and the Built Environment (CABE) and English Heritage, (2007) *Guidance on Tall Buildings*, Consultation Draft, CABE and English Heritage: London.

Couch, C., Fraser, C. and Percy, S. (2003) *Urban Regeneration in Europe*, Blackwell: Oxford.

Countryside Properties (2007) *Thinking Beyond Today*, accessed March 26 2008 at www.countryside-properties-corporate.com/sustainability.

Cowan, D. and McDermont, M. (2006) *Regulating Social Housing: Governing Decline*, Routledge-Cavendish: Oxon.

Cowan, R. (1979) 'Fun and survival in the inner city', *Town and Country Planning*, 48: 5–6.

Crilley, D., Bryce, C., Hall, R. and Ogden, P. (1991) *New Migrants in London's Docklands*, Department of Geography, Queen Mary and Westfield College: London.

Cruikshank, B. (1999) *The Will to Empower: Democratic Citizens and Other Subjects*, Cornell University Press: Ithaca, New York.

Cullingworth, J. and Nadin, V. (1997) *Town & Country Planning in the UK*, Routledge: London.

Daly, G., Mooney, G., Poole, L. and Davis, H. (2005) *Housing stock transfer in Birmingham and Glasgow: the contrasting experiences of two UK cities*, European Journal of Housing Policy, 5, 327–41.

Davidson, M. (2008) 'Spoiled mixture: where does state-led "positive" gentrification end?', *Urban Studies* (forthcoming November).

Davidson, M. and Lees, L. (2005) 'New-build "gentrification" and London's Riverside Renaissance', *Environment and Planning A*, 37: 1165–90.

Davies J. (2001) *Partnerships and Regimes: The Politics of Urban Regeneration in the UK*, Ashgate: Aldershot.

Davis, J. (1988), *Reforming London: The London Government Problem 1855-1900*, Clarendon Press: London.

De Certeau, M. (1984) *The Practice of Everyday Life*, University of California Press: Berkeley.

Deakin, N. (2001) *In Search of Civil Society*, Palgrave: Basingstoke.

Dean, J. and Hastings, A. (2000) *Challenging Images: Housing Estates, Stigma and Regeneration*, The Policy Press: Bristol.

Dean, M. (1999) *Governmentality: Power and Rule in Modern Societies*, Sage: London.

Dean, M. (2007) *Governing Societies*, Sage: London.

Defend Council Housing (2006) *The Case for Council Housing In 21st Century Britain*, Defend Council Housing: London.

Defilippis, J. and North, P. (2004) 'The emancipatory community: place, politics and collective action in cities', in L. Lees (ed.), *The Emancipatory City?*, Sage: London, pp.72–88.

Defilippis, J., Fisher, R. and Shragge, E. (2006) 'Neither romance nor regulation: re-evaluating community', *International Journal of Urban and Regional Research*, 30: 673–89.

Department for Communities and Local Government (DCLG) (2006) Strong *and Prosperous Communities – The Local Government White Paper*, HMSO: London.

Department for Communities and Local Government (DCLG) (2007a) *Indices of Deprivation*, accessed 18 May 2007 at: www.communities.gov.uk/communities/neighbourhoodrenewal/deprivation

Department for Communities and Local Government (DCLG) (2007b) *The Greater London Authority Act*, HMSO, London.

Department for Communities and Local Government (DCLG) (2007c) *Live Tables*, accessed 25 July at: www.communities.gov.uk/housing/housingresearch/housingstatistics/livetables/.

Department for Communities and Local Government (2007d) *Successful Large-scale Voluntary Transfers*, HMSO: London.

Department for Communities and Local Government (DCLG) (2007e) *Large-scale Voluntary Transfers: Negative Ballots*, HMSO: London.

Department for Communities and Local Government (DCLG) (2007f) *Homes for the Future: More Affordable, More Sustainable*, Cm. 7191, HMSO: London.

Department for Communities and Local Government (DCLG) (2008a) *The Planning Bill,* White Paper, HMSO: London.

Department for Transport (DfT) (1996) *Developing a Strategy for Walking*, HMSO: London.

Department for Transport (DfT) (2003) *On the Move: By Foot – A Discussion Paper*, HMSO: London.

Department for Transport (DfT) (2004) *Walking and Cycling: An Action Plan*, HMSO: London.

Department for Transport (DfT) (2005) *National Travel Survey: 2004*, HMSO: London.

Department for Transport (DfT) (2006) *National Travel Survey: 2005*, HMSO: London.

Department of Communities, Media and Sport (DCMS) (2007) 'Lottery and London to be repaid from sale of Olympic land', www.culture.gov.uk/reference_library/media_releases/2248.aspx

Department of the Environment, Transport and the Regions (DETR) (1998a) *A New Deal for Transport: Better for Everyone*, HMSO: London.

Department of the Environment, Transport and the Regions (DETR) (1998b) *Circular 6/98: Planning And Affordable Housing*, HMSO: London.

Department of the Environment, Transport and the Regions (DETR) (1998c) *A Mayor and Assembly for London: The Government's Proposals for Modernising the Governance of London*, HMSO: London.

Department of the Environment, Transport and the Regions (DETR) (1999) *Towards an Urban Renaissance: Final Report of the Urban Task Force UK*, HMSO: London.

Department of the Environment, Transport and the Regions (DETR) (2000a) *Our Towns and Cities: The Future: Delivering an Urban Renaissance*, HMSO: London.

Department of the Environment, Transport and the Regions (DETR) (2000b) *Encouraging Walking: Advice to Local Authorities*, HMSO: London.

Development Securities plc. (2005) *Towards Sustainability*, Development Securities: London.

Dicken, P. (1994) 'Modernity, alienation and environment: some aspects of housing tenure, design and social identity', in B. Danermark and I. Elander (eds), *Social Rented Housing In Europe: Policy, Tenure And Design*, Delft University Press, pp.90–106.

Dikeç, M (2002) 'Police, politics and the right to the city', *Geojournal*, 58: 91–8.

Dikeç, M (2005) 'Space, politics, and the political', *Environment and Planning D: Society and Space*, 23: 171–88.

Dikeç, M (2007) *Badlands of the Republic: Space, Politics and Urban Policy*, Blackwell: Oxford.

Dines, N., Cattell, V., Gesler, W. and Curtis, S. (2006) *Public Spaces, Social Relations and Well-being in East London*, The Policy Press: Bristol.

Dinham, A. (2005) 'Empowered or overpowered? The real experiences of participation in the New Deal for Communities', *Community Development Journal*, 40: 301–12.

Dinham, A. (2007) 'Raising expectations or dashing hopes? Well-being and participation in disadvantaged areas', *Community Development Journal*, 42: 181–93.

DiPasquale, D. and Wheaton, W. (1992) 'The markets for real estate assets and space: a conceptual framework', *Real Estate Economics*, 20, 181–98.

Dodman, D. (2004) 'Feelings of belonging? Young people's views on their surroundings in Kingston, Jamaica', *Children's Geographies*, 2: 185–98.

Dolton, M., 2006, PhD thesis, Department of Geography, Royal Holloway University of London, Egham, Surrey, TW20 0EX.

Donovan P. (2006) *East London's Economy and the Olympics*, Global Economic Perspectives: London.

Dorling, D. and Thomas, B. (2004) *People and Places: A 2001 Census Atlas of the UK*, The Policy Press: Bristol.

Dovey, K. (2005) *Fluid City: Transforming Melbourne's Urban Waterfront*, Routledge: Oxon.

Dowding, K., Dunleavy, P., King, D., Margetts, H. and Rydin, Y. (1999) 'Regime politics in London local government', *Urban Affairs Review*, 34: 515–45.

Duncan, A. (1992) *Taking On the Motorway: North Kensington Amenity Trust 21 Years*, Kensington and Chelsea Community History Group: London.

e-Politix (2007) *Thames Gateway Homes at Risk*, found at: www.epolitix.com/EN/News/200705/aaad-b9a9-f88c-490b-8cd6-6ee7e527659c.htm.

Edwards, C. (2001) 'Inclusion in regeneration: a place for disabled people?', *Urban Studies*, 38: 267–86.

Edwards, M. (2002) 'Wealth creation and poverty creation: global–local interactions in the economy of London', *City*, 6: 25–42.

Edwards, P. and Flatley, J. (1996) *The Capital Divided: Mapping Poverty and Social Exclusion in London*, London Research Centre: London.

Elsley, S. (2004) 'Children's experience of public space', *Children and Society*, 18: 155–64.

English Heritage (2004) *A Welcome Home: A Sense of Place in the Thames Gateway*, English Heritage: London.

Etzioni, A. (2004) *The Common Good*, Cambridge: Polity Press.

Fainstein, S. (1994) *The City Builders: Property, Politics, and Planning in London and New York*, Blackwell: Oxford.

Fainstein, S., Gordon, I. and Harloe, M. (eds) (1992) *Divided Cities. New York and London in the Contemporary World*, Blackwell: Oxford.

Farr, J. and Osborn, S. (1997) *High Hopes: Concierge, Controlled Entry and Similar Schemes For High-rise Blocks*, HMSO: London.

Fitzpatrick, S., Hastings, A. and Kintrea, K. (1998) *Including Young People in Urban Regeneration: A Lot to Learn?*, The Policy Press: Bristol.

Fitzpatrick, S., Hastings, A. and Kintrea, K. (2000) 'Youth involvements in urban regeneration: hard lessons, future directions', *Policy and Politics*, 28: 493–509.

Flint, J. (2002) 'Social housing agencies and the governance of anti-social behaviour', *Housing Studies*, 7: 619–37.

Flint, J. (2006) 'Housing and the new governance of conduct', in J. Flint (ed.), *Housing, Urban Governance and Anti Social Behaviour*, Polity Press: Bristol, pp.19–37.

Florida, R. (2005) *Cities and the Creative Class*, Routledge: Oxon.

Florio, S. and Brownill, S. (2000) 'Whatever happened to criticism? Interpreting the London Docklands Development Corporation's obituary', *City*, 4: 53–64.

Flynn, N., Leach, S., Vielba, C. (1985), *Abolition or Reform? The Greater London Council and the Metropolitan County Councils*, Harper Collins: London.

Flyvbjerg, B. (1998) *Rationality and Power*, Cambridge University Press: Cambridge.

Forrest, R. and Murie, A. (1991) *Selling the Welfare State*, Routledge: London.

Foster, J. (1999) *Docklands: Cultures in Conflict, Worlds in Collision*, UCL Press: London.

Frank, K. (2006) 'The potential of youth participation in planning', *Journal of Planning Literature*, 20: 351–71.

Fried, M. (1963) 'Grieving for a lost home', in L. Duhl (ed.), *The Urban Condition*, Basic Books: New York, pp.151–71.

Friends Of Queens Market (2005) *Towards a Forward-Looking, Traditional Street Market. Sensitive Solutions to a Precious London Asset*, Friends of Queen Market: London.

Frisby, D. (2001) *Cityscapes of Modernity*, The Policy Press: Oxford.

Fullilove, M. (2001) 'Root shock: the consequences of African American dispossession', *Journal of Urban Health*, 78: 72–80.

Furbey, R. (1999) 'Urban "regeneration": reflections on a metaphor', *Critical Social Policy*, 19: 419–45.

Geddes, M. (2000) 'Tackling social exclusion in the European Union? The limits to the new orthodoxy of local partnership', *International Journal of Urban and Regional Research*, 24: 782–800.

Geddes, M. (2006) 'Partnership and the limits to local governance in England: institutionalist analysis and neo-liberalism', *International Journal of Urban and Regional Research*, 30: 76–97.

Gehl Architects (2004) *Towards a Fine City for People: Public Spaces and Public Life – London*, Gehl Architects: London.

Gillan, A. (2005) 'Locals celebrate long jump from blight to boomtown', *The Guardian*, 7 July.

Gilroy, P. (1987) *There Ain't No Black in the Union Jack: The Cultural Politics of Race and Nation*, Hutchinson: London.

Ginsburg, N. (2005) 'The privatization of council housing', *Critical Social Policy*, 25: 115–35.

Ginsburg, N. And Watson, S. (1992) 'Issues of race and gender facing housing policy', in J. Birchall (ed.), *Housing Policy in the 1990s*, Routledge: London, pp.140–62.

Glancey, J. (2003) 'The Thames Gateway: here be monsters', *The Guardian*, 29 October.

Glancey, J. (2006) 'Poor people poor homes', *The Guardian*, 8 February.

Glass, R. (1964) *London: Aspects of Change*, Centre for Urban Studies: London.

Goffman, E. (1963) *Behaviour in Public Places: Notes on the Social Organisation of Gatherings*, Free Press of Glencoe/Collier-Macmillan: New York.

Gordon, I. (2003) 'Capital needs, capital growth, and global city rhetoric in Mayor Livingstone's London Plan', paper presented to the Association of American Geographers' Conference, New Orleans, March 2003 (copy available from the author).

Gordon, I. (2004a) 'A disjointed dynamo: the Greater South East and inter-regional relationships', *New Economy*, 11: 40–4.

Gordon, I. (2004b) 'Capital need, capital growth and global city rhetoric in Mayor Livingstone's London Plan', GAWC Research Bulletin, 145, www.lboro.ac.uk/gawc/rb/rb145.html.

Gordon, I. and Buck, N. (2005) 'Introduction: cities in the new conventional wisdom', in N. Buck, I. Gordon, A. Harding and I. Turok (eds), *Changing Cities: Rethinking Urban Competitiveness, Cohesion And Governance*, Palgrave: London, pp.1–24.

Gordon, I., Travers, T. and Whitehead, C. (2003) *London's Place in the UK Economy 2003*, London School of Economics for the Corporation of London: London.

Gordon, I., Travers, T. and Whitehead, C. (2004) *London's Place In The UK Economy 2004*, London School of Economics for the Corporation of London: London.

Government Office For London (2008) *Social Exclusion*, accessed 18 April 2008 at: www.gos.gov.uk/gol/People_sustain_comms/Socialinclusion/?a=42496.

Greater London Authority (GLA) (2001a) *Towards a London Plan: Initial Proposals for the Mayor's Spatial Development Strategy*, Mayor Of London: London.

Greater London Authority (GLA) (2001b) *The Mayor's Transport Strategy*, Greater London Authority: London.

Greater London Authority (GLA) (2002a) *London Divided: Income Inequality and Poverty in the Capital*, Greater London Authority: London.

Greater London Authority (GLA) (2002b) *The Draft London Plan: Spatial Development Strategy for Greater London*, Greater London Authority: London.

Greater London Authority (GLA) (2003a) 'Vauxhall Tower, Effra Site', *Planning Report Pdu/0434b/01*, 8 October, Greater London Authority: London.

Greater London Authority (GLA) (2003b) *Interim Strategic Planning Guidance on Tall Buildings*, Greater London Authority: London.

Greater London Authority (GLA) (2004a) *The London Plan: Spatial Development Strategy for Greater London*, Greater London Authority: London.

Greater London Authority (GLA) (2004b) *Making London Better for All Children and Young People: The Mayor's Children and Young People's Strategy*, Greater London Authority: London.

Greater London Authority (GLA) (2004c) *London Thames Gateway Development Framework*, April 2004, Greater London Authority: London.

Greater London Authority (GLA) (2006) *A Fairer London: The Living Wage In London*, Greater London Authority: London.

Green, A. (1994) *The Geography of Poverty and Wealth, 1981–1991*, Joseph Rowntree Foundation: York.

Green, A. and Owen, A. (2006) *The Geography of Poor Skills and Access to Work*, Joseph Rowntree Foundation: York.

Green, G., Gilberson, J. and Grimsley, M. (2002) 'Fear of crime and health in residential tower blocks: a case study in Liverpool UK', *European Journal of Public Health*, 12: 10–15.

Grosvenor Group Ltd. (2003) *Annual Report and Accounts 2003*, Grosvenor: London.

Groth, J. and Corijn, E. (2005) 'Reclaiming urbanity: indeterminate spaces, informal actors and urban agenda setting', *Urban Studies*, 42: 503–26.

Guy, S. and Henneberry, J. (2000) 'Understanding urban development processes: integrating the economic and the social in property research', *Urban Studies*, 37, 2399–2416.

Gyford, J. (1999) 'Politics and planning in London', in J. Simmie (ed.) *Planning London*, UCL Press: London, pp.71–89.

Hall, P. (1962) *The Industries of London since 1861*, Hutchinson: London.

Hall, P. (1963), *London 2000*, Faber and Faber: London.

Hall, P. (1974) 'The containment of urban England', *The Geographical Journal*, 140: 306–408.

Hall, P. (1989) *London 2001*, Unwin Hyman: London.

Hall, P. (1999) 'Planning in London: how we got from there to here', in J. Simmie (ed.), *Planning London*, UCL Press: London, pp.172–87.

Hall, P. (2006) 'London: a millennium long battle, a millennium truce?', in M. Tewdwr- Jones and P. Allmendinger (eds) *Territory, Identity and Spatial Planning*, Routledge: Oxon.

Hall, P. (2007) *London Voices, London Lives: Tales From A Working Capital*, The Policy Press: Bristol.

Hall, P., Pain, K. and Green, N. (2006) 'Anatomy of the polycentric metropolis', in P. Hall and K. Pain. (eds), *The Polycentric Metropolitan Region: Learning from Mega-city Regions in Europe*, Earthscan: London, pp.19–52.

Hamnett, C. (1994a) 'Social polarisation in global cities: theory and evidence', *Urban Studies*, 31: 401–24.

Hamnett, C. (1994b) 'Socio-economic change in London: professionalisation not polarisation', *Built Environment*, 20: 192–203.

Hamnett, C. (1996a) 'Social polarisation, economic restructuring and welfare state regimes', *Urban Studies*, 33: 1407–30.

Hamnett, C. (1996b) 'Why Sassen is wrong: a response to Burgers', *Urban Studies*, 33: 107–10.

Hamnett, C. (2003) *Unequal City: London in the Global Arena*, Routledge: London.

Hamnett, C. and Cross, D. (1998) 'Social polarisation and inequality in London: the earnings evidence 1979–1995', *Environment and Planning C: Government and Policy*, 16: 659–80.

Hamnett, C. and Randolph, W. (1982) 'How far will London's population fall?', *The London Journal*, 8: 95–100.

Hamnett, C. and Randolph, W. (1988) 'Labour and housing market changes in London: a longitudinal analysis', *Urban Studies*, 25: 380–98.

Hamnett, C. and Shoval, N. (2003) 'Museums as flagships', in Lily M. Hoffman, Susan S. Fainstein and Dennis R. Judd (eds), *Cities and Visitors*, Blackwell: Oxford, pp.219–38.

Hamnett, C., Ramsden, M. and Butler, T. (2007) 'Social background, ethnicity, school composition and educational attainment in east London', *Urban Studies*, 44: 1255–80.

Hannigan J. (1998) *Fantasy City: Pleasure and Profit in the Postmodern Metropolis*, Routledge: New York.

Hansard (2005) 'London 2012 Olympic Bid', 6 July 2005.

Harris, P., Lewis, J. and Adam, B. (2004) 'Time, sustainable transport and the politics of speed', *World Transport Policy and Practice*, 10: 5–11.

Harvey, D. (1973) *Social Justice and the City*, Edward Arnold: London

Harvey, D. (1989) 'From urban managerialism to urban entrepreneurialism: transformations in urban governance in late capitalism', *Georgafiska Annaler*, 71B: 3–17.

Harvey, D. (2000) *Space of Hope*, Edinburgh University Press: Edinburgh.

Harvey, D. (2005) *A Brief History of Neo-liberalism*, Oxford University Press: Oxford.

Hastings, A (1996) 'Unravelling the process of "partnership" in urban regeneration policy', *Urban Studies*, 33: 253–68.

Haworth, A. and Manzi, T. (1999) 'Managing the "underclass" interpreting the moral discourse of housing management', *Urban Studies*, 36: 153–66.

Hayden, D. (1995) *The Power of Place: Urban Landscapes as Public History*, MIT Press: Cambridge.

Hebbert, M. (1998), *London*, John Wiley and Sons: Chichester.

Heidegger, M. (1971) 'Building, dwelling, thinking', in *Poetry, Language, Thought*, trans. Albert Hofstadter, Harper And Row: London.

Hepworth, M., Binks A. and Ziemann, B. (2006) *Regional Employment and Skills in the Knowledge Economy: A Report for the Department of Trade and Industry*, Local Futures Group: London.

Her Majesty's Government (1960) *Royal Commission on Local Government in Greater London*, HMSO: London.

Her Majesty's Government (1983) *Streamlining the Cities*, HMSO: London.

Heynen, H. (2000) *Architecture and Modernity: A Critique*, MIT Press, Cambridge.

Hickman, P. and Robinson, D. (2006) 'Transforming social housing: taking stock of new complexities', *Housing Studies*, 21: 157–70.

Higgins Construction (2003) *Lord Rooker Is Our Special Guest*, accessed March 23 2007 at: www.higginsconstruction.co.uk/News_Detail.Cfm?News_Id=48.

Hill, S. (1997) 'A roll of the dice', *Roof*, July/August: 12.

Hillier, J. (2007) *Stretching Beyond the Horizon: A Multiplanar Theory of Spatial Planning and Governance*, Asghate Press: Ashgate.

Hills, J. (2007) *Ends and Means: The Future Role of Social Housing in England*, Case Report 34, Centre for the Analysis of Social Exclusion, London School of Economics: London.

His Royal Highness The Prince Of Wales (1993) *Architecture and the Environment*, St Martins Press: London.

Hoggart, K. (1991) 'London as an object of study', in K. Hoggart and D. Green (eds), *London: A New Metropolitan Geography*, Edward Arnold: London, pp.1–7.

Hoggett, P. (1997) 'Contested communities', in P. Hoggett (ed.), *Contested Communities*, The Policy Press: Bristol, pp.3–16.

Holcomb, H. B. and R. A. Beauregard (1981) *Revitalizing Cities*, Association of American Geographers: Washington, DC.

Holden, A. and Iveson, K. (2003) 'Designs on the urban: New Labour's urban renaissance and the spaces of citizenship', *City*, 7: 57–72.

Holmes, C. (2006) *A New Vision for Housing*, Routledge: Oxon.

Home Office (2001) *Community Cohesion: A Report to the Independent Review Team Chaired by Ted Cantle*, HMSO: London.

Horkheimer, M. (1993) 'Inaugural lecture at the Institute of Social Research (1930)', in S. Benhabib, W. Bonss and J. Mccole (eds), *On Max Horkheimer: New Perspectives*, MIT Press, London.

House of Commons Select Committee on Urban Affairs (2002) *Tall Buildings. Transport, Local Government and The Regions Committee, Sixteenth Report Of Session 2001–2*, HMSO: London.

Housing Corporation (2007) *Sector Study 52: Geographical Changes and Implications for Housing Associations*, Housing Corporation: London.

Hunt, T. (2004) *Building Jerusalem: The Rise and Fall of the Victorian City*, Weidenfield & Nicolson: London.

Huyssen, A. (2003) *Present Pasts Urban Palimpsests and the Politics of Memory*, Stanford University Press: Stanford.

Iles, A. and Seymour, B. (2006) 'The re-occupation', *Mute*, www.metamute.org/en/the-re-occupation.

Imrie, R. (2003) 'Architects' conceptions of the human body', *Environment and Planning D: Society and Space*, 21: 47–65.

Imrie, R. and Raco, M. (1999) 'How new is the new local governance? Lessons from the United Kingdom', *Transactions of the Institute of British Geographers*, 24: 45–63.

Imrie R and Raco, M. (2003), 'Community and the changing nature of urban policy', in R. Imrie and M. Raco, *Urban Renaissance? New Labour, Community and Urban Policy*, The Policy Press: Bristol, pp.3–36.

Imrie, R. and Thomas, H. (1993) 'The limits of property led regeneration', *Environment and Planning C: Government and Policy*, 11: 87–102.

Imrie, R. and Thomas, H. (eds) (1999) *British Urban Policy: An Evaluation of the Urban Development Corporations*, Sage: London.

Imrie, R., Thomas, H. and Marshall, T. (1995) 'Business organisations, local dependence and the politics of urban renewal in Britain', *Urban Studies*, 32: 31–47.

The Independent (2000), 'Blair: Livingstone would be a disastrous Mayor', 6 March, p.1.

Intelligent Space (2004) *London's Functional Walking Network*, available at www.intelligentspace.com/projects/10133.htm.

International Olympic Committee (IOC) (2006) *Report of the Evaluation Commission for the Games of the XXX Olympiad in 2012*, International Olympic Committee: Lausanne.

Islington Council (2007a) *Walking/Wayfinding Maps*, available at www.islington.gov.uk/Environment/Planning/maps/walkingwayfindingmaps.asp.

Islington Council (2007b) *Walk Islington: Explore the Unexpected*, Islington Council: London.

Jacobs, J. (1972) *The Death and Life of Great American Cities*, Penguin: London.

Jacobs, J. M. (1996) *Edge of Empire. Postcolonialism and the City*, Routledge: London.

Jacobs, J. M. (2003) 'The global domestic', in N. Alsayyad (ed.), *The End of Tradition?*, Routledge: London.

Jacobs, J. M. (2006) 'A geography of big things', *Cultural Geographies*, 13: 1–27.

Jacobs, J. M., Cairns, S. and Strebel, I. (2007) '"A tall storey . . . but, a fact just the same": The Red Road high-rise as a black box', *Urban Studies*, 44: 609–29.

Jacobs, K. (1999) *The Dynamics of Local Housing Policy*. Ashgate: Aldershot.

Jacobs, K (2001) 'Historical perspectives and methodologies: their relevance for housing studies?' *Housing, Theory and Society*, 18: 127–35.

Jacobs, S. (2000) 'In celebration of ordinariness', in *What If . . . ? Fifteen Visions of Change For Britain's Inner Cities*, The Short Book Company: London, pp.95–8.

Jager, M. (1986) 'Class definition and the esthetics of gentrification: Victoriana in Melbourne. gentrification of the city', in P. Williams and N. Smith (eds), Allen and Unwin: London, pp.78–91.

Jeffery, N (1997) 'Coin Street', *New Statesman*, 20 June.

Jencks, C. (1989) *Postmodernism: The New Classicism in Art and Architecture*, Academy Editions: London.

Jenkins, L. (2002) '11, Rue Due Conservatoire and the permeability of buildings', *Space and Culture*, 5: 222–36.

Jephcott, P. and Robinson, H. (1971) *Homes in High Flats: Some of the Human Problems Involved In High Flats*, Oliver And Boyd: Edinburgh.

Jessop B. (1999) *The Dynamics of Partnership and Governance Failure*, Department of Sociology, Lancaster University, www.lancs.ac.uk/fass/sociology/papers/jessop-dynamics-of-partnership.pdf.

Jessop B. (2002) *The Future of the Capitalist State*, Polity: Cambridge.

John, P., Tickell, A. and Musson, S. (2005) 'Governing the mega-region: governance and networks across London and the South-East of England', *New Political Economy*, 10: 91–106.

Johnston, R. (1994) 'World cities in a world system', *International Journal of Urban and Regional Research*, 18: 150–2.

Jonas, A. and Ward, K. (2007) 'Introduction to a debate on city-regions: new geographies of governance, democracy and social reproduction', *International Journal of Urban and Regional Research*, 31: 169–78.

Jones, D. (2005) Speech to Confederation of British Industry Congress, Birmingham, cited on *Channel 4 News*, Tuesday 4 October.

Jones, M. (1997) 'Spatial selectivity of the state? The regulationist enigma and local struggles over economic governance', *Environment and Planning A*, 29: 831–64.

Jones, P. and Evans, J. (2006) 'Urban regeneration, governance and the state: exploring notions of distance and proximity', *Urban Studies*, 43: 1491–1509.

Kearns, A. and Paddison, R. (2000), 'New challenges for urban governance', *Urban Studies*, 37: 845–50.

Keith, M. (2005) *After the Cosmopolitan: Multicultural Cities and the Future of Racism*, Routledge: Oxon.

Keith, M. (2007) 'Telling tales? Narratives and concepts of urban regeneration in the Thames Gateway', in P. Cohen and M. Rustin (eds), *London's Turning: The Prospect Of Thames Gateway*, Ashgate Press: Dover.

Kellerman, A. (2006) *Personal Mobilities*, Routledge: New York.

Kellett, J. (1969) *The Impact of Railways on Victorian Cities*, Routledge and Kegan Paul: London.

Kemp, P. (1989) 'Shifting the balance between state and market: the reprivatisation of rental housing provision in Britain', *Environment and Planning A*, 22: 792–810.

Kerr, J. (2003) 'Blowdown: The rise and fall of London's tower blocks', in J. Kerr and A. Gibson (eds), *London From Punk To Blair*, Reaktion Books: London, pp.188–97.

Keogh, G. and D'Arcy, E. (1999) 'Property market efficiency: an international economics perspective', *Urban Studies*, 36 (13): 2401–14.

Kintrea, K. (2007) 'Policies and programmes for disadvantaged neighbourhoods: recent English experience', *Housing Studies*, 22: 261–82.

Koolhaas, R. (2007) *Lagos: How It Works*, Lars Muller Press: Berlin.

Krueger, R. and Savage, L. (2007) 'City-regions and social reproduction: a "place" for sustainable development?', *International Journal of Urban and Regional Research*, 31: 215–33.

Kunzru, H. (2005), 'Market forces', *The Guardian*, 7 December.

Land Securities (2006) *Annual Report 2006*, Land Securities: London.

Larner, W. and Craig, D. (2005) 'After neo-liberalism? Community activism and local partnerships in Aotearoa, New Zealand', *Antipode*, 37: 402–24.

Larsen, J., Urry, J. and Axhausen, K. (2006) *Social Networks and Future Mobilities, Report to the Horizons Programme of the Department for Transport*, Department of Sociology, University of Lancaster and IVT, ETH Zurich: Lancaster and Zurich.

Latour, B. (1993) *We Have Never Been Modern*, Harvard University Press: Boston.

Latour, B. (1997) 'Where are the missing masses? The sociology of a few mundane artefacts', in W. Bijker and J. Law (eds), *Shaping Technology/Building Society: Studies In Sociotechnical Change*, The MIT Press: Cambridge, pp.225–58.

Latour, B. (2005) *Reassembling the Social: An Introduction to Actor-network Theory*, Oxford University Press: Oxford.

Lawless, P. (2006) 'Area-based urban initiatives: rationale and outcomes: the New Deal for Communities Programme in England', *Urban Studies*, 43: 1991–2011.

Lawless, P. (2007) 'Continuing dilemmas for area-based urban regeneration: evidence from the New Deal For Communities Programme in England', *People, Place & Policy Online*, 1: 14–21.

Leach, S. and Wilson, D. (2004) 'Urban elites in England: new models of executive governance', *International Journal of Urban and Regional Research*, 28: 134–49.

Learning and Skills Council (2005) *London East: Olympic Skills Dialogues. Draft Paper, September 2005*, Learning and Skills Council: London.

Lees, L. (2000) 'A reappraisal of gentrification: towards "geography of gentrification"', *Progress in Human Geography*, 24: 389–408.

Lees, L. (2001) 'Towards a critical geography of architecture: the case of an Ersatz Colosseum', *Ecumene: A Journal of Cultural Geographies*, 8: 51–86.

Lees, L. (2003a) 'Visions of "Urban Renaissance": the Urban Task Force Report and the Urban White Paper', in R. Imrie and M. Raco (eds.), *Urban Renaissance? New Labour, Community and Urban Policy*, The Policy Press: Bristol, pp.61–82.

Lees, L. (2003b) 'The ambivalence of diversity and the politics of urban renaissance: the case of youth in downtown Portland, Maine, USA', *International Journal of Urban and Regional Research*, 27: 613–34.

Lees, L., Slater, T. and Wyly, E. (2008) *Gentrification*, Routledge: New York.

Levitas, R. (1998) *The Inclusive Society? Social Exclusion and New Labour*, Macmillan: Basingstoke.

Levitas, R. (2005) *The Inclusive Society? Social Exclusion and New Labour*, 2nd edn, Palgrave Macmillan: Basingstoke.

Ley, D. (2004) 'Transnational spaces and everyday life', *Transactions of the Institute of British Geographers*, 29, 151–64.

Living Streets (2003) *A Response By Living Streets to the Draft Walking Plan for London*, Living Streets, available at www.livingstreets.org.uk.

Living Streets (2006) *Walkable London: A New Era for People On Foot*, available at www.livingstreets.org.uk.

Living Streets (2007) *Walking Works*, available at www.walkingworks.org.uk/content/for_the_media.php.

London Assembly (2003) *Access to the Thames: Scrutiny of the Thames Foreshore and Path*, Greater London Authority: London.

London Borough of Camden (LBC) (2001) *King's Cross: Towards an Integrated City*, London Borough of Camden: London.

London Borough of Camden (LBC) (2006) *Unitary Development Plan*, London Borough of Camden: London.

London Borough of Hackney (LBH) (1998) *Prime Minister Praises Holly Street as a Symbol for the Nation*, Press Release, 15 September (Pr. 285), London Borough of Hackney: London.

London Borough of Hackney (LBH) (1999a) *New-look Holly Street Gets the Thumbs up from Danish VIPs*, Press Release, 15 March (Pr. 100), London Borough of Hackney: London.

London Borough of Hackney (LBH) (1999b) *Holly Street: Blueprint for Success*, London Borough of Hackney: London.

London Borough of Hackney (LBH) (2007) *Neighbourhood Renewal Strategy*, London Borough of Hackney: London.

London Borough of Newham (LBN) (2002) *The Newham Story. A Short History of the London Borough of Newham*, available at www.newham.gov.uk/NR/rdonlyres/52364E5A-4560-4650-86AD-DA699BF7224E/0/NewhamStory.pdf.

London Borough of Newham (LBN) (2004a) *The Regeneration Tour: Welcome to Newham!*, London Borough of Newham: London.

London Borough of Newham (LBN) (2004b) *Newham Community Strategy*, London Borough of Newham: London.

London Borough of Newham (LBN) (2005) *Queens Market – Consultation and Progress Report*, accessed 23 June 2007 at http://moderngov.newham.gov.uk/published/c00000294/m00004358/ai00008111/$queensmarket.doca.ps.pdf.

London Borough of Newham (LBN) (2006) *Equality Impact Assessment on Queens Market Redevelopment Project*, London Borough of Newham: London.

London Borough of Newham (LBN) and MORI (2005) *Regeneration Developments In Queens Market, Newham. Survey of Residents, Shoppers, Market Traders and Businesses*, London Borough of Newham: London.

London Civic Forum (2007) *News and Reports, Sunday June 24*, accessed June 2007 at www.londoncivicforum.org.uk.news.

London Development Agency (LDA) (2006) *London's Communities*, accessed 15 January 2008 at www.lda.gov.uk/server/show/ConWebDoc.2382.

London Development Agency (LDA) (2008a) *Welcome to the LDA*, accessed 15 January 2008 at www.lda.gov.uk.

London Development Agency (LDA) (2008b) *What makes London a Global City?*, accessed 15 January 2008 at www.lda.gov.uk/server/show/ConWebDoc.1997.

London East Research Institute (LERI) (2006) *Thames Gateway Housing*, Davies Arnold Cooper: London.

London East Research Institute (LERI) (2007) *A Lasting Legacy for London?*, London Assembly: London.

London First (2007) *Keeping the UK Competitive*, London First Publications: London.

London Planning Advisory Committee (1991) *London: World City. World City Moving into the 21st Century*, HMSO: London.

London School of Economics (2007) *The Impact of Recent Immigration on the London Economy*, City of London: London.

Lovering J. (2003) 'MNCs and wannabes: inward investment, discourses of regional development and the regional service class', in N. Phelps and P. Raines (eds), *The Competition for Inward Investment*, Ashgate: Aldershot, pp.39–61.

Low, S. (2003) *Behind the Gates: Life, Security and the Pursuit of Happiness in Fortress America*, Routledge: New York.

Lund, H. (2002) 'Pedestrian environments and sense of community', *Journal of Planning Education and Research*, 21: 301–12.

Lupton, R. (2003) *Poverty Street: The Dynamics of Neighbourhood Decline and Renewal*, The Policy Press: Bristol.

Lyons, G. and Urry, J. (2005) 'Travel time use in the information age', *Transportation Research Part A: Policy and Practice*, 39: 257–76.

Maginn, P. (2004) *Urban Regeneration, Community Power and the (In)Significance of 'Race'*, Ashgate Press: Aldershot.

Malone, K. (2001) 'Children, youth and sustainable cities', *Local Environment*, 6: 5–12.

Malpass, P. (2000) *Housing Associations and Housing Policy: A Historical Perspective*, Macmillan: Basingstoke.

Malpass, P. (2005) *Housing and the Welfare State: The Development of Housing Policy in Britain*, Palgrave Macmillan: Basingstoke.

Malpass, P. and Mullins, D. (2002) 'Local authority housing stock transfer in the UK: from local initiative to national policy', *Housing Studies*, 17: 673–86.

Manzi, T. and Smith-Bowers, B. (2004) 'So many managers, so little vision: Registered Social Landlords and Consortium Schemes in the UK', *European Journal of Housing Policy*, 4: 57–75.

Marriott, O. (1969) *The Property Boom*, Macmillan: London.

Marvin, S., Harding, A. and Robson, B. (2006*) A Framework For City-regions, Working Paper 4, The Role Of City-regions In Regional Economic Development Policy*, Office of the Deputy Prime Minister: London.

Massey, D. (2004) *For Space*, Sage: London.

Massey, D, (2007) *World City*, Polity Press: Cambridge.

Matthews, H. (1992) *Making Sense of Place: Children's Understanding of Large-scale Environments*, Harvester Wheatsheaf: Hemel Hempstead.

Matthews, H (2001) *Children and Community Regeneration*, Save The Children: London.

Matthews, H. (2003) 'Children and regeneration: setting an agenda for community participation and integration', *Children and Society*, 17: 264–76.

Matthews, H., Limb, M. and Taylor, M. (1999) 'Young people's participation and representation in society', *Geoforum*, 30: 135–44.

May, J., Wills, J., Datta, K., Evans, Y., Herbert, J. and Mcilwaine, C. (2007) 'Keeping London working: global cities, the British State and London's new migrant division of labour', *Transactions of the Institute of British Geographers*, 32: 151–67.

Mayor of London (2005a) *Housing in London: The London Housing Strategy Evidence Base*, Greater London Authority: London.

Mayor of London (2005b) *Planning Report PDU/UDP30/SPG01/01: Ocean Estate, Stepney*, 9 February, Greater London Authority: London.

Mayor of London (2006a) *Alterations to the London Plan: Sustainability Statement*, Greater London Authority: London.

Mayor of London (2006b) *Towards The Mayor's Housing Strategy: Consultation Paper*, Greater London Authority: London.

Mayor of London (2007) *State of London's Children Report 2007*, Mayor of London: London.

McNeill, D. (2002a) 'Livingstone's London: left politics and the world city', *Regional Studies*, 36: 75–80.

McNeill, D. (2002b), 'The mayor and the world city skyline: London's tall buildings debate', *International Planning Studies*, 7: 325–34.

Merry, S. (1981) *Urban Danger: Life in a Neighbourhood of Strangers*, Temple University Press: Philadelphia.

Middleton, J. (2008), '"The walkable city": the dimensions of walking and overlapping walks of life', Unpublished PhD thesis, King's College London.

Monbiot, G. (1999) 'Drawbridge society', *The Guardian*, 24 June.

Morgan, K. (2002) 'The English question: regional perspectives on a fractured nation', *Regional Studies*, 36: 797–810.

Morgan, K. (2007) 'The polycentric state: new spaces of empowerment and engagement?', *Regional Studies*, 41: 1237–51.

Morphet, J. (2006) 'Embracing multiculturalism: the case of London', in W. Neill and HU Schwedler (eds) *Migration and Cultural Inclusion in the European City*, Palgrave Macmillan: Basingstoke, pp.167–78.

Morrison, Z. (2003) 'Cultural justice and addressing "social exclusion"', in R. Imrie and M. Raco (eds), *Urban Renaissance: New Labour, Community And Urban Policy*, The Policy Press: Bristol, pp.139–61.

Mouffe, C. (1999) 'Carl Schmitt and the paradox of Liberal Democracy', in C. Mouffe (ed.), *The Challenge of Carl Schmitt*, Verso: London, pp.1–7.

Mouffe, C. (2005) *On the Political*, Verso: London.

Muir H. (2005a) 'Sporting drive sees drop in crime for Olympic borough', *The Guardian*, 8 August.

Muir, H. (2005b) 'Equality means everyone. West Ham shows that all women shortlists need rethinking', *The Guardian*, 23 February.

Mullins, D. and Murie, A. (2006) *Housing Policy in the UK*, Palgrave Macmillan: Basingstoke.

Musson, S., John, P., and Tickell, A. (2006), 'Government, governance and decentralisation', in M. Tewdwr-Jones and P. Allmendinger (eds), *Territory, Identity and Spatial Planing*, Routledge: Oxon, pp.273–84.

National Audit Office (NAO) (1988) *Department of the Environment: Urban Development Corporations*, HMSO: London.

National Audit Office (NAO) (2007a) *Thames Gateway: Laying The Foundations*, HMSO: London.

National Audit Office (NAO) (2007b) *How European Cities Achieve Renaissance: A Companion to the National Audit Office's Report Laying The Foundations*, HMSO: London.

Newham Recorder (2006) 'Fish Island celebrates', 2 February.

Newman, J. (2001) *Modernising Governance: New Labour, Policy and Society*, Sage: London.

Newman, O. (1972) *Defensible Space: Crime Prevention through Urban Design*, Macmillan: New York.

Newman, P. and Smith, I. (2000), 'Cultural production, place and politics on the South Bank of the Thames', *International Journal of Urban and Regional Research*, 24: 9–24.

Newman, P. and Thornley, P. (1997) 'Fragmentation and centralisation in the governance of London: influencing the urban policy and planning agenda', *Urban Studies*, 34: 967–88.

Nolan P. (2004) *Transforming China*, Anthem Press: London.

North, D. and Syrett, S. (2006) *The Dynamics of Local Economies and Deprived Neighbourhoods*, Department for Communities and Local Government: London.

North, P. (2003) 'Communities at the heart? Community action and urban policy in the UK', in R. Imrie and M. Raco (eds), *Urban Renaissance? New Labour, Community and Urban Policy*, The Policy Press: Bristol, pp.121–38.

O'Brien, M. (2003) 'Regenerating children's neighbourhoods: what do children want?', in P. Christensen and M. O'Brien (eds) *Children in the City: Home, Neighbourhood and Community*, Routledge: London, pp.142–61.

O'Connor, J. (1973) *The Fiscal Crisis of the State*, St Martin's Press: New York.

Oatley, N. (1995) 'Competitive urban policy and the regeneration game', *Town Planning Review*, 66: 1–14.

Ocean New Deal For Communities (2002) *Ocean Eye: The New Deal for Communities Newsletter*, 1 July, Ocean NDC: London.

Ocean New Deal For Communities (2004) *Ocean Eye: The New Deal for Communities Newsletter*, 10 August, Ocean NDC: London.

Office of the Deputy Prime Minister (ODPM) (2001) *Better Places to Live by Design: A Companion Guide to PPG3*, HMSO: London.

Office of the Deputy Prime Minister (ODPM) (2003a) *Sustainable Communities: Building for the Future*, HMSO: London.

Office of The Deputy Prime Minister (ODPM) (2003b) *Improving the Delivery of Affordable Housing in London and the South East*, HMSO: London.

Office of the Deputy Prime Minister (ODPM) (2003c) *Factsheet 9: New Deal for Communities*, Neighbourhood Renewal Unit: London.

Office of the Deputy Prime Minister (ODPM) (2004) *The Egan Review: Skills for Sustainable Communities*, HMSO: London.

Office of the Deputy Prime Minister (ODPM) (2005) *Planning Policy Statement 6: Planning For Town Centres*, HMSO: London.

Office of Deputy Prime Minister (ODPM) (2006a) *Planning Policy Statement 3: Housing*, HMSO, London.

Office of the Deputy Prime Minister (ODPM) (2006b) *State of the English Cities*, HMSO, London.

Office of Deputy Prime Minister (ODPM) (2006c) *Olympic Delivery Authority (Planning Functions) Order 2006*, HMSO: London.

Opinion Research Services (ORS) (2004) *Greater London Housing Requirements Study*, Greater London Authority: London.

Paddison, R. (2001) 'Communities in the city', in R. Paddison (ed), *Handbook of Urban Studies*, Sage: London, pp.194–205.

Pahl, R. (1988) 'Employment, work and the domestic division of labour', *International Journal of Urban and Regional Research*, 4 (1): 1–20.

Parkes, A., Kearns, A. and Atkinson, R. (2002) 'What makes people dissatisfied with their neighbourhoods?', *Urban Studies*, 39: 2413–38.

Parliamentary Public Accounts Committee (PAC) (2007) *Uncorrected Transcript of Oral Evidence: To be Published as Hc 693-House of Commons Minutes of Evidence Taken before the Committee Of Public Accounts*, 13 June, HMSO: London.

Pawson, H. and Kintrea, K. (2002) 'Part of the problem or part of the solution? Social housing allocation policies and social exclusion in Britain', *Journal of Social Policy*, 31: 643–67.

Peck, J. (2005) 'Struggling with the creative class', *International Journal of Urban and Regional Research*, 29: 740–70.

Peck, J. and Tickell, A. (2002) 'Neo-liberalizing space', *Antipode* 34: 380–404.

Perrons, D. and Skyers, S. (2003) 'Empowerment through participation? Conceptual explorations and a case study', *International Journal of Urban and Regional Research*, 27: 265–85.

Perry, J. and Selden, M. (eds) (2000) *Chinese Society: Change, Conflict and Resistance*, 2nd edn, Routledge: London.

Peters, T. (1987) 'The rise of the skyscraper from the ashes of Chicago', *American Heritage: Invention and Technology Magazine*, 3 (Fall): 14–22.

Phillips, D., Davis, D. and Ratcliffe P. (2007) 'British Asian narratives of urban space', *Transactions of the Institute of British Geographers*, 32: 217–34.

Picard, Liza, (1997) *Restoration London*, Phoenix: London.

Pierson, J. and Worley, C. (2005) 'Housing and urban regeneration policy', in P. Somerville and N. Spirings (eds), *Housing and Social Policy*, Routledge: Oxon, pp.217–41.

Pile, S. (1996) *The Body and the City: Psychoanalysis, Space and Subjectivity*, Routledge: London.

Pimlott, B. and Rao, N. (2002), *Governing London*, Oxford University Press: Oxford.

Pinch, P. and Munt, I. (2002) 'Blue belts: an agenda for "waterspace" planning in the UK', *Planning, Practice and Research*, 17: 159–74.

Porter, R. (1989) *London: A Social History*, Pimlico Press: London.

Powell, M. (2000) 'New Labour and the third way in the British welfare state: a new and distinctive approach', *Critical Social Policy*, 20: 39–60.

Power, A. (1997) *Estates on the Edge: The Social Consequences of Mass Housing in Northern Europe*, Macmillan: New York.

Power, A. and Houghton, J. (2007) *Jigsaw Cities: Big Places, Small Spaces*, The Policy Press: Bristol.

Poynter G (1989) *Wall Street on the Water: Employment Patterns in London Docklands*, South East Region Trades Union Congress: London.

Poynter, G. (2006) *From Beijing to Bow Bells: Measuring the Olympic Effect*, London East Research Papers in Urban Studies, University Of East London: London.

Prasad, R. (2000) 'No safety in numbers for black and Asian families living in Newham', *The Guardian*, 22 November.

Preteceille, E. (2004). *La Division Sociale De L'espace Fancilien: Typologie Socioprofessionelle 1999 Et Transformation De L'espace Residentiel 1990–99*, Observatoire Sociologique Du Changement: Paris, 145.

Preuss H (2004) *The Economics of Staging the Olympics: A Comparison of the Games 1972–2008*, Edward Elgar: Cheltenham.

Price Waterhouse (1999) *An Evaluation of Dice (Design Improvement Controlled Experiment) Schemes, Commissioned by Office of the Deputy Prime Minster*, Price Waterhouse-Coopers: London.

Prime Minister's Strategy Unit (2003) *London Analytical Report*, Strategy Unit: London.

Putnam, R. (2000) *Bowling Alone: The Collapse and Revival of American Community*, Simon And Schuster: New York.

Rabinow, P. and Rose, N. (2003), *Thoughts on the Concept of Biopower Today*, accessed 10 May 2008 at www.molsci.org/research/publications_pdf/Rose_Rabinow_Biopower_Today.pdf.

Raco, M. (2003) 'New Labour, community and the future of Britain's urban renaissance', in R. Imrie and M. Raco (eds), *Urban Renaissance? New Labour, Community and Urban Policy*, Routledge: London, pp.235–49.

Raco, M. (2005) 'A step change or a step back? The Thames Gateway and the re-birth of the Urban Development Corporations', *Local Economy*, 20: 141–53.

Raco, M. (2007a) *Building Sustainable Communities: Spatial Policy and Labour Mobility in Post-War Britain*, The Policy Press: Bristol.

Raco, M. (2007b) 'The planning, design and governance of sustainable communities in the UK', in R. Atkinson and G. Helms (eds), *Securing an Urban Renaissance: Crime, Community and British Urban Policy*, The Policy Press: Bristol, pp.39–56.

Raco, M. (2008) 'Key worker housing, welfare reform and the new spatial policy in England', *Regional Studies*, available online at www.informaworld.com/smpp/content~content=a789783793~db=all.

Raco M. and Henderson, S. (2005) 'Sustainable urban planning and the brownfield development process in the United Kingdom', *Local Environment*, 11, 499–513.

Raco, M. and Imrie, R. (2000) 'Governmentality and rights and responsibilities in urban policy', *Environment and Planning A*, 32: 2187–2204.

Raco, M., Parker, G. and Doak, J. (2006) 'Reshaping spaces of local governance? Community Strategies and the modernisation of local governance in England', *Environment and Planning C: Government and Policy*, 24: 475–96.

Railway Lands Group (2006) *King's Cross Development: Campaigners Win Right to High Court Hearing*, accessed 1 April 2008 at www.kxrlg.org.uk/news/pressrelease070227.htm.

Rallings, C. and Thrasher, M. (2000), 'Personality politics and protest voting: the first elections to the Greater London Authority', *Parliamentary Affairs*, 53: 753–64.

Rancière, J (1998), *Disagreement*, University of Minnesota Press: Minneapolis.

Rancière, J (2003) *Ten Theses of Politics*, accessed 10 May 2007 at: http://muse.jhu.edu/journals/theory_and_event/v005/5.3ranciere.html.

Rancière, J (2007) *On the Shores of Politics*, Verso: London.

Rasmussen, S (1960) *The Unique City*, Penguin: London.

Rhodes, R. (2000) 'New Labour's civil service: summing-up joining-up', *Political Quarterly*, 71: 155–66.

Rhodes, R. (2003) *Understanding Governance*, Sage: London.

Richards, M. (2005) *Congestion Charging in London: The Policy and the Politics*, Palgrave Macmillan: Basingstoke.

Roberts. (2000) 'The evolution, definition and purpose of urban regeneration', in P. Roberts and H. Sykes (eds), *Urban Regeneration: A Handbook*, London, pp.295–315.

Robson, W. (1939) *The Government and Misgovernment of London*, G. Allen and Unwin: London.

Roche M. (2000) *Mega-events and Modernity*, Routledge: London.

Rose, D. (2004) 'Discourses and experiences of social mix in gentrifying neighbourhoods: a Montreal case study', *Canadian Journal of Urban Research*, 13: 278–316.

Rose, N. (1996) 'The death of the social? Re-figuring the territory of government', *Economy and Society*, 25: 327–56.

Rose, N. (2000), 'Community, citizenship and "the Third Way"', in D. Meredyth and J. Minson (eds), *Citizenship and Cultural Policy*, Sage: London, pp.1–17.

Rose, N. and Miller, P. (1992) 'Political power beyond the state: problematics of government', *British Journal of Sociology*, 43: 173–205.

Rossiter, B. and Gibson, K. (2003) 'Walking and performing "the City": a Melbourne chronicle', in G. Bridge and S. Watson (eds), *A Companion to the City*, Blackwell Publishing: Oxford, pp.437–47.

Rubin, G., Jatana, N. and Potts, R. (2006) *The World on a Plate: Queen's Market: The Economic and Social Value of London's Most Ethnically Diverse Street Market*, New Economics Foundation: London.

Rutheiser, C. (1996) *Imagineering Atlanta: The Politics of Place in the City of Dreams*, Verso: New York.

Rydin, Y., Thornley, A., Scanlon, K. and West, R. (2004), 'The Greater London Authority – a case of conflict of cultures? Evidence from the planning and environmental policy domains', *Environment and Planning C: Government and Policy*, 22: 55–76.

Sadek J (2002) *The Effectiveness of Government Regeneration Initiatives*, Select Committee on Office of the Deputy Prime Minister: Housing, Planning, Local Government and the Regions, Examination Of Witnesses, December 2: 232-239.

Saegert, S. (1976) 'Stress-inducing and stress-reducing qualities of environment', in W. Ittleson and L. Rulin (eds), *Environmental Psychology*, Holt Publications: New York, pp.218–23.

Sanders H. (1992) 'Building the convention city: politics, finance and public investment in urban America', *Journal of Urban Affairs*, 14: 135–60.

Sassen S. (1994) *Cities in a World Economy*, Pine Forge Press: Thousand Oaks, California.

Sassen, S. (2001) *The Global City. New York, London, Tokyo*, 2nd edn, Princeton University Press, Princeton.

Saunders, P. (1990) *A Nation of Home Owners*, Unwin Hyman: London.

Save Britain's Heritage (2001) *Memorandum To the Tall Buildings Inquiry of the House of Commons Select Committee on Urban Affairs*, accessed 24 August 2007 at: www.parliament.the-stationery-office.co.uk/pa/cm200102/cmselect/cmtlgr/482/48206.htm.

Scott, A. (2000) *The Cultural Economy of Cities*, Sage: London.

Select Committee on Environment, Transport and Regional Affairs (ETRA) (2001) *Walking in Towns and Cities, Eleventh Report*, HMSO: London.

Self, P. (1979) 'The siege of Coin Street', *Town and Country Planning*, 48: 149–50.

Sennett, R. (1977) *The Fall of the Public Man*, Cambridge: Cambridge University Press.

Sennett, R. (2000) *The Corrosion of Character*, W. W. Norton Series: New York.

Sennett, R. (2001) 'A flexible city of strangers', *Le Monde Diplomatique*, February, 23–5.

Sennett, R. (2007) *The Culture of the New Capitalism*, Yale University Press: New Haven.

Shaw, S., Bagwell, S. and Karmowska, J. (2004) 'Ethnoscapes as spectacle: re-imaging multicultural districts as new destinations for leisure and tourist consumption', *Urban Studies*, 41: 1983–2000.

Shelter (2004) *Crowded House: Cramped Living in England's Housing*, Shelter: London.

Shelter (2005) *Building Hope: The Case for More Homes Now*, Shelter: London.

Sherwood B. (2006) 'Games give push to regeneration', *Financial Times Special Report Thames Gateway*, 22 November, p.12.

Sibley, D. (1995) *Geographies of Exclusion: Society and Difference in the West*, Routledge: London.

Simmel, G. (1971) *The Metropolis and Mental Life*, University of Chicago Press: Chicago.

Simmie, J. (ed.) (1999), *Planning London*, UCL Press, London.

Simmons, R. (2006) 'The cost of bad design' in Commission For Architecture and the Built Environment, *The Cost of Bad Design*, CABE: London, pp.7–32.

Simone, M. (2004) *For the City Yet to Come: Changing African Life in Four Cities*, Duke University Press: London.

Sinclair, I. (2006) 'Lost treasure', *The Guardian*, 18 March.

Slater, T. (2006) 'The eviction of critical perspectives from gentrification research', *International Journal of Urban and Regional Research*, 30: 737–57.

Smith, D. (2005) *On the Margins of Inclusion*, The Policy Press: Bristol.

Bibliography

Social Exclusion Unit (SEU)(1998) *Bringing Britain Together: A National Strategy for Neighbourhood Renewal, Cm. 4045*, HMSO, London.

Speak, S. (2000) 'Children in urban regeneration: foundations for sustainable participation', *Community Development Journal*, 35: 31–40.

Spiker, P. (1987) 'Poverty and depressed estates: a critique of utopia on trial', *Housing Studies*, 2: 283–92.

St Modwen-London Borough of Newham (2004) *The New Queens Market: Towards a Safe, Clean, Vibrant and Lively Shopping and Living Environment, Preliminary Consultation Leaflet*, London Borough of Newham: London.

St Modwen-London Borough of Newham (2006) *Regeneration Proposals For Queens Market*, London Borough of Newham: London.

St Pierre, E. (1997) 'A critique of the rational individual of Liberal Democracy', paper presented at the Annual International Qualitative Research in Education Conference, Athens, Greece, 9–11 January.

Stallybrass, P. and White, A. (1986) *The Politics and Poetics of Transgression*, Cornell University Press: Ithaca.

Stedman Jones, G. (1984) *Outcast London*, 2nd edn, Penguin: London.

Stewart, J. and Rhoden, M. (2003) 'A review of social housing regeneration in the London Borough of Brent', *The Journal of the Royal Society for the Promotion of Health*, 123: 23–32.

Stoker, G. (1998) 'Governance as theory: five propositions', *International Social Science Journal*, 50: 17–28.

Stoker, G. (2000) 'Why mayors remain important', *The Scotsman*, 22 June.

Sweeting, D. (2002) 'Leadership in urban governance: the Mayor of London', *Local Government Studies*, 28: 3–20.

Swyngedouw, E (2005), 'Governance, innovation and the citizen: the Janus face of governance-beyond-the-state', *Urban Studies*, 42: 1991–2006.

Swyngedouw, E (2007), 'The post-political city', in I. Bavo (ed.), *Urban Politics Now. Re-imagining Democracy in the Neo-liberal City*, Nai Publishers: Amsterdam, pp.58–76.

Talen, E. (1999) 'Sense of community and neighbourhood form: an assessment of the social doctrine of new urbanism', *Urban Studies*, 36: 1361–79.

Taylor, J., Madrik M. and Collin, S. (2005) *Trading Places: The Economic Impact of Street Produce and Farmers' Markets*, New Economics Foundation and London Development Agency: London.

Taylor, M. (2007) 'Community participation in the real world', *Urban Studies*, 44: 297–317.

Taylor, P. (2004) *World City Network: A Global Urban Analysis*, Routledge: London.

Thompson, R. (2007) 'Strategic planning in London', in H. Dimitriou and R. Thompson (eds), *Strategic Planning for Regional Development in the UK*, Routledge: London, pp.251–70.

Thornley, A. (1991) *Urban Planning under Thatcherism*, Routledge: Oxon.

Thornley, A. (ed.) (1992), *The Crisis of London*, Routledge: London.

Thornley, A., Rydin, Y., Scanlon, K. and West, R. (2005) 'Business privilege and the strategic planning agenda of the Greater London Authority', *Urban Studies*, 42: 1947–69.

Thornton, P. (2005) 'Canary Wharf workers take home an average of £100,000', *The Independent*, 11 November, p.8.

Tiesdell, S. and Allmendinger, P. (2003) 'Neighbourhood regeneration and New Labour's third way', *Environment and Planning C: Government and Policy*, 19: 903–26.

Till, K. (2005) *The New Berlin: Memory, Politics, Place*, Minnesota University Press: Minnesota.

Tomaney, J. (2001) 'The new governance of London', *City*, 5: 225–48.

Towers, G. (2000) *Shelter Is Not Enough*, The Policy Press: Bristol.

Transport for London (TfL) (2004) *Making London a Walkable City: The Walking Plan for London*, Mayor of London: London.

Transport for London (TfL) (2005) *Improving Walkability*, Mayor of London: London.

Transport for London (TfL) (2007a) *London Travel Demand Survey Supplement, March 2007*, Mayor of London: London.

Transport for London (TfL) (2007b) *Smartmoves*, Issue 2, Mayor of London: London.

Travers, T. (2004), *The Politics of London: Governing an Ungovernable City*, Palgrave Macmillan: Basingstoke.

Travers, T., Jones, G., Hebbert, M. and Burnham, J. (1991) *The Government of London*, Joseph Rowntree Foundation: York.

Tuckett, I (1992), 'Coin Street: There is another way . . . ', in J. Montgomery and A. Thornley (eds) *Radical Planning Initiatives*, Gower: Aldershot, pp.137–49.

Turkington, R. (2004) 'High-rise as a doubtful guest', in R. Turkington, R. Van Kempen and F. Wassenberg (eds) *High-rise Housing In Europe: Current Trends And Future Prospects*, Delft University Press: Netherlands, pp.147–65.

Turok, I. (1992) 'Property-led urban regeneration: panacea or placebo?', *Environment and Planning A*, 24: 361–79.

Turok, I. and Edge, N. (1999) *The Jobs Gap*, Joseph Rowntree Foundation: York.

Uitermark, J. (2003) 'Social mixing and the management of disadvantaged neighbourhoods', *Urban Studies*, 40: 531–49.

Urban Splash (2006) *Annual Report, 2006*, Urban Splash: Manchester.

Valentine, G. (1996) 'Children should be seen and not heard: the production and transgression of adults' public space', *Urban Geography*, 17: 205–20.

Valentine, G. (1997) '"Oh yes I can." "Oh no you can't": children and parent's understandings of kids' competence to negotiate public space safely', *Antipode*, 29: 65–89.

Valentine, G. (2004) *Public Space and the Culture of Childhood*, Ashgate: London.

Van Kempen, R. (1994) 'High-rise living', in B. Danermark and I. Elander (eds), *Social Rented Housing in Europe: Policy, Tenure and Design*, Delft University Press: Delft, pp.159–80.

Vertovec, S. (2006) *The Emergence of Super-Diversity in Britain*, Compass Working Paper No. 25: Oxford.

Vicario, L. and Monje, P. (2003). 'Another "Guggenheim Effect"? The generation of a potentially gentrifi-able neighbourhood in Bilbao', *Urban Studies*, 40: 2383–400.

Walker, J. (2007) *The State of Walking in London*, paper presented at Annual Walking and Cycling Conference, 10 May 2007, London, available at www.walk21.com/uploads/File/WC%20conference%20 London%20100507.pdf.

Wallace, A. (2007) '"We have had nothing for so long that we don't know what to ask for": New Deal for Communities and the regeneration of socially excluded terrain', *Social Policy and Society*, 6: 1–12.

Warwick, E. (2008) 'Defensible space', in R. Kitchin and N. Thrift (chief eds), *International Encyclopaedia of Human Geography*, Elsevier, in press.

Wassenberg, F., Turkington, R. and van Kempen, R. (2004) 'Prospects for high-rise estates', in F. Wassenberg, R. Turkington and R. van Kempen (eds), *High Rise Housing in Europe*, Delft: Delft University Press, pp.265–80.

Watson, S. and Studdert, D. (2006) *Markets as Sites For Social Interaction: Spaces of Diversity*, The Policy Press: Bristol.

Watson, S. and Wells, K. (2005) 'Spaces of nostalgia: the hollowing out of a London market', *Social and Cultural Geography*, 6: 17–30.

Watt, P. (2001) 'The dynamics of social class and housing: a study of local authority tenants in the London Borough of Camden', unpublished PhD thesis, King's College London.

Watt, P. (2003) 'Urban marginality and economic restructuring: local authority tenants and employment in an inner London borough', *Urban Studies*, 40: 1769–89.

Watt, P. (2005) 'Housing histories and fragmented middle-class careers: the case of marginal professionals in London council housing', *Housing Studies*, 20: 359–81.

Watt, P. (2008a) 'Moving to a better place? Geographies of aspiration and anxiety in the Thames Gateway', in P. Cohen and M. Rustin (eds), *London's Turning: The Making of Thames Gateway*, Ashgate: Aldershot, pp.149–67.

Watt, P. (2008b) The 'only class' in town? Gentrification and the middle-class colonization of the city and the urban imagination, *International Journal of Urban and Regional Research*, 32: 206–11.

Bibliography

Watt, P. and Finn, T. (2000) *Residents' Attitudes to the Caretaking and Cleaning Service: A Study of the St. George's Estate, London Borough of Tower Hamlets*, Department of Sociology, University of East London: London.

Watt, P. and Jacobs, K. (2000) 'Discourses of social exclusion: an analysis of "Bringing Britain Together: a national strategy for neighbourhood renewal"', *Housing, Theory and Society*, 17: 14–26.

Weatherall (2000) *Feasibility Study. Queens Market, Green Street, Newham*, www.newham.gov.uk/nr/rdonlyres/2a0c08bc-deda-4b69-b013-751f285ba561/1881/queens_feasibility2000.pdf.

Weaver, M. (2002) 'What's the big deal in the end?', *The Guardian*, 7 July.

Weaver, M. (2006) 'Trouble in Prescottgrad', *The Guardian*, 15 February.

Westminster City Council (WCC) (2002) *Paddington Special Policy Area*, Department of Planning & Transport, City Of Westminster: London.

Westminster City Council (WCC) (2005) *Westminster One City: Excellent Services – Strong Communities, A White Paper For Westminster 2006–2011*, Westminster City Council: London.

While, A., Jonas, A. and Gibbs, D. (2004) 'The environment and the entrepreneurial city: searching for the urban sustainability fix in Manchester and Leeds', *International Journal of Urban and Regional Research*, 28: 549–69.

Whitehead, C. (2006) 'Housing demand, supply and the geography of inequality', in P. Malpass and L. Cairncross (eds), *Building on the Past: Visions of Housing Futures*, The Policy Press: Bristol.

Williams, T. (2007) *The Williams Report: Quality First: The Commission on the Design of Affordable Housing in the Thames Gateway*, The Housing Corporation: London.

Williams-Ellis, C. (1928) *England and the Octopus*, Beacon Books: London.

Willmott, P. and Young M. (1973) 'Social class and geography', in D. Donnison and D. Eversley (eds), *London: Urban Patterns, Problems And Policies*, Heinemann: London, pp.190–214.

Woodhysen, J. and Abley, I. (2004) *Why Is Construction So Backward?*, Chichester: John Wiley

Woodin Consultancies (1996) *Just What the Doctor Ordered: Housing, Health and Community Safety on Holly Street*, Woodin Consultancies: London.

Woodward, R. (1991) 'Mobilising opposition: the campaign Against Housing Action Trusts in Tower Hamlets', *Housing Studies*, 8: 44–56.

World Bank (2002) *Building Institutions for Markets*, World Bank: Washington, DC.

Worley, C. (2005) 'It's not about race. It's about the community: New Labour and "community cohesion"', *Critical Social Policy*, 25: 483–96.

Wright, P. (1985) *On Living in an Old Country*, Verso: London.

Young, C., Diep M. and Drabble, S. (2006) 'Living with difference? The "cosmopolitan city" and urban re-imaging in Manchester, UK', *Urban Studies*, 43: 1687–1714.

Young, I. (1990) *Justice and the Politics of Difference*, Princeton University Press: Princeton.

Young, K. (1984), 'Governing Greater London: the political aspects', *The Political Quarterly*, 55: 256–72.

Young, K. (2006), 'Postscript: back to the past?', *Local Government Studies*, 32: 373–80.

Young, K. and Garside, P. (1982) *Metropolitan London, Politics and Urban Change 1837–1981*, Holmes and Maier Publishers: London.

Young, L. and Barrett, H. (2001) 'Adapting visual methods: action research with Kampala street children', *Area*, 33: 141–52.

Young, M. and Willmott, P. (1990) *Family and Kinship in East London*, London, Penguin [originally published 1957].

Zimmerman, D. and Wieder, D. (1977) 'The diary: the diary interview method', *Urban Life*, 5: 479–98.

Žižek, S. (1999) *The Ticklish Subject*, Verso: London.

Zukin S. (1991) *Landscapes of Power: From Detroit to Disney World*, University of California Press: Berkeley.

Zukin, S. (1995) *The Cultures of Cities*, Blackwell: Oxford.

Index

Abercrombie Greater London Plan
(1946) 12, 59, 61
abolition of strategic government and
GLC 14, 63–65
activist experts 106–107, 95
actor network theory (ANT) 155–158,
171–172
administrative boundaries 58
advocacy 84
affordable housing: access to 42, 179,
182, 185; definitions of 182, 212;
demand for 171, 237; eligibility for
182; lack of 147, 227, 232; and
legislation 183; and local people
130; numbers of 178; and the
London 2012 Olympic Games
143; Paddington 124; provision of
10, 31, 88, 111, 130, 143, 178,
185–186, 190, 212, 222; riverside
development of 181–191; and
segregation 32, 184; and
separation from private housing
stock 184, 185, 186; and social
renting 228, 318; targets of 178;
Thames Gateway 232
Amsterdam 120
anti-social behavior: prevalence of 158,
319; characteristics of 167–169;
and crime 286; and design 300;
and liveability 171; orders
(ASBOs) 300; and Queen's
Market Newham 268, 270–271;
residents' experiences of
167–169; and security systems
168; and social housing 214; and
young people 290, 294, 298, 300
architecture 77, 80–83, 87–91, 96,
151–172, 179, 185, 270
area-based initiatives (ABIs) 126, 130,
199, 212, 213, 224, 232, 250
Argent Group plc 94–111
Arup 94, 96, 99, 103, 104, 110, 141, 211

aspirations 38, 77, 82, 90, 128, 141,
145, 148, 238–239, 260
Atlanta 134, 146
Audit Commission 95
Aylesbury Estate 219, 226, 232–233

banking 47, 50, 55
Barbican 49, 156, 158, 165, 171
Barcelona 48, 135, 153
Barker, Kate 34, 68, 82, 85, 86, 88, 89,
91, 320
Barking Reach 115
Barnsbury 30, 193, 194, 205, 209
Beckton 49, 263
Beijing 135, 146
Bengali 31, 272
Big Bang 24
Birmingham 9, 24, 26, 104, 140, 321
Blair, Tony (also Blairism) 27, 30–34,
46, 65, 66, 68, 232, 273, 278, 290
Blue Ribbon Network 20–21, 173–191
Boris Johnson viii, 72
Bristol 26, 51, 321
British Library 50
British Olympics Association 138, 140,
145
Brown, Gordon see Gordon Brown
Brussels 50
business services see financial
services

Cambridge 26, 259
Camden (London borough of) 107,
109–110, 111, 115, 172, 221–222
Canary Wharf Group 87
Canary Wharf 9, 36, 37, 41, 42, 45,
50–55, 64, 96, 135–136, 137, 146,
160, 174, 253
Canning Town 35, 260–261, 271
Capital City 16, 58–59, 103
CCTV 163–165, 184–185, 262, 301
Central London Partnership 103, 196

Centre Point 49

Channel Tunnel xi 50, 59, 101, 130

Chicago 134

children: and affluent households 49;
and democratic voice 289; focus
on 291; and inner city estates
290; and inner London 9–10,
289–309; and local schools 188;
and middle classes 32; Pakistani
and Bangledeshi 8; and Peabody
Trust 303–304; and play
equipment 305, 306; and poverty
8, 295; and primary schools 203;
and Queen's Market Newham
266; and regeneration 289–309;
and rented accommodation 295;
and riverside developments 188,
189; and self-development 295;
and Sure Start 309; and
universities 81; and urban space
290, 305, 307

citizenship 128, 289–290

City Challenge 96

City of London 11, 15, 24–25, 37,
40–41, 44–45, 52–53, 62, 113,
119, 132, 152, 172, 205, 315

civic engagement 12, 140

Clerkenwell 55

Coleman, Alice 156, 172, 301–302, 309

Commission for Architecture and the
Built Environment (CABE) 97, 169,
275

community turn to 12–15

community building 10, 12, 83, 97,
148, 272

community cohesion 93, 108, 192,
201, 209, 211, 261, 263, 271, 331;
also see social cohesion

community empowerment 22, 108,
275, 288

community engagement:
commitment to 110; and
developers 95, 97–99, 103, 110;
disruptive costs of 106; and

extra-local scale 104; and
government agendas 98; and
King's Cross 19, 102–111; lip
service to 110; and London 2012,
20, 144–148; management of
106; and Paddington 113, 114,
115–116, 127–129; place based
105; and political legitimacy 127;
and power 19

community involvement 22, 93–111,
138, 206, 275, 280, 283–288, 320

community participation 13, 103, 105,
212, 213, 224, 228–231, 233, 274,
275

communitarianism 274, 283

Comprehensive Estates Initiative (CEI)
22, 273–288

congestion charge 56, 67

consumption 8, 41, 44, 46, 48, 80, 84,
134, 148, 256, 314, 315

corporate responsibility 97

cost of living 18, 57

council housing 214, 218, 219, 230,
231, 288, 314

council tenants 162, 171, 215,
218–221, 230, 233

Countryside Properties 97

creative (also creative class) 10, 13–14,
47, 52, 281

creative industries 47, 52

crime: and anti-social behavior 167,
286; and disorder 130; and
dystopia 14; endemic 287; and
environmental design 276; fear of
185, 277; government strategy
relating to 273; high levels of 282,
295; and Holly Street 276; and
King's Cross 295; neighbourhood
251; petty 268; prevention 128;
and Queen's Market Newham
267–268; reduction of 260;
reported 277; and social housing
292–293; victims of 295; and
worklessness 224

Crossrail 17, 36, 38, 59, 90
Croydon 47, 55
culture: and agendas 20, 146; and
    economy 41, 44, 53–54; and
    industry 54, 315; and policy 42,
    54, 56; and quarters 44, 238–244;
    and regeneration 4, 53–54, 133,
    135, 137, 144; and transformation
    18, 271

defensible space 156, 165–166, 309
degeneration 18, 57
de-industrialisation 43
demolition 82, 116, 227, 262–268, 271
deprivation: and despair 282; and
    discrimination 178; economic
    239, 287; extent of 16; housing-
    related 229; indicators of 9–10,
    276; managing 224; multiple 228;
    neighbourhood 281; and
    Opportunity Areas 178;
    overcoming 177; and social
    exclusion 213; social 132, 134,
    135, 193, 195; and Tower Hamlets
    9–10, 228–229; urban 287
deregulation 24, 41, 316
design: and anti-social behavior 167;
    and class 258; and Coleman, Alice
    301–302; and community
    cohesion 263; and crime 276; and
    determinism 156, 300;
    eco-friendly 93; failure 275;
    female-sensitive 200; flaws of
    156, 161–162, 275–276, 28; and
    high-rises 155–158; inclusive 269;
    and London 2012, 143; and mass
    housing 82; modular 134; and
    new communities 94; and noise
    168–169; and obligations 92; open
    spaces 143; and play areas
    298–299; and poor construction
    161; and poor population 156;
    power of 156; and Queen's
    Market, Newham 263, 267–269;

and regeneration 22, 198,
    298–309; and relocation 263; and
    security 157, 163–167, 171, 85,
    319; and social problems 156; and
    strategy 176; technologies of 81;
    and waterside development 176
Development Securities plc 97, 120, 124
displacement 5, 42, 50, 52, 137, 146,
    183, 190, 227–228, 232
diversity: celebration of 54;
    community 202; cultural 31, 132;
    economic 144, 315; ethnic 22, 31,
    221, 227, 254–272, 292; and
    inclusion 13; and London 13, 46,
    155, 175; social 8, 188;
    understanding of 22; urban 3
divided city 313, 314, 317
Docklands, London 14, 16, 27, 40–42,
    45–50, 53, 64, 75, 89, 96, 112,
    119, 121, 129, 133, 140, 147–148,
    161, 173–174
Dockland's Light Railway (DLR) 50,
    55–56

earnings 52, 317
East End 14, 17, 49, 52, 91, 264
education 7, 9, 16, 32, 55, 59, 129,
    139, 144, 213, 224, 257
Egan, John (Egan Review) 97
employment 8, 47, 87, 89, 118, 129,
    134, 137, 139, 144, 239, 249,
    317–318
Education Action Zone 129
empowerment: and citizenship
    289–90; community 22, 108, 275,
    284–85, 288; and memory 78
English Heritage 122, 126, 154, 169;
    also see heritage
English Partnerships 91, 92
estate regeneration 218, 219
ethnic diversity 22, 221, 227, 254–272,
    292
extension to mayoral powers 60–61,
    68–72

faith communities 80

family (*also* families) 30, 34, 50, 81, 88, 111, 226, 295, 302, 307

financial services 25, 26, 40–41, 45, 47–51, 52, 87, 147–148, 221, 313

flagship developments 75–92, 93–111, 112–131, 13–148

Flyvbjerg, Bengt 103, 110

Foster, Norman 87

Foucault, Michel 83

Frankfurt, Germany 42, 79, 120

gated communities 86, 143, 183–186, 263

Gavron, Nicky 37, 175

gender 9, 193–194, 286

gentrification 3, 15, 18, 32–33, 41, 44, 45, 50, 52–53, 55–57, 81, 88, 143, 148, 183–190, 221, 227–228, 232, 241, 257, 258, 261, 271, 293, 318, 319, 321

Glancey, Jonathan 76

Glasgow 157

global cities 25–26, 51, 58, 175, 313

global city thesis 25, 51–52

globalisation vii, 6–7, 11, 24–25, 251, 321

Globe Theatre 54, 243

Gordon Brown 36, 37, 39

Governance: 'joined up approach' 66, 71, 278, 297; local 16, 84, 112, 130; urban vii, 280–281, 308

governmentality 275

Great Western Railway 116

Greater London Act (1999) 67

Greater London Authority (GLA): birth of 14, 136, 174; boundary of 70; budget of 65; and children 307; and community engagement 106; and developers 110; and development politics 6; and economy 29; and gentrification 319; and global development 6; and impact assessment 98; and

King's Cross 103; and London Plan 67, 169, 174–179, 196, 231; and the Mayor 65–68; and mixed communities 13; and new development 12; and the London 2012 Olympic Games 143; and Opportunity Areas 178; and partnership 250; and policy innovation 66; and regeneration 110; and renewable energy 109; and social housing 145; and social inclusion 171, 178; and social inequalities in London 8, 190, 317; and Transport Strategy 196, 198; and walking plans 192, 196–197; and waterfront renewal 174–179; and wealth generation 14

Greater London Council (GLC) 14, 17, 48, 54, 62–65, 113, 240–241, 252

Greater London Plan (1976) 118

Greycoats 240, 241

Grosvenor 94, 96, 97

Hackney 9, 21, 22, 42, 43, 45, 55, 132, 135, 143, 144, 163, 172, 193, 194, 199, 200–201, 204, 207–208, 210, 220, 221–222, 226, 231, 257, 258, 273–288, 320

Haringey 172, 226

Harvey, David 79

Hazel Blears 93

Herbert Commission, The (1960) 62, 63

heritage 78, 111, 114, 119, 177, 362, 203; *also see* English Heritage

high-rise *see* tower blocks

History of London Government 16, 17, 18–19, 59–72

Holly Street Estate, Hackney 22, 42, 273–288, 320

homelessness 214, 222, 225, 244

Horkheimer, Max 79

housing: affordability 3, 56, 222; Housing Action Trusts 218–219; and house prices 55, 57, 59, 143,

222, 225, 244; key worker 67, 153, 171; and tenure 45–46, 56, 160, 182, 186, 214–215, 217, 222, 225–226, 232, 314; mixed tenure 12, 151, 260, 263; and security of tenure 57, 221
Howard, Ebenazar 33, 62

income: and inequality 18, 24–25, 51–52; mixed 15, 187; structure 3, 32–33, 40–41, 51, 143, 171, 182–183, 190, 221–222, 227, 257, 271, 321
inequality: and dystopia 14; global 80; growing 313, 314, 317; housing 18, 57; income 24, 25, 51, 52; material 214; power 98; regional 315, 321; reproduction of 317; and social divisions 317; and social polarisation 52
inequity 13, 175, 183
internationalisation 40
immigration 25, 51, 53, 116, 261, 265, 318
Islington 9, 21, 43, 101, 102, 115, 172, 193, 194, 199–210, 220, 226, 289, 293, 295, 300, 309

Johnson, Boris see Boris Johnson
Jencks, Charles 82
Jubilee Line 55

Ken Livingstone viii, 17, 20, 27, 29, 36–37, 46, 53, 65, 67–69, 71–72, 113, 130, 136, 140, 142, 146, 151, 154, 307
key workers 182
King's Cross 6, 19, 28, 36, 42–43, 47, 50–51, 93–111, 115, 318–319
King's Cross Ten Estates 22, 289–309
Koolhaas, Rem 80

Lambeth 154, 172, 220, 226, 239–241, 250

Land Securities plc 97
Latour, Bruno 82, 83, 156–157, 171
Leeds 24, 26, 321
legacy 2012, 20, 132–148
Leicester 28
Leigh, Edward 75, 77
Lewisham 152, 172, 220, 226
liberal government 80, 86
Lille 50
liveability 20, 154, 158–160, 163, 167, 171, 176, 197
Living Streets 192, 197–198
local authority housing see council housing
local government 16, 40, 64–65, 71, 84, 91, 112–131, 134–135, 173, 276–279, 283–284, 319–320; see also LCC; GLC; GLA
Local Government Act 2003, 114
London 2012, 112, 137, 138, 140–148
London Bridge Tower 153
London Bridge 44, 192
London County Council (LCC) 12, 17, 34, 61
London Development Agency (LDA) 6, 7, 11, 12, 16, 103, 104, 110, 112, 136, 139, 142, 145, 146
London Docklands Development Corporations (LDDC) 41–42, 50, 64, 112, 115, 135, 173
London Fields 193, 204–207
London Motorway Box 116
London Olympic Games 2012 see London 2012
London Plan 10, 13, 37, 66–67, 68–69, 71, 91, 98, 113, 151, 169, 174–179, 190, 196, 231–232
London Planning Advisory Committee (LPAC) 64, 113, 321
London Regeneration Consortium 99–100, 101
London Urban Development Corporation 114
Los Angeles 25, 51, 78, 134, 135

Lower Lea Valley 29, 35, 36, 38, 137

Madrid 140
Manchester 9, 24, 25, 26, 28, 33, 104, 140, 321
manufacturing 7, 32, 40, 42–43, 47, 70–71, 134, 135
market freedom 94
Marshall, Alfred 33
Mayor of London viii, 6, 17–20, 27–29, 38, 46, 53, 55, 60–61, 65–71, 98, 112–114, 130, 136, 139–140, 145–146, 151, 174–176, 178–179, 201, 231, 260
mega events 132–148
Miami 134
middle classes: aspirant 32; changes in 51–52; and choice 32; and cosmopolitanism 53; divisions within 52; expansion of 148, 313, 314–315; and gentrification 33, 152, 190, 232, 239, 244, 257, 258; and home ownership 57; and inner city lifestyles 52; managerial 51, 314; new groups of 52; and outer eastern suburbs 52; and residential demand 52; and schools 32; and social capital 31; and an unequal city 52
Miliband, David 93
Milton Keynes 33
mixed-use 94, 101, 103, 110, 111, 123, 124, 126, 171
Montreal 144
mortgage debt 81
multicultural 256, 264–265, 308, 313

National Audit Office 75, 77, 86, 96, 173
neighbourhood: anonymity 202, 208, 209; and anti-social behavior 167, 319; and attachment 201, 208; characterisations of 169–170; communities 13, 31, 169–170,

171, 175, 186–191, 208, 251; definitions of 251; deprived 10, 14, 16, 213, 251; economic fabric of 97; empowered 187; encounters 170; facilities of 188, 229; feelings about 158, 207; and flagship projects 113, 116, 121; and gentrification 187, 241, 318; lived experiences of 157, 187–191; and mixed communities 12, 182, 187–191; planning 31; and post-political regeneration 252–253; problems of 276; railway suburb 5; and renewal programmes 8, 97, 98, 104, 130, 224, 225–226, 251, 259, 260–261, 264, 272, 278–279, 282, 308; and residential developments 180; riverside 180, 186, 187–191; segregation of 143, 184; and social capital 258; and social engineering 12; and social housing 213, 232, 280; and social inclusion vii, 14; social interactions in 187, 188, 210; survey of 155; Thames-side 20; units 12, 31; valuing 78, 284; visions for 238; and well-being 252; working class 5, 182–183, 190
neighbourhood renewal 8, 97–98, 104, 213, 251, 260–261, 278, 308
neo-liberal policy making 22, 288
neo-liberalism 20, 84, 147, 148, 213, 230, 242, 251–252, 271, 274, 81, 318
New Deal for Communities (NDC) 42, 212–213, 219, 224–233, 259, 260
New Labour see Blair, Tony and Blairism; Gordon Brown
New Right 63–64
New York 14, 25, 26, 40, 44, 51, 53, 81, 120, 134, 138
Newcastle-upon-Tyne 24, 26, 321

Newham 9, 22, 28, 75, 82, 132, 135, 143–145, 222, 226, 254–272

Newman, Oscar 156

North London Line 55

Nottingham 321

Olympic Delivery Authority (ODA) 112, 138–139, 145

Olympic Games *see* London 2012; mega events

Opportunity Areas 6, 103, 178, 187

organised opposition to regeneration 93–111, 120, 154, 218–219, 237–253, 254–272

Orlando 134

owner occupation 52–53, 171, 190, 217

Oxford 26, 282

Oxo Tower Wharf 44, 243

Paddington Basin 5, 42–51, 97, 188, 124, 319

Paddington Canal 117, 121, 127, 129

Paddington First Employment Scheme 125, 129, 131

Paddington Regeneration Partnership (PRP) 125, 129

Paddington Special Policy Area (PSPA) 122–129

Paddington Station 51, 117, 118, 124

Paddington Waterside Partnership 125

paradigms 92, 146, 252, 320

Paralympic Games Act (2007) 138

Paralympic Games 132, 140, 148

Peabody Trust 289–309

pedestrian policy 192–195, 198–207

People's Plan 100–101

physical renewal 96, 277

place identity/attachments 256, 262, 264

play areas 292, 298, 299, 305, 306

police 286, 292, 295, 300, 306

post-industrial city 12, 14, 18, 42–45, 54, 76–80, 84, 91, 134, 147, 173, 183, 240

post-political 21–22, 237–238, 245–253

poverty wage 214

poverty 8, 132, 152, 156, 183, 213, 214, 228–229, 260, 287, 292–293, 295, 314, 317

Prescott, John 76, 196

Prince Charles 83

private space 298, 302

privatisation 199, 219, 299, 258, 316.

professionalisation 8–9, 33, 51–53

property developers 19, 81, 88, 94–96, 111

property development 19, 34–36, 47, 82, 95–98, 107, 110, 111, 124, 221, 254.

property led redevelopment 41

prostitution 166–168, 292

Pruitt Igoe 82, 84

Public Accounts Committee 75, 77

public participation 12, 28, 289

public space: accessibility 183; availability of 206; Blue Ribbon Network 190–191; civic amenities 116; contested notions of 267–272; enhancement of 141; ethnic diversity 267–272; everyday life 264; good urban design 176; Greater London partnership 196; high quality of 263; homes 291; local democracy 258; meaning of 256–257; networks 256; play 296; politics of 145; provision of 22, 111, 126; representations of 264–272; riverside development 185–186; safety 249; social and therapeutic role of 259; social exclusion 21, 22; social interactions 192–211; struggles over 22; value of 264; walking 192–211; women 290; young people 22, 110, 289–309

Putnam, Robert 12, 168, 206

quality of life 9, 16, 45, 57, 59, 157, 160–162, 289–290, 295–297

Queen's Market, Newham 254–272
Queensbridge Community Trust 277, 282

rationality: and property development 119–121; and liberalism 111; and power 103, 110–111
Reading (Berkshire) 51
registered social landlords (RSLs): and changing housing stock 214–219; and development partnerships 91; and urban governance 280–281; and high-rise management 158
Richmond-on-Thames 55, 220
right-to-buy (RTB) 216, 217, 227, 228
River Thames 44, 55, 75, 176
riverside renaissance 173–191, 319
Rogers, Richard 20, 175–176, 183, 187, 240
Ronan Point 82, 84, 157
Royal Festival Hall 5, 54, 238, 242, 243

Salford 35, 224
San Francisco 134
Sassen, Saskia 41, 45, 60, 139, 314
schools 30–32, 188, 239, 242, 248, 252
Scotland 36
security: gated communities 183–186; high-rise housing 157, 163–171; housing tenure 12, 57, 221; investment 122; safety in public spaces 23, 197, 278, 294–302, 307, 319; social exclusion 214
Sennett, Richard 81, 148, 202, 204
Seoul 146
service class 139
Shanghai 102
Sheffield 321
Shoreditch 6, 43, 53, 226, 232, 233
Singapore 140
Single Regeneration Budget (SRB): and community-led regeneration 97, 105, 262; and holistic

regeneration 42, 224; and post-political planning 246–252, 262
social capital 7, 31, 98, 168, 258, 287
social change 51–53, 56, 314
social class 3, 18, 25, 31–34, 40, 42, 45–47, 51–52, 56, 116, 139, 182–184, 186–187, 190, 212, 217, 228, 232, 238, 244, 258, 264, 270, 292, 313–314, 318
social cohesion 53–54, 56; see also community cohesion
Social Exclusion Unit 97, 213
social exclusion: and area-based initiatives 42, 232; and community-led regeneration 232; and high-rise living 154; and participation 13; and social housing 212–214, 221–224; and young people 291, 293, 303; causes of 14, 21, 53, 97, 178–190, 278, 283; geographies of 314
social housing: and British spatial policy 85–89, 314, 320; and flagship regeneration projects 122, 181, 182, 190; and high-rise living 153, 154, 171; and mixed neighbourhoods 15, 20, 21, 31, 42–49, 52, 56, 278, 288, 292; and regeneration 212–233; and London Plan 34; and the London 2012 Olympic Games 145
social inclusion: and community participation 197; as a concept vii, 4, 12, 91, 160; and flagship regeneration 40, 42, 53, 54, 258; and the London 2012 Olympic Games 132, 141; and London Plan 175–178, 183, 186, 190; and walking the city 197; and social mixing 20; and economic competitiveness 261
social interaction: and civic engagement vii, 12; and high-rise

living 168; and urban sustainability 21; and the walkable city 201–210; patterns of 187, 188, 256, 258

social mixing: definitions of 14, 15, 210, 211, 227; and flagship regeneration projects 187, 192, 193; and gentrification 20, 21, 31, 232, 319

social polarisation: processes of vii, 8, 13; and London's global competitiveness 41; and the London 2012 Olympic Games 175; and professionalisation 51–52, 59; and social housing 84

social regeneration 137, 141, 151, 300, 320

social segregation 32, 143, 179, 184–185

South Bank 21, 43–44, 54, 112, 237–253, 319

South Bank Employers Group 243, 247, 248, 250, 253

South East Regional Planning Conference (SERPLAN) 64

Southwark 43, 172, 219, 220, 221–222, 226, 240, 241

St Pancras Station 43, 48, 50, 99

Square Mile 89, 152

stock transfer (LSVT) 217–220, 227–232, 288–288, 318

Stratford City 37, 115, 141, 143, 146, 259

Straw, Jack 140

street markets 256, 257, 267

sub-prime mortgages 81

suburbs: and Abercrombie Plan 31; and railways 5, 43, 55; and global city agenda 17; and social housing 219; and social mobility 45, 52, 81, 317, 318; and urban renaissance 90, 92; growth of 61; politics of 18

surveillance: and gated communities 163; and public spaces 165, 300–306; and young people 293

Sustainability: and the built environment 97; and brownfield regeneration 113, 133, 152; and development legacies 140–148, 177, 178, 225, 278, 280–287; and the environment 56, 94, 175; and London's global competitiveness vii, 3–6, 8–15, 19–21, 64, 126, 176, 191, 196; and manufacturing industry 7; and rights to the city 83, 262; and social sustainability 288; and urban liveability 151, 154, 170, 171, 195, 199, 201, 278, 280, 281, 288, 318

Sustainable Communities Plan 26, 33, 38, 87–91, 94, 97, 136, 316

sustainable communities: and growth corridors 30; and objects of urban policy 10–12, 202; and social housing estates 19, 21, 232, 297; and transport provision 38, 207; governance of 87, 90, 91

sustainable community building see community building

sustainable development vii, 66, 77, 93, 94, 110, 196,

Sydney 48, 140, 143

Taipei (Taiwan) 102

tall buildings 67, 151, 154, 169

Tate Modern 50, 54, 243

territorialising 22, 275, 288

terrorism, threat of 12

Thames Gateway: governance of 17, 28, 29, 75–92; history of 27, 59; regeneration projects in 19, 35, 42, 132, 136–146, 232, 259, 316, 32

Thames Gateway London Partnership 115

Thatcher, Margaret (also Thatcherism) 25, 45–46, 63–64, 84, 173, 241, 309

The London Plan (Spatial Development Strategy for London) 13, 37, 66,

71, 91, 98, 113, 118, 151, 169,
174–178, 190, 196, 231, 232, 238
Third Way 53, 247, 252
Thurrock 29, 91
Tokyo 25
Tooting 33
tower blocks 34, 42
Tower Bridge 76
Transport: and affordability 38; and
canals 40; corridors 30; costs of
59; Docklands 49–50; and
economic development 65;
effects of 127; and government
38; impacts of 126; infrastructure
10, 24, 43, 87, 91, 124, 124–125,
138; interchanges 30; and
investment 126; networks 315;
and the London 2012 Olympic
Games 144; and pedestrian policy
195–201; and planning 62, 63, 65,
195–201; and policy 42, 56, 66,
192–211; privatisation of 37;
public 29, 67, 70, 71, 90, 169, 193,
196, 197; and social interaction
209–210; strategy 66, 196;
sustainable modes of 195–196,
199–200; technologies 55; and
urban regeneration 54–56,
195–196; uses of 40; and walking
192–211; waterborne 177; *also
see* Crossrail; TfL; tube
Transport for London (TfL) 37, 65–68,
138, 192–210
tube (*also* tube stations) 24, 33, 37, 50,
55, 111, 141, 161, 198, 203, 255,
263

underground *see* tube
unemployment (*also* unemployed)
8–9, 25, 46, 52, 276, 318
Urban Development Corporations 17, 8,
29, 30, 64, 91, 96, 114, 115, 135
urban entrepreneurialism 95, 112, 134,
139, 173, 314

urban renaissance: and policy agenda
vii, 20, 31, 87, 92, 278, 317; and
high-rise developments 151; and
riverside developments 173, 185,
189–192, 319; and place-making
13, 182, 197, 263; and
suburbanisation 90; and
sustainable communities 201,
213, 270
Urban Splash 35, 94, 96
urban strangers 206, 209
Urban Task Force 34, 35, 151, 154,
183, 196
Urban White Paper 19, 35, 94, 95, 196,
297

value added tax 35
Vauxhall 154
voluntary sector 22, 215, 242, 260,
274, 280
Victoria Line 24, 55

Wales, South 26
Wandsworth 33, 172, 180, 181, 182,
187, 188
waterfront development 12, 49,
173–182
wealth 8, 11, 14, 132, 148, 193, 195,
317, 318
welfare 4, 11, 82, 84, 86, 115, 249,
260, 270
West End 41, 42–43, 47, 49, 51, 53,
55, 119–120, 146, 198, 205
Westminster (City Council) 113–130
Westminster (City of) 19, 44, 113, 115,
119–130, 172, 220, 238, 239, 241
Westway Motorway 116, 120, 121,
126
Willmott, Peter 43–44, 272
women 200, 251, 254, 290
Woolwich 55
Workfare 84
working class: anxieties of 232; and
cities 45; and class divisions 46;

communities 31; decline of 45, 52; displacement of 42, 228; and gentrification 33; and housing 43, 116, 182–183, 212, 217; and jobs 45; and multiculturalism 264; neighbourhoods 5, 52, 183, 186–187, 190, 238, 239, 244; and owner occupation 52; and quality of life 45; and revitalisation 14; and schools 32

Young people: and exclusion from public spaces 22, 200, 203, 205, 283; and gentrification 33, 50, 143, 152, 186; and public housing 225, 289–308; and regeneration 54, 266; and the London 2012 Olympic Games 140, 141

Young, Michael 43–44, 63, 64, 272